D1682123

Adobe Dreamweaver CS6

CERTIFIED ASSOCIATE
Approved Courseware

Revealed

Adobe Dreamweaver CS6

Revealed

Sherry Bishop

CERTIFIED ASSOCIATE
Approved Courseware

DELMAR
CENGAGE Learning

Australia • Brazil • Japan • Korea • Mexico • Singapore • Spain • United Kingdom • United States

DELMAR
CENGAGE Learning

Adobe Dreamweaver CS6 Revealed
Sherry Bishop

Vice President, Career and Professional Editorial: Dave Garza

Director of Learning Solutions: Sandy Clark

Senior Acquisitions Editor: Jim Gish

Managing Editor: Larry Main

Product Managers: Jane Hosie-Bounar, Nicole Calisi

Editorial Assistant: Sarah Timm

Vice President Marketing, Career and Professional: Jennifer Baker

Executive Marketing Manager: Deborah S. Yarnell

Associate Marketing Manager: Erin DeAngelo

Senior Production Director: Wendy Troeger

Production Manager: Andrew Crouth

Senior Content Project Manager: Kathryn B. Kucharek

Developmental Editor: Barbara Clemens

Technical Editor: John Shanley

Director of Design: Bruce Bond

Cover Design: Riezebos Holzbaur/Tim Heraldo

Cover Photo: Riezebos Holzbaur/Andrei Pasternak

Text Designer: Liz Kingslein

Production House: Integra Software Services Pvt. Ltd.

Proofreader: Harold Johnson

Indexer: Alexandra Nickerson

Technology Project Manager: Jim Gilbert

© 2013 Delmar, Cengage Learning

ALL RIGHTS RESERVED. No part of this work covered by the copyright herein may be reproduced, transmitted, stored, or used in any form or by any means graphic, electronic, or mechanical, including but not limited to photocopying, recording, scanning, digitizing, taping, web distribution, information networks, or information storage and retrieval systems, except as permitted under Section 107 or 108 of the 1976 United States Copyright Act, without the prior written permission of the publisher.

For product information and technology assistance, contact us at **Cengage Learning Customer & Sales Support, 1-800-354-9706**

For permission to use material from this text or product, submit all requests online at
www.cengage.com/permissions

Further permissions questions can be emailed to
permissionrequest@cengage.com

Adobe® Premiere Pro®, Adobe® After Effects®, Adobe® Bridge®, Adobe® Audition®, Adobe® Encore®, Adobe® Photoshop®, Adobe® InDesign®, Adobe® Illustrator®, Adobe® Flash®, Adobe® Dreamweaver®, Adobe® Fireworks®, and Adobe® Creative Suite® are trademarks or registered trademarks of Adobe Systems, Inc. in the United States and/or other countries. Third party products, services, company names, logos, design, titles, words, or phrases within these materials may be trademarks of their respective owners.

Adobe product screenshots reprinted with permission from Adobe Systems Incorporated.

The Adobe Certified Associate Approved Courseware logo is a proprietary trademark of Adobe. All rights reserved. Cengage Learning and Adobe Dreamweaver CS6—Revealed are independent from ProCert Labs, LLC and Adobe Systems Incorporated, and are not affiliated with ProCert Labs and Adobe in any manner. This publication may assist students to prepare for an Adobe Certified Associate exam, however, neither ProCert Labs nor Adobe warrant that use of this material will ensure success in connection with any exam.

The Adobe Approved Certification Courseware logo is a proprietary trademark of Adobe. All rights reserved. Cengage Learning and *Adobe Dreamweaver CS6—Revealed* are independent from ProCert Labs, LLC and Adobe Systems Incorporated, and are not affiliated with ProCert Labs and Adobe in any manner. This publication may assist students to prepare for an Adobe Certified Expert exam in Dreamweaver; however, neither ProCert Labs nor Adobe warrant that use of this material will ensure success in connection with any exam.

Library of Congress Control Number: 2011945471

ISBN-13: 978-1-133-69320-8
ISBN-10: 1-133-69320-2

Delmar
5 Maxwell Drive
Clifton Park, NY 12065-2919 USA

Cengage Learning is a leading provider of customized learning solutions with office locations around the globe, including Singapore, the United Kingdom, Australia, Mexico, Brazil, and Japan. Locate your local office at: **international.cengage.com/region**

Cengage Learning products are represented in Canada by Nelson Education, Ltd.

To learn more about Delmar, visit **www.cengage.com/delmar**

Purchase any of our products at your local college store or at our preferred online store **www.cengagebrain.com**

Notice to the Reader
Publisher does not warrant or guarantee any of the products described herein or perform any independent analysis in connection with any of the product information contained herein. Publisher does not assume, and expressly disclaims, any obligation to obtain and include information other than that provided to it by the manufacturer. The reader is expressly warned to consider and adopt all safety precautions that might be indicated by the activities described herein and to avoid all potential hazards. By following the instructions contained herein, the reader willingly assumes all risks in connection with such instructions. The publisher makes no representations or warranties of any kind, including but not limited to, the warranties of fitness for particular purpose or merchantability, nor are any such representations implied with respect to the material set forth herein, and the publisher takes no responsibility with respect to such material. The publisher shall not be liable for any special, consequential, or exemplary damages resulting, in whole or part, from the readers' use of, or reliance upon, this material.

Printed in the United States of America
1 2 3 4 5 6 7 16 15 14 13 12

SERIES VISION

Revealed Series Vision

The Revealed Series is your guide to today's hottest multimedia applications. For years, the Revealed Series has kept pace with the dynamic demands of the multimedia community, and continues to do so with the publication of 13 new titles covering the latest Adobe Creative Suite products. Each comprehensive book teaches not only the technical skills required for success in today's competitive multimedia market, but the design skills as well. From animation, to web design, to digital image-editing and interactive media skills, the Revealed Series has you covered.

We recognize the unique learning environment of the multimedia classroom, and we deliver text books that include:

- Comprehensive step-by-step instructions
- In-depth explanantions of the "why" behind a skill
- Creative projects for additional practice
- Full-color visuals for a clear explanation of concepts
- Comprehensive online material offering additional instruction and skills practice
- Video tutorials for skills reinforcement as well as the presentation of additional features
- NEW icons to highlight features that are new since the previous release of the software

With the Revealed Series, we've created books that speak directly to the multimedia and design community—one of the most rapidly growing computer fields today.

—The Revealed Series

New to This Edition

The latest edition of Adobe Dreamweaver CS6 Revealed includes many exciting new features, some of which are listed below:

- The new HTML5 layouts
- Media queries and Multiscreen support
- W3C Validator support with the W3C CSS Validation Service
- All Data Files are HTML5 compliant
- New coverage for inserting video and sound
- CSS level 3 coverage
- New Coverage of Adobe Bridge

CourseMate

A CourseMate is available with *Adobe Dreamweaver CS6 Revealed*, which helps you make the grade!

The CourseMate includes:

- An interactive eBook, with highlighting, note-taking, and search capabilities
- Interactive learning tools including:
  - Chapter quizzes.
  - Flash cards.
  - Instructional video lessons from Total Training, the leading provider of video instruction for Adobe software. These video lessons are integrated with the book, and include assessment.
  - And more!

Go to login.cengagebrain.com to access these resources.

AUTHOR'S VISION

This book will introduce you to a fascinating program that will hopefully inspire you to create rich and exciting websites. Although the world of technology is always spinning more quickly than we would sometimes like, we are in a particularly exciting time in the realm of web design. With HTML5 and CSS3, we are challenged to learn more efficient, sleek methods for designing sites. I hope you will find this as fascinating as I do.

Through the work of many talented and creative individuals, this text was created for you. Our Product Manager, Jane Hosie-Bounar, guided and directed the team from start to finish. She is a talented and tireless individual—the ultimate professional and visionary. She is rock solid—someone I can always count on for sage advice and guidance. Barbara Clemens, my Development Editor, is an example of so many things I value: joy, kindness, patience, and determination. I miss both of these friends and mentors each time we finish a book project.

The copyright content was generously provided by my dear friend Barbara Waxer. Additional information on locating media on the Internet and determining its legal use is available in her Revealed Series book *Internet Surf and Turf Revealed: The Essential Guide to Copyright, Fair Use, and Finding Media*. Barbara contributed even more for this edition by editing the Bridge chapter and did a wonderful job, as usual.

John Shanley did double duty this time. As the Dreamweaver Technical Editor for both Mac and PC, he carefully tested each step to make sure that the end product was error-free. He gave exceptional feedback as he reviewed each chapter. This part of the publishing process is what truly sets Delmar Cengage Learning apart from other publishers.

Suwathiga Velayutham, Kathy Kucharek, Delmar Content Project Manager, and Nicole Calisi, Delmar Product Manager, worked on the layout and kept the schedule on track. We thank them for keeping up with the many details and deadlines. The work is beautiful.

Kathleen Ryan patiently contacted the websites we used as examples to obtain permission for their inclusion. This component adds much to the content of the book and would not have been possible without her good work. Thank you to each of you that allowed us to use images of your websites.

Harold Johnson quietly worked behind the scenes to ensure that all grammatical and punctuation errors were corrected. He also provided valuable insight in regard to the accuracy of content specifics.

Special thanks go to Jim Gish, Senior Acquisitions Editor, and Sandy Clark, the Director of Learning Solutions. They have embraced the Revealed books with enthusiasm and grace and provided us with such excellent resources to produce books that make us all proud. Attending Adobe MAX was beyond expectation and a tremendous boost for my research efforts.

Thanks to the Beach Club in Gulf Shores, Alabama, beachclubal.com, for being such a delightful place to visit. Several photographs of their beautiful property appear in The Striped Umbrella website.

Typically, your family is the last to be thanked. My husband, Don, supports and encourages me every day, as he has for the last forty-two years. Our travels with our children and grandchildren provide happy memories for us and content for the websites. You will see the faces of my precious grandchildren Jacob, Emma, Thomas, and Caroline peeking out from some of the pages.

—Sherry Bishop

PREFACE

Introduction to Adobe Dreamweaver CS6—Revealed

Welcome to *Adobe Dreamweaver CS6—Revealed*. This book offers complete coverage of basic to intermediate Dreamweaver skills, helping you to create polished, professional-looking websites. Use this book both in the classroom and as your own reference guide.

This text is organized into 13 chapters. In these chapters, you will explore the many options Dreamweaver provides for creating dynamic Dreamweaver websites. You'll also work with many of the exciting features new to this release of the software. New features are marked with a NEW in the text.

What You'll Do

A What You'll Do figure begins every lesson. This figure gives you an at-a-glance look at what you'll do in the chapter, either by showing you a file from the current project or a tool you'll be using.

Comprehensive Conceptual Lessons

Before jumping into instructions, in-depth conceptual information tells you "why" skills are applied. This book provides the "how" and "why" through the use of professional examples. Also included in the text are tips and sidebars to help you work more efficiently and creatively, or to teach you a bit about the history or design philosophy behind the skill you are using.

DREAMWEAVER VII

Step-by-Step Instructions

This book combines in-depth conceptual information with concise steps to help you learn Dreamweaver CS6. Each set of steps guides you through a lesson where you will create, modify, or enhance a Dreamweaver CS6 file. Step references to large colorful images and quick step summaries round out the lessons. The Data Files for the steps are provided on Cengage Brain. For information on how to access Cengage Brain, see "Read This Before You Begin."

Projects

This book contains a variety of end-of-chapter materials for additional practice and reinforcement. The Skills Review contains hands-on practice exercises that mirror the progressive nature of the lesson material. The chapter concludes with four projects: two Project Builders, one Design Project, and one Portfolio Project. The Project Builders require you to apply the skills you've learned in the chapter. The Design Project incorporates critical thinking skills while evaluating live websites. The Portfolio Project encourages you to address and solve challenges based on the content explored in the chapter in order to create portfolio-quality work.

INSTRUCTOR RESOURCES

What Instructor Resources Are Available with This Book?

The Instructor Resources are Delmar's way of putting the resources and information needed to teach and learn effectively into your hands. All the resources are available for both Macintosh and Windows operating systems. These resources can be found online at **http://login.cengage.com**. Once you log in or create an account, search for the title under 'My Dashboard' using the ISBN. Then select the instructor companion site resources and click 'Add to my Bookshelf.'

Instructor's Manual

The Instructor's Manual includes chapter overviews and detailed lecture topics for each chapter, with teaching tips.

Sample Syllabus

The Sample Syllabus includes a suggested syllabus for any course that uses this book.

PowerPoint Presentations

Each chapter has a corresponding PowerPoint presentation that you can use in lectures, distribute to your students, or customize to suit your course.

Data Files for Students

To complete most of the chapters in this book, your students will need Data Files, which are available online. Instruct students to use the Data Files List at the end of this book. This list gives instructions on organizing files.

To access the Data Files for this book, take the following steps:

1. Open your browser and go to http://www.cengagebrain.com
2. Type the author, title, or ISBN of this book in the Search window. (The ISBN is listed on the back cover.)
3. Click the book title in the list of search results.
4. When the book's main page is displayed, click the Access button under Free Study Tools.
5. To download Data Files, select a chapter number and then click on the Data Files tab on the left navigation bar to download the files.

Solutions to Exercises

Solution Files are Data Files completed with comprehensive sample answers. Use these files to evaluate your students' work. Or distribute them electronically so students can verify their work. Sample solutions to all lessons and end-of-chapter material are provided, with the exception of some Portfolio Projects.

Bridge Solution Files

The solution files for the Bridge chapter are figures of Bridge screen captures. As you complete each set of steps, you can compare your screen to its related figure.

ACA Certification

This book covers the objectives necessary for Adobe Dreamweaver ACA certification. Use the Certification Grid at the back of the book to find out where an objective is covered. Be sure to review the Glossary pages referenced in the ACA grid at the back of the book for complete coverage of the objectives.

Additional Resources and Certification

To access additional resources for this book, including information about ACE certification, follow Steps 1 through 4 under Data Files for Students, above, and then click ACE information or, to access additional materials, click the Additional Materials tab under Book Resources to download the files.

Test Bank and Test Engine

ExamView is a powerful testing software package that allows instructors to create and administer printed and computer (LAN-based) exams. ExamView includes hundreds of questions that correspond to the topics covered in this text, enabling students to generate detailed study guides that include page references for further review. The computer-based and LAN-based/online testing component allows students to take exams using the EV Player, and also saves the instructor time by grading each exam automatically.

DREAMWEAVER IX

BRIEF CONTENTS

BRIDGE

Chapter 1 Using Adobe Bridge to Manage Assets
- Lesson 1 Explore the Bridge Workspace 1-4
- 2 Use Metadata, Ratings, and Labels 1-8

DREAMWEAVER

Chapter 1 Getting Started with Dreamweaver
- Lesson 1 Explore the Dreamweaver Workspace 1-4
- 2 View a Web Page and Use Help 1-12
- 3 Plan and Set Up a Website 1-18
- 4 Add a Folder And Pages 1-26

Chapter 2 Developing a Web Page
- Lesson 1 Create Head Content and Set Page Properties 2-4
- 2 Create, Import, and Format Text 2-10
- 3 Add Links to Web Pages 2-18
- 4 Use the History Panel and Edit Code 2-24
- 5 Modify and Test Web Pages 2-30

Chapter 3 Working with Text and Cascading Style Sheets
- Lesson 1 Create Unordered and Ordered Lists 3-4
- 2 Create, Apply, and Edit Cascading Style Sheets 3-10
- 3 Add Rules and Attach Cascading Style Sheets 3-20
- 4 Use Coding Tools to View and Edit Rules 3-26

Chapter 4 Adding Images
- Lesson 1 Insert and Align Images 4-4
- 2 Enhance an Image and Use Alternate Text 4-12
- 3 Insert a Background Image and Perform Site Maintenance 4-18
- 4 Add Graphic Enhancements 4-24

Chapter 5 Working with Links and Navigation
- Lesson 1 Create External and Internal Links 5-4
- 2 Create Internal Links to Named Anchors 5-10
- 3 Create, Modify, and Copy a Spry Menu Bar 5-16
- 4 Create an Image Map 5-26
- 5 Manage Website Links 5-30
- 6 Incorporate Web 2.0 Technology 5-34

Chapter 6 Positioning Objects with CSS and Tables
- Lesson 1 Create a Page Using CSS Layouts 6-4
- 2 Add Content to CSS Layout Blocks 6-8
- 3 Edit and Format CSS Layout Blocks 6-14
- 4 Create a Table 6-22
- 5 Resize, Split, and Merge Cells 6-26
- 6 Insert and Align Images in Table Cells 6-30
- 7 Insert Text and Format Cell Content 6-34

Chapter 7 Managing a Web Server and Files
- Lesson 1 Perform Website Maintenance 7-4
- 2 Publish a Website and Transfer Files 7-14
- 3 Check Files Out and In 7-22
- 4 Cloak Files 7-28
- 5 Import and Export a Site Definition 7-32
- 6 Evaluate Web Content For Legal Use 7-36
- 7 Present a Website to a Client 7-40

Chapter 8 Using Styles and Style Sheets for Design
- Lesson 1 Create and Use Embedded Styles 8-4
- 2 Modify Embedded Styles 8-12
- 3 Use CSS3 and Media Queries 8-18
- 4 Work with Conflicting Styles 8-26

DREAMWEAVER XI

Chapter 9   **Collecting Data with Forms**
Lesson 1   Plan and Create a Form   9-4
2   Edit and Format a Form   9-10
3   Work with Form Objects   9-16
4   Test and Process a Form   9-30

Chapter 10   **Positioning Objects with AP Divs**
Lesson 1   Insert an AP Div   10-4
2   Set the Position and Size of an AP Div   10-8
3   Add Content to an AP Div   10-14
4   Set AP Div Properties   10-20

Chapter 11   **Adding Media and Interactivity**
Lesson 1   Add and Modify Flash Objects   11-4
2   Add Rollover Images   11-10
3   Add Behaviors   11-14
4   Add Video   11-18
5   Add Sound   11-22

Chapter 12   **Creating and Using Templates**
Lesson 1   Create Templates with Editable Regions   12-4
2   Use Templates to Create Pages   12-10
3   Use Templates to Update a Site   12-16
4   Use Advanced Template Options   12-20

Chapter 13   **Working with Library Items and Snippets**
Lesson 1   Create and Modify Library Items   13-4
2   Add Library Items to Pages   13-14
3   Add and Modify Snippets   13-20

ACA Grid   1
Data Files List   20
Glossary   36
Index   50

CONTENTS

BRIDGE CHAPTER 1: USING ADOBE BRIDGE TO MANAGE ASSETS

INTRODUCTION   1-2
Accessing Adobe Bridge   1-2

LESSON 1
Explore the Bridge Workspace   1-4
Examining the Adobe Bridge Workspace   1-4
Tasks   Start Adobe Bridge   1-6
         Change modes   1-7

LESSON 2
Use Metadata, Ratings, and Labels   1-8
Tasks   Add and view metadata   1-9
         Filter files with keywords   1-11
         Label and rate files   1-12
         Filter files with labels and ratings   1-13

CHAPTER 1: GETTING STARTED WITH DREAMWEAVER

INTRODUCTION   1-2
Using Dreamweaver Tools   1-2

LESSON 1
Explore the Dreamweaver Workspace   1-4
Examining the Dreamweaver Workspace   1-4
Working with Dreamweaver Views   1-6
Tasks   Start Dreamweaver (Windows)   1-7
         Start Dreamweaver (Macintosh)   1-8
         Change views and view panels   1-9

LESSON 2
View a Web Page and Use Help   1-12
Opening a Web Page   1-12
Viewing Basic Web Page Elements   1-12
Getting Help   1-13
Tasks   Open a web page and view basic page
         elements   1-14
         Use Dreamweaver Help   1-16

LESSON 3
Plan and Set Up a Website   1-18
Understanding the Website Development Process   1-18
Planning a Website   1-18
Planning the Basic Structure   1-19
Creating the Web Pages and Collecting the Page Content   1-20
Testing the Pages   1-21
Modifying the Pages   1-21
Publishing the Site   1-21
Tasks   Select the location for your website   1-22
         Create a local site folder   1-23
         Set up a website   1-24
         Set up web server access   1-25

LESSON 4
Add a Folder And Pages   1-26
Adding a Folder to a Website   1-26
Creating the Home Page   1-27
Adding Pages to a Website   1-27
Tasks   Add a folder to a website (Windows)   1-28
         Add a folder to a website (Macintosh)   1-28
         Set the default images folder   1-29
         Create the home page   1-30
         Save an image file in the assets folder   1-31
         Add pages to a website (Windows)   1-32
         Add pages to a website (Macintosh)   1-33

CHAPTER 2: DEVELOPING A WEB PAGE

INTRODUCTION 2-2
Understanding Page Layout 2-2

LESSON 1
Create Head Content and Set Page Properties 2-4
Creating the Head Content 2-4
Setting Web Page Properties 2-4
Choosing Colors to Convey Information 2-5
Tasks Edit a page title 2-6
Enter keywords 2-7
Enter a description 2-8
Set the page background color 2-9

LESSON 2
Create, Import, and Format Text 2-10
Creating and Importing Text 2-10
Formatting Text Two Ways: HTML vs. CSS 2-10
Changing Fonts 2-11
Changing Font Sizes 2-11
Formatting Paragraphs 2-11
Tasks Enter text 2-12
Format text 2-13
Save an image file in the assets folder 2-14
Import text 2-15
Set text properties 2-16
Check spelling 2-17

LESSON 3
Add Links to Web Pages 2-18
Adding Links to Web Pages 2-18
Using Menu Bars 2-18
Following WCAG Accessibility for Navigation 2-19
Tasks Create a menu bar 2-20
Insert a horizontal rule 2-20
Add links to web pages 2-21
Create an email link 2-22
View the email link in the Assets panel 2-23

LESSON 4
Use the History Panel and Edit Code 2-24
Using the History Panel 2-24
Viewing HTML Code in the Code Inspector 2-24
Tasks Use the History panel 2-26
Use the Code Inspector 2-27
Use the Reference panel 2-28
Insert a date object 2-29

LESSON 5
Modify and Test Web Pages 2-30
Testing and Modifying Web Pages 2-30
Testing a Web Page Using Different Browsers and Screen Sizes 2-30
Using Adobe BrowserLab 2-31
Testing a Web Page as Rendered in a Mobile Device 2-31
Tasks Modify a web page 2-32
Test web pages by viewing them in a browser 2-33

CHAPTER 3: WORKING WITH TEXT AND CASCADING STYLE SHEETS

INTRODUCTION 3-2
Using Cascading Style Sheets 3-2
Formatting Text as Lists 3-2

LESSON 1
Create Unordered and Ordered Lists 3-4

Creating Unordered Lists 3-4
Formatting Unordered Lists 3-4
Creating Ordered Lists 3-5
Formatting Ordered Lists 3-5
Creating Definition Lists 3-5
Tasks Create an unordered list 3-6
Create an ordered list 3-8
Format an ordered list heading 3-9

LESSON 2
Create, Apply, and Edit Cascading Style Sheets 3-10

Understanding Cascading Style Sheets 3-10
Using the CSS Styles Panel 3-10
Understanding the Advantages of Using Style Sheets 3-11
Understanding CSS Code 3-11
Tasks Create a Cascading Style Sheet and add a rule 3-12
Apply a rule 3-14
Edit a rule 3-15
View code with the Code Navigator 3-16
Use the Code Navigator to edit a rule 3-17
Add a Tag selector to an existing style sheet 3-18

LESSON 3
Add Rules and Attach Cascading Style Sheets 3-20

Understanding External and Embedded Style Sheets 3-20
Understanding Related Page Files 3-21
Tasks Add a class rule to a Cascading Style Sheet 3-22
Attach a style sheet 3-24
Use the Related Files toolbar to view styles 3-25

LESSON 4
Use Coding Tools to View and Edit Rules 3-26

Coding Tools in Dreamweaver 3-26
Using Coding Tools to Navigate Code 3-27
Using Code Hints to Streamline Coding 3-27
Converting Styles 3-27
Tasks Collapse code 3-28
Expand code 3-29
Move an embedded style to an external CSS 3-30

CHAPTER 4: ADDING IMAGES

INTRODUCTION 4-2
Using Images to Enhance Web Pages 4-2
Graphics Versus Images 4-2

LESSON 1
Insert and Align Images 4-4

Understanding Graphic File Formats 4-4
Understanding the Assets Panel 4-4
Inserting Files with Adobe Bridge 4-5
Aligning Images 4-5
Tasks Insert an image 4-6
Insert an image placeholder 4-8
Replace an image placeholder with an image 4-9
Use Adobe Bridge 4-10
Align an image 4-11

LESSON 2
Enhance an Image and Use Alternate Text 4-12

Enhancing an Image 4-12
Using Alternate Text 4-13
Tasks Add a border 4-14
Add horizontal and vertical space 4-14
Edit image settings 4-15
Edit alternate text 4-16
Set the alternate text accessibility option 4-17

LESSON 3
Insert a Background Image and Perform Site Maintenance 4-18

Inserting a Background Image 4-18
Managing Images 4-18
Creating a Website Color Palette 4-19
Tasks Insert a background image 4-20
Remove a background image from a page 4-21
Delete files from a website 4-22
Add a color to your design palette 4-23

LESSON 4
Add Graphic Enhancements 4-24

Adding a Link to a Larger Image 4-24
Adding Favicons 4-24
Adding a No Right-Click Script 4-25
Tasks Use an image to link to another image 4-26
Insert a favicon on a page 4-27

DREAMWEAVER XV

CHAPTER 5: WORKING WITH LINKS AND NAVIGATION

INTRODUCTION 5-2

Understanding Internal and External Links 5-2

LESSON 1
Create External and Internal Links 5-4

Creating External Links 5-4
Creating Internal Links 5-4
Tasks Create an external link 5-6
      Create an internal link 5-8
      View links in the Assets panel 5-9

LESSON 2
Create Internal Links to Named Anchors 5-10

Inserting Named Anchors 5-10
Creating Internal Links to Named Anchors 5-10

Tasks Insert a named anchor 5-12
      Create an internal link to a named anchor 5-14

LESSON 3
Create, Modify, and Copy a Spry Menu Bar 5-16

Creating a Spry Menu Bar 5-16
Copying and Modifying a Menu Bar 5-17
Tasks Create a Spry menu bar 5-18
      Add items to a menu bar 5-20
      Use CSS to format a menu bar 5-21
      Copy and paste a menu bar 5-25

LESSON 4
Create an Image Map 5-26

Understanding Image Maps 5-26
Tasks Create an image map 5-28

LESSON 5
Manage Website Links 5-30

Managing Website Links 5-30
Tasks Manage website links 5-31
      Update a page 5-32

LESSON 6
Incorporate Web 2.0 Technology 5-34

What Exactly Is Web 2.0? 5-34

CHAPTER 6: POSITIONING OBJECTS WITH CSS AND TABLES

INTRODUCTION 6-2

Using Div Tags Versus Tables for Page Layout 6-2

LESSON 1
Create a Page Using CSS Layouts 6-4

Understanding Div Tags 6-4
Using CSS Page Layouts 6-4
Viewing CSS Layout Blocks 6-5
Tasks Create a page with a CSS layout 6-6

LESSON 2
Add Content to CSS Layout Blocks 6-8

Understanding Div Tag Content 6-8
Understanding CSS Code 6-9
Tasks Add text to a CSS container 6-10
      Add images to a CSS block 6-12

LESSON 3
Edit and Format CSS Layout Blocks 6-14

Editing Content in CSS Layout Blocks 6-14
Tasks Edit block properties to align content 6-15
      Edit type properties in CSS layout blocks 6-17
      Edit CSS layout block properties 6-18
      Edit page properties 6-20

LESSON 4
Create a Table 6-22

Understanding Table Modes 6-22
Creating a Table 6-22
Using Expanded Tables Mode 6-23
Setting Table Accessibility Preferences 6-23
Tasks Create a table 6-24
      Set table properties 6-25

LESSON 5
Resize, Split, and Merge Cells 6-26

Understanding Table Tags 6-27

Tasks Split cells 6-28
      Merge cells 6-29

LESSON 6
Insert and Align Images in Table Cells 6-30

Inserting Images in Table Cells 6-30
Aligning Images in Table Cells 6-30
Tasks Insert images in table cells 6-32
      Align graphics in table cells 6-33

LESSON 7
Insert Text and Format Cell Content 6-34

Inserting Text in a Table 6-34
Formatting Cell Content 6-34
Formatting Cells 6-34
Tasks Insert text 6-35
      Format cell content 6-36
      Format cell 6-37
      Modify cell content 6-39
      Check layout 6-40
      Validate HTML5 markup 6-41

CHAPTER 7: MANAGING A WEB SERVER AND FILES

INTRODUCTION 7-2
Preparing to Publish a Site 7-2

LESSON 1
Perform Website Maintenance 7-4
Maintaining a Website 7-4
Using the Assets Panel 7-4
Checking Links Sitewide 7-4
Using Site Reports 7-4
Validating Markup 7-5
Testing Pages 7-5
Tasks Check for broken links 7-6
  Check for orphaned files 7-6
  Check for untitled documents 7-7
  Check for missing alternate text 7-7
  Validate for HTML5 standards 7-8
  Validate CSS 7-9
  Enable Design Notes 7-10
  Associate a Design Note with a file 7-11
  Edit a Design Note 7-12

LESSON 2
Publish a Website and Transfer Files 7-14
Defining a Remote Site 7-14
Viewing a Remote Site 7-15
Transferring Files to and from a Remote Site 7-15
Synchronizing Files 7-16
Tasks Set up a web server connection on an FTP site 7-17
  Set up a web server connection to a local or network folder 7-18
  View a website on a remote server 7-19
  Upload files to a remote server 7-20
  Synchronize files 7-21

LESSON 3
Check Files Out and In 7-22
Managing a Website with a Team 7-22
Checking Out and Checking In Files 7-22
Enabling the Check Out Feature 7-23
Using Subversion Control 7-23
Tasks Activate the Enable file check-out feature 7-24
  Check out a file 7-25
  Check in a file 7-26
  Edit site preferences 7-27

LESSON 4
Cloak Files 7-28
Understanding Cloaking Files 7-28
Cloaking a Folder 7-28
Cloaking Selected File Types 7-29
Tasks Cloak and uncloak a folder 7-30
  Cloak selected file types 7-31

LESSON 5
Import and Export a Site Definition 7-32
Exporting a Site Definition 7-32
Importing a Site Definition 7-32
Tasks Export a site definition 7-33
  Import a site definition 7-34
  View the imported site 7-35

LESSON 6
Evaluate Web Content For Legal Use 7-36
Can I Use Downloaded Media? 7-36
Understanding Intellectual Property 7-36
What Exactly Does the Copyright Owner Own? 7-36
Understanding Fair Use 7-37
How Do I Use Work Properly? 7-37
Understanding Licensing Agreements 7-37
Obtaining Permission or a License 7-38
Posting a Copyright Notice 7-38

LESSON 7
Present a Website to a Client 7-40
Are You Ready to Present Your Work? 7-40
What Is the Best Way to Present Your Work? 7-41

DREAMWEAVER XVII

CHAPTER 8: USING STYLES AND STYLE SHEETS FOR DESIGN

INTRODUCTION 8-2

LESSON 1
Create and Use Embedded Styles 8-4

Understanding Embedded Styles 8-4
Creating and Applying Embedded Styles 8-4
Tasks Replace the folder for The Striped Umbrella website (Win) 8-8
Replace the folder for The Striped Umbrella website (Mac) 8-9
Create a class style 8-10
Apply a class style 8-11

LESSON 2
Modify Embedded Styles 8-12

Editing Embedded Styles 8-12
Redefining HTML Tags 8-12
Using the CSS Styles Panel 8-12
Tasks Modify a class style 8-14
Redefine an HTML tag 8-15
Edit an embedded style in the Properties pane 8-17
Delete an embedded style 8-17

LESSON 3
Use CSS3 and Media Queries 8-18

Understanding CSS3 Features 8-18
Using Media Queries and Fluid Grid Layouts 8-19
Validating for CSS3 Standards 8-20
Testing Browser Compatibility with Adobe BrowserLab 8-21
Tasks Add CSS3 tags for enhanced appearance 8-22
Modify CSS3 tags 8-24
Upload files for CSS3 validation 8-25

LESSON 4
Work with Conflicting Styles 8-26

Understanding the Order of Precedence 8-26
Using Tools to Manage Your Styles 8-27
Tasks Compare conflicting styles 8-28
Check for errors with Browser Compatibility Check 8-29

CHAPTER 9: COLLECTING DATA WITH FORMS

INTRODUCTION 9-2

Using Forms to Collect Information 9-2

LESSON 1
Plan and Create a Form 9-4

Planning a Form 9-4
Creating Forms 9-4
Setting Form Properties 9-5
Understanding CGI Scripts 9-7
Tasks Insert a form 9-8
Set form properties 9-9

LESSON 2
Edit and Format a Form 9-10

Using Tables to Lay Out a Form 9-10
Adding Labels to Form Objects 9-10
Using CSS to Format the Form 9-11
Tasks Add a table to a form 9-12
Add form labels to table cells 9-13
Add form labels using the Label button 9-14
Create a rule for the form table 9-15

LESSON 3
Work with Form Objects 9-16

Understanding Form Objects 9-16
Setting Form Object Attributes 9-17
Using Dreamweaver Exchange 9-18
Tasks Insert single-line text fields 9-19
Insert a multiple-line text field 9-21
Insert a Checkbox Group 9-22
Add radio groups to a form 9-24
Add a menu 9-26
Insert a hidden field 9-28
Add Submit and Reset buttons 9-29

LESSON 4
Test and Process a Form 9-30

Creating User-Friendly Forms 9-30
Tasks Check spelling and create visual clues for required fields 9-31
Link a file 9-32

CHAPTER 10: POSITIONING OBJECTS WITH AP DIVS

INTRODUCTION 10-2
Using AP Divs 10-2

LESSON 1
Insert an AP Div 10-4

Understanding AP Elements 10-4
Using HTML Tags to Create AP Divs 10-5
Understanding AP Div Content 10-5
Formatting AP Divs 10-5
Tasks Draw an AP div 10-6
Define an AP div 10-7

LESSON 2
Set the Position and Size of an AP Div 10-8

Understanding Absolute Positioning 10-8
Setting Positioning Attributes 10-8
Tasks Set the Left and Top positions of an AP div 10-10
Set AP div height and width 10-11
Set the Z-Index value for AP divs 10-12

LESSON 3
Add Content to an AP Div 10-14

Understanding AP Element Content 10-14
Tasks Add an image to an AP div 10-16
Set a background image 10-18
Add and format text on an AP div 10-19

LESSON 4
Set AP Div Properties 10-20

Using the AP Elements Panel 10-20
Setting AP Divs Relative to Containers 10-20
Tasks Rename an AP element 10-22
Control AP div visibility 10-23
Adjust the position of AP elements relative to a CSS container 10-24
Add borders to AP elements 10-25

CHAPTER 11: ADDING MEDIA AND INTERACTIVITY

INTRODUCTION 11-2
Understanding Media Objects 11-2

LESSON 1
Add and Modify Flash Objects 11-4

Understanding Adobe Flash 11-4
Inserting Flash Content 11-4
Tasks Insert Flash movies 11-6
Play a Flash movie in Dreamweaver and in a browser 11-7
Modify a Flash file from Dreamweaver 11-8

LESSON 2
Add Rollover Images 11-10

Understanding Rollover Images 11-10
Adding Rollover Images 11-10
Tasks Add a rollover image 11-12

LESSON 3
Add Behaviors 11-14

Adding Interactive Elements 11-14
Using the Behaviors Panel 11-14
Understanding Actions and Events 11-14
Using the Spry Framework 11-15
Tasks Add a behavior 11-16
Edit a behavior 11-17

LESSON 4
Add Video 11-18

Inserting Video 11-18
Tasks Add video 11-20

LESSON 5
Add Sound 11-22

Adding Sound 11-22
Using Controllers 11-23
Tasks Add sound 11-24

DREAMWEAVER XIX

CHAPTER 12: CREATING AND USING TEMPLATES

INTRODUCTION 12-2
Understanding How to Use Templates 12-2

LESSON 1
Create Templates with Editable Regions 12-4
Creating a Template from an Existing Page 12-4
Defining Editable Regions 12-4
Defining Optional Regions 12-4
Defining Editable Optional Regions 12-5
Tasks Create a template from an existing page 12-6
Create an editable region 12-7
Modify a template 12-8

LESSON 2
Use Templates to Create Pages 12-10
Creating Pages with Templates 12-10
Modifying Editable Regions 12-10
Creating Links in Template-Based Pages 12-11
Attaching a Template to an Existing Page 12-12
Tasks Create a new page based on a template 12-13
Modify editable regions in a template 12-14
Add a link 12-14
Convert existing pages to template-based pages 12-15

LESSON 3
Use Templates to Update a Site 12-16
Making Changes to a Template 12-16
Updating All Pages Based on a Template 12-17
Tasks Make changes to a template 12-18
Update all template-based pages in a site 12-18

LESSON 4
Use Advanced Template Options 12-20
Setting Parameters for Optional Regions 12-20
Nesting Templates 12-20
Creating Editable Attributes 12-21

CHAPTER 13: WORKING WITH LIBRARY ITEMS AND SNIPPETS

INTRODUCTION 13-2
Understanding Library Items 13-2
Understanding Snippets 13-2

LESSON 1
Create and Modify Library Items 13-4
Understanding the Benefits of Library Items 13-4
Viewing and Creating Library Items 13-4
Modifying Library Items 13-5
Tasks Create a text-based library item 13-6
Create an image-based library item 13-8
Edit an image-based library item 13-10
Update library items 13-11
Edit a text-based library item 13-12

LESSON 2
Add Library Items to Pages 13-14
Adding Library Items to a Page 13-14
Making Library Items Editable on a Page 13-14
Deleting and Recreating Library Items 13-15
Tasks Add a library item to a page 13-16
Make a library item editable on a page 13-18
Delete a library item 13-19
Recreate a library item 13-19

LESSON 3
Add and Modify Snippets 13-20
Using the Snippets Panel 13-20
Inserting and Modifying Snippets 13-20
Creating New Snippets 13-21
Tasks Add a predefined snippet to a page 13-22
Modify snippet text 13-23
Modify snippet links 13-24
Create a new snippet 13-24

ACA GRID 1
DATA FILES LIST 20
GLOSSARY 36
INDEX 50

DREAMWEAVER XX

READ THIS BEFORE YOU BEGIN

Intended Audience

This text is designed for the beginner or intermediate user who wants to learn how to use Dreamweaver. The book is designed to provide basic and in-depth material that not only educates, but also encourages you to explore the nuances of this exciting program. Features new to Dreamweaver CS6 and covered in this book are indicated by NEW.

Approach

The text allows you to work at your own pace through step-by-step tutorials. A concept is presented and the process is explained, followed by the actual steps. To learn the most from the use of the text, you should adopt the following habits:

- Proceed slowly: Accuracy and comprehension are more important than speed.
- Understand what is happening with each step before you continue to the next step.
- After finishing a skill, ask yourself if you could do it on your own, without referring to the steps. If the answer is no, review the steps.

General

Throughout the initial chapters, students are given precise instructions regarding saving their work. Students should feel that they can save their work at any time, not just when instructed to do so.

Icons, Buttons, and Pointers

Symbols for icons, buttons, and pointers are shown in the step each time they are used. Icons may look different in the files panel depending on the file association settings on your computer.

Skills Reference

As a bonus, a Power User Shortcuts table is included at the end of chapters. This table contains the quickest method of completing tasks covered in the chapter. It is meant for the more experienced user, or for the user who wants to become more experienced.

Fonts

The Data Files contain a variety of commonly used fonts, but there is no guarantee that these fonts will be available on your computer. In a few cases, fonts other than those common to a PC or a Macintosh are used. If any of the fonts in use is not available on your computer, you can make a substitution, realizing that the results may vary from those in the book.

Windows and Macintosh

Adobe Dreamweaver CS6 works virtually the same on Windows and Macintosh operating systems. In those cases where there is a significant difference, the abbreviations (Win) and (Mac) are used.

Data Files

To complete the lessons in this book, you need the Data Files. To access the Data Files for this book, take the following steps:

1. Open your browser and go to http://www.cengagebrain.com
2. Type the author, title, or ISBN of this book in the Search window. (The ISBN is listed on the back cover.)
3. Click the book title in the list of search results.
4. When the book's main page is displayed, click the Access button under Free Study Tools.
5. To download Data Files, select a chapter number and then click on the Data Files tab on the left navigation bar to download the files.
6. To access additional materials, including information about ACE certification, click the Additional Materials tab under Book Resources to download the files.

Your instructor will tell you where to store the files as you work, such as the hard drive, a network server, or a USB drive. The instructions in the lessons will refer to "the drive and folder where you store your Data Files" when referring to the Data Files for the book.

When you copy the Data Files to your computer, you may see lock icons that indicate that the files are read-only when you view them in the Dreamweaver Files panel. To unlock the files, right-click on the locked file name in the Files panel, then click Turn off Read Only.

Images vs. Graphics

Many times these terms seem to be used interchangeably. For the purposes of this book, the term images is used when referring to pictures on a web page. The term graphics is used as a more encompassing term that refers to non-text items on a web page such as photographs, logos, navigation bars, Flash animations, graphs, background images, and drawings. You may define these terms in a slightly different way, depending on your professional background or business environment.

Dreamweaver Preference Settings

All Data and Solution Files in this edition are of the HTML5 document type. To follow the steps correctly, it is easier if you set your Dreamweaver Default Document Type (DTD) setting to HTML5. To do this, use the Edit, Preferences, New Document command, then choose HTML5 for the Default Document Type (DTD).

System Preference Settings

The learning process will be much easier if you can see the file extensions for the files you will use in the lessons. To do this in Windows, open Windows Explorer, click Organize, Folder and Search Options, click the View tab, then uncheck the box Hide Extensions for Known File Types. To do this for a Mac, go to Finder, click the Finder menu, and then click Preferences. Click the Advanced tab, then select the Show all file extensions check box. In Windows 8, open Windows Explorer, click the View tab, and then select the File name extensions check box in the Show/Hide group.

The figures in the book were taken using the Windows setting of Smaller - 100% (default). If you want to match the figures exactly, change your system to match this setting. It is located in the Control Panel, Appearance and Personalization, Display dialog box.

Creating a Portfolio

The Portfolio Project and Project Builders allow you to use your creativity to come up with original Dreamweaver designs. It is a good idea to create a portfolio in which you can store your original work.

System Requirements

For a Windows operating system:

- Intel Pentium® 4 or AMD Athlon® 64 processor
- Microsoft Windows® XP with Service Pack 2 (Service Pack 3 recommended); Windows Vista® Home Premium, Business, Ultimate, or Enterprise with Service Pack 1; or Windows 7
- 512 MB of RAM
- 1 GB of available hard-disk space for installation; additional free space required during installation (cannot install on removable flash-based storage devices)
- 1280 × 800 display with 16-bit video card
- Java(TM) Runtime Environment 1.6 (included)
- DVD-ROM drive
- QuickTime 7.6.6 software required for HTML5 media playback
- This software will not operate without activation.
- Broadband Internet connection and registration are required for software activation, validation of subscriptions, and access to online services. Phone activation is not available.

For a Macintosh operating system:

- Multicore Intel® processor
- Mac OS X v10.6 or v10.7
- 512 MB of RAM
- 1.8 GB of available hard-disk space for installation; additional free space required during installation (cannot install on a volume that uses a case-sensitive file system or on removable flash storage devices)
- 1280 × 800 display with 16-bit video card
- Java Runtime Environment 1.6
- DVD-ROM drive
- QuickTime 7.6.6 software required for HTML5 media playback
- This software will not operate without activation.
- Broadband Internet connection and registration are required for software activation, validation of subscriptions, and access to online services. Phone activation is not available.

Memory Challenges

If, instead of seeing an image on an open page, you see an image placeholder with a large X across it, your RAM is running low. Try closing any other applications that are running to free up memory.

Building a Website

You will create and develop several websites named The Striped Umbrella, Blooms & Bulbs, TripSmart, and Carolyne's Creations in the lesson material and end of unit exercises in this book. Because each chapter builds from the previous chapter, it is recommended that you work through the chapters in consecutive order.

Websites Used in Figures

Each time a website is used for illustration purposes in a lesson, where necessary, a statement acknowledging that we obtained permission to use the website is included, along with the URL of the website. Sites whose content is in the public domain, such as federal government websites, are acknowledged as a courtesy.

ADOBE BRIDGE CS6

CHAPTER 1

USING ADOBE BRIDGE TO
MANAGE ASSETS

1. Explore the Bridge workspace
2. Use metadata, ratings, and labels

CHAPTER 1
USING ADOBE BRIDGE TO
MANAGE ASSETS

Introduction

Adobe Bridge is a media content manager integrated with many of the Adobe products for quick access to project files. Bridge is very easy to use as your "bridge" between your library of assets and your project files you are developing in programs such as Dreamweaver, Photoshop, Fireworks, Flash, Illustrator, and InDesign. In Bridge, you can open and preview any file format that Adobe recognizes such as JPGs, SWFs, PNGs, and PDFs. Although the most common use of Bridge is to organize and view media, it has many powerful features that you will find useful, such as adding metadata and keywords to files. **Metadata** is file information you add to a file with tags (words) that are used to identify and describe the file. **Keywords** are words you add to a file to identify, group, and sort files.

Accessing Adobe Bridge

Adobe Bridge is packaged with the Adobe Creative Suite. There are several ways to access the program: by opening it directly from your Applications or Program Files folder on your computer's hard drive, or within Adobe Illustrator, Photoshop, Fireworks, Flash, or InDesign by using the Go to Bridge button on the Menu bar (in Windows, this is on the Menu bar next to the Help, on Mac it is on the Application bar), or by choosing File on the Menu bar, and then clicking Browse in Bridge within the program. A streamlined version of Bridge called Mini Bridge is also available in Photoshop, InDesign, and InCopy; it appears as a panel that opens directly within the application work area. You can always use Bridge as your primary tool for viewing, copying, and moving media files similar to the way you use Windows Explorer or Macintosh Finder. You can also configure Bridge to start automatically each time you log in or start your computer or device by choosing Start Bridge At Login on the Advanced tab in the Adobe Bridge Preferences dialog box. You can enable (or disable) a script that enables other applications to communicate with Bridge when you start Bridge by checking the Adobe Bridge CS6 check box on the Startup Scripts tab in the Preferences dialog box. To access the Preferences dialog box, click Edit on the Menu bar, then choose Preferences (Win) or click the Adobe Bridge CS6 menu and then choose Preferences (Mac).

TOOLS YOU'LL USE

LESSON 1

Explore the Bridge WORKSPACE

What You'll Do

In this lesson, you will start Bridge, examine the components that make up the Bridge workspace, and change modes.

Examining the Adobe Bridge Workspace

When you start Bridge, you see the Bridge **Essentials workspace**, the default workspace that includes all of the menus, panels, buttons, and panes that you use to organize your media files. Other workspace choices are the Filmstrip, Metadata, Output, Keywords, Preview, Light Table, and Folders workspaces. You can change workspaces by using the Window menu or by clicking one of the Workspace buttons on the Application bar. You can also arrange the panes and panels to create a custom workspace and then assign it a unique name using the Window > Workspace > New Workspace command. You can work in **Compact mode**, which is a mode with a smaller, simplified workspace window. Press [Ctrl][Enter] (Win) or [⌘][return] (Mac) to switch back and forth between your workspace and Compact mode.

The Essentials workspace is divided into three panes, which are arranged in columns and further divided into panels. Each panel can be expanded or collapsed by clicking the panel title bar. You can also hide panels using the Windows > Display or Hide command.

Refer to Figure 1 as you locate the components described below.

> **QUICK TIP:**
> You can resize panels by dragging the horizontal divider bar between panels or the vertical divider bar on either side of the Content panel. You can also lighten the Bridge interface by choosing a different color theme on the General tab in the Preferences dialog box. From this point forward, the light gray theme is used for maximum readability.

The left pane includes the Favorites, Folders, Filter, Collections, and Export panels. You can use the **Favorites panel** to quickly access folders that you designate as folders you use frequently. You can use the **Folders panel** to navigate through and select a folder, and review its contents. The **Filter panel** is used for filtering files to view in the Content panel. The **Collections panel** is used to group assets located in different locations into a single collection. The **Export panel** is used to optimize images by saving them as JPEGs for use on the web.

The center pane is the **Content panel**, where thumbnails of the files from the selected drive and folder in the Folders panel appear.

You can change the size of the thumbnails by using the Thumbnail slider at the bottom of the workspace.

The right pane includes the Preview, Metadata, and Keywords panels. The **Preview panel** is where a preview of a selected file appears. The **Metadata panel** lists the metadata for a selected file. You use the Metadata panel to assign new metadata to a file. The **Keywords panel** lists the keywords assigned to a file. You use the Keywords panel to add new keywords to a file.

The **Menu bar** with the program commands is at the top of the Bridge workspace. Below the Menu bar is the **Application bar** that contains navigation buttons, the Workspace buttons, and the Search text box. Under the Application bar is the **Path bar**, where you see the path for the selected folder in the Folders panel that you are currently viewing. The Path bar makes it easy to navigate quickly from folder to folder.

Figure 1 *The Bridge Essentials workspace*

Lesson 1   Explore the Bridge Workspace

Start Adobe Bridge

To start Adobe Bridge directly using Windows:

1. Click the **Start button** on the taskbar.
2. Point to **Programs** (if necessary), then click **Adobe Bridge CS6**, as shown in Figure 2.

To start Adobe Bridge directly using Macintosh:

1. Click **Finder** in the Dock, then click **Applications**.
2. Click the **Adobe Bridge CS6 folder**, then double-click the **Adobe Bridge CS6 application**.

TIP Once Bridge is running, you can add it to the Dock permanently by [control]-clicking the Bridge icon, clicking Options, then clicking Keep in Dock.

To start Adobe Bridge from an Adobe Creative Suite 6 component that is integrated with Bridge:

1. Click **File** on the Menu bar, then click **Browse in Bridge**.

   Or

   Click the **Adobe Bridge button** on the Menu bar.

   The button you use to start Bridge varies by Adobe application. There is no Browse in Bridge button in Dreamweaver on a Mac.

TIP Photoshop users can also click Mini Bridge in iconic panels.

You started Bridge CS6.

Figure 2 *Starting Adobe Bridge*

Adobe Bridge CS6

BRIDGE 1-6

Using Adobe Bridge to Manage Assets

Figure 3 *Viewing the Bridge Data Files folder*

Essentials workspace button

Breadcrumb trail

Folders panel

Bridge folder in Data Files folder

Figure 4 *Using Review Mode and the Loupe tool*

Thumbnail slider

Loupe tool placed over an image

Loupe tool

Lesson 1   Explore the Bridge Workspace

Change modes

1. Verify that you are in the Essentials workspace.
2. Use the breadcrumb trail across the top of the Bridge window on the Path panel or use the Folders panel to navigate to and select the **Bridge folder** from the drive and folder where you store your Data Files, as shown in Figure 3.

   Thumbnails of each file in the Bridge Data Files folder appear in the Content panel.
3. Use the **Thumbnail slider** on the bottom of the Bridge window to adjust the size of the thumbnails, as shown in Figure 3.
4. Click **View** on the Menu bar, click **Review Mode** to display the contents of the Bridge folder in a carousel arrangement, then use the keyboard arrow keys to shuffle through the images.

   TIP You can also press [Ctrl][B] (Win) or ⌘ [B] (Mac) to change to Review Mode.
5. Click the **Loupe tool** in the lower-right corner of the window, then click and drag the **mouse pointer** over the image to magnify a selected area so you can examine the detail more closely, as shown in Figure 4.

   TIP You can also activate the Loupe tool by moving the mouse pointer over an image, then clicking the image.
6. Press **[Esc]** (Win) or ⌘ **[W]** (Mac) to exit Review Mode, then click a blank area of the Content panel to deselect the files.

You viewed the Data Files, used the Thumbnail slider to adjust the size of the thumbnails, changed to Review Mode, used the Loupe tool to magnify a selected area in an image, then exited Review Mode.

BRIDGE 1-7

LESSON 2

Use Metadata, Ratings, AND LABELS

What You'll Do

In this lesson, you will add and view metadata, use keywords to filter files, label and rate files, then filter files with labels and ratings.

The Metadata panel is a rich source of information about a file, including the camera settings used (descriptive information that you cannot change) and copyright information (additive data that you can change). You can view and edit the copyright information in the IPTC (International Press Telecommunications Council) Core section of the Metadata panel. Image resolution, author name, and keywords are also examples of metadata you can view in the Metadata panel.

Metadata is saved using the **Extensible Metadata Platform (XMP) standard**. XMP metadata is used by Adobe products, such as Illustrator, InDesign, Flash, and Photoshop, and is usually stored with the file name. If a file contains metadata, XMP allows the metadata to stay with the file when the file is converted to a different file type or placed in a project. You can add metadata using the File > File Info command.

QUICK TIP

You cannot add metadata to .gif files.

You use the Keywords panel to view and add keywords to a file to help group, organize, and sort files. There are two types of keywords: **parent keywords** and **child keywords**. Child keywords are also referred to as **sub keywords**. Child keywords are subcategories of parent keywords. For instance, you could have a parent keyword "food" and a child keyword "desserts." After you have added keywords to files, you can use the Filter panel to sort files by their keywords.

QUICK TIP

In the following steps, you will create keywords for the four websites used in the Dreamweaver lessons. After assigning the keywords, you can sort them by website, copy all of the files for each website, then paste them in the assets folders you will create when you set up the websites. This will save you some time as you work through the lessons, but it is not necessary if you choose not to do so.

You can also identify groups of files by using labels. Labels allow you to assign a file a color or a star rating from zero to five stars. This is an easy way to mark the files you want to keep and others you may want to delete.

Figure 5 *Viewing the metadata for the blooms_banner.jpg file*

Metadata for the blooms_banner.jpg file

Figure 6 *Viewing the keywords for the blooms_banner.jpg file*

Keywords for the blooms_banner.jpg file

Figure 7 *Adding a keyword and a sub keyword*

Website keyword

blooms sub keyword added and applied to the file

Lesson 2 Use Metadata, Ratings, and Labels

Add and view metadata

1. Open the Metadata panel, click the first file listed, **blooms_banner.jpg**, then click **File Properties** (if necessary) to expand the panel to view the file size, dimensions, and resolution of the selected file, as shown in Figure 5.

2. Click the **Keywords panel**, then view the keywords for the selected file, as shown in Figure 6.

   Each file is assigned one or more chapter numbers that correspond to the chapter or chapters the file is used in. The blooms_banner.jpg file is used in chapters five, four, one, and two. It would also be nice to include a keyword for each file that corresponds to the website the file is used with.

3. Click the **New Keyword button** on the lower-right corner of the panel.

4. Type **Website** in the New Keyword text box, then press **[Enter]** (Win) or **[return]** (Mac).

   Keywords let you search for and quickly locate files with common characteristics.

TIP If you want to delete the default keywords and sub keywords, click the keyword you want to delete, then click the Delete Keyword button. The default keywords have been deleted in Figure 7.

5. With the Website keyword selected, click the **New Sub Keyword button**, type **blooms** in the Keywords text box, press **[Enter]** (Win) or **[return]** (Mac), then click to place a check mark in the check box next to the new keyword.

   The check mark applies the keyword to the file, as shown in Figure 7.

(continued)

BRIDGE 1-9

6. Repeat Step 5 to add three more sub keywords under the Website keyword: **striped_umbrella**, **carolynes**, and **tripsmart**, as shown in Figure 8.

7. Using Table 1 as a reference, apply the striped_umbrella sub keyword to each image listed in the table to associate them with The Striped Umbrella website.

   There are four files that will be used in The Striped Umbrella website that you cannot add the striped_umbrella sub keyword to: cafe_logo.gif, spacer_30px.gif, su_logo.gif, and su_banner.gif.

8. Using Table 2 as a reference, repeat Step 7 to add sub keywords for the Blooms & Bulbs website.

   There is one file you cannot add a sub keyword to: gardening_gloves.gif.

Figure 8 *Adding three additional sub keywords*

Four sub keywords added

TABLE 1
Add the striped_umbrella sub keyword to these files:

boardwalk.png	map_large.jpg
boats.jpg	map_small.jpg
cafe_photo.jpg	pool.jpg
chocolate_cake.jpg	sea_spa_logo.png
club_house.jpg	two_dolphins_small.jpg
family_sunset.jpg	water.jpg
fisherman.jpg	

© Cengage Learning 2013

TABLE 2
Add the blooms sub keyword to these files:

blooms_banner.jpg	rose_bloom.jpg
butterfly.jpg	ruby_grass.jpg
chives.jpg	trees.jpg
coleus.jpg	tulips.jpg
fiber_optic_grass.jpg	two_roses_large.jpg
lady_in_red.jpg	two_roses.jpg
plants.jpg	water_lily.jpg
rose_bud.jpg	

© Cengage Learning 2013

BRIDGE 1-10

Using Adobe Bridge to Manage Assets

Figure 9 *Viewing files with the striped_umbrella sub keyword*

striped_umbrella keyword is selected

13 files are listed and appear in the Content panel

Figure 10 *Viewing files with the blooms sub keyword*

blooms keyword is selected

15 files are listed and appear in the Content panel

Filter files with keywords

1. Click the **Filter panel title bar** to expand the panel if necessary, then click to select **striped_umbrella** under the Keywords criteria.

   13 files appear in the Content panel, as shown in Figure 9.

   TIP If the files are not listed in alphabetical order, click View > Sort > By Filename.

2. Click to select **blooms** under the Keywords criteria, then click to deselect **striped_umbrella**.

   The Content panel now shows 15 files listed for the Blooms & Bulbs website, as shown in Figure 10.

3. Click to deselect **blooms** under the Keywords criteria.

   All 52 files appear in the Content panel.

You used the Filter panel to view the Data files with the keywords striped_umbrella and blooms. You then removed the filter to view all Data files.

Lesson 2   Use Metadata, Ratings, and Labels

BRIDGE 1-11

Label and rate files

1. On the Content panel, click the **blue_footed_booby.jpg** file, hold down **[Ctrl]** (Win) or **[⌘]** (Mac), click **iguana_and_lizard.jpg**, then click **sea_lions_in_surf.jpg**.

   TIP Use the scroll bar to scroll to select the files if necessary.

   Three files are selected in the Content panel.

2. Click **Label** on the Menu bar, then click *********, as shown in Figure 11.

   Each of the three files is labeled with a five-star rating. The stars appear under the thumbnail and above the filename in the Content panel and Preview panel.

   TIP To remove a rating, use the Label > No Rating command.

3. Click the **brunch.jpg file**, click **Label** on the Menu bar, then click **Approved**.

   The Approved label could be used to indicate art that has been approved for a project. A green label appears between the thumbnail and the filename in the Content panel and Preview panel, as shown in Figure 12.

   TIP To remove a label, use the Label > No Label command.

You applied a five-star label to three files. You then added an Approved label to one file.

Figure 11 *Applying a five-star rating to three selected files*

Five-star rating

Preview panel shows three files are selected

Figure 12 *Applying an Approved label to a file*

Approved label

Approved green label appears in Content panel and Preview panel

BRIDGE 1-12

Using Adobe Bridge to Manage Assets

Figure 13 *Filter showing file with Approved label*

Approved criteria

One file appears in Content panel and Preview panel

Figure 14 *Viewing files with a ***** rating*

***** criteria

Three files appear in Content panel

Lesson 2   Use Metadata, Ratings, and Labels

Filter files with labels and ratings

1. On the Filter panel, click to select **Approved** under the Labels criteria.

   One file appears in the Content panel and Preview panel, as shown in Figure 13.

2. On the Filter panel, click to deselect **Approved** under the Labels criteria.

3. On the Filter panel, click to select ***** under the Ratings criteria.

   Three files appear in the Content panel, as shown in Figure 14.

4. On the Filter panel, click the **Clear Filter button** at the bottom of the panel to remove the filter.

   All files appear in the Content panel.

5. Close Adobe Bridge.

BRIDGE 1-13

SKILLS REVIEW

Explore the Bridge workspace.

1. Start Adobe Bridge, then use the Folders panel or the Path bar to display the Bridge Data Files folder.
2. Use the buttons on the Application bar to switch to the Filmstrip workspace.
3. Return to the Essentials workspace.
4. Press [Ctrl][Enter] (Win) or [⌘][return] (Mac) to switch to Compact mode.
5. Repeat Step 4 to switch back to the Essentials workspace.

Use metadata, ratings, and labels.

1. Refer to Table 3 to add the sub keyword **carolynes** to the files that will be used in the Carolyne's Creations website.
2. Refer to Table 4 to add the sub keyword **tripsmart** to the files that will be used in the TripSmart website.
3. Filter the files in the Bridge folder to show only the files for the Carolyne's Creations website.
4. Filter the files in the Bridge folder to show only the TripSmart website files.
5. Clear the filter to show all files.
6. Add a four-star rating to the fish.jpg file.
7. Add an approved label to the family_sunset.jpg file.
8. Filter the files in the Bridge folder to show the five GIF images that you were not able to add keywords to, then compare your screen to Figure 15.
9. Clear all filters, then exit Bridge.

[TABLE 3]

Add the carolynes sub keyword to these files:

brunch.jpg	fish.jpg
cc_banner_with_text.jpg	marshmallows.jpg
cc_banner.jpg	peruvian_appetizers.jpg
children_cooking.jpg	peruvian_glass.jpg
cookies_oven.jpg	pie.jpg

© Cengage Learning 2013

[TABLE 4]

Add the tripsmart sub keyword to these files:

blue_footed_booby.jpg	sea_lions_in_surf.jpg
iguana_and_lizard.jpg	tripsmart_banner.jpg
llama.jpg	tripsmart_gradient.jpg
machu_picchu_from_high.jpg	walking_stick.jpg
machu_picchu_ruins.jpg	

© Cengage Learning 2013

SKILLS REVIEW
(CONTINUED)

Figure 15 *Completed Skills Review*

Using Adobe Bridge to Manage Assets

BRIDGE 1-15

ADOBE DREAMWEAVER CS6

CHAPTER 1

GETTING STARTED WITH
DREAMWEAVER

1. Explore the Dreamweaver workspace
2. View a web page and use Help
3. Plan and set up a website
4. Add a folder and pages

CHAPTER 1
GETTING STARTED WITH DREAMWEAVER

Introduction

Adobe Dreamweaver CS6 is a web development tool that lets you create dynamic web pages containing text, images, hyperlinks, animation, sounds, video, and interactive elements. You can use Dreamweaver to create individual web pages or complex websites consisting of many web pages. A **website** is a group of related web pages that are linked together and share a common interface and design. Dreamweaver lets you create design elements such as text, forms, rollover images, and interactive buttons, or import elements from other software programs. You can also save Dreamweaver files in many different file formats, including XHTML, HTML, JavaScript, CSS, or XML, to name a few. **XHTML** is the acronym for eXtensible HyperText Markup Language, the current standard language used to create web pages. You can still use **HTML** (HyperText Markup Language) in Dreamweaver; however, it is no longer considered the standard language. You use a web browser to view your web pages on the Internet. A **web browser** is a program, such as Microsoft Internet Explorer, Google Chrome, Apple Safari, or Mozilla Firefox, which displays web pages.

Using Dreamweaver Tools

Creating a robust website is a complex task. Fortunately, Dreamweaver has an impressive number of tools that can help. Using Dreamweaver design tools, you can create dynamic and interactive web pages without writing a word of code. However, if you prefer to write code, Dreamweaver makes it easy to enter and edit the code directly and see the visual results of the code instantly. Dreamweaver also contains organizational tools that help you work with a team of people to create a website. You can also use the Dreamweaver management tools to help you manage a website. For instance, you can use the **Files panel** to create folders to organize and store the various files for your website, and to add pages to your website.

TOOLS YOU'LL USE

Property inspector

Collapse to Icons button

Show Code and Design views button

Switch Design view to Live view button

Show Code view button

Show Design view button

DREAMWEAVER 1-3

LESSON 1

Explore the
DREAMWEAVER WORKSPACE

What You'll Do

In this lesson, you will start Dreamweaver, examine the components that make up the Dreamweaver workspace, and change views.

Examining the Dreamweaver Workspace

After you start Dreamweaver, you see the **Dreamweaver workspace**, the screen that includes all of the menus, panels, buttons, inspectors, and panes that you use to create and maintain websites. It is designed to give you easy access to all the tools you need to create web pages. Refer to Figure 1 as you locate the components described below.

The **Document window** is the large area in the Dreamweaver program window where you create and edit web pages. The **Menu bar** (also called the **Application bar**), located above the Document window, includes menu names, a Workspace switcher, and other application commands. The Menu bar appears on either one bar or two bars, depending on your screen size and resolution. To choose a menu command, click the menu name to open the menu, then click the menu command. The Insert panel appears at the top of the Dreamweaver workspace on the right side of the screen. The **Insert panel**, sometimes called the Insert bar, includes nine categories of buttons displayed through a drop-down menu: Common, Layout, Forms, Data, Spry, jQuery Mobile, InContext Editing, Text, and Favorites. Clicking a category in the Insert panel displays the buttons and menus for inserting objects associated with that category. For example, if you click the Layout category, you find buttons for using div tags for creating blocks of content on pages; for inserting Spry interactive page elements such as buttons or drop-down menus; and for inserting and editing tables.

QUICK TIP

Two additional options are available through the Insert panel drop-down menu. To display the icons in color, click Color Icons, or right-click the Insert panel, then click Color Icons. To hide the button labels, click Hide Labels.

The **Document toolbar** contains buttons and drop-down menus you can use to change the current work mode, check browser compatibility, preview web pages, debug web pages, choose visual aids, and view file-management options. One of the buttons on the Document toolbar, the Switch Design view to Live view button, is used to view the current page in Live view.

DREAMWEAVER 1-4

Getting Started with Dreamweaver

Live view displays an open document as if you were viewing it in a browser, with interactive elements active and functioning. When you switch to Live view, navigation buttons are added to the Document toolbar.

Two additional toolbars do not appear by default: the Standard toolbar and the Style Rendering toolbar. The **Standard toolbar** contains buttons you can use to execute frequently used commands that are also available on the File and Edit menus. The **Style Rendering toolbar** contains buttons that you can use to display data for different platforms, such as a cell phone or television. To display or hide the Document, Standard, and Style Rendering toolbars, right-click an empty area of an open toolbar, then click the toolbar name you wish to display or hide. You can also use the View > Toolbars menu.

The **Related Files toolbar** is located below an open document's filename tab and displays the names of any related files. **Related files** are files that are linked to a document and are necessary for the document to display and function correctly. An external style sheet, which contains formatting rules that control the appearance of a document, is a good example of a related file. The **Coding toolbar** contains buttons you can use when working directly in

Figure 1 *Dreamweaver CS6 workspace*

Lesson 1 Explore the Dreamweaver Workspace

DREAMWEAVER 1-5

the code and is not visible unless you are in Code view. When visible, it appears on the left side of the Document window.

The **Property inspector**, sometimes referred to as the **Properties pane**, located at the bottom of the Dreamweaver window, lets you view and change the properties (characteristics) of a selected object. The Property inspector is context sensitive, which means it changes according to what is selected in the Document window. The **status bar** is located below the Document window. The left side of the status bar displays the **tag selector**, which shows the HTML tags used at the insertion point location. The right side displays the Select tool, used for page editing; the Hand tool, used for panning; the Zoom tool, used for magnifying; and the Set Magnification menu, used to change the percentage of magnification. It also displays the window size and estimated download time for the current page.

A **panel** is a tabbed window that displays information on a particular topic or contains related commands. **Panel groups** are sets of related panels that are grouped together. A collection of panels or panel groups is called a **dock**. To view the contents of a panel in a panel group, click the panel's tab. Panels are docked by default on the right side of the screen. You can undock or "float" them by dragging the panel tab to another screen location. To collapse or expand a panel group, double-click the panel tab, as shown in Figure 2. When you first start Dreamweaver, the Adobe BrowserLab, Insert, CSS Styles, AP Elements, Business Catalyst, Files, and Assets panels appear by default. You can open panels using the Window menu commands or the corresponding shortcut keys.

QUICK TIP
The Collapse to Icons button above the top panel lets you collapse all open panels to icons to enlarge the workspace.

Working with Dreamweaver Views

A **view** is a particular way of displaying page content. Dreamweaver has three working views. **Design view** shows the page as it would appear in a browser and is primarily used for designing and creating a web page. **Code view** shows the underlying HTML code for the page; use this view to read or edit the underlying code.

QUICK TIP
You can also split Code view to enable you to work on two different sections of code at once. To change to Split Code view, click View on the Menu bar, then click Split Code.

Show Code and Design views is a combination of Code view and Design view. Show Code and Design views is the best view for **debugging** or correcting errors because you can immediately see how code modifications change the appearance of the page. The view buttons are located on the Document toolbar. If you want to switch to the same view for all open documents, hold down the Ctrl key (Win) or Control key (Mac) while you click a view button.

Figure 2 *Panels in panel group*

Figure 3 *Starting Dreamweaver CS6 (Windows)*

Click Adobe Dreamweaver CS6

Hiding and Displaying Toolbars

To hide or display the Style Rendering, Document, or Standard toolbars, click View on the Menu bar, point to Toolbars, then click Style Rendering, Document, or Standard. The Coding toolbar is available only in Code view and the Code window in Split view, and appears vertically in the Document window. By default, the Document toolbar appears in the workspace.

Start Dreamweaver (Windows)

1. Click the **Start button** on the taskbar.
2. Point to **All Programs**, then click **Adobe Dreamweaver CS6**, as shown in Figure 3.
3. If the Default Editor dialog box opens, click **OK**.

You started Dreamweaver CS6 for Windows.

Lesson 1 Explore the Dreamweaver Workspace

DREAMWEAVER 1-7

Start Dreamweaver (Macintosh)

1. Click **Finder** in the Dock, then click **Applications**.
2. Click the **Adobe Dreamweaver CS6 folder**, then double-click the **Adobe Dreamweaver CS6 application**, as shown in Figure 4.

TIP Once Dreamweaver is running, you can add it to the Dock permanently by [control]-clicking the Dreamweaver icon, clicking Options, then clicking Keep In Dock.

You started Dreamweaver CS6 for Macintosh.

Figure 4 *Starting Dreamweaver CS6 (Macintosh)*

DREAMWEAVER 1-8

Getting Started with Dreamweaver

Figure 5 *Code view for new document*

Show Code view button | *Show Code and Design views button* | *Show Design view button* | *Switch Design view to Live view button* | *Menu bar may be displayed as two bars* | *Click to collapse all panels to icons*

Coding toolbar

Your panel arrangement may differ depending on the last placement

Using Two Monitors for Optimum Workspace Layout

One option you have for workspace layout is Dual Screen layout. **Dual Screen layout** is the layout you would choose when you are using two monitors while working with Dreamweaver. The Document window and Property inspector appear on the first monitor and the panels appear on the second monitor. It is seamless to work between the two monitors and optimizes your workspace by allowing you to have multiple panels open without compromising your Document window space.

Change views and view panels

1. Click **HTML** in the Create New category on the Dreamweaver Welcome Screen.

   The Dreamweaver Welcome Screen provides shortcuts for opening files and for creating new files or websites.

   TIP If you do not want the Dreamweaver Welcome Screen to appear each time you start Dreamweaver, click the Don't show again check box on the Welcome Screen or remove the check mark next to Show Welcome Screen in the General category in the Preferences dialog box.

2. Click the **Show Code view button** Code on the Document toolbar.

   The default code for a new document appears in the Document window, as shown in Figure 5.

   TIP The Coding toolbar is available only in Code view and in the Code window in Split view.

3. Click the **Show Code and Design views button** Split on the Document toolbar.

4. Click the **Show Design view button** Design on the Document toolbar.

   TIP If your icons appear in black-and-white and you would like to display them in color, click the Insert panel drop-down menu, then click Color Icons.

   (continued)

Lesson 1   Explore the Dreamweaver Workspace

DREAMWEAVER 1-9

5. Click the **Assets panel tab**, then compare your screen to Figure 6.

   TIP If the Assets panel is not visible, click Window on the Menu bar, then click Assets.

6. Click the **Files panel tab** to display the contents of the Files panel.
7. Double-click **Assets** to collapse the panel group.
8. View the contents of the CSS Styles and AP Elements panels.
9. Click and drag the **blank area** next to the AP Elements tab to the middle of the document window.

   The panel group is now in a floating window.

   (continued)

Figure 6 *Displaying a panel group*

Files and Assets panels docked together in one panel group

Drag title bar or blank area next to tabs to undock or "float" panel group

Drag either panel name to undock or "float" panel separately from group

Choosing a Workspace Layout

The Dreamweaver interface is an integrated workspace, which means that all of the document windows and panels appear in a single application window. Each open document appears as a tab below the document toolbar. (In the Mac OS, documents can either be tabbed together in a single window or displayed in separate windows.) To view a tabbed document, click the tab with the document's filename. The **Workspace switcher**, a drop-down menu in the top right corner on the Menu bar, lets you change the workspace layout. The default layout is the Designer workspace layout, where the panels are docked on the right side of the screen and Split view is the default view. Other workplace layouts include App Developer, App Developer Plus, Business Catalyst, Classic, Coder, Coder Plus, Designer Compact, Dual Screen, Fluid Layout and Mobile Applications. To change the workspace layout, click the Workspace switcher, then click the desired layout. You can also rearrange the workspace using your own choices for panel placement and save the workspace with a unique name using the "New Workspace" and "Manage Workspaces" commands on the Workspace switcher. The Reset 'Current view' option resets the workspace layout to return to the default positions on the screen for the selected view.

Figure 7 *Docking a panel group*

Blue drop zone appears as a horizontal line

Panel group being docked

10. Click and drag the **panel title bar** back to its original position, then drop it to dock the panel group below the Insert panel.

    Release the mouse only when you see the blue drop zone. The **blue drop zone** is a heavy blue line that appears when the panel is in the correct position to be docked. See Figure 7. If the blue drop zone appears as a box, releasing the button adds the panel to the boxed panel group.

    TIP If you have rearranged the panels from their original positions and want to reset them back to their default positions, click the Workspace switcher drop-down menu, then click Reset 'Designer'. You will also have to reset the Color Icons, as color icons are not part of the default Designer workspace.

11. Click **File** on the Menu bar, then click **Close** to close the open document.

You viewed a new web page using three views, opened panel groups, viewed their contents, then closed panel groups.

Viewing Your Page in Live View

When you view your web pages in Dreamweaver, the page elements appear similar to the way they will appear on the web, but not exactly. To get a better idea of how it will look, you can use the Switch Design view to Live view button on the Document toolbar. This button causes the open document to appear as it would in a browser, with interactive elements active and functioning. If you are viewing the page in Live view, the Shows the Live view source in code view button will appear to the right of the Switch Design view to Live view button. This button will display the code as read-only; it cannot be modified without exiting "Shows the Live view source in code view." The code is highlighted in yellow and allows you to see the dynamic changes in the code while you interact with the dynamic content on the page. When the Switch Design view to Live view button is active, the Shows the Live view source in code view button can be toggled on or off. If Live view is not active, the Shows the Live view source in code view button will not appear. When you click the Live view button the first time, you may see a message that you need to install the Flash plug-in from the Adobe website, www.adobe.com. Download the plug-in and your page can then be viewed using Live view.

LESSON 2

View a Web Page
AND USE HELP

What You'll Do

In this lesson, you will open a web page, view several page elements, and access the Help system.

Opening a Web Page

After starting Dreamweaver, you can create a new website, create a new web page, or open an existing website or web page. The first web page that appears when users go to a website is called the **home page**. The home page sets the look and feel of the website and directs users to the rest of the pages in the site.

Viewing Basic Web Page Elements

There are many elements that make up web pages. Web pages can be very simple and designed primarily with text, or they can be media-rich with images, sound, and movies, creating an enhanced interactive web experience. Figure 8 shows a web page with text and graphics that work together to create a simple and attractive page.

Most information on a web page is presented in the form of text. You can type text directly onto a web page in Dreamweaver or import text created in other programs. You can then use the Property inspector to format text so that it is attractive and easy to read. Text should be short and to the point to engage users and prevent them from losing interest and leaving your site.

Hyperlinks, also known as **links**, are images or text elements on a web page that users click to display another location on the page, another web page on the same website, or a web page on a different website.

Images add visual interest to a web page. The saying that "less is more" is certainly true with images, though. Too many images cause the page to load slowly and discourage users from waiting for the page to download. Many pages have **banners**, which are images that appear across the top or down the side of the screen that can incorporate a company's logo, contact information, and links to the other pages in the site.

Menu bars, also called navigation bars, are bars that contain multiple links that are usually organized in rows or columns. Sometimes menu bars are used with an image map. An **image map** is an image that has been divided into sections, each of which serves as a link. The way that menu bars and other internal links are used on your pages is referred to as the **navigation structure** of the site.

Rich media content is a comprehensive term that refers to attractive and engaging images,

Getting Started with Dreamweaver

interactive elements, video, or animations. Some of this content can be created in Dreamweaver, but much of it is created with other programs such as Adobe Flash, Fireworks, Photoshop, or Illustrator.

Getting Help

Dreamweaver has an excellent Help feature that is comprehensive and easy to use. When questions or problems arise, you can use the commands on the Help menu to find the answers you need. Clicking the Dreamweaver Help command opens the Dreamweaver Help page that contains a list of topics and subtopics by category. The Help feature in Dreamweaver CS6 is based on Adobe AIR technology. **Adobe AIR** is an Adobe product used for developing content that can be delivered with a browser or as a desktop application.

The Search text box at the top of the window lets you enter a keyword to search for a specific topic. Context-specific help can be accessed by clicking the Help button on the Property inspector.

Figure 8 *Common web page elements*

National Endowment for the Arts website – www.arts.endow.gov

Lesson 2   View a Web Page and Use Help

DREAMWEAVER 1-13

Open a web page and view basic page elements

1. Click **File** on the Menu bar, then click **Open**.
2. Click the **Look in list arrow** (Win), or **navigation list arrow** (Mac), locate the drive and folder where you store your Data Files, then double-click the **chapter_1 folder** (Win), or click the **chapter_1 folder** (Mac).
3. Click **dw1_1.html**, then click **Open**. You may not see the .html file extension if the option for hiding file extensions for known file types is selected on your operating system.

   TIP If you want your screen to match the figures in this book, make sure the Document window is maximized and the Windows display setting is 100% (Win).

4. Click **Window** on the Menu bar, then click **Hide Panels** to temporarily hide the panels.

   Hiding the panels gives you a larger viewing area for your web pages. You can also press [F4] to show or hide the panels.

   Note to Mac users: On the newest Mac OS, the F-keys are assigned to system functions. (F1=monitor brightness and F4=widgets) You can change this in your system preferences. Newer keyboards have an "FN" or "fn" key that can be used in conjunction with the F-keys so that they function "normally."

5. Locate each of the web page elements shown in Figure 9.

   TIP Because you are opening a single page that is not in a website with access to the other pages, the links will not work.

   (continued)

Figure 9 *Viewing web page elements (Win)*

Links to the main pages in the website   *Banner*   *Text*   *Image*

Figure 9 *Viewing web page elements (Mac)*

Banner

Links to the main pages in the website

Text

Image

6. Press **[F4]** to show the panels.
7. Click the **Show Code view button** [Code] to view the code for the page.
8. Scroll down to view all the code, if necessary, then click the **Show Design view button** [Design] to return to Design view.

TIP To show and highlight the code for a particular page element, select the page element in Design view, then click the Show Code view button.

9. Click **File** on the Menu bar, then click **Close** to close the open page without saving it.

TIP You can also click the Close button (the X) on the filename tab to close the page.

You opened a web page, located several page elements, viewed the code for the page, then closed the page without saving it.

Lesson 2 View a Web Page and Use Help

DREAMWEAVER 1-15

Use Dreamweaver Help

1. Click **Help** on the Menu bar, then click **Dreamweaver Help**.

   The Dreamweaver Help window opens in your browser window. Since the help feature is online content, you must have Internet access to use it. Also, because help is online, the pages are "live," and subject to change. So your screens may not match the figures in these steps exactly.

2. Click the drop-down menu next to the Adobe Community Help search text box, select **Dreamweaver** if necessary, click to place the insertion point in the Adobe Community Help search text box, then type **"CSS Property inspector"**, as shown in Figure 10.

3. Press [**Enter**] (Win) or [**Return**] (Mac).

   The Search Community Help window opens with results from the search.

4. Click to select the **Only Adobe content** option button, click the **Toggle the product filter menu visibility drop-down menu**, then click **Dreamweaver**, if necessary, as shown in Figure 11.

   The Help topic list changes to display only Dreamweaver help from the Adobe website.

   (continued)

Figure 10 *Dreamweaver Help window*
Copyright © 2012 Adobe Systems Incorporated. All rights reserved.

Search text box

Drop-down menu

Figure 11 *Displaying Help content*
Copyright © 2012 Adobe Systems Incorporated. All rights reserved.

Only Adobe content option button

Click a topic to open related content

Toggle the product filter menu visibility drop-down menu

DREAMWEAVER 1-16

Getting Started with Dreamweaver

Figure 12 *Searching for a topic in Help*
Copyright © 2012 Adobe Systems Incorporated. All rights reserved

Scroll to read content

5. Scroll down to scan the list of topics, click one of the links to read information about a topic of your choice, then follow several sublinks to learn more.

    The content appears on the right side of the window. The left side of the window shows the Dreamweaver versions to which the current topic relates, and a link for other contact support options, as shown in Figure 12.

6. Close the Adobe Community Help window.

You used Adobe Help to read information in the Adobe Dreamweaver CS6 documentation.

Using Adobe Help

When you access the Help feature in Dreamweaver, you have the choice of downloading a PDF for offline help (which is similar to searching in a Dreamweaver manual) or using online help. The online help feature is called Adobe Community Help. Adobe Community Help is a collection of materials such as tutorials, published articles, or blogs, in addition to the regular help content. All content is monitored and approved by the Adobe Community Expert program.

Lesson 2 View a Web Page and Use Help

LESSON 3

Plan and Set Up
A WEBSITE

What You'll Do

In this lesson, you will review a website plan for The Striped Umbrella, a beach resort and spa. You will also create a local site folder for The Striped Umbrella website, and then set up the website.

Understanding the Website Development Process

Creating a website is a complex process. It can often involve a large team of people working in various roles to ensure that the website contains accurate information, looks good, and works smoothly. Figure 13 illustrates the phases in a website development project.

Planning a Website

Planning is probably the most important part of any successful project. Planning is an essential part of creating a website, and is a continuous process that overlaps the subsequent phases. To start planning your website, you need to create a checklist of questions and answers about the site. For

Figure 13 *Phases of a website development project*

Develop a plan → Create the basic structure → Create the content → Test ⇄ Modify → Publish example, what are your goals for the site? Who is the audience you want to target? Teenagers? Children? Sports enthusiasts? Senior citizens? How can you design the site to appeal to the target audience? What content is appropriate for the target audience? What content is relevant to the purpose of the website? The more questions you can answer about the site, the more prepared you will be when you begin the developmental phase. Because of the public demand for up-to-date information, your plan should include not just how to get the site up and running, but how to keep it current. Table 1 lists some of the basic questions you need to answer during the planning phase for almost any type of website. From your checklist, you should create a statement of purpose and scope, a timeline for all due dates, a budget, a task list with work assignments, and a list of resources needed. You should also include a list of deliverables, such as page prototypes and art for approval. The due dates for each deliverable should be included in the timeline.

Planning the Basic Structure

Once you complete the planning phase, you need to determine the structure of the site by creating a wireframe. A **wireframe**, sometimes referred to as a storyboard, is an illustration that represents every page in a website. Like a flowchart, a wireframe shows the relationship of each page in the site to all the other pages. Wireframes also show how each page element is to be placed on each page. Wireframes are helpful when planning a website, because they allow you to visualize how each page in the site links to others. They are also an important tool to help the client see how the pages will look and work together. Make sure that the client and all other interested stakeholders approve the wireframe before the site construction actually begins. Wireframes range from very simple (known as low-fidelity wireframes) to interactive and multidimensional (known as high-fidelity wireframes). You can create a simple wireframe by using a pencil and paper or by using a graphics program on a computer, such as Adobe Illustrator, Adobe Fireworks, or Microsoft PowerPoint. To create more complex wireframes that simulate the site

TABLE 1: WEBSITE PLANNING CHECKLIST

Question	Examples
1. Who is the target audience?	Seniors, teens, children
2. How can I tailor the site to reach that audience?	Specify an appropriate reading level, decide the optimal amount of media content, use formal or casual language
3. What are the goals for the site?	Sell a product, provide information
4. How will I gather the information?	Recruit other employees, write it myself, use content from in-house documents
5. What are my sources for media content?	Internal production department, outside production company, my own photographs
6. What is my budget?	Very limited, well financed
7. What is the timeline?	Two weeks, one month, six months
8. Who is on my project team?	Just me, a complete staff of designers
9. How often should the site be updated?	Every 10 minutes, once a month
10. Who will update the site?	Me, other team members

© Cengage Learning 2013

navigation and user interaction, use a high-fidelity wireframe program such as OverSite, ProtoShare, Microsoft Visio, or Adobe Proto. The basic wireframe shown in Figure 14 shows all the The Striped Umbrella website pages that you will create in this book. The home page appears at the top of the wireframe, and it has four pages linked to it. The home page is called the **parent page**, because it is at a higher level in the web hierarchy and has pages linked to it. The pages linked below it are called **child pages**. The Activities page, which is a child page to the home page, is also a parent page to the Cruises and Fishing pages. You can refer to this wireframe as you create the actual links in Dreamweaver. More detailed wireframes also include all document names, images, text files, and link information. Use your wireframe as your guide as you develop the site to make sure you follow the planned site structure.

In addition to creating a wireframe for your site, you should also create a folder hierarchy on your computer for all of the files that will be used in the site. Start by creating a folder for the site with a descriptive name, such as the name of the company. This folder, known as the **local site folder**, will store all the pages or HTML files for the site. Traditionally, this folder has been called the **root folder** and many people still use this term; in this book we will call it the local site folder. Then create a subfolder, often called **assets** or **images**, in which you store all of the files that are not pages, such as images and sound files.

QUICK TIP

You should avoid using spaces, special characters, or uppercase characters in your folder names to ensure that all your files can be read and linked successfully on all web servers, whether they are Windows- or UNIX-based.

Figure 14 *The Striped Umbrella website wireframe*

After you create the local site folder, you are ready to set up your site. When you **set up** a site, you use the Dreamweaver Site Setup dialog box to assign your site a name and specify the local site folder. After you have set up your site, the site name and any folders and files it contains appear in the **Files panel**, the panel you use to manage your website's files and folders. Using the Files panel to manage your files ensures that the site links work correctly when the website is published. You also use the Files panel to add or delete pages.

Creating the Web Pages and Collecting the Page Content

This is the fun part! After you create your wireframe, obtain approvals, and set up your site, you need to gather the files you'll need to create the pages, including text, images, buttons, video, and animations. You will import some of these pages from other software programs, and some you will create in Dreamweaver. For example, you can create text in a word-processing program and import or paste it into Dreamweaver, or you can create and format text in Dreamweaver.

Images, tables, colors, and horizontal rules all contribute to making a page attractive and interesting, but they can increase file size.

In choosing your page elements, carefully consider the file size of each page. A page with too many graphic elements might take a long time to load, which could cause visitors to leave your site.

Testing the Pages

Once all your pages are completed, you need to test the site to make sure all the links work and that everything looks good. It is important to test your web pages using different browser software. The four most common browsers are Microsoft Internet Explorer, Mozilla Firefox, Google Chrome, and Apple Safari. Test your site using different versions of each browser, because older versions may not support the latest web technology. You should also test your site using a variety of screen sizes. Some users may have small monitors, while others may have large, high-resolution monitors. Also consider connection download time. Although most people use cable modems or DSL (digital subscriber line), some in rural areas still use slower dial-up modems. Testing is a continuous process, for which you should allocate plenty of time.

Modifying the Pages

After you create a website, you'll probably find that you need to keep making changes to it, especially when information on the site needs to be updated. Each time you make a change, such as adding a new button or image to a page, you should test the site again. Modifying and testing pages in a website is an ongoing process.

Publishing the Site

Publishing a website refers to the process of transferring all the files for the site to a **web server**, a computer that is connected to the Internet with an IP (Internet Protocol) address, so that it is available for viewing on the Internet. A website must be published so that Internet users can view it. There are several options for publishing a website. For instance, many **Internet Service Providers (ISPs)** provide space on their servers for customers to publish websites, and some commercial websites provide limited free space for their users. Although publishing happens at the end of the process, it's a good idea to set up web server access in the planning phase. Use the Files panel to transfer your files using the Dreamweaver FTP capability. **FTP (File Transfer Protocol)** is the process of uploading and downloading files to and from a remote site.

Managing a Project with a Team

When working with a team, it is essential that you define clear goals for the project and a list of objectives to accomplish those goals. Your plan should be finalized after conferring with both the clients and other team members to make sure that the purpose, scope, and objectives are clear to everyone. Establish the **deliverables**, or products that will be provided to the client at the product completion such as new pages or graphic elements created, and a timeline for their delivery. You should present the web pages at strategic times in the development process to your team members and to your clients for feedback and evaluation. Analyze all feedback objectively, incorporating both the positive and the negative comments to help you make improvements to the site and meet the clients' expectations and goals. A common pitfall in team management is **scope creep**. Scope creep means making impromptu changes or additions to a project without corresponding increases in the schedule or budget. Proper project control and communication between team members and clients can minimize scope creep and achieve the successful and timely completion of a project.

Select the location for your website

1. Open or expand the Files panel if necessary to view the contents.

   TIP If the Background File Activity dialog box opens, click Close. It is just indicating the status of any current file activity.

2. Click the **drive or folder** that is currently displayed in the pop-up menu in the Files panel. See Figure 15.

3. Click to select the **drive or folder** (or subfolder) in the list where you will store your folders and files for your websites.

   You will store all of the folders and files you create inside this drive or folder.

You selected the drive or folder where you will create your website.

Figure 15 *Selecting a drive in the Files panel*

Click to select the drive that you will use to store your files (your drive or folder may differ)

Click to display the pop-up menu

Understanding IP Addresses and Domain Names

To be accessible over the Internet, a website must be published to a web server with a permanent IP address. An **IP address** is an assigned series of numbers, separated by periods, that designates an address on the Internet. To access a web page, you can enter either an IP address or a domain name in the address text box of your browser window. A **domain name** is a web address that is expressed in letters instead of numbers and usually reflects the name of the business represented by the website. For example, the domain name of the Adobe website is www.adobe.com, but the IP address is 192.150.16.117. Because domain names use descriptive text instead of numbers, they are much easier to remember. Compare an IP address to your Social Security number and a domain name to your name. Both your Social Security number and your name are used to refer to you as a person, but your name is much easier for your friends and family to use than your Social Security number. You can type the IP address or the domain name in the address text box of the browser window to access a website. The domain name is also referred to as a **URL** or Uniform Resource Locator.

Figure 16 *Creating a local site folder using the Files panel*

Your drive or folder may differ

striped_umbrella folder will become the root folder after the site is defined (the folder is yellow)

If you just see a drive or folder name here, you do not currently have a website open

Figure 17 *Viewing an open website in the Files panel*

striped_umbrella root folder (the folder is green)

The open website name appears here

If you see the word "Site" here, you do have a website open

Create a local site folder

1. Verify that the drive or folder where you want to store your site is selected in the Files panel, right-click (Windows) or control-click (Macintosh) the **drive or folder**, then click **New Folder**.

2. Type **striped_umbrella** to rename the folder, then press **[Enter]**.

   The folder is renamed striped_umbrella, as shown in Figure 16. You have not created a website yet. You have just created the folder that will serve as the local site folder after you set up the site.

   The folder color is currently yellow (Mac users will see blue folders), but after you set up the site in the next section, it will change to green. Notice the difference between Figure 16 and Figure 17. In Figure 16, you have only created the local site folder, not the website, and the color of the folder is yellow. In Figure 17, The Striped Umbrella website has been created and is open, so the local site folder is green.

You created a new folder to serve as the local site folder for The Striped Umbrella website.

Lesson 3 Plan and Set Up a Website

DREAMWEAVER 1-23

Set up a website

1. Click **Site** on the Menu bar, then click **New Site**.
2. Click **Site** in the category list in the Site Setup for Unnamed Site dialog box (if necessary), then type **The Striped Umbrella** in the Site name text box.

   TIP You can use uppercase letters and spaces in the site name because it is not the name of a folder or a file.

3. Click the **Browse for folder icon** next to the Local Site Folder text box, click the **Select list arrow** (Win) or the **navigation list arrow** (Mac) in the Choose Root folder dialog box, navigate to and click the **drive and folder** where your website files will be stored, then click the **striped_umbrella folder**.
4. Click **Open** (Win) or **Choose** (Mac), then click **Select** (Win). See Figure 18.

You created a website and set it up with the name The Striped Umbrella. You then told Dreamweaver the folder name and location to use for the local site folder.

Figure 18 *Site Setup for The Striped Umbrella dialog box*

Site category

Site name

Local Site Folder text box — your drive may differ

Browse for File icon

Understanding the Process of Publishing a Website

Before publishing a website so that web users can access it, you should first create a **local site folder**, also called the **local root folder**, to house all the files for your website, as you did on page 1-23. This folder usually resides on your hard drive. Next, you need to gain access to a remote server. A **remote server** is a web server that hosts websites and is not directly connected to the computer housing the local site. Many Internet Service Providers, or ISPs, provide space for publishing websites on their servers. Once you have access to a remote server, you can then use the Servers category in the Site Setup dialog box to enter information such as the FTP host, host directory, login, and password. After entering this information, you can then use the Put File(s) button in the Files panel to transfer the files to the designated remote server. Once the site is published to a remote server, it is called a **remote site**.

Figure 19 *Adding a server for Remote Access for The Striped Umbrella website*

Servers category

Add new Server icon

Figure 20 *Entering server information for The Striped Umbrella website*

Enter Server name here

Choices for publishing a website

Set up web server access

1. Click **Servers** in the Category list, then click the **Add new Server icon** ✚, as shown in Figure 19.

   TIP If you do not have the information to publish your website, skip step 2 and continue to step 3. You can specify this information later.

2. Click the **Connect using: list arrow**, choose the method you will use to publish your website, as shown in Figure 20, enter any necessary information in the Site Setup for The Striped Umbrella dialog box based on the setting you chose, then click **Save**.

   TIP Your network administrator or web hosting service will give you the necessary information to publish your website.

3. Click **Save** to close the Site Setup dialog box.

You set up the remote access information to prepare you for publishing your website.

Lesson 3 Plan and Set Up a Website

DREAMWEAVER 1-25

LESSON 4

Add a Folder
AND PAGES

What You'll Do

In this lesson, you will use the Files panel to create a new folder and new pages for the website.

Adding a Folder to a Website

After setting up a website, you need to create folders to organize the files that will make up the site. Creating a folder called **assets** is a good beginning. There is nothing magic about the word "assets," though. You can name your folder anything that makes sense to you, as long as you follow proper folder naming conventions such as avoiding the use of spaces. You can use the assets folder to store all non-HTML files, such as images or sound files. Many designers name this folder "images" and use additional folders to store other types of supporting files. After you create the assets folder, it is a good idea to set it as the default location to store the website images. This saves a step when you import new images into the website.

> **DESIGN TIP**
>
> **Creating an Effective Navigation Structure**
>
> When you create a website, it's important to consider how your users will navigate from page to page within the site. A menu bar, or navigation bar, is a critical tool for moving around a website, so it's important that all text, buttons, and icons used in a menu bar have a consistent look across all pages. If you use a complex menu bar, such as one that incorporates JavaScript or Flash, it's a good idea to include plain text links in another location on the page for accessibility. Otherwise, users might become confused or lost within the site. A navigation structure can include more links than those included in a menu bar, however. For instance, it can contain other sets of links that relate to the content of a specific page and which are placed at the bottom or sides of a page in a different format. No matter which navigation structure you use, make sure that every page includes a link back to the home page. Don't make users rely on the Back button on the browser toolbar to find their way back to the home page. It's possible that the user's current page might have opened as a result of a search and clicking the Back button will then take the user out of the website.

QUICK TIP

Because complex websites might contain many types of files, you might want to create subfolders within the assets folder for each type of file. For instance, you could create subfolders named text, images, or sounds.

Creating the Home Page

The **home page** of a website is the first page that users see when they visit your site. Most websites contain many other pages that all connect back to the home page. The home page filename usually has the name index.html (.htm), or default.html (.htm).

Adding Pages to a Website

Websites might be as simple as one page or might contain hundreds of pages. When you create a website, you can add all the pages and specify where they should be placed in the website folder structure in the local site folder. Once you add and name all the pages in the website, you can then add the content, such as text and graphics, to each page. One method is to add as many blank pages as you think you will need in the beginning, rather than adding them one at a time with all the content in place. This enables you to set up the navigation structure of the website at the beginning of the development process and view how each page is linked to others. When you are satisfied with the overall structure, you can then add the content to each page. This is strictly a personal preference, however. You can also choose to add and link pages as you create them, and that will work just fine, too.

You have a choice of several default document types you can generate when you create new HTML pages. The default document type is designated in the Preferences dialog box. XHTML 1.0 Transitional is the default document type when you install Dreamweaver, but you can change it to HTML5 or any other document type. It's important to understand the terminology—the pages are still called HTML pages and the file extension is still HTML, but the document type will be XHTML 1.0 Transitional. We will use HTML5 as our standard document type for the files we create in each lesson.

QUICK TIP

You can also convert existing HTML documents into XHTML-compliant documents. To do this, open an existing HTML document, click File, point to Convert, then choose the XHTML document type.

Using the Files Panel for File Management

You should use the Files panel to add, delete, move, or rename files and folders in a website. It is very important that you perform these file-maintenance tasks in the Files panel rather than in Windows Explorer (Win) or in the Finder (Mac). Working outside of Dreamweaver, such as in Windows Explorer, can cause linking errors. You cannot take advantage of the simple, yet powerful, Dreamweaver site-management features unless you use the Files panel for all file-management activities. You might choose to use Windows Explorer (Win) or the Finder (Mac) only to create the local site folder or to move or copy the local site folder of a website to another location. If you move or copy the local site folder to a new location, you will have to set up the site again in the Files panel, as you did in Lesson 3 of this chapter. Setting up a site is not difficult and will become routine for you after you practice a bit. If you are using Dreamweaver on multiple computers, such as in labs or at home, you will have to set up your sites the first time you change to a different computer.

Add a folder to a website (Windows)

1. Right-click **Site - The Striped Umbrella** in the Files panel, then click **New Folder**.
2. Type **assets** in the folder text box, then press **[Enter]**.

   TIP To rename a folder, click the folder name once, pause, click again, then type the new name.

3. Compare your screen to Figure 21.

You used the Files panel to create a new folder in the striped_umbrella folder and named it "assets".

Add a folder to a website (Macintosh)

1. Press and hold **[control]**, click the **striped_umbrella folder**, then click **New Folder**.
2. Type **assets** in the new folder name text box, then press **[return]**.

   TIP To rename a folder, click the folder name text box, type the new name, then press **[return]**.

3. Compare your screen to Figure 22.

You used the Files panel to create a new folder in the striped_umbrella folder and named it "assets".

Figure 21 *The Striped Umbrella site in Files panel with assets folder created (Windows)*

New assets folder

Local site folder for The Striped Umbrella website

Figure 22 *The Striped Umbrella site in Files panel with assets folder created (Macintosh)*

Local site folder for The Striped Umbrella website

New assets folder

Figure 23 *Site Setup for The Striped Umbrella dialog box with the assets folder set as the default images folder*

Advanced Settings category

Default Images folder text box

Browse for folder button

Set the default images folder

1. Click the **Site pop-up menu** in the Files panel, click **Manage Sites**, then click the **Edit the currently selected site button** .
2. Click **Advanced Settings** in the category list in the Site Setup dialog box, then click **Local Info** if necessary.
3. Click the **Browse for folder button** next to the Default Images folder text box.
4. If necessary, navigate to your striped_umbrella folder, double-click the **assets folder** (Win) or click the **assets folder** (Mac) in the Choose Image Folder dialog box, then click **Select** (Win) or **Choose** (Mac).

   Compare your screen to Figure 23.
5. Click **Save**, then click **Done**.

You set the assets folder as the default images folder so that imported images will be automatically saved in it.

Lesson 4 Add a Folder and Pages

Create the home page

1. Open **dw1_2.html** from the drive and folder where you store your Data Files.

   The file has several elements in it, including a banner image.

2. Click **File** on the Menu bar, click **Save As**, click the **Save in list arrow** (Win) or the **Where list arrow** (Mac), navigate to your striped_umbrella folder, select **dw1_2.html** in the File name text box (Win) or select **dw1_2** in the Save As text box (Mac), then type **index.html**.

   Windows users do not have to type the file extension. It will be added automatically.

3. Click **Save**, then click **No** when asked to update links.

   As shown in Figure 24, the drive where the local site folder is stored, the local site folder name, and the page's filename are displayed to the right of the document tab and in the Address text box in the Browser Navigation toolbar. This information is called the **path**, or location of the open file in relation to other folders in the website.

   The banner image is no longer visible and a gray broken link placeholder appears in its place. This is because although you saved the .html file under a new name in the website's local site folder, you have not yet copied the image file into the website's assets folder. The banner image is still linked to the Data Files folder. You will fix this in the next set of steps.

You opened a file, then saved it with the filename index.

Figure 24 *index.html saved in the striped_umbrella local site folder*

Broken Link icon

Link to banner is broken because the banner is not yet saved in the website

Path for file (Mac users will not see the path)

Root folder

index.html

DREAMWEAVER 1-30

Getting Started with Dreamweaver

Figure 25 *Property inspector showing properties of The Striped Umbrella banner*

Property inspector provides details about the selected image — *Src text box* — *Browse for file button* — *Image file has been copied to the assets folder* — *The Striped Umbrella banner* — *Selection handles*

Save an image file in the assets folder

1. Click the **broken link placeholder** to select it.

   Small, black selection handles appear around the broken link. To correct the broken link, you must copy the image file from the Data Files folder into the assets folder of your website.

2. Click the **Browse for File button** next to the Src text box in the Property inspector, navigate to the assets folder In your Data Files folder for this chapter, click **su_banner.gif**, click **OK** (Win) or **Open** (Mac), then click on a blank part of the page. (Click the banner placeholder image again if the banner still doesn't appear.)

   The file for The Striped Umbrella banner, su_banner.gif, is automatically copied to the assets folder of The Striped Umbrella website, the folder that you designated as the default images folder. When the image is selected, the Src text box shows the path of the banner to the assets folder in the website, and the banner image is visible on the page.

   TIP If you do not see the su_banner.gif file listed in the Files panel, click the Refresh button on the Files panel toolbar.

3. Select the banner to view the banner properties in the Property inspector, then compare your screen to Figure 25.

   TIP Until you copy an image from an outside folder to your website, the image is not part of the website and will appear as a broken link.

You saved The Striped Umbrella banner in the assets folder.

Lesson 4 Add a Folder and Pages

DREAMWEAVER 1-31

Add pages to a website (Windows)

1. Click the **plus sign** to the left of the assets folder (if necessary) to open the folder and view its contents, su_banner.gif.

   TIP If you do not see a file listed in the assets folder, click the Refresh button on the Files panel toolbar.

2. Right-click the **striped_umbrella local site folder**, click **New File**, type **about_us** to replace untitled, then press **[Enter]**.

   Each new file is a page in the website. This page does not have page content or a page title yet.

   TIP If you create a new file in the Files panel, use care to make sure the .html file extension is not deleted or that the file does not end up with a double file extension.

3. Repeat Step 2 to add five more blank pages to The Striped Umbrella website, naming the new files **spa.html**, **cafe.html**, **activities.html**, **cruises.html**, and **fishing.html**.

   TIP Make sure to add the new files to the site folder, not the assets folder. If you accidentally add them to the assets folder, just drag them to the site folder.

4. Click the **Refresh button** on the Files panel to list the files alphabetically, then compare your screen to Figure 26.

5. Click **File**, **Save**, to save the index.html file, if necessary, close both open files, click **File** on the Menu bar then click **Exit**.

   TIP If you are prompted to save changes to the dw1_1.html file, click No.

You added the following six pages to The Striped Umbrella website: about_us, activities, cafe, cruises, fishing, and spa.

DREAMWEAVER 1-32

Figure 26 *New pages added to The Striped Umbrella website (Windows)*

su_banner.gif in the assets folder

New pages added in the striped_umbrella local site folder

DESIGNTIP

Adding Page Titles

When you view a web page in a browser, its page title appears in the browser window title bar. (The page title is different from the filename, the name used to save the page on a computer.) The page title reflects the page content and sets the tone for the page. It is especially important to use words in your page title that are likely to match keywords users might enter when using a search engine. Search engines compare the text in page titles to the keywords typed into the search engine. When a title bar displays "Untitled Document," the designer has neglected to give the page a title. This is like giving up free "billboard space" and looks unprofessional.

Getting Started with Dreamweaver

Figure 27 *New pages added to The Striped Umbrella website (Macintosh)*

assets folder

New pages added in the striped_umbrella local site folder

Add pages to a website (Macintosh)

1. Click the **triangle** to the left of the assets folder to open the folder and view its contents.

   TIP If you do not see a file listed in the assets folder, click the Refresh button on the Files panel.

2. [control]-click the **striped_umbrella local site folder**, click **New File**, type **about_us** to replace untitled, then press **[return]**.

   TIP If you create a new file in the Files panel, use care to make sure the .html file extension is not deleted or that the file does not end up with a double file extension.

3. Repeat Step 2 to add five more blank pages to The Striped Umbrella website, naming the new files **spa.html**, **cafe.html**, **activities.html**, **cruises.html**, and **fishing.html**.

   TIP Make sure to add the new files to the site folder, not the assets folder. If you accidentally add them to the assets folder, just drag them to the site folder.

4. Click the **Refresh button** to list the files alphabetically, then compare your screen to Figure 27.

5. Click **File**, **Save**, to save the index.html file, then close both open files.

6. Click **Dreamweaver** on the Menu bar, and then click **Quit Dreamweaver**.

   TIP If you are prompted to save changes, click No.

You added six pages to The Striped Umbrella website: about_us, activities, cafe, cruises, fishing, spa.

POWER USER SHORTCUTS	
To do this:	**Use this shortcut:**
Open a file	[Ctrl][O] (Win) or ⌘ [O] (Mac)
Close a file	[Ctrl][W] (Win) or ⌘ [W] (Mac)
Create a new file	[Ctrl][N] (Win) or ⌘ [N] (Mac)
Save a file	[Ctrl][S] (Win) or ⌘ [S] (Mac)
Get Dreamweaver Help	[F1]
Show/Hide panels	[F4]
Switch between Code view and Design view	[Ctrl][`] (Win) or [control] [`] (Mac)

© Cengage Learning 2013

SKILLS REVIEW

Explore the Dreamweaver workspace.
1. Start Dreamweaver.
2. Create a new HTML document.
3. Change the view to Code view.
4. Change the view to Code and Design views.
5. Change the view to Design view.
6. Collapse the panels to icons.
7. Expand the panels.
8. Undock the Files panel and float it to the middle of the document window. Dock the Files panel back to its original position.
9. View the Assets panel.
10. Close the page without saving it.

View a web page and use Help.
1. Open the file dw1_3.html from where you store your Data Files.
2. Locate the following page elements: a banner, an image, and text.
3. Change the view to Code view.
4. Change the view to Design view.
5. Use the Dreamweaver Help command to search for information on docking panels.
6. Display and read one of the topics you find.
7. Close the Dreamweaver Help window.
8. Close the page without saving it.

Plan and set up a website.
1. Use the Files panel to select the drive and folder where you store your website files.
2. Create a new local site folder in this folder or drive called **blooms**.
3. Create a new site called **Blooms & Bulbs**.
4. Specify the blooms folder as the local site folder.
5. Use the Servers Info category in the Site Setup for Blooms & Bulbs dialog box to set up web server access. (*Hint*: Skip this step if you do not have the necessary information to set up web server access.)
6. Click Save to close the Site Setup dialog box.

Add a folder and pages.
1. Create a new folder in the blooms local site folder called **assets**.
2. Edit the site to set the assets folder as the default location for the website images.
3. Open the file dw1_4.html from where you store your Data Files, save this file in the blooms local site folder as **index.html**, then click No to updating the links.
4. Select the broken image for the Blooms & Bulbs banner on the page.
5. Use the Property inspector to browse for blooms_banner.jpg, then select it to automatically save it in the assets folder of the Blooms & Bulbs website. (Remember to click off of the banner anywhere else on the page to show the banner as it replaces the broken image if necessary.)
6. Create seven new pages in the Files panel, and name them: **plants.html**, **workshops.html**, **newsletter.html**, **annuals.html**, **perennials.html**, **water_plants.html**, and **tips.html**.
7. Refresh the view to list the new files alphabetically, then compare your screen to Figure 28.
8. Close all open pages.

SKILLS REVIEW
(CONTINUED)

Figure 28 *Completed Skills Review*

PROJECT BUILDER 1

You have been hired to create a website for a travel outfitter called TripSmart. TripSmart specializes in travel products and services. In addition to selling travel products, such as luggage and accessories, they organize trips and offer travel advice. Their clients range from college students to families to vacationing professionals. The owner, Thomas Howard, has requested a dynamic website that conveys the excitement of traveling.

1. Using the information in the preceding paragraph, create a wireframe for this website, using either a pencil and paper or a program such as Microsoft Word. Include the home page with links to four child pages named **catalog.html**, **newsletter.html**, **services.html**, and **tours.html**. Include two child pages under the tours page named **peru.html** and **galapagos.html**.
2. Create a new local site folder named **tripsmart** in the drive and folder where you store your website files.
3. Start Dreamweaver, if necessary, then create a site with the name **TripSmart**. Set the tripsmart folder as the local site folder for the site.
4. Create an assets folder and set it as the default location for images.
5. Open the file dw1_5.html from where you store your Data Files, then save it in the tripsmart local site folder as **index.html**. (Remember not to update links.)
6. Correct the path for the banner by selecting the banner on the page, browsing to the original source in the Data Files folder, then selecting the file to copy it automatically to your TripSmart assets folder.
7. Create six additional pages for the site, and name them as follows: **catalog.html**, **newsletter.html**, **services.html**, **tours.html**, **peru.html**, and **galapagos.html**. Use your wireframe and Figure 29 as a guide.
8. Refresh the Files panel.
9. Close all open pages.

Figure 29 *Completed Project Builder 1*

PROJECT BUILDER 2

Your company has been selected to design a website for a catering business called Carolyne's Creations. In addition to catering, Carolyne's services include cooking classes and daily specials available as take-out meals. She also has a retail shop that stocks gourmet treats and kitchen items.

1. Create a wireframe for this website that includes a home page and child pages named **shop.html**, **classes.html**, **catering.html**, and **recipes.html**. Create two more child pages under the classes.html page called **children.html** and **adults.html**.
2. Create a new local site folder for the site in the drive and folder where you save your website files, then name it **cc**.
3. Create a website with the name **Carolyne's Creations**, using the cc folder for the local site folder.
4. Create an assets folder for the site and set the assets folder as the default location for images.
5. Open dw1_6.html from the where you store your Data Files then save it as **index.html** in the cc folder.
6. Reset the source for the banner to automatically save the cc_banner.jpg file in the assets folder.
7. Using Figure 30 and your wireframe as guides, create the additional pages shown for the website.
8. Refresh the Files panel to sort the files alphabetically.
9. Close all open pages.

Figure 30 *Completed Project Builder 2*

Getting Started with Dreamweaver

DREAMWEAVER 1-37

DESIGN PROJECT

Figure 31 shows the Department of Defense website, a past selection for the Adobe Site of the Day. To visit the current Department of Defense website, connect to the Internet, then go to www.defense.gov. The current page might differ from the figure because dynamic websites are updated frequently to reflect current information. The main navigation structure is under the banner. The page title is The Official Home of the Department of Defense.

Go to the Adobe website at www.adobe.com, click the Customer Showcase link under the Company menu, then choose one of the sites listed to visit. Explore the site and answer the following questions:

1. Do you see page titles for each page you visit?
2. Do the page titles accurately reflect the page content?
3. Is the navigation structure clear?
4. How is the navigation structure organized?
5. Why do you think this site was chosen as a Site of the Day?

Figure 31 *Design Project*
United State Department of Defense website – www.defense.gov

PORTFOLIO PROJECT

The Portfolio Project will be an ongoing project throughout the book, in which you will plan and create an original website without any Data Files supplied. The focus of the site can be on any topic, organization, sports team, club, or company that you would like. You will build on this site from chapter to chapter, so you must do each Portfolio Project assignment in each chapter to complete your website. When you finish this book, you should have a completed site that would be an excellent addition to a professional portfolio.

1. Decide what type of site you would like to create. It can be a personal site about you, a business site that promotes a fictitious or real company, or an informational site that provides information about a topic, cause, or organization.
2. Write a list of questions and answers about the site you have decided to create.
3. Create a wireframe for your site to include at least four pages. The wireframe should include the home page with at least three child pages under it.
4. Create a local site folder and an assets folder to house the assets, then set up your site using the local site folder as the website local site folder and the assets folder as the default images folder.
5. Create a blank page named **index.html** as a placeholder for the home page.
6. Begin collecting content, such as pictures or text to use in your website. You can use a digital camera to take photos, use a scanner to scan pictures, or create your own graphics using a program such as Adobe Fireworks or Adobe Illustrator. Gather the content in a central location that will be accessible to you as you develop your site.

ADOBE DREAMWEAVER CS6

CHAPTER 2 DEVELOPING A
WEB PAGE

1. Create head content and set page properties
2. Create, import, and format text
3. Add links to web pages
4. Use the History panel and edit code
5. Modify and test web pages

CHAPTER 2
DEVELOPING A WEB PAGE

Introduction

The process of developing a web page requires a lot of thought and planning. Besides developing the page content, you also need to write descriptive head content. Head content does not appear on the page but in the HTML code; it contains information search engines use to help users find your website. Next, choose the page background and text colors. Then add the page content, format it attractively, and add links to let users navigate between the site pages. Finally, to ensure that all links work correctly and are current, test them regularly.

Understanding Page Layout

Before you add content to a page, consider the following guidelines for laying out pages:

Use white space effectively. A room with too much furniture makes it difficult to appreciate the individual pieces. The same is true of a web page. Too many text blocks, links, animations, and images can be distracting. Consider leaving white space on each page. **White space**, which is not necessarily white, is the area on a page with no content.

Limit media elements. Too many media elements, such as images, video clips, or sounds, can result in a page that takes too long to load. Users might leave your site before the entire page finishes loading. Use media elements only if they serve a purpose.

Keep it simple. Often the simplest websites are the most appealing and are also the easiest to create and maintain. A simple, well-designed site that works well is far superior to a complex one that contains errors.

Use an intuitive navigation structure. Make sure your site's navigation structure is easy to use. Users should always know where they are in the site and be able to easily find their way back to the home page. If users get "lost," they might leave the site rather than struggle to find their way around.

Apply a consistent theme. To help give pages in your website a consistent appearance, consider designing your pages using elements that relate to a common theme. Consistency in the use of color and fonts, the placement of the navigation links, and the overall page design gives a website a unified look and promotes greater ease of use and accessibility. Style sheets and pre-developed page layouts called **templates** can make this easier.

TOOLS YOU'LL USE

LESSON 1

Create Head Content and
SET PAGE PROPERTIES

What You'll Do

In this lesson, you will learn how to enter titles, keywords, and descriptions in the head content section of a web page. You will also change the background color for a web page.

Creating the Head Content

A web page is composed of two distinct sections: the head content and the body. The **head content** includes the page title that appears in the title bar of the browser and some important page elements, called meta tags, that are not visible in the browser.

Meta tags are HTML codes that include information about the page, such as keywords and descriptions. Meta tags are read by screen readers for users who have visual impairments. **Keywords** are words that relate to the content of the website. A **description** is a short paragraph that describes the content and features of the website. For instance, the words "beach" and "resort" would be appropriate keywords for The Striped Umbrella website. Search engines find web pages by matching the title, keywords, and description in the head content of web pages with keywords that users enter in search engine text boxes. Therefore, it is important to include concise, useful information in the head content. The **body** is the part of the page that appears in a browser window. It contains all the page content that is visible to users, such as text, images, and links.

> **QUICK TIP**
> Don't confuse page titles with filenames, the names used to store files on the server.

Setting Web Page Properties

When you create a web page, one of the first design decisions that you should make is to choose properties that control the way the page appears in a browser, such as the **background color**, the color that fills the entire page. The background color should complement the colors used for text, links, and images on the page. Often, backgrounds consist of images for either the entire page or a part of the page, such as a Cascading Style Sheet (CSS) layout block. A **CSS layout block** is a section of a web page that is defined and formatted using a Cascading Style Sheet, a set of formatting characteristics you can apply to text, links, and other page objects. You will learn more about CSS layout blocks in Chapter 6. When you use the Page Properties dialog box to set page properties such as the background color, Dreamweaver automatically creates a style that modifies the body tag to include the properties you added.

Developing a Web Page

A strong contrast between the text color and the background color makes it easier for users to read your text. One of the Web Content Accessibility Guidelines (WCAG), Version 2.0, from the World Wide Web Consortium (W3C) states that contrast will "make it easier for users to see content including separating foreground from background." You can choose a light background color with dark text, or a dark background color with light text. A white background with dark text, though not terribly exciting, provides good contrast and is easiest to read for most users. Another design decision you need to make is whether to change the **default font** and **default link colors**, which are the colors used by the browser to display text, links, and visited links. The default color for **unvisited links**, or links that the user has not clicked yet, is blue. Unvisited links are usually simply called **links**. The default color for **visited links**, or links that have been previously clicked, is purple. You change the background color, text, and link colors using the color picker in the Page Properties dialog box. You can choose colors from one of the five Dreamweaver color palettes, as shown in Figure 1.

Choosing Colors to Convey Information

Before 1994, colors appeared differently on different types of computers. In 1994, Netscape developed the first web-safe color palette, a set of colors that appears consistently in all browsers and on Macintosh, Windows, and UNIX platforms. The evolution of video cards has made this less relevant today, but use of appropriate colors is an important factor in creating accessible pages. Be sure to use only colors that provide good contrast on your pages. Dreamweaver has two web-safe color palettes, Color Cubes and Continuous Tone, each of which contains 216 web-safe colors. Color Cubes is the default color palette. To choose a different color palette, open the color picker. You can find the color picker on the CSS Property inspector, in various dialog boxes, and in various panels. Click the color picker list arrow, then click the color palette you want.

Another WCAG guideline states that color should never be the only visual means of conveying information. Never refer to a page object solely by the color, like the "red" box.

Figure 1 *Color picker showing color palettes*

Available color palettes
Click list arrow to choose a color palette
Web-safe palettes

DESIGN TIP

Making Pages Accessible
Not all of your users will have perfect vision and hearing or full use of both hands. There are several techniques you can use to ensure that your website is accessible to individuals with disabilities. These techniques include using text alternatives for any non-text content, making text readable and understandable, and providing ways to help users navigate through the site easily. Adobe provides much information about website compliance with Section 508 accessibility guidelines. For more information, visit the Adobe website at www.adobe.com/accessibility/. Here you will find suggestions for creating accessible websites, an explanation of Section 508, and information on how people with disabilities use assistive devices to navigate the Internet.

The World Wide Web Consortium (W3C) provides the Web Content Accessibility Guidelines (WCAG) 2.0 as the standard for designing sites that are accessible to users of all abilities. The levels of accessibility are grouped into three priority level checkpoints. All websites must complete all of the Priority 1 checkpoints, such as providing a text equivalent for every non-text element. These guidelines are published at www.w3.org. To read rationale behind creating accessible sites, go to http://www.webaim.org to find information about the POUR principles (Putting People at the Center of the Process) of making a website accessible. The WebAIM site also has a free accessibility evaluation tool called WAVE (Web Accessibility Evaluation Tool). Simply type in a URL or upload a file to test for accessibility.

Lesson 1 Create Head Content and Set Page Properties

Edit a page title

1. Start Dreamweaver, click the **Site list arrow** on the Files panel, then click **The Striped Umbrella** if necessary.
2. Double-click **index.html** in the Files panel to open The Striped Umbrella home page, click **View** on the Menu bar, then click **Head Content**.

   The Meta icon, Title icon, and CSS icon are now visible in the head content section. See Figure 2.
3. Click the **Title icon** in the head content section.

   The page title The Striped Umbrella appears in the Title text box in the Property inspector.
4. Click after the end of The Striped Umbrella text in the Title text box in the Property inspector, press **[Spacebar]**, type **beach resort and spa, Ft. Eugene, Florida,** press **[Enter]** (Win) or **[return]** (Mac), then click in the title text box.

   Compare your screen with Figure 3. The new title is better, because it incorporates the words "beach resort" and "spa" and the location of the resort—words that potential customers might use as keywords when using a search engine.

   TIP You can also change the page title using the Title text box on the Document toolbar. To view hidden text in the Title box, click in the title and scroll using the left and right keyboard arrow keys.

You opened The Striped Umbrella website, opened the home page, viewed the head content section, and changed the page title.

Figure 2 *Viewing the head content*

Meta icon   Title icon   CSS icon
Head content section
Title text box on Document toolbar

Figure 3 *Property inspector displaying new page title*

Click in the title and scroll with an arrow key to see the rest of the title

---

DESIGN TIP

Designing Appropriate Content for Your Target Audience

When you begin developing the content for your website, you need to decide what content to include and how to arrange each element on each page. You must design the content with the target audience in mind. What is the age group of your audience? What reading level is appropriate? Should you use a formal or informal tone? Should the pages be simple, consisting mostly of text, or rich with images and media files? Evaluate the font sizes, the number and size of images and animations, the reading level, and the amount of technical expertise necessary to navigate your site, and make sure they fit your audience. Usually, the first page that your audience will see when they visit your site is the home page. Design the home page so that users will understand your site's purpose and feel comfortable finding their way around your site's pages.

To ensure that users do not get "lost" in your site, design all the pages with a consistent look and feel. You can use templates and Cascading Style Sheets to maintain a common look for each page. **Templates** are web pages that contain the basic layout for each page in the site, including the location of a company logo or a menu of buttons. You'll learn more about Cascading Style Sheets in Lesson 2 and templates in Chapter 12.

Figure 4 *Insert panel displaying the Common category*

Figure 5 *Keywords dialog box*

Common category

Keywords

Head list arrow

Your icon may differ depending on what was last selected

Keywords command

DESIGN TIP

Entering Keywords and Descriptions

Search engines use keywords, descriptions, and titles to find pages based on search terms a user enters. Therefore, it is very important to anticipate the search terms your potential customers would use and include these words in the keywords, description, and title. Many search engines display page titles and descriptions in their search results. Some search engines limit the number of keywords that they will index, so make sure you list the most important keywords first. Keep your keywords and descriptions short and concise to ensure that all search engines will include your site. To choose effective keywords, many designers use focus groups to learn which words potential customers or clients might use. A **focus group** is a marketing tool that asks a group of people for feedback about a product, such as the impact of a television ad or the effectiveness of a website design.

Lesson 1   Create Head Content and Set Page Properties

Enter keywords

1. Click the **Insert panel list arrow**, then on the dropdown menu, click the **Common category** (if it is not already selected).

2. Click the **Head list arrow**, as shown in Figure 4, then click **Keywords**.

   TIP Some buttons on the Insert panel include a list arrow indicating that there is a menu of choices available. The button that you selected last will appear on the Insert panel until you select another.

3. Type **The Striped Umbrella**, **beach resort**, **spa**, **Ft. Eugene**, **Florida**, **Gulf of Mexico**, **fishing**, **golf**, **golfing**, **cruises** in the Keywords text box, as shown in Figure 5, then click **OK**

   The Keywords icon appears in the head content section, indicating that there are keywords associated with this page. When you click the icon to select it, the keywords appear in the Keywords text box in the Property inspector.

You added keywords relating to the resort to the head content of The Striped Umbrella home page.

DREAMWEAVER 2-7

Enter a description

1. Click the **Head list arrow** on the Insert panel, then click **Description**.
2. In the Description text box, type **The Striped Umbrella is a full-service resort and spa just steps from the Gulf of Mexico in Ft. Eugene, Florida.**

   Your screen should resemble Figure 6.
3. Click **OK**.

   The description appears in the Description text box in the Property inspector.
4. Click the **Show Code view button** on the Document toolbar, then click on the page to deselect the text.

   The title, keywords, and description tags appear in the HTML code in the document window, as shown in Figure 7. The order of your lines of code may vary slightly from the figures that show Code view, but this is usually not a problem unless the code is in the wrong section.

   TIP You can enter and edit the title tag and the meta tags directly in the code in Code view.

5. Click the **Show Design view button** to return to Design view.

   The Description icon appears in the head content section, indicating that this page includes a description.
6. Click **View** on the Menu bar, then click **Head Content** to close the head content section.

You added a description of The Striped Umbrella resort to the head content of the home page. You then viewed the page in Code view and the head content in the HTML code.

DREAMWEAVER 2-8

Figure 6 *Description dialog box*

Figure 7 *Head Content displayed in Code view*

Your head content line numbers may differ — Opening Head tag — Title tag

```
1  <!doctype html>
2  <html>
3  <head>
4  <meta charset="utf-8">
5  <title>The Striped Umbrella beach resort and spa, Ft. Eugene, Florida</title>
6  <meta name="keywords" content="The Striped Umbrella, beach resort, spa, Ft. Eugene, Florida, Gulf of Mexico, fishing, golf, golfing, cruises">
7  <meta name="description" content="The Striped Umbrella is a full-service resort and spa just steps from the Gulf of Mexico in Ft. Eugene, Florida.">
```

Keywords meta tag — Description meta tag

Using Descriptions for POWDER Authentication

A website description can be stored in an XML file to provide POWDER authentication. **XML** stands for Extensible Markup Language, a type of file that is used to develop customized tags to store information. **POWDER** is the acronym for **Protocol for Web Description Resources**. This is an evaluation system for web pages developed with the World Wide Web Consortium (W3C) that provides summary information about a website. Examples include the date the site was created, the name of the person or company responsible for the content on the site, and a description of the content. It is designed to help users determine if a site would be considered a trustworthy resource of value and interest. It replaces the previous system called PICS, or Platform for Internet Content Selection.

Developing a Web Page

Figure 8 *Page Properties dialog box*

Background color box showing existing page background color

White

Default Color button

Hexadecimal code for white is preceded with a # sign — you may have a different color format selected

Understanding Hexadecimal Values

Each color is assigned a **hexadecimal RGB value**, a value that represents the amount of red, green, and blue present in the color. For example, white, which is made of equal parts of red, green, and blue, has a hexadecimal value of FFFFFF. This is also called an RGB triplet in hexadecimal format (or a **hex triplet**). Each pair of characters in the hexadecimal value represents the red, green, and blue values. The hexadecimal number system is based on 16, rather than 10 in the decimal number system. Because the hexadecimal number system includes only numbers up to 9, values after 9 use the letters of the alphabet. "A" represents the number 10 in the hexadecimal number system. "F" represents the number 15. The hexadecimal values can be entered in the code using a form of shorthand that shortens the six characters to three characters. For instance: FFFFFF become FFF; 0066CC becomes 06C. The number value for a color is preceded by a pound sign (#) in HTML code.

Set the page background color

1. Click **Modify** on the Menu bar, then click **Page Properties** to open the Page Properties dialog box.

2. Click the **Background color box** to open the color picker, as shown in Figure 8.

   The background color box in the Page Properties dialog box changes color based on the currently selected color. It is now blue, reflecting the current page background color, rather than the default icon color shown in the step instructions.

3. Click the rightmost color in the bottom row (white), as shown in Figure 8.

4. Click **Apply**, then click **OK**.

   Clicking Apply lets you see the changes you made to the web page without closing the Page Properties dialog box.

   TIP If you don't like the color you chose, either click the Default Color button in the color picker to switch to the default color or click a different color. Not all browsers apply the same default colors for page backgrounds, so if you want your pages to display a specific color for the background, use style sheets to specify which color to use. You can also specify transparent (rather than a color) as a background. Black is generally the default text color used by browsers, but specify that also in your style sheets just to be safe.

   The background color of the web page is now white. The black text against the white background provides a nice contrast and makes the text easy to read.

5. Save your work.

You used the Page Properties dialog box to change the background color to white.

LESSON 2

Create, Import, AND FORMAT TEXT

What You'll Do

In this lesson, you will create a new page to replace the blank spa page, enter and format text, import text, set text properties, and check the spelling on the Striped Umbrella home page.

Creating and Importing Text

Most information in web pages is presented in the form of text. You can type text directly on a page in Dreamweaver, import, or copy and paste it from another software program. (Macintosh users do not have the option to import text. They must open a text file, copy the text, then paste it into an HTML document.) When using a Windows computer to import text from a Microsoft Word file, it's best to use the Import Word Document command. Not only will the formatting be preserved, but Dreamweaver will generate clean HTML code. **Clean HTML code** is code that does what it is supposed to do without using unnecessary instructions, which take up memory.

When you format text, it is important to keep in mind that your site users must have the same fonts installed on their computers as the fonts you use. Otherwise, the text might appear incorrectly. To avoid font compatibility and accessibly issues, you can use TypeKit, a company acquired by Adobe in 2011, that provides access to web fonts through the Adobe Creative Cloud. TypeKit offers fonts though a subscription-based service that can be read correctly by all browsers and devices. To learn more about TypeKit, go to typekit.com.

QUICK TIP

Some software programs can also convert text into images so that the text retains the same appearance, no matter which fonts are installed. However, text converted into images is no longer editable.

If text does not have a font specified, the default font on the user's computer will be used to display the text. Keep in mind that some fonts might not appear the same on both a Windows and a Macintosh computer. The way fonts are **rendered** (drawn) on the screen differs because Windows and Macintosh computers use different technologies to render them. If you are not using embedded fonts, it is wise to stick to the standard fonts that work well with both systems. Test your pages using both operating systems.

Formatting Text Two Ways: HTML vs. CSS

Because text is more difficult and tiring to read on a computer screen than on a printed page, you should make the text in your website attractive and easy to read. One way to do this is to format text by changing its font, size, and color. Previously web designers used the Property inspector to apply formatting attributes, such as font type, size, color, alignment, and indents. This created HTML tags in the code that directed the way the fonts would appear in a browser. **Tags** are the parts of the code that specify the appearance for all page content when viewed in a browser.

The more accepted method today is to create Cascading Style Sheets (CSS) to format and place web page elements. **Cascading Style Sheets** are sets of formatting attributes that you use to format web pages to provide a consistent presentation for content across the site. Cascading Style Sheets make it easy to separate page content from the page design. The content is placed in the body section on web pages, and the styles are placed in either an external style sheet file or in the page head content. Separating content from design is preferable because editing content and formatting content are two separate tasks. Creating the page content is a separate process from formatting the content. So when you use CSS styles, you can update or change the page content without disturbing the page formatting.

You can apply some formatting without creating styles by using the Bold and Italic HTML tags. You can also use HTML heading tags, which determine the relative size and boldness of text, and which help to show the importance of text relative to the rest of the text on the page.

To apply CSS or HTML formatting, you use the Property inspector, which has a panel for each method: the CSS Property inspector and the HTML Property inspector. You display them by clicking the CSS or the HTML button on the left side of the Property inspector. Some coding options are unique to each one and some coding options are available on both. For instance, HTML heading tags are only available on the HTML Property inspector. Font tags are only available on the CSS Property inspector. The Bold tag is available on both. Regardless of which Property inspector you use, CSS styles will be created when you format page objects.

Because CSS is a lot to learn when you are just beginning, we are going to begin by using HTML tags for formatting. Although they are not the currently preferred formatting method, it's still a good idea to know about HTML tags because you might "inherit" a web page that contains them. Then in Chapter 3, we will use the preferred method, CSS.

> **QUICK TIP**
> Even if you use the Property inspector to format text with HTML tags, Dreamweaver automatically creates styles when you apply most formatting attributes.

Changing Fonts

You can format your text with different fonts by choosing a font combination from the Font list in the CSS Property inspector. A **Font-combination** is a set of font choices that specify which fonts a browser should use to display the text on your web page. Font combinations ensure that if one font is not available, the browser will use the next one specified in the font combination. For example, if text is formatted with the font combination Arial, Helvetica, sans serif, the browser will first look on the user's system for Arial. If Arial is not available, then it will look for Helvetica. If Helvetica is not available, then it will look for a sans-serif font to apply to the text. Using fonts within the default settings is wise, because fonts set outside the default settings might not be available on all users' computers.

Changing Font Sizes

There are two ways to change the size of text using the Property inspector. When the CSS option is selected, you can select a numerical value for the size from 9 to 36 pixels (or type a smaller or larger number). Or you can use a size expressed in words from xx-small to larger, which sets the size of selected text relative to other text on the page. On the HTML Property inspector, you do not have font sizes available.

Formatting Paragraphs

The HTML Property inspector displays options to format blocks of text as paragraphs or as different sizes of headings. To format a paragraph as a heading, click anywhere in the paragraph, and then select the heading size you want from the Format list in the HTML Property inspector. The Format list contains six different heading formats. Heading 1 is the largest size, and Heading 6 is the smallest size. Browsers display text formatted as headings in bold, setting them off from paragraphs of text. It is considered good practice to use headings because heading tags give the user an idea of the importance of the heading relative to other text on the page. Text with a level 1 heading would be at a higher importance level than text with a level 2 heading. You can also align paragraphs with the alignment buttons on the CSS Property inspector and indent paragraphs using the Blockquote and Remove Blockquote buttons on the HTML Property inspector.

> **QUICK TIP**
> Mixing too many different fonts and formatting attributes on a web page can result in pages that are visually confusing or difficult to read.

Enter text

1. Position the insertion point directly after "want to go home." at the end of the paragraph, press **[Enter]** (Win) or **[return]** (Mac), then type **The Striped Umbrella**.

    Pressing [Enter] (Win) or [return] (Mac) creates a new paragraph.

    TIP If the new text does not assume the formatting attributes as the paragraph above it, click the Show Code and Design views button Split , position the insertion point right after the period after "home", then go back to the page in Design view and insert a new paragraph.

2. Press and hold **[Shift]**, press **[Enter]** (Win) or **[return]** (Mac), then type **25 Beachside Drive**.

    Pressing and holding [Shift] while you press [Enter] (Win) or [return] (Mac) creates a line break. A **line break** places a new line of text on the next line down without creating a new paragraph. Line breaks are useful when you want to add a new line of text directly below the current line of text and keep the same formatting.

3. Add the following text below the 25 Beachside Drive text, using line breaks after each line:

    Ft. Eugene, Florida 33775

    555-594-9458

4. Compare your screen with Figure 9.

You entered text for the address and telephone number on the home page.

Figure 9 *Entering the address and telephone number on The Striped Umbrella home page*

Come enjoy the best of both worlds, a secluded sandy beach populated with beautiful birds, yet a short drive down the road from world-class shopping, restaurants, and entertainment. Bring a good book and leave your laptop at the office. You won't want to go home.

The Striped Umbrella
25 Beachside Drive
Ft. Eugene, Florida 33775
555-594-9458

Copyright 2002 - 2015
Last updated on January 1, 2015

Single-spaced lines created by using line breaks

Pressing [Enter] (Win) or [return] (Mac) creates a new paragraph

TABLE 1: HTML FORMATTING TAGS

HTML tag	Represents
<p> </p>	Opening and closing paragraph tag
 	Line break tag (does not require a closing tag)
<em> </em>	Opening and closing italic (emphasis) tag
<strong> </strong>	Opening and closing bold tag
<u> </u>	Opening and closing underline tag

© Cengage Learning 2013

Using Keyboard Shortcuts

When working with text, the keyboard shortcuts for Cut, Copy, and Paste are very useful. These are [Ctrl][X] (Win) or ⌘ [X] (Mac) for Cut, [Ctrl][C] (Win) or ⌘ [C] (Mac) for Copy, and [Ctrl][V] (Win) or ⌘ [V] (Mac) for Paste. You can view all Dreamweaver keyboard shortcuts using the Keyboard Shortcuts dialog box, which lets you view existing shortcuts for menu commands, tools, or miscellaneous functions, such as copying HTML or inserting an image. You can also create your own shortcuts or assign shortcuts that you are familiar with from using them in other software programs. To view or modify keyboard shortcuts, click the Keyboard Shortcuts command on the Edit menu (Win) or Dreamweaver menu (Mac), then select the shortcut key set you want. Each chapter in this book includes Power User shortcuts, a list of keyboard shortcuts relevant to that chapter.

Developing a Web Page

Figure 10 *Formatting the address on The Striped Umbrella home page*

Selected address text — *HTML button displays formatting options on Property inspector* — *body_text rule* — *Italic button*

Figure 11 *Viewing the HTML code for the address and phone number*

<p> tag begins a new paragraph

"body_text" tag defines the CSS style in the original data file

Closing </em> tag ends italic text

Opening <em> tag begins italic text

Closing </p> tag ends a paragraph

*
 tags show line breaks from pressing [Shift][Enter] at the end of each line*

Format text

1. Select the entire address and telephone number, then click the **HTML button** `<> HTML` in the Property inspector (if it is not already selected) to change to the HTML Property inspector, as shown in Figure 10.

2. Click the **Italic button** *I* in the Property inspector to italicize the text, then click after the text to deselect it.

3. Click the **Show Code view button** `Code` to view the HTML code, as shown in Figure 11.

   It is always helpful to learn what the HTML code means. Refer to Table 1 to locate some basic HTML formatting tags. As you edit and format your pages, read the code to see how it appears for each element. The more familiar you are with the code, the more comfortable you will feel with Dreamweaver and web design. A strong knowledge of HTML is a necessary skill for professional web designers.

4. Click the **Show Design view button** `Design` to return to Design view.

5. Save your work, then close the page.

You changed the Property inspector options from CSS to HTML, then formatted the address and phone number for The Striped Umbrella by changing the font style to italic.

Lesson 2 Create, Import, and Format Text

DREAMWEAVER 2-13

Save an image file in the assets folder

1. Click **File** on the Menu bar, click **New**, click **Blank Page** (if necessary), click **HTML** in the Page Type column, click **<none>** as shown in Figure 12, click the **DocType list arrow**, click **HTML5**, click **Create**, then click the **Show Design view button** Design if necessary.

   A new blank page opens in the Document window.

2. Click **File**, click **Save As**, navigate to your Striped Umbrella site root folder, then save the file as **spa.html**, overwriting the existing (blank) spa.html file.

3. Click the **Insert bar menu**, click **Common**, click the **Images list arrow**, then click **Image**.

   The Select Image Source dialog box opens, as shown in Figure 13.

4. Browse to and open the website assets folder, double-click **su_banner.gif**, type **The Striped Umbrella banner** in the Image Tag Accessibility Attributes dialog box, then click **OK**.

   The banner appears at the top of the new page. You will learn more about the Image Tag Accessiblity Attributes dialog box in Chapter 4.

   TIP You can also drag the banner image from the Files panel onto the page since it is already saved in the website assets folder.

5. Click to the right of the image to deselect it, press **[Shift][Enter]** (Win) or **[Shift][Return]** (Mac), repeat Step 3 to open the Select Image Source dialog box, then navigate to the assets folder in your chapter_2 data files folder.

6. Double-click **sea_spa_logo.png**, type **The Sea Spa logo** in the Image Tag Accessibility Attributes dialog box, then click **OK**.

   (continued)

Figure 12 *Creating a new HTML document with the New Document dialog box*

Blank Page   HTML Page Type   <none> Layout   Create button   DocType: HTML5

Figure 13 *Selecting the source file for the banner*

Double-click the filename to select the file and close the dialog box

Path for image

DREAMWEAVER 2-14

Developing a Web Page

Figure 14 *Image file added to the Striped Umbrella assets folder*

Images placed on page

Images listed in assets folder

Figure 15 *Clean Up Word HTML dialog box*

Clean up HTML from list arrow

Settings

Choosing Filenames for Web Pages

When you choose a name for a web page, you should use a short, simple descriptive name that reflects the contents of the page. For example, if the page is about your company's products, you could name it products.html. You should also follow some general rules for naming web pages, such as naming the home page index.html. Most file servers look for the file named index.html or default.html to use as the initial page for a website. Do not use spaces, special characters, or punctuation in filenames for files or folders that you will use in your site. Use underscores rather than spaces for readability; for example: use sea_spa_logo.jpg rather than sea spa logo.jpg. Just to be totally safe for all file servers, use only letters, numbers, or underscores in file or folder names. Many designers also avoid the use of uppercase letters.

7. Save your work.

   A copy of the sea_spa_logo.png file appears in the assets folder, along with the banner image, as shown in Figure 14.

You created a new file to replace the blank spa file, inserted the website banner image, then inserted the spa logo under the banner image and saved it in the website assets folder.

Import text

1. Click to place the insertion point to the right of the spa graphic on the spa.html page.

2. Click **File** on the Menu bar, point to **Import**, click **Word Document**, navigate to the **chapter_2 folder** from the location where you store your Data Files, then double-click **spa.doc** (Win); or double-click **spa.doc** from where you store your Data Files, select all, copy, close spa.doc, then paste the copied text on the spa page in Dreamweaver (Mac).

3. Click **Commands** on the Menu bar, then click **Clean Up Word HTML**.

   TIP If a dialog box appears stating that Dreamweaver was unable to determine the version of Word used to generate this document, click OK, click the Clean up HTML from list arrow, then choose the Word 2000 and newer version of Word if it isn't already selected.

4. Make sure each check box in the Clean Up Word HTML dialog box is checked, as shown in Figure 15, click **OK**, then click **OK** again to close the results window.

You imported a Word document, then used the Clean Up Word HTML command.

Set text properties

1. Select the Common category on the Insert panel if necessary, then scroll up the page and select the text "The Sea Spa Services."

2. Click the **Format list arrow** in the HTML Property inspector, then click **Heading 1**.

    The Heading 1 format is applied to the paragraph. Even a single word is considered a paragraph if there is a paragraph break (also known as a hard return) after it. The HTML code for a Heading 1 tag is <h1>. The tag is then closed with </h1>. For headings, the level of the heading tag follows the h, so the code for a Heading 2 tag is <h2>.

3. Select the text **Massages**, **Facials**, and **Body Treatments**, click the **Format list arrow** in the HTML Property inspector, click **Heading 2**, then click outside the heading to deselect the text.

    The H1 and H2 tags make the text a little large for the page, but it is more in keeping with semantic markup to begin with level 1 headings and work down. **Semantic markup** means coding to emphasize meaning. You can change the size of the text for each heading using style sheets if you want to change the default settings. We will do this in Chapter 3.

4. Click after the word "Treatments", insert a line break, click the **Show Code and Design views button** Split on the Document toolbar, then compare your screen to Figure 16.

    The word "Massages" after the words "Body Treatments" may be in a different position on your screen. Figure 16 was sized down, so your page will be much wider than the figure shows.

    (continued)

Figure 16 *Viewing the heading tags in Show Code and Design views*

You may see more or less of your windows depending on your document window size

Heading tags

Headings with <h2> tags

Heading with <h1> tags

Importing and Linking Microsoft Office Documents (Windows)

Adobe makes it easy to transfer data between Microsoft Office documents and Dreamweaver web pages. When importing a Word or Excel document, click File on the Menu bar, point to Import, then click either Word Document or Excel Document. Select the file you want to import, then click the Formatting list arrow to choose among importing Text only; Text with structure (paragraphs, lists, and tables); Text, structure, basic formatting (bold, italic); or Text, structure, full formatting (bold, italic, styles) before you click Open. The option you choose depends on the importance of the original structure and formatting. Always use the Clean Up Word HTML command after importing a Word file.

You can also create a link to a Word or Excel document on your web page. To do so, browse to locate the Word or Excel document you want to add as a link, then drag the file name to the location on the page where you would like the link to appear. (If the document is located outside the site, you can browse for it using the Site list arrow on the Files panel, Windows Explorer, or Mac Finder.) Next, select the Create a link option button in the Insert Document dialog box, then save the file in your site root folder so it will be uploaded when you publish your site. If it is not uploaded, the link will be broken.

Figure 17 *Check Spelling dialog box*

```
Facials

Revitalizing Facial
A light massage with a customized essential oil blend that moisturizes the skin and restores circulation.

Gentlemen's Facial
A cleansing facial that restores a healthy glow. Includes a neck and shoulder massage.

Milk Mask
A soothing mask that softens and moisturizes the face. Leaves your skin looking

Body Treatments

Salt Glow
Imported sea salts are massaged into the skin, exfoliating and cleansing the pore

Herbal Wrap
Organic lavender blooms create a detoxifying and calming treatment to relieve a

Seaweed Body Wrap
Seaweed is a natural detoxifying agent that also helps improve circulation.

Call The Sea Spa desk for prices and reservations. Any of our services can be p
until 9:00 p.m. Call 555-594-9458, extension 39.
```

Check Spelling dialog box with "masage" highlighted, suggestions listed including massage, manage, ma-sage, mas-age, mas age, ma sage, sage.

Click "Change" to correct spelling

Checking for Spelling Errors

It is very important to check for spelling and grammatical errors before publishing a page. A page that is published with errors will cause the user to immediately judge the site as unprofessional and carelessly made, and the accuracy of the page content will be in question. If you have text in a word processing file that you plan to import into Dreamweaver, check the spelling in the word processor first. Then check the spelling in the imported text again in Dreamweaver. This allows you to add words such as proper names to the Dreamweaver dictionary so the program will not flag them again. Click the Add to Personal button in the Check Spelling dialog box to add a new word to the dictionary. Even though you might have checked a page using the Check Spelling feature, you still must proofread the content yourself to catch usage errors such as misuse of "to," "too," and "two." Accuracy in both content and delivery is critical.

Tip: If your <h1> tag is before the image tag rather than before "The Sea Spa Services" heading, cut and paste it to match the code in Figure 16.

You applied two heading formats, then viewed the HTML code.

Check spelling

1. Click the **Show Design view button** Design to return to Design view.
2. Place the insertion point in front of the text "The Sea Spa Services".

   It is a good idea to start a spelling check at the top of the document because Dreamweaver searches from the insertion point down. If your insertion point is in the middle of the document, you will receive a message asking if you want to check the rest of the document. Starting from the beginning saves time.
3. Click **Commands** on the Menu bar, then click **Check Spelling**.

   The word "masage" is highlighted on the page as a misspelled word and suggestions are listed to correct it in the Check Spelling dialog box, as shown in Figure 17.
4. Click **massage**. in the Suggestions list if necessary, then click **Change**.

   The word is corrected on the page. If the Check Spelling dialog box highlights "exfoliating" click Ignore.
5. Click **OK** to close the Dreamweaver dialog box stating that the Spelling Check is completed.
6. Save and close the spa page.

You checked the spa page for spelling errors.

LESSON 3

Add Links
TO WEB PAGES

What You'll Do

In this lesson, you will open the home page and add links to the menu bar that link to the About Us, Spa, Cafe, and Activities pages. You will then insert an email link at the bottom of the page.

Adding Links to Web Pages

Links, or hyperlinks, provide the real power for web pages. Links make it possible for users to navigate all the pages in a website and to connect to other pages anywhere on the web. Users are more likely to return to websites that have a user-friendly navigation structure. Users also enjoy websites that have interesting links to other web pages or other websites.

To add links to a web page, first select the text or image that you want to serve as a link, and then, in the Link text box in the Property inspector, specify a path to the page to which you want to link.

When you create links on a web page, it is important to avoid **broken links**, or links that cannot find their intended destinations. You can accidentally cause a broken link by typing the incorrect address for the link in the Link text box. Broken links can be caused by companies merging, going out of business, or simply moving their website addresses.

In addition to adding links to your pages, you should provide a **point of contact**, or a place on a web page that provides users with a means of contacting the company. A common point of contact is a **mailto: link**, which is an email address that users with questions or problems can use to contact someone at the company's headquarters.

Using Menu Bars

A **menu bar**, or **navigation bar**, is an area on a web page that contains links to the main pages of a website. Menu bars are usually located at the top or side of each page in a website and can be created with text, images, or a combination of the two. Menu bars are the backbone of a website's navigation structure, which includes all navigation aids for moving around a website. To make navigating a website as easy as possible, you should place menu bars in the same position on each page. The web page in Figure 18 shows a menu bar that contains a set of main links with additional links that appear when a user moves a mouse pointer over (known as a rollover) each main link. You can create a simple menu bar by typing text representing each of your site's pages at the top of your web page, formatting the text, and then adding links to each of the text references. It is always a good idea to provide plain text links like this for accessibility, regardless of the type of navigation structure you choose to use. For example, if you use Flash for your navigation links, it is a good idea to include a duplicate set of text with links to the same pages. Most websites typically have links at the bottom of each page for accessing company contact information, terms of use, copyright, and terms of use statements.

Following WCAG Accessibility for Navigation

The WCAG Guideline 2.4 lists ways to ensure that all users can successfully and easily navigate a website. It states: "Provide ways to help users navigate, find content, and determine where they are." Suggestions include limiting the number of links on a page, using techniques to allow users to quickly access different sections of a page, and making sure that links are readable and easily distinguishable.

Figure 18 *The CIA website*
Central Intelligence Agency website – www.cia.gov

Additional links appear when mouse pointer rolls over a main link

Lesson 3   Add Links to Web Pages

DREAMWEAVER 2-19

Create a menu bar

1. Open **index.html**.
2. Position the insertion point to the left of "A" in About Us, then drag to select **About Us - Spa - Cafe**.
3. Type **Home - About Us - Spa - Cafe - Activities**, as shown in Figure 19.

   These five text labels will serve as a menu bar. You will add the links later.

You created a new menu bar using text, replacing the original menu bar.

Insert a horizontal rule

1. Click in front of the word "Welcome".
2. Click **Horizontal Rule** in the Common category on the Insert panel to insert a horizontal rule between the menu bar and the first paragraph.

   A horizontal rule is a line used to separate page elements or to organize information on a page.
3. Compare your screen to Figure 20, then save your work.

TIP An asterisk after the filename in the title bar indicates that you have altered the page since you last saved it. After you save your work, the asterisk no longer appears.

You added a horizontal rule to separate the menu bar from the page content.

Figure 19 *Viewing the new menu bar*

Figure 20 *Inserting a horizontal rule*

- Asterisk indicates page has not been saved
- Horizontal Rule command
- Horizontal rule
- Properties for horizontal rule

Preventing Data Loss

It is always a good idea to save your files frequently. A good practice is to save a file after you have completed a successful edit, before you attempt a difficult edit, and when you have finished working on an open file. It is also a good idea to close a file when you are not working on it. Having unnecessary files open can be a distraction to your work flow. Do not open files from a different website other than the open site in the Files panel, or you might accidentally save them in the wrong folder!

Figure 21 *Selecting text for the Home link*

Selected text

Link text box
Browse for file button

Figure 22 *Select File dialog box*

Striped Umbrella site root folder

index.html file

Click OK to set link

Relative to: list arrow

Figure 23 *Links added to menu bar*

Menu bar with links added

Add links to web pages

1. Double-click **Home** to select it, as shown in Figure 21.
2. Click the **Browse for File button** next to the Link text box in the HTML Property inspector, then navigate to the striped_umbrella local site folder if necessary.
3. Verify that the link is set Relative to Document in the Relative to: list.
4. Click **index.html** as shown in Figure 22, click **OK** (Win) or **Open** (Mac), then click anywhere on the page to deselect Home.

TIP Your file listing might differ depending on your view settings.

Home now appears in blue with an underline, indicating it is a link. If users click the Home link, a new page will not open, because the link is on the home page. It might seem odd to create a link to the same page on which the link appears, but this will be helpful when you copy the menu bar to other pages in the site. Always provide users a link to the home page.

5. Repeat Steps 1–4 to create links for About Us, Spa, Cafe, and Activities to their corresponding pages in the striped_umbrella site folder.
6. When you finish adding the links that link to the other four pages, deselect all, then compare your screen to Figure 23.

You created a link for each of the five menu bar elements to their respective web pages in The Striped Umbrella website.

Lesson 3 Add Links to Web Pages

DREAMWEAVER 2-21

Create an email link

1. Place the insertion point after the last digit in the telephone number, then insert a line break.
2. Click **Email Link** in the Common category on the Insert panel to insert an email link.
3. Type **Club Manager** in the Text text box, type **manager@stripedumbrella.com** in the Email text box, as shown in Figure 24, then click **OK** to close the Email Link dialog box.

   TIP If the text does not retain the formatting from the previous line use the Edit, Undo command to undo Steps 1–3. Switch to Code view and place the insertion point immediately to the right of the telephone number, then repeat the steps again in Design view.

4. Save your work.

   The text "mailto:manager@stripedumbrella.com" appears in the Link text box in the HTML Property inspector. See Figure 25. When a user clicks this link, a blank email message window opens in the user's default email software, where the user can type a message.

   TIP You must enter the correct email address in the Email text box for the link to work. However, you can enter any descriptive name, such as customer service or Bob Smith in the Text text box. You can also enter the email address as the text if you want to show the actual email address on the web page.

You inserted an email link to serve as a point of contact for The Striped Umbrella.

Figure 24 *Email Link dialog box*

Text for e-mail link on the page (this could also be a person's name or position or the actual e-mail link)

Link information

Figure 25 *mailto: link on the Property inspector*

mailto: link

Figure 26 *The Assets panel URL category*

URLs button

E-mail link on home page

Refresh button

View the email link in the Assets panel

1. Click the **Assets panel tab** to view the Assets panel.
2. Click the **URLs button** to display the URLs in the website.
3. Click the **Refresh button** at the bottom of the Assets panel, if necessary, to view the code for the link, then compare your screen to Figure 26.

   URL stands for **Uniform Resource Locator**. The URLs listed in the Assets panel show all of the **external links**, or links pointing outside of the website. An email link is outside the website, so it is an external link. You will learn more about URLs and links in Chapter 5. The links you created to the site pages are internal links (inside the website), and are not listed in the Assets panel.

4. Click the **Files panel tab** to view the Files panel.

You viewed the email link on the home page in the Assets panel.

Lesson 3   Add Links to Web Pages

LESSON 4

Use the History
PANEL AND EDIT CODE

What You'll Do

In this lesson, you will use the History panel to undo formatting changes you make to a horizontal rule. You will then use the Code Inspector to view the HTML code for the horizontal rule. You will also insert a date object and then view it using the Code Inspector.

Using the History Panel

Throughout the process of creating a web page, you will make mistakes along the way. Fortunately, you have a tool named the History panel to undo your mistakes. The **History panel** records each editing and formatting task you perform and displays them in a list in the order in which you completed them. Each task listed in the History panel is called a **step**. You can drag the **slider** on the left side of the History panel to undo or redo steps, as shown in Figure 27. You can also click in the bar to the left of a step to undo all steps below it. You click the step to select it. By default, the History panel records 20 steps. You can change the number of steps the History panel records in the General category of the Preferences dialog box. However, keep in mind that setting this number too high will require additional memory and could affect Dreamweaver's performance.

Viewing HTML Code in the Code Inspector

If you enjoy writing code, you occasionally might want to make changes to web pages by writing the code rather than using the panels and tools in Design view. Often it is actually easier to make editing or formatting corrections in the code. You can view the code in Dreamweaver using Code view, Code and Design views, or the Code Inspector. The **Code Inspector**,

---

Understanding Other History Panel Features

Dragging the slider up and down in the History panel is a quick way to undo or redo steps. However, the History panel offers much more. It has the capability to "memorize" certain tasks and consolidate them into one command. This is a useful feature for steps that you perform repetitively on web pages. The History panel does not show steps performed in the Files panel or any program-wide changes, such as editing preferences or changing panel arrangements.

shown in Figure 28, is a separate window that displays the current page in Code view. The advantage of using the Code Inspector is that you can see a full-screen view of your page in Design view while viewing the underlying code in a floating window that you can resize and position wherever you want.

You can add advanced features, such as JavaScript functions, to web pages by copying and pasting code from one page to another using the Code Inspector. A **JavaScript** function is a block of code that adds dynamic content such as rollovers or interactive forms to a web page. A **rollover** is a special effect that changes the appearance of an object when the mouse moves over it.

QUICK TIP

If you are new to HTML, you can use the Reference panel to find answers to your HTML questions. The Reference panel contains many resources besides HTML help, such as JavaScript help. You can open the Reference panel from the Code Inspector or the Results panel.

Figure 27 *The History panel*

- Drag slider up to undo steps
- Click in the bar next to a step to undo to that step

Figure 28 *The Code Inspector*

- Code displayed in the Code Inspector
- Page displayed in Design view behind the Code Inspector
- Selected text with corresponding code

Lesson 4 Use the History Panel and Edit Code

DREAMWEAVER 2-25

Use the History panel

1. Click **Window** on the Menu bar, then click **History**.

   The History panel opens and displays steps you have recently performed.

2. Click the **Panel options button**, click **Clear History**, as shown in Figure 29, then click **Yes** to close the warning box.

3. Select the **horizontal rule** on the index page.

   The Property inspector shows the properties of the selected horizontal rule.

4. Click the **W text box** in the Property inspector, type **900**, click the **Align list arrow**, click **Left**, then compare your Property inspector to Figure 30.

   Horizontal rule widths can be set in pixels or as a percent of the width of the window. If the width is expressed in pixels, the code will only show the number, without the word "pixels". Pixels is understood as the default width setting.

5. Using the Property inspector, change the W text box value to **80**, change the measurement unit to **%**, click the **Align list arrow**, then click **Center**.

6. Drag the **slider** on the History panel up to Set Alignment: left, as shown in Figure 31.

   The bottom three steps in the History panel appear gray, indicating that these steps have been undone.

7. Right-click (Win) or Control-click (Mac) the **History panel title bar**, then click **Close** to close the History panel.

You formatted the horizontal rule, made changes to it, then used the History panel to undo some of the changes.

Figure 29 *Clearing the History panel*

You may see different steps depending on your keystrokes

Panel options button

Clear History command

Figure 30 *Property inspector settings for horizontal rule*

Width set to 900 pixels

Alignment of horizontal rule set to left side of page

Figure 31 *Undoing steps using the History panel*

Slider

Set Alignment: left

Steps that have been undone

DREAMWEAVER 2-26

Developing a Web Page

Figure 32 *Viewing the View Options menu*

— View Options button
— Options menu

Code for Horizontal rule

POWER USER SHORTCUTS	
To do this:	**Use this shortcut:**
Select All	[Ctrl][A] (Win) or ⌘[A] (Mac)
Copy	[Ctrl][C] (Win) or ⌘[C] (Mac)
Cut	[Ctrl][X] (Win) or ⌘[X] (Mac)
Paste	[Ctrl][V] (Win) or ⌘[V] (Mac)
Line Break	[Shift][Enter] (Win) or [Shift][return] (Mac)
Show or hide the Code Inspector	[F10] (Win) or [fn][option][F10] (Mac)
Preview in browser	[F12] (Win) or [fn][option][F12] (Mac)
Check spelling	[Shift][F7] (Win) or [fn][Shift][F7] (Mac)

© Cengage Learning 2013

Lesson 4 Use the History Panel and Edit Code

Use the Code Inspector

1. Click the **horizontal rule** to select it if necessary, click **Window** on the Menu bar, then click **Code Inspector**.

   Because the horizontal rule on the page is selected, the corresponding code is highlighted in the Code Inspector.

   TIP You can also press [F10](Win) or [fn][option][F10] (Mac) to display the Code Inspector.

2. Click the **View Options button** on the Code Inspector toolbar to display the View Options menu, then if **Word Wrap** is unchecked, click it once to activate it.

   The Word Wrap feature forces text to stay within the confines of the Code Inspector window, allowing you to read without scrolling sideways.

3. Repeat Step 2 to activate Line Numbers, Highlight Invalid Code, Syntax Coloring, Auto Indent, and Coding Toolbar as shown in Figure 32.

4. Select **900** in the horizontal rule width code, type **950**, then press **[Tab]**.

You changed the width of the horizontal rule by changing the code in the Code Inspector.

DREAMWEAVER 2-27

Use the Reference panel

1. With the horizontal rule still selected, click the **Reference button** on the Code Inspector toolbar, as shown in Figure 33, to open the Results Tab Group below the Property inspector, with the Reference panel visible.

   TIP If the horizontal rule is not still selected, you will not see the horizontal rule description in the Reference panel.

2. Read the information about horizontal rules in the Reference panel, as shown in Figure 34, right-click in an empty area of the **Results Tab Group title bar**, then click **Close Tab Group** (Win) or click the **Panel options button** then click **Close Tab Group** (Mac and Win) to close the Results Tab Group.

   The preferred method of formatting and positioning horizontal rules is to use CSS, rather than use the Property inspector. After you learn how to use CSS, you will then use them to format your horizontal rules.

3. Close the Code Inspector.

You read information about horizontal rule settings in the Reference panel.

Figure 33 *Reference button on the Code Inspector toolbar*

Reference button

Figure 34 *Viewing the Reference panel*

Information on <HR> (horizontal rule tag)

DREAMWEAVER 2-28

Developing a Web Page

Figure 35 *Insert Date dialog box*

Update automatically on save check box
Date formats

Figure 36 *Viewing the date object code*

Code for date object (if the date object is selected, your code will be highlighted in blue instead of yellow)

```
39  Last updated on
40     <!-- #BeginDate format:Am1 -->December 19, 2011<!--
       #EndDate -->
41  </p>
42  <p> </p>
43  </body>
44  </html>
```

Inserting Comments

It is easy to insert comments into HTML code in Dreamweaver. Comments can provide helpful information describing portions of the code, such as a JavaScript function. You can create comments in any Dreamweaver view, but you must turn on Invisible Elements to see them in Design view. Use the Edit (Win) or Dreamweaver (Mac) > Preferences > Invisible Elements > Comments command to enable viewing of comments; then use the View > Visual Aids > Invisible Elements command to display them on the page. To create a comment, select the Common category on the Insert panel, click Comment, type a comment in the Comment dialog box, and then click OK. Comments are not visible in browser windows.

Insert a date object

1. Scroll down the page, if necessary, to select **January 1, 2015**, then press **[Delete]** (Win) or **[delete]** (Mac).
2. Click **Date** in the Common category in the Insert panel, then click **March 7, 1974** if necessary in the Date format list.
3. Check the **Update automatically on save check box**, as shown in Figure 35, click **OK**, then deselect the text.
4. Change to Code and Design views.

   The code has changed to reflect the date object, which is set to today's date, as shown in Figure 36. (Your date will be different.) The new code is highlighted with a light yellow background, indicating that it is a date object, automatically coded by Dreamweaver, rather than a date that has been manually typed on the page by the designer or developer.

5. Return to Design view, then save the page.

You inserted a date object that will be updated automatically when you open and save the home page.

Lesson 4 Use the History Panel and Edit Code

DREAMWEAVER 2-29

LESSON 5

Modify and Test
WEB PAGES

What You'll Do

In this lesson, you will preview the home page in the browser to check for typographical errors, grammatical errors, broken links, and overall appearance. After previewing, you will make slight formatting adjustments to the page to improve its appearance.

Testing and Modifying Web Pages

Testing web pages is a continuous process. You never really finish a website, because there are always additions and corrections to make. As you add and modify pages, you must test each page as part of the development process. The best way to test a web page is to preview it in Live view or in a browser window to make sure that all text and image elements appear the way you expect them to. You should also test your links to make sure they work properly. You need to proofread your text to make sure it contains all the necessary information for the page with no typographical or grammatical errors. Designers typically view a page in a browser, return to Dreamweaver to make necessary changes, and then view the page in a browser again. They repeat this process many times before the page is ready for publishing. In fact, it is sometimes difficult to stop making improvements to a page and move on to another project. You need to strike a balance among quality, creativity, and productivity.

Testing a Web Page Using Different Browsers and Screen Sizes

Because users access the Internet using a wide variety of computer systems, it is important to design your pages so that all browsers and screen sizes can display them well. You should test your pages using different browsers and a wide variety of screen sizes to ensure the best

DESIGN TIP

Using "Under Construction" or "Come Back Later" Pages

Many people are tempted to insert an unfinished page as a placeholder for a page that they intend to finish later. Rather than have real content, these pages usually contain text or an image that indicates the page is not finished, or "under construction." You should not publish a web page that has a link to an unfinished page. It is frustrating to click a link for a page you want to open only to find an "under construction" note or image displayed. You want to make the best possible impression on your users. If you cannot complete a page before publishing it, at least provide enough information on it to make it "worth the trip."

DREAMWEAVER 2-30

Developing a Web Page

view of your page by the most people possible. Most web users today use a desktop computer with a screen resolution above 1024 by 768. Very few users use a resolution below this. So design your pages for this higher resolution. However, you'll also need to accommodate users who will view your pages with laptops, tablets, and mobile phones, so make sure your pages look good at these sizes, as well. To view your page using different screen sizes, click the Window Size pop-up menu on the status bar, then choose the setting you want to use.

QUICK TIP NEW

You can also use the Mobile size, Tablet size, and Desktop size buttons (introduced in Dreamweaver version 5.5) on the status bar to view your pages.

To view your pages using several different browsers, click the Preview/Debug in Browser button on the Menu bar, click Edit Browser List, then use the Add icon to add additional browsers installed on your computer to the list. You can also designate which browser to use as the default browser, the browser which opens when users press the F12 key. Remember also to check your pages using Windows and Macintosh platforms. Some page elements such as fonts, colors, table borders, layers, and horizontal rules might not appear consistently in both.

Using Adobe BrowserLab

Adobe BrowserLab is a tool that checks pages by simulating multiple browsers and platforms. You can use it to test your pages in browsers that are not installed on your computer. For example, if you are using a PC, you can use BrowserLab to test your pages with Apple Safari. BrowserLab is a great way to test your pages with multiple browsers and multiple versions of the same browser, which would be impossible otherwise without using multiple computers. You can access BrowserLab through the Adobe BrowserLab panel or the Preview/Debug in Browser button. To use BrowserLab, you need an Adobe ID. Visit the Adobe website to obtain an Adobe ID.

Testing a Web Page as Rendered in a Mobile Device

Dreamweaver has another preview feature (introduced in Dreamweaver version 5.5) that allows you to see what a page would look like if it were viewed on a mobile hand-held device, such as a phone or tablet. This is a new feature called the **Multiscreen Preview**. The Multiscreen button is located on the Document toolbar. With the Multiscreen Preview, you can view a page in three device sizes in one window, as shown in Figure 37. The Viewport Sizes button is used to change the default size settings to sizes of your choice.

Figure 37 *Using the Multiscreen Preview*

Viewport Sizes button

Phone preview   *Tablet preview*   *Desktop preview*

Lesson 5   Modify and Test Web Pages

DREAMWEAVER 2-31

Modify a web page

1. Click the **Tablet size button** ▫ on the status bar to see how the page would appear on a tablet using the default tablet settings, as shown in Figure 38.

    A user viewing this page on a tablet will be forced to use the horizontal scroll bar to view the entire page.

    NEW As you develop your pages with CSS, you can use **Media Queries** (introduced in Dreamweaver version 5.5) to detect which type of device is displaying your pages. By customizing your style sheets for different screen size and orientations, you can control how your pages will look when viewed with different devices. We will learn more about Media Queries in Chapter 8.

2. Replace the period after the last sentence, "You won't want to go home." with an exclamation point.

3. Click the **Multiscreen button** on the Document toolbar, then click **Full Size**.

    The page returns to full Design view.

4. Save your work.

You viewed the home page using two different window sizes and made a simple edit.

Figure 38 *Using Tablet preview to view the page*

Multiscreen button   *Page viewed in default tablet size setting*   *Tablet size (768 x 1024) button*

Using Smart Design Principles in Web Page Layout

As you view your pages in the browser, take a critical look at the symmetry of the page. Is it balanced? Are there too many images compared to text, or vice versa? Does everything "heavy" seem to be on the top or bottom of the page, or do the page elements seem to balance with the weight evenly distributed between the top, bottom, and sides? Use design principles to create a site-wide consistency for your pages. Horizontal symmetry means that the elements are balanced across the page. Vertical symmetry means that they are balanced down the page. Diagonal symmetry balances page elements along the invisible diagonal line of the page. Radial symmetry runs from the center of the page outward, like the petals of a flower. These principles all deal with balance; however, too much balance is not good, either. Sometimes it adds interest to place page elements a little off center or to have an asymmetric layout. Color, white space, text, and images should all complement each other and provide a natural flow across and down the page. The **rule of thirds**—dividing a page into nine squares like a tic-tac-toe grid—states that interest is increased when your focus is on one of the intersections in the grid. The most important information should be at the top of the page where it is visible without scrolling, or "above the fold," as they say in the newspaper business.

Figure 39 *Viewing The Striped Umbrella home page in the Firefox browser*

Visited links

Edited text

Test web pages by viewing them in a browser

1. Click the **Preview/Debug in browser button** on the Document toolbar, then choose your browser from the menu that opens.

   The Striped Umbrella home page opens in your default browser.

2. Click each link on the menu bar, then after each click, use the Back button on the browser toolbar to return to the home page.

   Pages with no content at this point will appear as blank pages. Compare your screen to Figure 39. The links in Figure 39 have all been clicked, which made them visited links. So they appear in purple rather than blue, the color of unvisited links.

3. Close your browser window, then close all open pages in Dreamweaver.

You viewed The Striped Umbrella home page in your browser and tested each link on the menu bar.

DESIGN TIP

Choosing a Window Size

Today, most users use a screen resolution of 1024 × 768 or higher. Because of this, more content can be displayed at one time on a computer monitor. Some people might use their whole screen to view pages on the Internet. Others might choose to allocate a smaller area of their screen to the browser window. In other words, people tend to use their "screen real estate" in different ways. The ideal web page will not be so small that it tries to spread out over a larger screen size or so large that the user has to use horizontal scroll bars to read the page content. The WCAG guideline 1.4.8 states that " … Text can be resized without assistive technology up to 200 percent in a way that does not require the user to scroll horizontally to read a line of text on a full-screen window." Achieving the best balance and meeting accessibility guidelines is one of the design decisions that you must make during the planning process.

SKILLS REVIEW

Create head content and set page properties.

1. Open the Blooms & Bulbs website.
2. Open the index page and view the head content.
3. Edit the page title so it reads **Blooms & Bulbs - Your Complete Garden Center**.
4. Insert the following keywords: **garden, plants, nursery, flowers, landscape, bulbs, Blooms & Bulbs, Alvin, Texas**.
5. Insert the following description: **Blooms & Bulbs is a premier supplier of plants, trees, and shrubs for both professional and home gardeners**.
6. Switch to Code view to view the HTML code for the head content, then switch back to Design view.
7. Open the Page Properties dialog box to view the current page properties.
8. Change the background color to a color of your choice and use the Apply button to view the change.
9. Change the background color to white, then save your work.

Create, import, and format text.

1. Create a new paragraph after the second paragraph of text and type the following text, inserting a line break after each line.
   Blooms & Bulbs
   Highway 43 South
   Alvin, Texas 77511
   555-248-0806
2. Verify that the HTML button is selected in the Property inspector, and select it if it is not.
3. Italicize the name, address and phone number lines.
4. Change to Code view to view the formatting code for the italicized text.
5. Return to Design view, save your work, hide the head content, then close the home page.
6. Create a new blank HTML5 file and save it as **tips.html** in the Blooms & Bulbs website, overwriting the existing file.
7. Insert the blooms & bulbs banner (from your website assets folder) at the top of the page, add appropriate alternate text, then enter a paragraph break after the banner. Insert the file butterfly.jpg from the chapter_2 assets folder where you store your Data Files, then add appropriate alternate text.
8. Place the insertion point to the right of the butterfly image, then insert a paragraph break.
9. Import gardening_tips.doc from where you store your Data Files, using the Import Word Document command (Win) or copy and paste the text (Mac).
10. Use the Clean Up Word HTML command to correct or remove any unnecessary code.
11. Click inside the Seasonal Gardening Checklist heading, then use the Property inspector to apply a Heading 1 format.
12. Click inside the Basic Gardening Tips heading, then use the Property inspector to format the selected text with a Heading 1 format.
13. Place the insertion point at the top of the document, then check the page for spelling errors by using the Check Spelling command, and make any necessary corrections.
14. Save your work and close the tips page.

Add links to web pages.

1. Open the index page, then select the current menu bar and replace it with **Home - Featured Plants - Garden Tips - Workshops - Newsletter**. Use a hyphen with a space on either side to separate the items.
2. Add a horizontal rule between the menu bar and the first paragraph of text.
3. Use the Property inspector to link Home on the menu bar to the index.html page in the Blooms & Bulbs website.
4. Link Featured Plants on the menu bar to the plants.html page.
5. Link Garden Tips on the menu bar to the tips.html page.
6. Link Workshops on the menu bar to the workshops.html page.
7. Link Newsletter on the menu bar to the newsletter.html page.
8. Create a line break after the telephone number and then use the Insert panel to create an email link, with **Customer Service** as the text and **mailbox@bloomsandbulbs.com** as the email address. (*Hint*: If your text does not retain the formatting from the previous line, reapply the settings.)
9. Save your work.
10. View the email link in the Assets panel, refreshing it if necessary, then view the Files panel.

Use the History panel and edit code.

1. Open the History panel, then clear its contents.
2. Select the horizontal rule under the menu bar, then change the width to 900 pixels and the alignment to Left.
3. Change the width to 70% and the alignment to Center.

SKILLS REVIEW
(CONTINUED)

4. Use the History panel to restore the horizontal rule settings to 900 pixels wide, left aligned.
5. Close the History panel.
6. Open the Code Inspector and verify that Word Wrap is selected.
7. Edit the code in the Code Inspector to change the width of the horizontal rule to 950 pixels.
8. Open the Reference panel and scan the information about horizontal rules.
9. Close the Code Inspector and close the Reference panel tab group.
10. Delete the current date in the Last updated on statement on the home page and replace it with a date using the March 7, 1974 format that will update automatically when the file is saved.
11. Examine the code for the date at the bottom of the page to verify that the code that forces it to update on save is included in the code. (*Hint*: The code should be highlighted with a light yellow background if it is not selected, or a blue background if it is selected.)
12. Return to Design view, then save your work.

Modify and test web pages.

1. View the index page with the Tablet size and Mobile size settings, then return to Desktop size.
2. View the page in your browser.
3. Verify that all links work correctly, then close the browser.
4. On the home page, add the text "We are happy to deliver or ship your purchases." to the end of the first paragraph.
5. Save your work, then view the pages in your browser, comparing your pages to Figure 40 and Figure 41.
6. Close your browser, then close the open page.

Figures 40 & 41 *Completed Skills Review, home page and tips page*

PROJECT BUILDER 1

You have been hired to create a website for TripSmart, a travel outfitter. You have created the basic framework for the website and are now ready to format and edit the home page to improve the content and appearance.

1. Open the TripSmart website, then open the home page.
2. Enter the following keywords: **TripSmart, travel, trips, vacations, Fayetteville, Arkansas,** and **tours**.
3. Enter the following description: **TripSmart is a comprehensive travel service. We can help you plan trips, make travel arrangements, and supply you with travel gear.**
4. Change the page title to **TripSmart - Serving all your travel needs**.
5. Replace the existing menu bar with the following text: **Home**, **Catalog**, **Services**, **Tours**, and **Newsletter**. Between each item, use a hyphen with a space on either side to separate the items.
6. Replace the date in the last updated statement with a date that will update automatically on save.
7. Add a paragraph break after the last paragraph, then type the following address, using line breaks after each line:
   TripSmart
   1106 Beechwood
   Fayetteville, AR 72704
   555-848-0807
8. Insert an email link in the line below the telephone number, using **Contact Us** for the text and **mailbox@tripsmart.com** for the email link.
9. Italicize TripSmart, the address, phone number, and email link.
10. Link the menu bar entries to index.html, catalog.html, services.html, tours.html, and newsletter.html.
11. View the HTML code for the page, then return to Design view.
12. Insert a horizontal rule above the address.
13. Change the horizontal rule width to 950 pixels and align it to the left side of the page.
14. Save your work.
15. View the page using two different window sizes, then test the links in your browser window.
16. Compare your page to Figure 42, close the browser, then close all open pages.

Figure 42 *Completed Project Builder 1*

PROJECT BUILDER 2

Your company has been selected to design a website for a catering business named Carolyne's Creations. You are now ready to add content to the home page and apply formatting options to improve the page's appearance, using Figure 43 as a guide.

1. Open the Carolyne's Creations website, then open the home page.
2. Edit the page title to read **Carolyne's Creations: Premier Gourmet Food Shop**.
3. Add the description **Carolyne's Creations is a full-service gourmet food shop. We offer cooking classes, take-out meals, and catering services. We also have a retail shop that stocks gourmet items and kitchen accessories.**
4. Add the keywords **Carolyne's Creations, gourmet, catering, cooking classes, kitchen accessories, take-out, Seven Falls, Virginia**.
5. Place the insertion point in front of the sentence in the second paragraph beginning "Give us a call" and type **We also have a pick-up window on the right side of the building for take-out orders**.
6. Add the following address below the second paragraph using line breaks after each line:
   **Carolyne's Creations
   496 Maple Avenue
   Seven Falls, Virginia 52404
   555-963-8271**
7. Enter another line break after the telephone number and type **Email**, add a space, then add an email link using **Carolyne Kate** for the text and **carolyne@carolynescreations.com** for the email address.
8. Create links from each menu bar element to its corresponding web page.
9. Replace the date that follows the text "Last updated on" with a date object that will automatically update on save, then save your work.
10. Insert a horizontal rule between the menu bar and the Welcome heading.
11. Set the width of the horizontal rule to 400 pixels, then left-align the horizontal rule.
12. Save your work, view the completed page in your default browser, then test each link.
13. Close your browser.
14. Close all open pages.

Figure 43   *Completed Project Builder 2*

DESIGN PROJECT

Albert Iris is looking for a durable laptop case that he can use for the frequent trips he takes with his laptop. He is searching the Internet looking for one that is attractive, strong, and that provides quick access for removing the laptop for airport security. He knows that websites use keywords and descriptions in order to receive "hits" with search engines. He is curious about how they work. Follow the steps below and write your answers to the questions.

1. Connect to the Internet, then go to **www.sfbags.com** to view the WaterField Designs website's home page, as shown in Figure 44.
2. View the page source by clicking View on the Menu bar, then clicking Source (Internet Explorer) or Tools > Web Developer > Page Source (Mozilla Firefox).
3. Can you locate a description and keywords? If so, what are they?
4. How many keyword terms do you find?
5. Is the description appropriate for the website? Why or why not?
6. Look at the numbers of keyword terms and words in the description. Is there an appropriate number?
7. Use a search engine such as Google at www.google.com, then type the words **laptop bag** in the Search text box.
8. Click a link in the list of results and view the source code for that page. Do you see keywords and a description? Do any of them match the words you used in the search?

Figure 44 *Design Project*
Waterfield Designs website used with permission from Waterfield Designs – www.sfbags.com

PORTFOLIO PROJECT

In this assignment, you will continue to work on the website you defined in Chapter 1. In Chapter 1, you created a wireframe for your website with at least four pages. You also created a local site folder for your site and an assets folder to store the site asset files. You set the assets folder as the default storage location for your images. You began to collect information and resources for your site and started working on the home page.

1. Think about the head content for the home page. Add the title, keywords, and a description.
2. Create the main page content for the home page.
3. Add the address and other contact information to the home page, including an email address.
4. Consult your wireframe and design the menu bar.
5. Link the menu bar items to the appropriate pages.
6. Add a last updated on statement to the home page with a date that will automatically update when the page is saved.
7. Edit the page content until you are satisfied with the results. You will format the content after you have learned to use Cascading Style Sheets in the next chapter.
8. Verify that all links, including the email link, work correctly.
9. When you are satisfied with the home page, review the checklist questions shown in Figure 45, then make any necessary changes.
10. Save your work.

Figure 45 *Portfolio Project*

Website Checklist
1. Does the home page have a page title?
2. Does the home page have a description and keywords?
3. Does the home page contain contact information, including an email address?
4. Does the home page have a menu bar that includes a link to itself?
5. Does the home page have a "last updated on" statement that will automatically update when the page is saved?
6. Do all paths for links and images work correctly?
7. Does the home page look good using at least two different browsers and screen resolutions?

ADOBE DREAMWEAVER CS6

CHAPTER 3

**WORKING WITH TEXT AND
CASCADING STYLE SHEETS**

1. Create unordered and ordered lists
2. Create, apply, and edit Cascading Style Sheets
3. Add rules and attach Cascading Style Sheets
4. Use coding tools to view and edit rules

CHAPTER 3
WORKING WITH TEXT AND CASCADING STYLE SHEETS

Introduction

Most web pages depend largely on text to convey information. Dreamweaver provides many tools for working with text that you can use to make your web pages attractive and easy to read. These tools can help you format text quickly and make sure it has a consistent look across all your web pages.

Using Cascading Style Sheets

You can save time and ensure that all your page elements have a consistent appearance by using **Cascading Style Sheets (CSS)**. CSS are sets of formatting instructions, usually stored in a separate file, that control the appearance and position of text and graphics on a web page or throughout a website. CSS are a great way to define consistent formatting attributes for page elements such as paragraph text, lists, and table data. You can then apply the formatting attributes to any element in a single document or to all of the pages in a website.

Formatting Text as Lists

If a web page contains a large amount of text, it can be difficult for viewers to digest it all. You can break up the monotony of large blocks of text by dividing them into smaller paragraphs or by organizing them as lists. You can create three types of lists in Dreamweaver: unordered lists, ordered lists, and definition lists.

Lists are also excellent for creating simple navigation bars. You can format list items to look like buttons by applying styles to assign background colors for each list item. You can even create rollover effects for list items by having the background color change when the user rolls the mouse over them. This technique gives your links a more professional look than plain text links without requiring the use of JavaScript, Spry, or Flash. Cascading Style Sheets are indeed a powerful tool. This chapter will focus on using Cascading Style Sheets to format text.

TOOLS YOU'LL USE

LESSON 1

Create Unordered
AND ORDERED LISTS

What You'll Do

- Salt Glow
  Imported sea salts are massaged into the skin, exfoliating and cleansing the pores.
- Herbal Wrap
  Organic lavender blooms create a detoxifying and calming treatment to relieve aches and pains.
- Seaweed Body Wrap
  Seaweed is a natural detoxifying agent that also helps improve circulation.

Call The Sea Spa desk for prices and reservations. Any of our services can be personalized according to your needs. Our desk is open from 7:00 a.m. until 9:00 p.m. Call 555-594-9458, extension 39.

Questions You May Have

1. How do I schedule Spa services?
   Please make appointments by calling The Club desk at least 24 hours in advance. Please arrive 15 minutes before your appointment to allow enough time to shower or use the sauna.
2. Will I be charged if I cancel my appointment?
   Please cancel 24 hours before your service to avoid a cancellation charge. No-shows and cancellations without adequate notice will be charged for the full service.
3. Are there any health safeguards I should know about?
   Please advise us of medical conditions or allergies you have. Heat treatments like hydrotherapy and body wraps should be avoided if you are pregnant, have high blood pressure, or any type of heart condition or diabetes.
4. What about tipping?
   Gratuities are at your sole discretion, but are certainly appreciated.

In this lesson, you will create an unordered list of spa services on the spa page. You will also import text with questions and format them as an ordered list.

Creating Unordered Lists

Unordered lists are lists of items that do not need to appear in a specific sequence, such as a grocery list, which often lists items in a random order. Items in unordered lists are usually preceded by a **bullet**, a small dot or similar icon. Unordered lists that contain bullets are sometimes called **bulleted lists**. Although you can use paragraph indentations to create an unordered list, bullets can often make lists easier to read. To create an unordered list, first select the text you want to format as an unordered list, then use the Unordered List button in the HTML Property inspector to insert bullets at the beginning of each paragraph of the selected text.

Formatting Unordered Lists

In Dreamweaver, the default bullet style is a round dot. To change the bullet style to a square, use Cascading Style Sheets. You can create a rule to modify the <ul> tag that will apply to all unordered lists in a website, as shown in Figure 1 or you can create an

Figure 1 *Using CSS to format all unordered lists in a website*

Unordered list style type = square

DREAMWEAVER 3-4

Working with Text and Cascading Style Sheets

inline rule to only modify one unordered list as shown in Figure 2. You will learn about Cascading Style Sheets in the next lesson.

Creating Ordered Lists

Ordered lists, which are sometimes called **numbered lists**, are lists of items that are presented in a specific sequence and that are preceded by sequential numbers or letters. An ordered list is appropriate for a list in which each item must be executed according to its specified order. A list that provides numbered directions for driving from Point A to Point B or a list that provides instructions for assembling a bicycle are both examples of ordered lists.

Formatting Ordered Lists

You can format an ordered list to show different styles of numbers or letters by using Cascading Style Sheets, as shown in Figure 3. You can apply numbers, Roman numerals, lowercase letters, or uppercase letters to an ordered list.

Creating Definition Lists

Definition lists are similar to unordered lists but have a hanging indent and are not preceded by bullets. They are often used with terms and definitions, such as in a dictionary or glossary. To create a definition list, select the text to use for the list, click Format on the Menu bar, point to List, and then click Definition List.

Figure 2 *Using CSS to format only one unordered list in a website*

```
17    <p class="list_headings">Massages</p>
18    <ul style="list-style:square">
19      <li class="body_text">Sports Massage<br />
20        Our deepest massage for tense and sore muscles. Not
      recommended for first-time massage  clients.</li>
21      <li class="body_text">Swedish Massage<br />
22        A gentle, relaxing massage. Promotes balance and wellness.
      Warms muscle tissue  and increases circulation.</li>
```

Unordered list style type = square

Figure 3 *Using CSS to format all ordered lists in a website*

Ordered list style type = lower alpha

Lesson 1 Create Unordered and Ordered Lists

Create an unordered list

1. Open the spa page in The Striped Umbrella website.
2. Select the three items and their descriptions under the Massages heading.
3. Click the **HTML button** <> HTML in the Property inspector to switch to the HTML Property inspector if necessary, click the **Unordered List button** to format the selected text as an unordered list, click anywhere to deselect the text, then compare your screen to Figure 4.

   Each spa service item and its description are separated by a line break. That is why each description is indented under its corresponding item, rather than formatted as a new list item. You must enter a paragraph break to create a new list item.

4. Repeat Step 3 to create unordered lists with the three items under the Facials and Body Treatments headings, being careful not to include the contact information in the last paragraph on the page as part of your last list.

TIP Pressing [Enter] (Win) or [return] (Mac) once at the end of an unordered list creates another bulleted item. To end an unordered list, press [Enter] (Win) or [return] (Mac) twice.

(continued)

Figure 4 *Creating an unordered list*

Unordered list   A line break does not create a new list item   Unordered List button   A paragraph break creates a new list item

DESIGN TIP

Coding for the Semantic Web

You may have heard the term "semantic web." The word "semantics" refers to the study of meanings of words or sentences. So the term "semantic web" refers to the way page content can be coded to convey meaning to other computer programs such as search engines. One example is to use the <em> tag which means "emphasis" rather than the <i> tag which means "italic" to show emphasis. Another example would be to use font size attributes such as <small> or <medium> rather than using font size attributes expressed in pixels. Cascading Style Sheets are used to define the appearance of semantic tags. For instance, you can specify the attributes of the <h1> heading tag by choosing the Selector Type: Tag (redefines an HTML element) rules in the New CSS Rules dialog box. CSS and semantic coding work together to enhance the meaning of the page content and provide well-designed pages that are attractive and consistent throughout the site. An ideal website would incorporate semantic coding with external style sheets to format all website content. This approach will enable "Semantic Web" programs to interpret the content presented, make it easier for web designers to write and edit, and enhance the overall experience for site users.

Figure 5 *Viewing the three unordered lists*

Massages

- Sports Massage
  Our deepest massage for tense and sore muscles. Not recommended for first-time massage clients.
- Swedish Massage
  A gentle, relaxing massage. Promotes balance and wellness. Warms muscle tissue and increases circulation.
- Hot Stone Massage
  Uses polished local river rocks to distribute gentle heat. Good for tight, sore muscles. Balances and invigorates the body muscles. Advance notice required.

Facials

- Revitalizing Facial
  A light massage with a customized essential oil blend that moisturizes the skin and restores circulation.
- Gentlemen's Facial
  A cleansing facial that restores a healthy glow. Includes a neck and shoulder massage.
- Milk Mask
  A soothing mask that softens and moisturizes the face. Leaves your skin looking younger.

Body Treatments

- Salt Glow
  Imported sea salts are massaged into the skin, exfoliating and cleansing the pores.
- Herbal Wrap
  Organic lavender blooms create a detoxifying and calming treatment to relieve aches and pains.
- Seaweed Body Wrap
  Seaweed is a natural detoxifying agent that also helps improve circulation.

5. Save your work, then compare your page to Figure 5.
6. Position the insertion point to the left of the first item in the first unordered list, then click the **Show Code view button** Code on the Document toolbar to view the code for the unordered list, as shown in Figure 6.

    A pair of HTML tags surrounds each type of element on the page. The first tag in each pair begins the code for a particular element, and the last tag ends the code for the element. For instance, the tag <ul> begins the unordered list, and the </ul> tag ends it. The tags <li> and </li> surround each item in the list.
7. Click the **Show Design view button** Design on the Document toolbar.
8. Save your work.

You opened the spa page in Design view and formatted three spa services lists as unordered lists. You then viewed the HTML code for the unordered lists in Code view.

Figure 6 *HTML tags in Code view for unordered lists*

```
17  <p class="list_headings">Massages</p>
18  <ul>
19    <li class="body_text">Sports Massage<br />
20      Our deepest massage for tense and sore muscles. Not recommended for first-time massage  clients.</li>
21    <li class="body_text">Swedish Massage<br />
22      A gentle, relaxing massage. Promotes balance and wellness. Warms muscle tissue  and increases circulation.</li>
23    <li class="body_text">Hot Stone Massage<br />
24      Uses polished local river rocks to distribute gentle heat. Good  for tight, sore muscles. Balances and invigorates the body
    muscles. Advance  notice required. </li>
25  </ul>
26  <p class="list_headings">Facials</p>
27  <ul>
28    <li class="body_text">Revitalizing Facial<br />
29      A light massage with a customized essential oil blend that  moisturizes the skin and restores circulation. </li>
30    <li class="body_text">Gentlemen&rsquo;s Facial<br />
31      A cleansing facial that restores a healthy glow. Includes a  neck and shoulder massage.</li>
32    <li class="body_text">Milk Mask<br />
33      A soothing mask that softens and moisturizes the face. Leaves  your skin looking younger.</li>
34  </ul>
```

Beginning and ending tags for unordered list

First pair of tags for the first list item in the list

Lesson 1   Create Unordered and Ordered Lists

DREAMWEAVER 3-7

Create an ordered list

1. Place the insertion point at the end of the page, after the words "extension 39."
2. Click the **Word Document** command on the File, Import menu, browse to the location where you store your Data Files, then double-click **questions.doc** (Win) or open **questions.doc** from where you store your Data Files, select all, copy, then paste the copied text on the page (Mac).

    The inserted text appears on the same line as the existing text.

3. Click **Commands** on the menu bar, click **Clean Up Word HTML**, click **OK** to close the Clean Up Word HTML dialog box, click **OK** to close the Dreamweaver dialog box, place the insertion point to the left of the text "Questions you may have," then click **Horizontal Rule** in the Common category on the Insert panel.

    A horizontal rule appears and separates the unordered list from the text you just imported.

4. Select the text beginning with "How do I schedule" and ending with the last sentence on the page.
5. Click the **Ordered List button** in the HTML Property inspector to format the selected text as an ordered list.
6. Deselect the text, then compare your screen to Figure 7.

You imported text on the spa page. You also added a horizontal rule to help organize the page. Finally, you formatted selected text as an ordered list.

Figure 7 *Creating an ordered list*

- Seaweed Body Wrap
  Seaweed is a natural detoxifying agent that also helps improve circulation.

Call The Sea Spa desk for prices and reservations. Any of our services can be personalized according to your needs. Our desk is open from 7:00 a.m. until 9:00 p.m. Call 555-594-9458, extension 39.

Questions You May Have

1. How do I schedule Spa services?
   Please make appointments by calling The Club desk at least 24 hours in advance. Please arrive 15 minutes before your appointment to allow enough time to shower or use the sauna.
2. Will I be charged if I cancel my appointment?
   Please cancel 24 hours before your service to avoid a cancellation charge. No-shows and cancellations without adequate notice will be charged for the full service.
3. Are there any health safeguards I should know about?
   Please advise us of medical conditions or allergies you have. Heat treatments like hydrotherapy and body wraps should be avoided if you are pregnant, have high blood pressure, or any type of heart condition or diabetes.
4. What about tipping?
   Gratuities are at your sole discretion, but are certainly appreciated.

Ordered list items

Figure 8 *Formatting a list heading*

Formatted heading for list *Bold button* *Italic button* *Indent button*

Format an ordered list heading

1. Click to place the insertion point in the heading "Questions you may have," then use the HTML Property inspector to apply the **Heading 3** format, as shown in Figure 8.

TIP You could show emphasis by using the Bold button **B** or the Italic button *I* on the HTML Property inspector, as shown in Figure 8, but the heading code shows the significance (semantics) of the phrase more clearly. It shows that the phrase is a heading related to the text that follows it. The three headings on the page are formatted with three different heading tags that indicate their order of importance on the page: Heading 1 first, then Heading 2, followed by Heading 3.

2. Save your work.

You formatted the "Questions you may have" heading.

Lesson 1 Create Unordered and Ordered Lists

DREAMWEAVER 3-9

LESSON 2

Create, Apply, and
EDIT CASCADING STYLE SHEETS

What You'll Do

In this lesson, you will create a Cascading Style Sheet file for The Striped Umbrella website. You will also create a rule named list_headings and apply it to the list item headings on the spa page.

Understanding Cascading Style Sheets

Cascading Style Sheets (CSS) are made up of sets of formatting attributes called **rules**, which define the formatting attributes for page content. Rules are sometimes referred to as styles. Style sheets are classified by where the code is stored. The code can be saved in a separate file (**external style sheet**), as part of the head content of an individual web page (**internal or embedded styles**), or as part of the body of the HTML code (**inline styles**). External CSS are saved as files with the .css extension and are stored in the website's directory structure. Figure 9 shows an external style sheet named su_styles.css listed in the Files panel. External style sheets are the preferred method for creating and using styles.

CSS are also classified by their type. A **Class type** can be used to format any page element. An **ID type** and a **Tag type** are used to redefine an HTML tag. A **Compound** type is used to format a selection. In this chapter, we will use the class type and the tag type, both stored in an external style sheet file.

Using the CSS Styles Panel

You use buttons on the CSS Styles panel to create, edit, and apply rules. To add a rule, use the New CSS Rule dialog box to name the rule and specify whether to add it to a new or existing style sheet. You then use the CSS Rule definition dialog box to set the formatting attributes for the rule. Once you add a new rule to a style sheet, it appears in a list in the CSS Styles panel. To apply a rule, you select the text to which you want to apply the rule, and then choose a rule from the Targeted Rule list in the CSS Property inspector. You can apply CSS rules to elements on a single web page or to all of the pages in a website. When you edit a rule, such as changing the font size it specifies, all page elements formatted with that rule are automatically updated. Once you create an external CSS, you should attach it to the remaining pages in your website.

Use the CSS Styles panel to manage your styles. The Properties pane displays properties for a selected rule at the bottom of the panel. You can easily change a property's value by clicking an option from a drop-down menu.

Understanding the Advantages of Using Style Sheets

You can use CSS styles to save an enormous amount of time. Being able to define a rule and then apply it to page elements on all the pages of your website means that you can make hundreds of formatting changes in a few minutes. In addition, style sheets create a more uniform look from page to page and they generate cleaner code. Using style sheets separates the development of content from the way the content is presented. Pages formatted with CSS styles are much more compliant with current accessibility standards than those with manual formatting.

> **QUICK TIP**
>
> For more information about Cascading Style Sheets, visit www.w3.org/Style.

Understanding CSS Code

You can see the properties for a CSS rule by looking at the style sheet code. A CSS rule consists of two parts: the selector and the declaration. The **selector** is the name of the tag to which the style declarations have been assigned. The **declaration** consists of a property (such as font-size or font-weight) and a value (such as 14 px or bold). For example, Figure 10 shows the code for an internal style that sets the background color for a page. In this example, the selector is the body tag. The only property assigned to this selector is background-color. The value for this property is #FFF, or white. The property and value together comprise the declaration. When there is more than one property, each additional property and value are separated by a semicolon.

When you create a new external CSS file, you will see it as a related files document in the Document window. Save this file as you make changes to it.

Figure 9 *Cascading Style Sheet file created in striped_umbrella site root folder*

Figure 10 *Viewing CSS code*

Lesson 2   Create, Apply, and Edit Cascading Style Sheets

DREAMWEAVER 3-11

Create a Cascading Style Sheet and add a rule

1. Click the **CSS button** in the Property inspector to switch to the CSS Property inspector, as shown in Figure 11.
2. If the CSS Styles panel is not open, click **Window** on the Menu bar, then click **CSS Styles** to open the CSS Styles panel or click the **CSS Styles panel tab**.
3. Click the **Switch to All (Document) Mode button** on the CSS Styles panel if it's not already active, then click the **New CSS Rule button** in the CSS Styles panel to open the New CSS Rule dialog box.
4. Verify that Class (can apply to any HTML element) is selected under Selector Type, then type **list_headings** in the Selector Name text box.

   TIP Class selector names are preceded by a period in the code and in the CSS panel. If you don't enter a period when you type the name, Dreamweaver will add the period for you when the rule is created.

5. Click the **Rule Definition list arrow**, click **(New Style Sheet File)**, compare your screen with Figure 12, then click **OK**.

   This indicates that you want to create a new style sheet file, which will contain your list_headings rule and any other rules you may create for this site. The Save Style Sheet File As dialog box opens.

   (continued)

Figure 11 *CSS Property inspector*

CSS button

Options in the Property inspector change depending on whether the HTML or CSS button is selected

Figure 12 *New CSS Rule dialog box*

Class option for Selector Type

New rule name

Rule Definition list arrow

DREAMWEAVER 3-12

Working with Text and Cascading Style Sheets

Figure 13 *CSS Rule Definition for .list_headings in su_styles.css dialog box*

Type category selected

Figure 14 *CSS Styles panel with list_headings rule added*

list_headings rule

Properties for list_headings rule

DESIGN TIP

Choosing Fonts

There are two classifications of fonts: sans-serif and serif. **Sans-serif** fonts are block-style characters that are often used for headings and subheadings. The headings in this book and the text you are reading now use a sans-serif font. Examples of sans-serif fonts include Arial, Verdana, and Helvetica. **Serif** fonts are more ornate and contain small extra strokes at the beginning and end of the characters. Serif fonts are considered easier to read in printed material, because the extra strokes lead your eye from one character to the next. Examples of serif fonts include Times New Roman, Times, and Georgia. The paragraph text on the first page of each chapter in this book is in a serif font. Many designers feel that a sans-serif font is preferable when the content of a website is primarily intended to be read on the screen, but that a serif font is preferable if the content will be printed. When you choose fonts, you need to keep in mind the amount of text each page will contain and whether most viewers will read the text on-screen or print it. A good rule of thumb is to limit each website to no more than three font variations.

6. Type **su_styles** in the File name text box (Win) or the Save As text box (Mac), verify that the striped_umbrella folder appears in the Save in box, then click **Save** to open the CSS Rule Definition for .list_headings in su_styles.css dialog box.

   The .list_headings rule will be stored within the su_styles.css file in the Striped Umbrella local site folder. Next, you define the properties for the rule.

7. Verify that Type is selected in the Category list, set the Font-family to **Arial**, **Helvetica**, **sans-serif**, set the Font-size to **12 px**, set the Font-weight to **bold**, set the Font-style to **normal**, set the Color to **#006**, compare your screen to Figure 13, then click **OK**.

   TIP You can modify the font combinations in the Font-family list by clicking Modify on the Menu bar then clicking Font Families.

   Other interesting type options that are available in the CSS Rule Definition dialog box are Line-height, which changes the height of each line measured in pixels; Text-decoration, which adds text effects, Font-variant, which allows you to change the text to small caps, and Text-transform, which has options to change text to all upper-case or all lower-case.

8. Click the **plus sign** (Win) or the **expander arrow** (Mac) next to su_styles.css in the CSS Styles panel and expand the panel, if necessary, to see the .list_headings rule displayed, then select the **.list_headings rule**.

   The CSS rule named .list_headings and its properties appear in the CSS Styles panel, as shown in Figure 14.

You created a Cascading Style Sheet file named su_styles.css and a rule called .list_headings within the style sheet.

Lesson 2 Create, Apply, and Edit Cascading Style Sheets

DREAMWEAVER 3-13

Apply a rule

1. Click **View** on the Menu bar, point to **Toolbars**, then click **Style Rendering**.

   TIP You can also right-click an empty area on an open toolbar to see the displayed and hidden toolbars listed in a drop-down menu. The displayed toolbars have a check next to them. To display or hide a toolbar, click its name on the menu.

2. Verify that the Toggle Displaying of CSS Styles button on the Style Rendering toolbar is active, as shown in Figure 15.

   TIP You can determine if the Toggle Displaying of CSS Styles button is active if it has a dark outline around the button. As long as this button is active, you do not have to display the toolbar on the screen.

   You use the Toggle Displaying of CSS Styles button to see how styles affect your page. If it is not active, you will not see the effects of your styles and the default browser settings will be used to display the content.

3. Select the paragraph heading "Massages," click the **Targeted Rule list arrow** in the Property inspector, then click **list_headings**, as shown in Figure 16.

4. Repeat Step 3 to apply the list_headings rule to each of the spa services unordered list headings, click anywhere in the document to deselect the text, then compare your screen to Figure 17.

   TIP You can use the keyboard shortcut [Ctrl][Y] (Win) or [Command][Y] (Mac) to repeat the previous action.

You applied the list_headings rule to each of the Spa Services category headings.

Figure 15 *Style Rendering toolbar*

Figure 16 *Applying a CSS rule to selected text*

Figure 17 *Unordered list with list_headings rule applied*

DREAMWEAVER 3-14

Working with Text and Cascading Style Sheets

Figure 18 *Editing a rule*

Properties of the list_headings rule

font-size list arrow

Click 14 on this menu

Figure 19 *Viewing the changes made to the list_headings rule*

Text with the list_headings rule applied is now larger

Edit a rule

1. Click **.list_headings** in the CSS Styles panel.

    The rule's properties and values appear in the Properties pane, the bottom part of the CSS Styles panel.

    TIP Click the plus sign (Win) or expander arrow (Mac) to the left of su_styles.css in the CSS Styles panel if you do not see .list_headings. Click the plus sign (Win) or expander arrow (Mac) to the left of <style> if you do not see su_styles.css. You may have to resize the CSS Styles panel to see the Properties pane.

2. Click **12 px** in the CSS Styles panel, click the **font-size list arrow**, click **14** as shown in Figure 18, then compare your screen to Figure 19.

    All of the text to which you applied the list_headings rule is larger, reflecting the changes you made to the list_headings rule. You can also click the **Edit Rule button** in the CSS Styles panel to open the CSS Rule Definition for .list_headings dialog box.

    TIP If you position the insertion point in text that has a CSS rule applied to it, that rule is displayed in the Targeted Rule text box in the CSS Property inspector or the Class text box in the HTML Property inspector.

3. Click **File** on the menu bar, then click **Save All** to save the spa page and the style sheet file.

4. Hide the Style Rendering toolbar.

You edited the list_headings rule to change the font size to 14 pixels. You then viewed the results of the edited rule in the unordered list.

View code with the Code Navigator

1. Click in the paragraph heading "Massages", then [Alt]-click (Win) or [Command] [Option]-click (Mac) to display the Code Navigator.

   A window opens, as shown in Figure 20, with the name of the style sheet that is linked to this page (su_styles.css) and the name of the rule in the style sheet that has been applied to this text (list_headings).

2. Position the mouse pointer over the list_headings rule name until you see a box with the rule's properties, as shown in Figure 21.

   TIP You can disable the Code Navigator by clicking the Disable check box as shown in Figure 21.

You displayed the Code Navigator to view the properties of the list_headings rule.

Figure 20 *Viewing the rule name in the Code Navigator*

Window displays the name of the style sheet file and rule applied from the style sheet

Figure 21 *Viewing the rule properties in the Code Navigator*

Hover the mouse pointer over the rule name to see its properties

Check box to disable Code Navigator

Figure 22 *Using Code and Design views to view rule properties*

Figure 23 *Using Code and Design views to edit a rule*

Replace color "006" with "003"

Using the Style Rendering Toolbar

The Style Rendering toolbar allows you to display your page as it would appear for different media types, such as print, TV, or handheld. To display it when a page is open, click View on the Menu bar, point to Toolbars, and then click Style Rendering. The buttons on the Style Rendering toolbar allow you to see how your page will look as you select different media types. The seventh button on the toolbar is the Toggle Displaying of CSS Styles button, which you can use to view how a page looks with styles applied. It works independently of the other buttons. The next button to the right is the Design-time Style Sheets button, which you can use to show or hide particular combinations of styles while you are working in the Document window. The buttons on the right side of the toolbar can be used to change the text size or show the link properties for links in the active document.

Use the Code Navigator to edit a rule

1. Click **.list_headings** in the Code Navigator. The document window splits into two panes. The left pane displays the code for the CSS file and the right section displays the HTML page in Design view, as shown in Figure 22.

   TIP The default setting for Show Code and Design views in Dreamweaver CS6 splits the two windows vertically, rather than horizontally. To view the two windows split horizontally on the screen, click View on the Menu bar, then click Split Vertically to uncheck the option and split the screens horizontally.

2. Type directly in the code to replace the color "006" with the color "**003**" as shown in Figure 23.

   TIP You can also edit the rule properties in the CSS Styles panel.

3. Click the **Refresh button** [Refresh] in the CSS Styles panel, then save all files.

4. Click the **Show Design view button** [Design].

   The font color has changed in Design view to reflect the new shade of blue in the rule.

You changed the color value in the .list_headings rule.

Add a Tag selector to an existing style sheet

1. Click the **New CSS Rule button** in the CSS Styles panel.
2. Click the **Selector Type list arrow**, then select **Tag (redefines an HTML element)**.
3. Type **h1** in the Selector Name text box, verify that su_styles.css appears in the Rule Definition text box, compare your screen to Figure 24, then click **OK**.

   The CSS Rule Definition for H1 in su_styles.css dialog box opens.

4. With the Type Category selected, change the Font-family to **Arial**, **Helvetica**, **sans-serif**; the Font-size to **24**; the Font-weight to **bold**, as shown in Figure 25; then click **OK**.

   The Sea Spa Services heading on the page changes in appearance to reflect the new h1 properties specified in the new rule.

TIP The Remove Font from Favorites button next to the Font-family list box can be used to remove fonts from the menu list.

(continued)

Figure 24 *Creating a Tag selector*

Select Tag (redefines an HTML element)

Type or select h1

Verify that su_styles.css will be the location for the new rule

Figure 25 *CSS Rule Definition for h1 in su_styles.css*

Remove Font from Favorites button

Transitioning to a Real-World Work Process

As you learn Dreamweaver throughout the chapters in this book, you practice its many features in a logical learning sequence. You will develop an understanding of both current concepts like CSS3 and older, but still used, features such as HTML formatting and embedded styles. Once you learn Dreamweaver and start using it to create your own websites, you would ideally format all pages with rules from one external style sheet. You would move all of the embedded styles in the predesigned CSS layouts to the external style sheet because the embedded styles on each page would be redundant. After you have worked through this book, you should have the skills and understanding to design sites built entirely and efficiently with CSS.

Figure 26 *Viewing the headings with new rules applied*

Headings formatted with selector rules

New rules added to style sheet

5. Repeat Steps 1 through 4 to create a new Tag selector that redefines the h2 tag with a Font-family of **Arial**, **Helvetica**, **sans-serif**; a Font-size of **18**; and a Font-weight of **normal**.

6. Repeat Step 5 to create a new Tag selector that redefines the h3 tag with a Font-family of **Arial**, **Helvetica**, **sans-serif**; a Font-size of **16**; and a Font-weight of **bold**.

7. Save all files, then compare your screen to Figure 26.

You added three tag selectors to your style sheet that modify the appearance of the h1, h2, and h3 tags.

Using Web Open Font Format (WOFF)

The Mozilla Foundation developed the Web Open Font Format (WOFF), in concert with several other organizations, as another option for formatting text on the World Wide Web. WOFF fonts are embedded in web pages with the CSS3 property @font-face. This allows browsers to access external font libraries and deliver a font when a page is viewed in a browser that does not have that font installed. Because WOFF is a compressed format, it allows WOFF-formatted content to download faster. Currently Firefox Version 3.6 and up, Internet Explorer Version 9 and up, Google Chrome Version 5 and up, and Safari Version 5.1 and up support the WOFF format. You can convert fonts to a WOFF format using Font Squirrel, a free online service at www.fontsquirrel.com/fontface/generator. Examples of font libraries are typekit.com and www.google.com/webfonts#HomePlace:home.

Lesson 2 Create, Apply, and Edit Cascading Style Sheets

DREAMWEAVER 3-19

LESSON 3

Add Rules and Attach
CASCADING STYLE SHEETS

What You'll Do

In this lesson, you will add a rule to a Cascading Style Sheet. You will then attach the style sheet file to the index page and apply one of the rules to text on the page.

Understanding External and Embedded Style Sheets

When you are first learning about CSS, the terminology can be confusing. In the last lesson, you learned that external style sheets are separate files in a website, saved with the .css file extension. You also learned that CSS can be part of an HTML file, rather than a separate file. These are called internal, or embedded, style sheets. External CSS files are created by the web designer. Embedded style sheets are created automatically in Dreamweaver if the designer does not create them, using default names for the rules. The code for these rules resides in the head content for that page. These rules are automatically named style1, style2, and so on. You can rename the rules as they are created to make them more recognizable for you to use, for example, paragraph_text, subheading, or address. Embedded style sheets apply only to a single page, although you can copy them into the code in other pages or move them to an external style sheet. Remember that style sheets can be used to format much more than text objects. They can be used to set the page background, link properties, or determine the appearance of almost any object on the page. Figure 27 shows the code for some embedded rules and a link to an external style sheet. The code resides in the head content of the web page.

When you have several pages in a website, you will probably want to use the same styles for each page to ensure that all your elements have a consistent appearance. To attach a style sheet to another document, click the Attach Style Sheet button on the CSS Styles panel to open the Attach External Style Sheet dialog box, make sure the Add as Link option is selected, browse to locate the file you want to attach, and then click OK. The rules contained in the attached style sheet will appear in the CSS Styles panel, and you can use them to apply rules to text on the page. External style sheets can be attached, or linked, to any page. This is an extremely powerful tool. If you decide to edit a rule, the changes will automatically be made to every object on every page that it formats.

Understanding Related Page Files

When an HTML file is linked to other files necessary to display the page content, these files are called **related files.** When a file that has related files is open in the Document window, each related file name is displayed in the Related Files toolbar above the Document window. A Cascading Style Sheet file is an example of a related file. When an HTML document has an attached CSS file but the CSS file is not available, the page file will appear in the browser, but will not be formatted correctly. It takes both the HTML file and the CSS file working together to display the content properly. When you upload HTML files, remember also to upload all related page files. Other examples of related page files are Flash player, video files, and JavaScript files.

When an HTML file with a linked CSS file is open in Dreamweaver, the name of the CSS filename appears below the page tab. When you click on the CSS filename, the screen changes to Split view, with the right side displaying the open HTML page in Design view and the left side displaying the CSS file. If you click Source Code next to the related page filename, the code for the top level document (open HTML file) will appear on the left side. You can edit both Code view windows by typing directly in the code.

Figure 27 *Code for embedded rules and a link to an external style sheet*

Style sheet name in the Related Files toolbar

Embedded rules are embedded in the head content

Link to external style sheet

Lesson 3   Add Rules and Attach Cascading Style Sheets

DREAMWEAVER 3-21

Add a class rule to a Cascading Style Sheet

1. Click the **New CSS Rule button** in the CSS Styles panel.
2. Verify that Class (can apply to any HTML element) is the Selector Type, type **body_text** in the Selector Name text box, verify that su_styles.css appears in the Rule Definition text box, as shown in Figure 28, then click **OK**.

   The new rule will be saved in the su_styles.css file as an external style.

3. Set the Font-family to **Arial**, **Helvetica**, **sans-serif**, set the Font-size to **12**, set the Color to **#000**, compare your screen to Figure 29, then click **OK**.
4. Select the three list items and their descriptions under the Massages heading, click the **Targeted Rule list arrow** in the CSS Property inspector, then click **body_text** to apply it to the three massage names and descriptions.

   The rule is applied to the text, but the text would be easier to read if it were a little larger.

5. Click the **Edit Rule button** in the CSS Styles panel.
6. Change the font size to **medium** in the Type category of the CSS Rule Definition for body_text in su_styles.css dialog box, as shown in Figure 30, then click **OK**.

   There are several ways to define font size rather than using pixels. Using a size of small, medium, large, etc., is one of them. Other choices include using em, pt, or a percentage.

   (continued)

Figure 28 *Adding a class rule to a CSS*

New rule name

su_styles.css is displayed in the Rule Definition list box

Figure 29 *Formatting options for body_text rule*

Figure 30 *Editing the body_text rule*

Change the Font-size to medium

Figure 31 *Spa page with style sheet applied to rest of text on page*

Text formatted with the body_text rule

7. Repeat Step 4 to apply the body_text rule to the rest of the text on the page except for the text that has already been formatted with the list_headings rule or heading tags, as shown in Figure 31.
8. Click **File** on the Menu bar, then click **Save All**, to save both the spa page and the su_styles.css file.

The rule is saved in the style sheet file and applied to the text in the HTML file.

TIP You must save the open su_styles.css file after editing it, or you will lose your changes.

You added a new rule called body_text to the su_styles.css file. You then applied the rule to selected text.

Lesson 3 Add Rules and Attach Cascading Style Sheets

DREAMWEAVER 3-23

Attach a style sheet

1. Close the spa page and open the index page.
2. Click the **Attach Style Sheet button** on the CSS Styles panel.
3. Click **Browse** then navigate to the file su_styles.css, if necessary, click the **su_styles.css** file, click **OK** (Win) or click **Open** (Mac), verify that the **Link option button** is selected, as shown in Figure 32, then click **OK**.

   There are now two rules named body_text. One is an internal style that was in the data file when you brought it into the website and one is in the external style sheet. Since these rules have duplicate names, it would be better to delete the internal style and let the external style format the text.

4. Select the **body_text rule** under the <style> section of the CSS Styles panel, as shown in Figure 33, then click the **Delete CSS Rule button** on the CSS Styles panel.
5. Click the **Show Code view button** and view the code that links the su_styles.css file to the index page, as shown in Figure 34.
6. Click the **Show Design view button**, then save your work.

You attached the su_styles.css file to the index.html page and deleted the body_text internal style, allowing the body_text external style to format the page text.

Figure 32 *Attaching a style sheet to a file*

Link option button   su_styles.css style sheet selected

Figure 33 *Deleting an internal style*

Delete the internal body_text rule

External styles   Internal styles   Delete CSS Rule button

Figure 34 *Viewing the internal styles and code to link the CSS file*

Internal styles listed in head content

Code linking external style sheet file to the index page in head content

DREAMWEAVER 3-24

Working with Text and Cascading Style Sheets

Figure 35 *Using the Related Files toolbar to view an external style sheet file*

Left pane displays code for external style sheet

Click su_styles.css to view external style sheet file

Right pane content will vary according to the placement of your insertion point

Figure 36 *Using the Related Files toolbar to view embedded styles*

Click Source Code to view embedded styles

Left pane displays code for embedded styles

Use the Related Files toolbar to view styles

1. Click **su_styles.css** on the Related Files toolbar.

   The document window changes to Show Code and Design views with the external CSS file in the left pane and the HTML page in Design view in the right pane, as shown in Figure 35.

2. Click **Source Code** on the Related Files toolbar.

   The code for the HTML file appears on the left with the code for the embedded styles as shown in Figure 36.

3. Click the **Show Design view button** Design to return to Design view.

You viewed the external and embedded styles using the Related Files toolbar.

Lesson 3 Add Rules and Attach Cascading Style Sheets

DREAMWEAVER 3-25

LESSON 4

Use Coding Tools to
VIEW AND EDIT RULES

What You'll Do

Coding Tools in Dreamweaver

In Code view, you can see the Coding toolbar, shown in Figure 37. It contains a number of handy tools that help you navigate through and view your code in different ways. It has buttons that expand or collapse code, buttons for changing the way the code is displayed, and buttons for inserting and removing comments. The Coding toolbar appears on the left side of the Document window. Although you cannot move it, you can hide it, using the Toolbars command on the View menu in Code view.

As you learned in Chapter 2, you can customize the way your page code appears in Code view. You can wrap the lines of code, display or hide line numbers and hidden characters, or highlight invalid code so you can fix it. You can also have different code types appear in different colors, indent lines of code, and display syntax error alerts. In Chapter 2, you viewed these options using the View Options button on the Code Inspector toolbar. You can also view and change them on the Code View options menu under the View menu on the Menu bar.

Figure 37 *Coding toolbar*

In this lesson, you will collapse, then expand the code for the index page to view the code for the embedded and external styles. You will then move embedded styles to the external style sheet file.

DREAMWEAVER 3-26

Working with Text and Cascading Style Sheets

Using Coding Tools to Navigate Code

As your pages get longer and the code more complex, it is helpful to collapse sections of code, much as you can collapse and expand panels, folders, and styles. Collapsing code lets you temporarily hide code between two different sections of code that you would like to read together. To collapse selected lines of code, you can click the minus sign (Win) or the triangle (Mac) next to the line number. You can also use the Collapse Full Tag or Collapse Selection buttons on the Coding toolbar. This will allow you to look at two different sections of code that are not adjacent to each other.

Adding comments is an easy way to add documentation to your code, which is especially helpful when you are working in a team environment and other team members will be working on pages with you. For example, you might use comments to communicate instructions like "Do not alter code below this line." or "Add final schedule here when it becomes available." Comments are not visible in the browser.

Using Code Hints to Streamline Coding

If you are typing code directly into Code view, Dreamweaver can speed your work by offering you code hints. **Code hints** are lists of tags that appear as you type, similar to other auto-complete features that you have probably used in other software applications. As you are typing code, Dreamweaver will recognize the tag name and offer you choices to complete the tag simply by double-clicking a tag choice in the menu, as shown in Figure 38. You can also add your own code hints to the list using JavaScript. Code hints are stored in the file CodeHints.xml.

Converting Styles

You can also convert one type of style to another. For instance, you can move an embedded style to an external style sheet or an inline style to either an embedded style or a style in an external style sheet. To do this, select the style in Code view, right-click the code, point to CSS Styles, then click Move CSS Rules. You can also move styles in the CSS Styles panel by selecting the style, right-clicking the style, and choosing the action you want from the shortcut menu.

Figure 38 *Using code hints*

As you begin typing code, the shortcut menu appears when Dreamweaver recognizes the code

Double-click from the list to complete your tag

Collapse code

1. Verify that the index page is open, then change to Code view.
2. Scroll up the page, if necessary, to display the code that ends the embedded styles (</style>).

   The code will probably be on or close to line 18 in the head section.
3. Select this line of code, then drag up to select all of the code up to and including the beginning tag for the embedded style sheet (<style type="text/css">, as shown in Figure 39.

   TIP If your code is in a slightly different order, scroll to find the meta tags to select them.
4. Click the **minus sign** (Win) or **vertical triangle** (Mac) in the last line of selected code to collapse all of the selected code.

   You can now see code above and below the collapsed code section as shown in Figure 40. The plus sign (Win) or horizontal triangle (Mac) next to the line of code indicates that there is hidden code. You also see a gap in the line numbers where the hidden code resides.

You collapsed a block of code in Code view to be able to see two non-adjacent sections of the code at the same time.

Figure 39 *Selecting lines of code on the index page to collapse*

Clicking either minus sign will collapse the selected code

Select the code in lines 8 through 18 (your line numbers may vary slightly)

Figure 40 *Collapsed code in Code view*

Lines 9 through 18 are hidden

Plus sign shows that there is collapsed code

DREAMWEAVER 3-28

Working with Text and Cascading Style Sheets

Figure 41 *Expanded code for index page*

```
1   <!doctype html>
2   <html>
3   <head>
4   <meta charset="utf-8">
5   <title>The Striped Umbrella beach resort and spa, Ft. Eugene, Florida</title>
6   <meta name="keywords" content="The Striped Umbrella, beach resort, spa, Ft. Eugene, Florida, Gulf of Mexico, fishing, golf, golfing, cruises">
7   <meta name="description" content="The Striped Umbrella is a full-service resort and spa just steps from the Gulf of Mexico in Ft. Eugene, Florida.">
8   <style type="text/css">
9   .nav_bar { font-size: large;
10      font-family: Arial, Helvetica, sans-serif;
11  }
12  .small_text { font-size: 10px;
13      font-family: Arial, Helvetica, sans-serif;
14  }
15  body {
16      background-color: #FFF;
17  }
18  </style>
19  <link href="su_styles.css" rel="stylesheet" type="text/css">
20  </head>
21
22  <body>
23  <img src="assets/su_banner.gif" alt="The Striped Umbrella banner" width="950" height="139">
```

Code is expanded again

Expand code

1. Click the **plus sign** (Win) or **horizontal triangle** (Mac) on line 8 to expand the code.
2. Compare your screen to Figure 41, then click in the page to deselect the code.

   All line numbers are visible again.

You expanded the code to display all lines of the code again.

POWER USER SHORTCUTS	
To do this:	**Use this shortcut:**
Switch views	[Ctrl][`] (Win) or [control][`] (Mac)
Indent text	[Ctrl][Alt][]] (Win) or ⌘ [option][]] (Mac)
Outdent text	[Ctrl][Alt][[] (Win) or ⌘ [option][[] (Mac)
Align Left	[Ctrl][Alt][Shift][L] (Win) or ⌘ [option][shift][L] (Mac)
Align Center	[Ctrl][Alt][Shift][C] (Win) or ⌘ [option][shift][C] (Mac)
Align Right	[Ctrl][Alt][Shift][R] (Win) or ⌘ [option][shift][R] (Mac)
Align Justify	[Ctrl][Alt][Shift][J] (Win) or ⌘ [option][shift][J] (Mac)
Bold	[Ctrl][B] (Win) or ⌘ [B] (Mac)
Italic	[Ctrl][I] (Win) or ⌘ [I] (Mac)
Refresh	[F5]

© Cengage Learning 2013

Lesson 4 Use Coding Tools to View and Edit Rules

Move an embedded style to an external CSS

1. Select the lines of code in the head section with the properties of the small_text rule (including the closing bracket) on the index page.

   The code will be on or close to lines 12 through 14.

2. Right-click (Win) or control-click (Mac) the **selected code**, point to **CSS Styles**, then click **Move CSS Rules**, as shown in Figure 42.

   TIP You can also convert a rule in the CSS Styles panel. To do this, right-click the rule name, then click Move CSS Rules.

3. In the Move To External Style Sheet dialog box, verify that su_styles.css appears in the Style Sheet text box, as shown in Figure 43, then click **OK**.

4. Repeat Steps 1 through 3 to move the nav_bar and body rules to the external style sheet.

   Since all styles are now in the external style sheet, they are available to be used for formatting all of the pages in the site.

   (continued)

Figure 42 *Moving the embedded small_text rule to the external style sheet file*

Selected code for small_text rule

Move CSS Rules command

Figure 43 *Moving the embedded style to the external style sheet file*

The embedded small_text rule will move to the su_styles file

DREAMWEAVER 3-30

Working with Text and Cascading Style Sheets

Figure 44 *Viewing the three rules moved to the external style sheet*

This code fragment is no longer needed and can be deleted

The body_text, small_text, and nav_bar rules are now in the su_styles.css file

Figure 45 *Viewing the CSS Styles panel after removing code*

5. Expand the su_styles.css style in the CSS Styles panel, if necessary, to display its rules, then compare your panel with Figure 44 to verify that the styles have been moved to the external style sheet file.

   The opening and closing tags for the internal style sheet are still in the code and can be removed now. When you delete the <style> tag in the CSS Styles panel, the opening and closing tags in the code will be removed.

6. Click **<style>** in the CSS Styles panel, press **[Delete]**, then compare your screen to Figure 45.

   You can also delete this code on the page in Code view if you prefer.

7. Return to Design view, then save and close all open files.

You moved three embedded rules to the external style sheet. You then deleted the remaining code left from the internal style sheet.

The evolution of CSS3

The use of Cascading Style Sheets has evolved over the years from CSS Level 1 to the present CSS Level 3. Cascading Style Sheets revisions are referenced by "levels" rather than "versions." Each new level builds on the previous level. CSS Level 1 is obsolete today. CSS Level 2 is still used, but CSS Level 3 is the latest W3C (World Wide Web Consortium) standard. With CSS3, several properties are available that promote website accessibility such as the @font-face rule. For more information about CSS3, go to www.w3.org/TR/CSS/.

Lesson 4 Use Coding Tools to View and Edit Rules

DREAMWEAVER 3-31

SKILLS REVIEW

Create unordered and ordered lists.
1. Open the Blooms & Bulbs website.
2. Open the tips page.
3. Select the text items below the Seasonal Gardening Checklist heading and format them as an unordered list. (*Hint*: There are no paragraph breaks between each item. To correct this, enter a paragraph break between each line, then remove any extra spaces.)
4. Select the lines of text below the Basic Gardening Tips heading and format them as an ordered list. (Refer to the Step 3 hint if each line does not become a separate list item.)
5. Save your work.

Create, apply, and edit Cascading Style Sheets.
1. Create a new CSS rule named **bullet_term**, making sure that the Class option button is selected in the Selector Type section and that the (New Style Sheet File) option is selected in the Rule Definition section of the New CSS Rule dialog box.
2. Click OK, name the style sheet file **blooms_styles** in the Save Style Sheet File As dialog box, then click Save.
3. Choose the following settings for the bullet_term rule: Font-family = Arial, Helvetica, sans-serif; Font-size = large; Font-style = normal; Font-weight = bold; and Color = #333.
4. Apply the bullet_term rule to the names of the seasons in the Seasonal Gardening Checklist: Fall, Winter, Spring, and Summer.
5. Edit the bullet_term rule by changing the font size to 16 pixels.

Add rules and attach Cascading Style Sheets.
1. Create a new class rule named **intro_text** in the blooms_styles.css file using following font settings: Font-family, Verdana, Geneva, sans-serif; Font-size 14 px; Color #333.
2. Apply the intro_text rule to the first paragraph on the page, then save the page.
3. Add a new Tag selector rule to the blooms_styles.css file that formats the h1 tag with the following properties: Font-family: Arial, Helvetica, sans-serif; Font-size: 16 px; Font-weight: bold.
4. Save the tips page, open the index page, and attach the blooms_styles.css file.
5. Apply the body_text rule to the rest of the text on the page that is not formatted with a rule.
6. Use the Save All command on the File menu to save both open pages and the style sheet, then preview both pages in the browser.
7. Close the browser.

Use coding tools to view and edit rules.
1. Switch to the index page if necessary, then change to Code view.
2. Display the code that ends the four embedded styles.
3. Select the lines of code for all of the embedded styles, including the opening and closing tags.
4. Collapse all of the selected code.
5. Expand the code.
6. Select the lines of code that define the small_text rule properties in the head section (including the closing bracket), then move the rule to the blooms_styles external style sheet.
7. Repeat Step 6 to move the body_text, nav_bar, and body rules to the external style sheet.
8. Delete the remaining code fragments for the beginning and ending embedded styles tags.
9. Apply the body_text rule to any remaining text on the tips page that is not formatted with a rule.
10. Save all open files, compare your pages to Figures 46 and 47, then close all open files.

SKILLS REVIEW
(CONTINUED)

Figure 46 & 47 *Completed Skills Review*

PROJECT BUILDER 1

Use Figures 48 and 49 as a guide to continue your work on the TripSmart website that you began in Project Builder 1 in Chapter 1, and continued to work on in Chapter 2. (Your finished pages will look different if you choose different formatting options.) You are now ready to create some rules to use for the text on the newsletter and index pages.

1. Open the TripSmart website.
2. Open dw3_1.html from where you store your Data Files and save it in the tripsmart site folder as **newsletter.html**, overwriting the existing newsletter.html file and not updating the links.
3. Verify that the path for the banner is correctly set to the assets folder of the TripSmart website, then type the title **Travel Tidbits** in the Title text box on the Document toolbar.
4. Create an unordered list from the text beginning "Be organized." to the end of the page.
5. Create a new CSS rule called **paragraph_text** making sure that the Class option is selected in the Selector Type section and that the (New Style Sheet File) option is selected in the Rule Definition section of the New CSS Rule dialog box.
6. Save the style sheet file as **tripsmart_styles.css** in the TripSmart website site folder.
7. Choose a font family, size, style, weight, and color of your choice for the paragraph_text style.
8. Apply the paragraph_text rule to all of the text on the page except the "Ten Tips for Stress-Free Travel" heading.
9. Create a Tag selector rule in the tripsmart_styles.css file that formats the h1 tag with a font, size, style, color, and weight of your choice, and assign the Heading 1 format to the "Ten Tips for Stress-Free Travel" heading.
10. Create another Class selector rule in the external style sheet called **list_term** with a font, size, style, color, and weight of your choice and apply it to each of the item names in the list such as "Be organized."
11. Close the dw3_1.html page, then save the newsletter page and the style sheet.
12. Open the index page, then attach the tripsmart_styles style sheet.
13. Select the two paragraphs and contact information, then apply the paragraph_text rule.
14. Delete the body_text embedded rule, then move the remaining embedded rules to the external style sheet. Delete any remaining code fragments from the embedded styles.
15. Save and preview the index and newsletter pages in your browser, using Figures 48 and 49 as examples.
16. Close your browser, then close all open files.

Figures 48 & 49 *Sample Project Builder 1*

PROJECT BUILDER 2

In this exercise, you continue your work on the Carolyne's Creations website that you started in Project Builder 2 in Chapter 1, and continued to build in Chapter 2. You are now ready to add a page to the website that will showcase a recipe. Figures 50 and 51 show a possible solution for these pages in this exercise. Your finished pages will look different if you choose different formatting options.

1. Open the Carolyne's Creations website
2. Open dw3_2.html from the location where you store your Data Files, save it to the website site folder as **recipes.html**, overwriting the existing file and not updating the links. Close the dw3_2.html file.
3. Select the pie image broken link placeholder, then use the Property inspector to browse for the pie.jpg image in the assets folder where you store your Data Files.
4. Format the list of ingredients on the recipes page as an unordered list.
5. Create a CSS rule named **body_text** and save it in a style sheet file named **cc_styles.css** in the website root folder. Use any formatting options that you like, then apply the body_text rule to all text except the menu bar and the text "Caramel Coconut Pie," "Ingredients," and "Directions."
6. Create a Tag selector rule that defines the properties for a Heading 1 rule and another one that defines the properties for a Heading 2 rule, using appropriate formatting options.
7. Apply the <h1> format to the "Caramel Coconut Pie" heading and the <h2> rule to the "Ingredients" and "Directions" headings, then save your work.
8. Open the index page, then attach the cc_styles.css to the file.
9. Delete the embedded body_text rule. The body_text rule in the external style sheet will format the text.
10. Convert the nav_bar rule and the small_text rule to external rules in the cc_styles style sheet, then switch back to the recipes page and format the menu bar with the nav_bar rule.
11. Delete any unnecessary code fragments left from the embedded styles.
12. Save all open files, then preview both pages in the browser.
13. Close your browser, then close all open pages.

Figures 50 and 51 *Sample Project Builder 2*

Working with Text and Cascading Style Sheets

DREAMWEAVER 3-35

DESIGN PROJECT

Charles Chappell is a sixth-grade history teacher. He is reviewing educational websites for information he can use in his classroom.

1. Connect to the Internet, then navigate to the Library of Congress website at www.loc.gov. The Library of Congress website is shown in Figure 52.
2. Which fonts are used for the main content on the home page—serif or sans-serif? Are the same fonts used consistently on the other pages in the site?
3. Do you see ordered or unordered lists on any pages in the site? If so, how are they used?
4. Use the View > Source (IE) or the Tools > Web Developer > Page Source (Firefox) command to view the source code to see if a style sheet was used.
5. Do you see the use of Cascading Style Sheets noted in the source code?

Figure 52 *Design Project*
The Library of congress website – www.loc.gov

PORTFOLIO PROJECT

In this assignment, you will continue to work on the website that you started in Chapter 1, and continued to build in Chapter 2. No Data Files are supplied. You are building this site from chapter to chapter, so you must do each Portfolio Project assignment in each chapter to complete your website.

You continue building your website by designing and completing a page that contains a list, headings, and paragraph text. During this process, you will develop a style sheet and add several rules to it

1. Consult your wireframe and decide which page to create and develop for this chapter.
2. Plan the page content for the page and make a sketch of the layout. Your sketch should include at least one ordered or unordered list, appropriate headings, and paragraph text. Your sketch should also show where the paragraph text and headings should be placed on the page and what rules should be used for each type of text. You should plan on creating at least two CSS rules.
3. Create the page using your sketch for guidance.
4. Create a Cascading Style Sheet for the site and add to it the rules you decided to use. Apply the rules to the appropriate content.
5. Attach the style sheet to the index page you developed in Chapter 2 and consider converting any existing embedded styles to the external style sheet.
6. Preview the new page in a browser, then check for page layout problems and broken links. Make any necessary corrections in Dreamweaver, then preview the page again in the browser. Repeat this process until you are satisfied with the way the page looks in the browser.
7. Use the checklist in Figure 53 to check all the pages in your site.
8. Close the browser, then close all open pages.

Figure 53 *Portfolio Project*

Website Checklist
1. Does each page have a page title?
2. Does the home page have a description and keywords?
3. Does the home page contain contact information?
4. Does every completed page in the site have consistent navigation links?
5. Does the home page have a last updated statement that will automatically update when the page is saved?
6. Do all paths for links and images work correctly?
7. Is there a style sheet with at least two rules?
8. Did you apply the rules to all text blocks?
9. Do all pages look good using at least two different browsers?

ADOBE DREAMWEAVER CS6

CHAPTER 4 ADDING IMAGES

1. Insert and align images
2. Enhance an image and use alternate text
3. Insert a background image and perform site maintenance
4. Add graphic enhancements

CHAPTER 4
ADDING IMAGES

Introduction

The majority of web page information appears in the form of text. But pages are much more interesting if they also contain images that enhance or illustrate the information. A well-designed web page usually includes a balanced combination of text and images. Dreamweaver provides many tools for working with images that you can use to make your web pages attractive and easy to understand.

Using Images to Enhance Web Pages

Images make web pages visually stimulating and more exciting than pages that contain only text. However, you should use images with an eye on both the purpose of each page and the overall design plan. There is a fine balance between using too many images that overwhelm the user and not providing enough images to enhance the text. There are many ways to work with images so that they complement the content of pages in a website.

You can use specific file formats used to save images for websites to ensure maximum quality with minimum file size.

Graphics Versus Images

Two terms that designers sometimes use interchangeably are graphics and images. For the purposes of discussion in this text, we will use the term **graphics** to refer to the appearance of most non-text items on a web page, such as photographs, logos, menu bars, Flash animations, charts, background images, and drawings. Files for items such as these are called graphic files. They are referred to by their file type, or graphic file format, such as JPEG (Joint Photographic Experts Group), GIF (Graphics Interchange Format), or PNG (Portable Network Graphics). We will refer to the actual pictures that you see on the pages as images. But don't worry about which term to use. Many people use one term or the other according to habit or region, or use them interchangeably.

TOOLS YOU'LL USE

Alt text box

LESSON 1

Insert and ALIGN IMAGES

What You'll Do

In this lesson, you will insert three images on the about_us page in The Striped Umbrella website. You will then adjust the alignment of the images on the page to make the page more visually appealing.

Understanding Graphic File Formats

When you choose graphics to add to a web page, it's important to use graphic files in the appropriate file format. Keep in mind the different types of devices that may be used to view the pages, such as tablets or smart phones. The three primary graphic file formats used in web pages are **GIF** (Graphics Interchange Format), **JPEG** or **JPG** (Joint Photographic Experts Group), and **PNG** (Portable Network Graphics). GIF files download quickly, making them ideal to use on web pages. Though limited in the number of colors they can represent, GIF files have the ability to show transparent areas. JPG files can display many colors. Because they often contain many shades of the same color, photographs are often saved in JPG format. Files saved with the PNG format can display many colors and use various degrees of transparency, called **opacity**. However, not all older browsers support the PNG format. JPGs and GIFS are best used when targeting mobile devices.

QUICK TIP
The Dreamweaver status bar shows the total download time for the open web page. Each time you add a new graphic to the page, you can see how much additional download time that graphic has added to the total.

Understanding the Assets Panel

When you add a graphic to a website, Dreamweaver automatically adds it to the Assets panel. The **Assets panel**, located in the Files panel group, displays all the assets in a website. The Assets panel contains nine category buttons that you use to view your assets by category. These include Images, Colors, URLs, SWF, Shockwave, Movies, Scripts, Templates, and Library. To view a particular type of asset, click the appropriate category button.

The Assets panel is divided into two panes. When you click the Images button, as shown in Figure 1, the lower pane displays a list of all the images in your site and is divided into five columns. You might need to resize the Assets panel to see all five columns. To resize the Assets panel, undock the Files tab group and drag a side or corner of the panel border.

The top pane displays a thumbnail of the selected image in the list. You can view assets in each category in two ways. You can use the Site option button to view all the assets in a website, or you can use the Favorites option button to view those assets that you have designated as **favorites**, or assets that

DREAMWEAVER 4-4

Adding Images

you expect to use repeatedly while you work on the site.

You can use the Assets panel to add an asset to a web page by dragging the asset from the Assets panel to the page or by using the Insert button on the Assets panel. If you are working on a page layout without final images ready to place, you can insert an image placeholder to hold the image position on the page. An **image placeholder** is a graphic the size of an image you plan to use. You can place it on a page until the actual image is finalized and ready to place on the page. To insert an image placeholder, use the Image Placeholder command on the Insert > Image Objects menu. When the final image is ready, simply replace the image placeholder with the final image.

Inserting Files with Adobe Bridge

You can manage project files, including video and Camera Raw files, with a file-management tool called Adobe Bridge. **Camera Raw** file formats are files that contain unprocessed data and are not yet ready to be printed. **Adobe Bridge** is an image file management program that is used across the Adobe suite applications. Bridge is an easy way to view files in their original locations before bringing them into the website. Bridge is an integrated application, which means you can use it to manage files among other Adobe programs such as Photoshop and Illustrator. You can also use Bridge to add meta tags and search text to your files. To open Bridge, click the Browse in Bridge command on the File menu or click the Browse In Bridge button on the Standard toolbar.

Aligning Images

When you insert an image on a web page, you need to position it in relation to other page elements such as text or other images. Positioning an image is also called **aligning** an image. By default, when you insert an image in a paragraph, its bottom edge aligns with the baseline of the first line of text or any other element in the same paragraph. When you first place images on a page, they do not include code to align them, so they appear at the insertion point, with no other page elements next to them. You add alignment settings with CSS. By adding a new rule to modify the <img> tag, you can add an alignment property and value. If you use an external style sheet, the <img> tag will apply globally to all images on pages with a link to the style sheet.

Figure 1 Assets panel

- Images button
- Category buttons
- Drag any panel border or corner to resize
- Drag title bar to undock tab group
- Site option button
- Favorites option button
- Thumbnail of selected image
- List of images in website

Lesson 1 Insert and Align Images

Insert an image

1. Open The Striped Umbrella website, open dw4_1.html from the drive and folder where you store your Data Files, then save it as **about_us.html** in the striped_umbrella site root folder.

2. Click **Yes** (Win) or **Replace** (Mac) to overwrite the existing file, click **No** to Update Links, then close dw4_1.html.

3. Click the **Attach Style Sheet button** in the CSS Styles panel, then attach the su_styles.css style sheet to the page.

4. Select the two large paragraphs of text on the page, click the **HTML button** on the Property inspector, verify that the Format is set to Paragraph, click the **CSS button**, then apply the body_text rule to the selected text.

5. Click the **HTML button**, then apply the Heading 1 tag to the text "Welcome guests!"

6. Place the insertion point before "When" in the first paragraph, click the **Images list arrow** in the Common category in the Insert panel, then click **Image** to open the Select Image Source dialog box.

7. Navigate to the assets folder in the drive and folder where you store your Data Files, double-click **club_house.jpg**, type the alternate text **Club House** if prompted, click **OK**, open the Files panel if necessary, then verify that the file was copied to your assets folder in the striped_umbrella site root folder.

   Compare your screen to Figure 2.

   (continued)

Figure 2 *Striped Umbrella about_us page with the inserted image*

club_house.jpg file inserted

Path should begin with the word "assets"

Click Image list arrow, then click Image to insert an image

Style sheet is attached

Inserted file listed in the assets folder

Figure 3 *Image files for The Striped Umbrella website listed in Assets panel*

- Images button
- Thumbnail of selected image
- List of images in The Striped Umbrella website
- Refresh Site List button

8. Click the **Assets panel tab** in the Files tab group, click the **Images button** in the Assets panel (if necessary), then click the **Refresh Site List button** in the Assets panel to update the list of images in The Striped Umbrella website.

The Assets panel displays a list of all the images in The Striped Umbrella website, as shown in Figure 3. If you don't see the new image listed, press and hold [CTRL] (Win) or ⌘ (Mac) before you click the Refresh Site List button.

You inserted one image on the about_us page and copied it to the assets folder of the website.

Organizing Assets for Quick Access

Your can organize the assets in the Assets panel in two ways, using the Site and Favorites options buttons. The Site option lists all of the assets in the website in the selected category in alphabetical order. But in a complex site, your asset list can grow quite large. To avoid having to scroll to search for frequently used items, you can designate them as Favorites. To add an asset to the Favorites list, right-click (Win) or [control]-click (Mac) the asset name in the Site list, and then click Add to Favorites. When you place an asset in the Favorites list, it still appears in the Site list. To delete an asset from the Favorites list, click the Favorites option button in the Assets panel, select the asset you want to delete, and then press [Delete] or the Remove from Favorites button on the Assets panel. If you delete an asset from the Favorites list, it still remains in the Site list. You can further organize your Favorites list by creating folders for similar assets and grouping them inside the folders.

Lesson 1 Insert and Align Images

Insert an image placeholder

1. Click to place the insertion point before the word "After" at the beginning of the second paragraph.
2. Click the **Images list arrow** in the Common category in the Insert panel, then click **Image Placeholder** to open the Image Placeholder dialog box.
3. Type **boardwalk** in the Name text box, **350** in the Width text box, **218** in the Height text box, and **Boardwalk to the beach** in the Alternate text text box, as shown in Figure 4.
4. Click **OK** to accept these settings, then compare your screen to Figure 5.

You inserted an image placeholder on the about_us page to hold the location on the page until the final image is ready to insert.

Figure 4 *Image Placeholder dialog box*

Figure 5 *Image placeholder on the about_us page*

Image placeholder

Click to insert an image placeholder

DREAMWEAVER 4-8

Adding Images

Figure 6 *The about_us page with the boardwalk image inserted*

Settings remain from the image placeholder settings

Boardwalk image replaces placeholder image

Src Browse for File button

Replace an image placeholder with an image

1. Click to select the **image placeholder** on the about_us page, if necessary.
2. Click the **Browse for File button** next to the Src text box on the Property inspector and browse to the assets folder where you store your Data Files if necessary.

   TIP You can also double-click an image placeholder to open the Select Image Source dialog box.

3. Double-click **boardwalk.png** to replace the image placeholder with the boardwalk image.

   The alternate text and the height and width settings on the Property inspector are the same that you entered in the Image Placeholder dialog box, as shown in Figure 6.

4. Save your work.

You replaced an image placeholder on the about_us page with a final image.

Lesson 1 Insert and Align Images

DREAMWEAVER 4-9

Use Adobe Bridge

1. Click to place the insertion point at the end of the last sentence on the page, then enter a paragraph break.

2. Click **File** on the Menu bar, click **Browse in Bridge**, close the dialog box asking if you want the Bridge extension for Dreamweaver to be enabled, answer **Yes** (if necessary), click the **Folders tab**, navigate to where you store your Data Files, then click the thumbnail image **su_logo.gif** in the assets folder, as shown in Figure 7.

   The Bridge window is divided into several panels; files and folders are listed in the Folders panel. The files in the selected folder appear in the Content panel. A picture of the selected file appears in the Preview panel. The Metadata and Keywords panels list any tags that have been added to the file. Your Content panel background may be lighter or darker depending on your Bridge settings.

3. Click **File** on the Menu bar, point to **Place**, then click **In Dreamweaver**.

4. Type the alternate text **The Striped Umbrella logo**, if prompted, then click **OK**.

   The image appears on the page.

   TIP You can also click the Browse in Bridge button on the Standard toolbar to open Bridge.

   After refreshing, your Assets panel should resemble Figure 8.

You inserted an image on the about_us page using Adobe Bridge.

Figure 7 *Using Adobe Bridge*

Folders tab Folders panel Your path may differ

su_logo.gif image is selected in Content panel

Your Content panel may be darker or lighter depending on your settings

Preview panel

Metadata and Keywords panels

Figure 8 *Assets panel with five images*

Five image files saved in the Striped Umbrella website

Click Refresh Site List button to refresh file list

DREAMWEAVER 4-10

Adding Images

Figure 9 New CSS Rule dialog box

Select the Class Selector Type

New Selector name is img_left_float

The new rule will be saved in the su_styles.css style sheet

Figure 10 CSS Rule Definition for img_left_float in su_styles.css dialog box

Select the Box Category

Select the left Float value

Figure 11 Clubhouse image with img_left_float rule applied

Text floats to the right of the image

Img_left_float rule is applied

Img_left_float rule is listed in the style sheet

Lesson 1 Insert and Align Images

Align an image

1. Scroll to the top of the page, then click the **club house image**.

   Because an image is selected, the Property inspector displays tools for setting the properties of an image.

2. Click the **New CSS Rule button** in the CSS Styles panel, click **Class** in the Selector type list box, type **img_left_float** for the Selector name, verify that it will be saved in the su_styles.css file, compare your screen to Figure 9, then click **OK**.

3. Click the **Box Category**, click the **Float list arrow**, click **left** as shown in Figure 10, then click **OK**.

   The Float property tells the browser to "float" the image to the left of whatever follows it on the page.

4. Click the **clubhouse image** if necessary, click the **Class list arrow** on the right side of the Property inspector, then click **img_left_float**.

   The text moves to the right side of the image, as shown in Figure 11.

5. Repeat Steps 2 through 4 to create another rule named **img_right_float** with a Float value of **right**.

6. Apply the img_right_float rule to the boardwalk image.

   TIP You can also right-click an image, point to CSS Styles, then click the rule you want to apply.

7. Save your work, then close Adobe Bridge.

You created two new CSS rules: one to use to align the image to the left with (text to the right of it) and one to use to align the image to the right with (text to the left of it).

DREAMWEAVER 4-11

LESSON 2

Enhance an Image and
USE ALTERNATE TEXT

What You'll Do

In this lesson, you will add borders to images, add horizontal and vertical space to set them apart from the text, and then add or edit alternate text to each image on the page.

Enhancing an Image

After you place an image on a web page, you have several options for enhancing it, or improving its appearance. To make changes to the image itself, such as removing scratches from it, or erasing parts of it, you need to use an image editor such as Adobe Fireworks or Adobe Photoshop.

> **QUICK TIP**
> You can copy a Photoshop PSD file and paste it directly into Dreamweaver. After inserting the image, Dreamweaver will prompt you to optimize the image for the web.

You can use Dreamweaver to enhance how images appear on a page. For example, you can modify the brightness and contrast, add borders around an image or add horizontal and vertical space. **Borders** are frames that surround an image. Horizontal and vertical space is blank space above, below, and on the sides of an image that separates the image from text or other elements on the page. Adding horizontal or vertical space is the same as adding white space, and helps images stand out on a page. In the web page from the First Federal Bank website shown in Figure 12,

> **DESIGN TIP**
>
> **Resizing Graphics Using an External Editor**
>
> Each image on a web page takes a specific number of seconds to download, depending on the size of the file. Larger files (in kilobytes, not width and height) take longer to download than smaller files. It's important to determine the smallest acceptable size for an image on a page. Then, if you need to resize an image to reduce the file size, use an external image editor to do so, instead of resizing it in Dreamweaver. Decreasing the size of an image using the H (height) and W (width) settings in the Property inspector does not reduce the file size or the time it will take the file to download. Ideally you should use images that have the smallest file size and the highest quality possible, so that each page downloads as quickly as possible.

DREAMWEAVER 4-12

Adding Images

the horizontal and vertical space around the images helps make these images more prominent. Adding horizontal or vertical space does not affect the width or height of the image. The best way to add horizontal and vertical space is with CSS. Spacing around web page objects can also be created by using "spacer" images, or transparent images that act as placeholders. In the First Federal site, spacer images were used to provide space between several of the page elements.

Using Alternate Text

One of the easiest ways to make your web page viewer-friendly and accessible to people of all abilities is to use alternate text. Alternate text is descriptive text that appears in place of an image while the image is downloading or not displayed. Screen readers, devices used by persons with visual impairments to convert written text on a computer monitor to spoken words, can "read" alternate text and make it possible for viewers to have an image described to them in detail. You should also use alternate text when inserting form objects, text displayed as graphics, buttons, frames, and media files. Without alternate text assigned to these objects, screen readers will not be able to read them.

One of the default preferences in Dreamweaver is to prompt you to enter alternate text whenever you insert an image on a page. You can set alternate text options in the Accessibility category of the Preferences dialog box. You can program some browsers to display only alternate text and to download images manually. Earlier versions of some browsers used to show alternate text when the mouse was placed over an image, such as Internet Explorer versions before version 8.0.

The use of alternate text is the first checkpoint listed in the Web Content Accessibility Guidelines (WCAG), Version 2.0, from the World Wide Web Consortium (W3C). The 12 WCAG guidelines are grouped together under four principles: perceivable, operable, understandable, and robust. The first guideline under perceivable states that a website should "Provide text alternatives for any non-text content so that it can be changed into other forms people need, such as large print, Braille, speech, symbols, or simpler language." To view the complete set of accessibility guidelines, go to the Web Accessibility Initiative page at w3.org/WAI/. You should always strive to meet these criteria for all web pages.

Figure 12 *First Federal Bank website*
First Federal Bank website used with permission from First Federal Bank – www.ffbh.com

Add a border

1. Click the **img_left_float** rule in the CSS Syles panel, click the **Edit Rule button**, click the **Border Category**, enter the rule properties shown in Figure 13, then click **OK**.

   You will not see the border displayed properly until you preview the page in a browser.

2. Repeat Step 1 to add a border to the img_right_float rule.

You edited two rules to add a border around the two images on the about_us page.

Add horizontal and vertical space

1. Edit the img_left_float rule again to add vertical and horizontal space by unchecking the "Same for all" check box under Margin in the Box category, then setting the Box Right Margin to **10 px** as shown in Figure 14.

   The text is more evenly wrapped around the image and is easier to read, because it is not so close to the edge of the image.

2. Repeat Step 1 to add a 10 px left margin to the img_right_float rule.

3. Save your work, click the **Switch Design View to Live view button**, then compare your screen to Figure 15.

4. Return to Design view, then open the spa page.

5. Click the **sea_spa_logo image**, then apply the img_left_float rule to it.

(continued)

Figure 13 CSS Rule Definition for img_left_float dialog box

Same for all check boxes are checked

Border Category

Top = solid

Color = #666

Width = thin

Figure 14 CSS Rule Definition for img_left_float dialog box

Click to uncheck

Right Margin = 10px

Figure 15 Viewing the images with borders and margins

Both images have borders and horizontal space separating them from the text

DREAMWEAVER 4-14

Adding Images

Figure 16 *Viewing the Image Optimization dialog box*

Format options — [Image Optimization dialog box showing Format dropdown with options: PNG 32, PNG 24, PNG 8, JPEG, GIF. File size: 92 K]

Format list arrow

Original file size

Integrating Photoshop CS6 with Dreamweaver

Dreamweaver has many functions integrated with Photoshop CS6. For example, you can copy and paste a Photoshop PSD file directly from Photoshop into Dreamweaver. Dreamweaver will prompt you to optimize the image by choosing a file format and settings for the web. Then it will paste the image on the page. If you want to edit the image later, select the image, then click the Edit button in the Property inspector to open the image in Photoshop. (The appearance of the Edit button will change according to the default image editor you have specified.) Photoshop users can set Photoshop as the default image editor in Dreamweaver for specific image file formats. Click Edit on the Menu bar, click Preferences (Win), or click Dreamweaver, click Preferences (Mac), click File Types/Editors, click the Extensions plus sign button, select a file format from the list, click the Editors plus sign button, then use the Select External Editor dialog box to browse to Photoshop (if you don't see it listed already), and then click Make Primary. You can also edit an image in Photoshop and export an updated Smart Object instantly in Dreamweaver. A **Smart Object** is an image layer that stores image data from raster or vector images. Search the Adobe website for a tutorial on Photoshop and Dreamweaver integration. Fireworks is another commonly used default image editor. Use the same steps to select it rather than Photoshop.

6. Save and close the spa page.

   The spacing under each picture differs because of the difference in the lengths of the paragraphs.

You added horizontal spacing and vertical spacing around three images on the about_us page and spa page by adding margin values to the img_left_float rule and the img_right_float rule.

Edit image settings

1. Select the **boardwalk image** on the about_us page.
2. Click the **Edit Image Settings button** in the Property inspector, then click the **Format list arrow**, as shown in Figure 16.

   You can use the Image Optimization dialog box to save a copy of the image in a different file format. File property options vary depending on which graphics format you choose. When you choose a different file format, then edit and save it, the program creates a copy and does not alter the original file.

3. Choose the JPEG format, then notice that the file size that appears at the bottom of the dialog box is much smaller than the PNG image.
4. Click **OK** to save the changes and close the Image Optimization dialog box.

   The Save Web Image dialog box opens. Here you choose the location where you want to save the image with the new file format.

5. Navigate to the website assets folder in the Save Web Image dialog box, then click **Save** to save the boardwalk.jpg image.

   There are now two copies of this image in the assets folder. One is a PNG and one is a JPG. If you don't see the new image, refresh the Assets panel.

You experimented with file format settings in the Image Optimization dialog box, then saved the image as a JPG file.

Lesson 2 Enhance an Image and Use Alternate Text

Edit alternate text

1. Select the club house image, select **Club House** in the Alt text box in the Property inspector (if necessary), type **The Striped Umbrella Club House** as shown in Figure 17, then press **[Enter]** (Win) or **[return]** (Mac).

   TIP You can tell when an image is selected when you see selection handles on its edges.

2. Select the boardwalk image, replace the alternate text with **The boardwalk to the beach** in the Alt text box, then press **[Enter]** (Win) or **[return]** (Mac).

   You added "The" to the beginning of the existing alternate text.

3. Save your work.

4. Preview the page in your browser, compare your screen to Figure 18, then close your browser.

You edited the alternate text for two images on the page.

Figure 17 *Alternate text setting in the Property inspector*

Alt text box

Figure 18 *about_us page viewed in browser*

DREAMWEAVER 4-16

Adding Images

Figure 19 *Preferences dialog box with Accessibility category selected*

Accessibility category

Check boxes for Form objects, Frames, Media, and Images

These options are not available in Mac OS X

POWER USER SHORTCUTS	
To do this:	**Use this shortcut:**
Switch views	[Ctrl][`] (Win) or ⌘ [`] (Mac)
Insert image	[Ctrl][Alt][I] (Win) or ⌘ [option][I] (Mac)
Refresh	[F5]
Browse in Bridge	[Ctrl][Alt][O] (Win) or ⌘ [option][O] (Mac)

© Cengage Learning 2013

Displaying Alternate Text in a Browser

There is a simple method you can use to force alternate text to appear in a browser when a mouse is held over an image. To do this, add a title tag to the image properties using the same text as the alt tag. Example: <img src="assets/club_house.jpg" alt="The Striped Umbrella Club House" title="The Striped Umbrella Club House" width="350" height="246" hspace="10" vspace="10" border="1" align="left" /> This method will work in Internet Explorer 8 and later versions and Mozilla Firefox.

Set the alternate text accessibility option

1. Click **Edit** on the Menu bar (Win) or **Dreamweaver** on the Menu bar (Mac), click **Preferences** to open the Preferences dialog box, then click the **Accessibility category**.

2. Verify that the four attributes check boxes are checked, as shown in Figure 19, check them if they are not checked, then click **OK**.

TIP Once you set the Accessibility preferences, they will be in effect for all websites that you develop, not just the one that's open when you set them.

You set the Accessibility preferences to prompt you to enter alternate text each time you insert a form object, frame, media, or image on a web page.

Lesson 2 *Enhance an Image and Use Alternate Text*

LESSON 3

Insert a Background Image and
PERFORM SITE MAINTENANCE

What You'll Do

In this lesson, you will insert two types of background images. You will then use the Assets panel to delete them both from the website, along with the boardwalk.png file. You will also check for non-web-safe colors in the Assets panel.

Inserting a Background Image

You can insert a background image on a web page to provide depth and visual interest to the page, or to communicate a message or mood. **Background images** are image files used in place of background colors. Although you can use background images to create a dramatic effect, you should avoid inserting them on web pages where they would not provide the contrast necessary for reading page text. Even though they might seem too plain, standard white backgrounds are usually the best choice for web pages. If you choose to use a background image on a web page, it should be small in file size. You can choose a single image that fills the page background, or you can choose a tiled image. A **tiled image** is a small image that repeats across and down a web page, appearing as individual squares or rectangles. A tiled image will download much faster than a large image.

When you create a web page, you can use either a background color or a background image, unless you want the background color to appear while the background image finishes downloading. You can also use background images for some sections of your page and solid color backgrounds for other sections.

The NASA home page shown in Figure 20 uses a night sky image for the page background, but individual sections have solid gray or black backgrounds. Since the solid backgrounds are dark, NASA used white or light blue text to provide contrast. The stars in the background tie in well with the rest of the page design and help to set a dramatic mood.

Background images or background colors are inserted using CSS. To add them to a single page, use the Modify > Page Properties dialog box, which adds an internal rule to modify the body tag. To use them as a global setting for the entire site, create an external rule to modify the <body> tag.

Managing Images

As you work on a website, you might find that you have files in your assets folder that you don't use in the website. To avoid accumulating unnecessary files, it's a good idea to look at an image first, before you place it on the page, and copy it to the assets folder. If you inadvertently copy an unwanted file to the assets folder, you should delete it or move it to another location. This is a good website management practice that will prevent the assets folder from filling up with unwanted image files.

> **QUICK TIP**
>
> Remember that Adobe Bridge is an excellent tool for organizing and managing your images.

Removing an image from a web page does not remove it from the assets folder in the local site folder of the website. To remove an asset from a website, if you have a lot of files, it is faster to locate the file you want to remove in the Assets panel. You then use the Locate in Site command to open the Files panel with the unwanted file selected. If you don't have many images in your site, it is faster to locate them in the Files panel. You can then use the Delete command to remove the file from the site. If you designate frequently used image files as favorites, you can locate them quickly in the Assets panel by selecting the Favorites option.

It is a good idea to store original unedited copies of your website image files in a separate folder, outside the assets folder of your website. If you edit the original files, resave them using different names. Doing this ensures that you will be able to find a file in its original, unaltered state. You may have files on your computer that you are currently not using at all; however, you may want to use them in the future. Storing currently unused files helps keep your assets folder free of clutter. Storing copies of original website image files in a separate location also ensures that you have back-up copies in the event that you accidentally delete a file from the website.

> **QUICK TIP**
>
> You cannot use the Assets panel to delete a file. You must use the Files panel to delete files and perform all file management tasks.

Creating a Website Color Palette

With monitors today that display millions of colors, you are not as limited with the number of colors you can use, and you may choose to select colors outside of the web-safe palette color space. You can experiment by choosing colors outside the default color palettes to create a color scheme that complements your website content. You can use the eyedropper tool to pick up a color from a page element, such as the background of an image. To do this, click a color box from an open dialog box, such as a CSS Rule Definition dialog box, then place the pointer over a color on the page. Click the color, and this color will then replace the previous color in the color box and apply it to the page element. If you are designing pages that will be displayed with a web device such as a PDA or mobile phone, be aware that many of these devices have more limited color displays and, in these cases, it might be wise to stick to web-safe colors instead.

> **QUICK TIP**
>
> To see the colors used in your site, click the Colors button on the Assets panel.

Figure 20 *NASA website*
NASA website – www.nasa.gov

Lesson 3 Insert a Background Image and Perform Site Maintenance

DREAMWEAVER 4-19

Insert a background image

1. Click **Modify** on the Menu bar, then click **Page Properties** to open the Page Properties dialog box.
2. Click the **Appearance (CSS) category**, if necessary.
3. Click **Browse** next to the Background image text box, navigate to the assets folder in the chapter_4 folder in the drive and folder where you store your Data Files, then double-click **water.jpg**.
4. Click **OK** to close the Page Properties dialog box, then click the **Refresh Site List button** to refresh the file list in the Assets panel. The water.jpg file is automatically copied to The Striped Umbrella assets folder.

   The white background is replaced with a muted image of water, as shown in Figure 21. The color of the water is close to the shades of blue in the website banner, so the image fits in well with the other page colors. However, since it flows directly behind the text, it does not provide the good contrast that the white background did.

5. Expand the CSS Styles panel if necessary, then compare your screen to Figure 22.

   Since you used the Modify > Page Properties command to set the image background, Dreamweaver created an internal <body> rule that tells the browser to use the water.jpg file as the page background. Your external style sheet

   (continued)

Figure 21 *The about_us page with a background image*

The water image flows behind the page content

Figure 22 *The CSS Styles panel with the new embedded body rule added*

Internal body style added to style sheet

DREAMWEAVER 4-20

Adding Images

Figure 23 *Removing a background image*

Selected filename

Figure 24 *Deleting the embedded style sheet*

Selected embedded stylesheet

Understanding HTML Body Tags

When you set page preferences, it is helpful to understand the HTML tags that are being generated. Sometimes it's easier to make changes to the code, rather than use menus and dialog boxes. The code for the page background color is located in the head section. If you want to change the page properties, you add additional codes to the body tag. Adding a color to the background will add a style to the page; for example, "body { background-color: #000; }". If you insert an image for a background, the code will read "body { background-image: url assets/water.jpg); }".

also has a <body> rule that tells the browser to use the color white for the page background. The internal style takes precedence over the external style, so for this page only, the white background will be replaced with the water background.

You created an internal style to apply an image background to the about_us page. You then viewed the CSS Styles panel. It now includes both an external style sheet and an internal style sheet.

Remove a background image from a page

1. Click **Modify** on the Menu bar, click **Page Properties**, then click **Appearance (CSS)**.

   Notice that the Page Properties dialog box shows both the background color from the external style sheet and the background image from the embedded style sheet. Remember that an embedded rule overrides a conflicting external rule. If both settings were in an external style sheet, the Background image property would override the Background color property.

2. Select the text in the Background image text box, as shown in Figure 23, press **[Delete]**, then click **OK**.

   The background of the about_us page is white again. However, the background image file, water.jpg, was not deleted. It is still in the website assets folder.

3. Save your work.

4. Click **<style>** in the CSS Styles panel, as shown in Figure 24, then click the **Delete Embedded Stylesheet button**.

   The embedded style sheet is deleted, since you no longer need it.

You deleted the link to the background image file to change the about_us page background back to white. You then deleted the embedded style sheet.

Delete files from a website

1. Click the **Assets panel tab** if necessary, then click the **Images button** if necessary.
2. With the Site option selected, refresh the Assets panel, right-click (Win) or [control]-click (Mac) **boardwalk.png** in the Assets panel, click **Locate in Site** to open the Files panel, select **boardwalk.png** on the Files panel, if necessary, press **[Delete]**, then click **Yes** in the dialog box that appears.

   You deleted the boardwalk.png file, since you optimized it and are now using the optimized version, boardwalk.jpg. You no longer need the larger version of the file. However, the original photograph for this file should not be deleted, but stored in a separate folder in case you need it later.

3. Click the **Assets panel tab**, then refresh the Assets panel.

   TIP If you delete a file on the Files panel that has an active link to it, you will receive a warning message. If you rename a file on the Files panel that has a link to it, the Files panel will update the links to correctly link to the renamed file. To rename a file, right-click (Win) or [control]-click (Mac) the file you want to rename, point to Edit, click Rename, then type the new name.

   Your Assets panel should resemble Figure 25.

You removed an image file from The Striped Umbrella website, then refreshed the Assets panel.

Figure 25 *Images listed in Assets panel*

Images button

Images file list after removing boardwalk.png

Using Color in Compliance with Accessibility Guidelines

Web Content Accessibility Guidelines (WCAG), Version 2.0, from the World Wide Web Consortium (W3C), states that a website should not rely on the use of color alone. This means that if your website content depends on your viewer correctly seeing a color, then you are not providing for those people who cannot distinguish between certain colors or do not have monitors that display color. Be especially careful when choosing color used with text, so you provide a good contrast between the text and the background.

If you are typing in the code or in a text box, it is better to reference colors as numbers, rather than names. For example, use "#FFF" instead of "white." Using style sheets for specifying color formats is the preferred method for coding. For more information, see the complete list of accessibility guidelines listed on the W3C website, www.w3.org.

Figure 26 *New color selected with the Eyedropper*

Preview of the color that will be used if you click here with the Eyedropper

Color code changes as you move the Eyedropper over the image

Apply button applies the color without closing the dialog box

Figure 27 *Colors listed in the Assets panel*

Colors button

Drag the border to the left to expand panel width

Web-safe colors

Non-web-safe background color — your color may differ

Lesson 3 Insert a Background Image and Perform Site Maintenance

Add a color to your design palette

1. Click the **body rule** in the CSS Styles panel, click the **Edit Rule button**, then click the **Background-color box**.

    The Color Picker opens.

2. Scroll to find the club house image on the page, move the pointer over it, click to select one of the lightest sections of the cupola, as shown in Figure 26, then click **Apply**.

    The color you sampled appears in the Background-color text box in the CSS Rule Definition for body in su_styles.css dialog box. It will be difficult to exactly match the color in Figure 26 unless you type it in the Background-color text box. Just experiment and choose a light color that provides good contrast with the text.

3. Click **OK** to close the CSS Rule Definition dialog box, then save your work.

    Because you set the background color with the body rule in the external style sheet, every page will now use this color for the background.

4. Click the **Colors button** in the Assets panel to display the colors used in the website, refresh the Assets panel, then drag the left border of the Assets panel to display the second column, if necessary, as shown in Figure 27.

    All of the colors are web-safe except the page background color.

5. Preview the page in your browser, then close your browser.

You edited the body rule in the su_styles.css file to change the body background color to a light cream color. You then viewed the colors listed in the Assets panel, and previewed the new page background color in the browser.

DREAMWEAVER 4-23

LESSON 4

Add Graphic
ENHANCEMENTS

What You'll Do

In this lesson, you will use a small image to link to a larger image and add a favicon to a page.

Adding a Link to a Larger Image

Sometimes designers want to display a small image on a page with an option for the user to click on the image to display a larger image. You frequently see this practice on retail sites with multiple items for sale. It is done both to conserve space and to keep the page size as small as possible. These sites will display a **thumbnail image**, or small version of a larger image, so that more images will fit on the page. Another technique is to link from one image to a second image that incorporates the first image. For example, a furniture site may create a link from an image of a chair to an image of the chair in a furnished room. An additional enhancement is often added to allow users to click on the larger image to magnify it even more

To accomplish this, you need two versions of the same image using an image editor such as Photoshop: one that is small (in dimensions and in file size) and one that is large (in dimensions and in file size.) After you have both images ready, place the small image on your page, select it, then link it to the large image. When a user clicks the small image in a browser, the large image opens. Another option is to place the large image on a new web page so you can also include additional descriptive text about the image or a link back to the previous page.

Adding Favicons

In most browsers today, when you add a web page to your favorites list or bookmarks, the page title will appear with a small icon that represents your site, similar to a logo, called a **favicon** (short for favorites icon). This feature was introduced in Microsoft Internet Explorer 5. Most browsers now also display favicons in the browser address bar. Favicons are a nice way to add branding, or recognition, for your site. To create a favicon, first create an icon that is 16 pixels by 16 pixels. Second, save the file as an icon file with the .ico file extension in your site root folder. Do not save it in a subfolder such as an assets or images folder.

> **QUICK TIP**
> There are plug-ins available for Photoshop that will save files with an icon file format, or you can search the Internet for programs that will generate icons.

Third, add HTML code to the head section of your page to link the icon file. The browser will then find the icon and load it in the address bar when the page loads.

QUICK TIP

The Firefox and Opera browsers can read a .jpg or a .png file, in addition to an .ico file.

Figure 28 shows a favicon in the Snapfish by HP website. Notice that the favicon is displayed both on the address bar and on the page tab. The design of the favicon ties in with the name of the company and other images of fish that are used in the page content. This is a nice touch to complete a well-designed site.

Adding a No Right-Click Script

On most websites, users are able to save an image on a page by right-clicking an image, then clicking Save on the shortcut menu. If you would like to prevent viewers from having this option, you can add a **no right-click script**, or JavaScript code that will not allow users to display the shortcut menu by right-clicking an image. To do this, locate JavaScript code that will add this option and copy and paste it into the head content of your page. To locate JavaScript code, use a search engine to search the Internet with a term such as "no right-click script." You will find scripts that prevent users from saving any image on the page, or all content of any kind on the page. Some scripts return a message in the browser such as "This function is disabled," and some do not return a message at all. These scripts will keep many users from saving your images, but they will not stop the most serious and knowledgeable perpetrators.

You can also protect website images by inserting the image as a table, cell, or CSS block background and then placing a transparent image on top of it. When a user attempts to save it with the shortcut menu, they will only save the transparent image.

Figure 28 *Snapfish website*
© 2009 The Snapfish by HP website used with permission from Snapfish by HP—www.snapfish.com

Favicon displayed in the address bar and on the page tab

Favicon is a smaller version of the logo used on the page

Use an image to link to another image

1. Click to place the insertion point to the right of the su_logo image, insert the image **map_small.jpg** from the assets folder where you store your Data Files, type **Map to The Striped Umbrella** in the Image Tag Accessibility Attributes dialog box, then click **OK**.

2. Select the **map_small image**, press the **left arrow key** ←, insert **spacer_30px.gif** from the assets folder where you store your data files, type **spacer image** in the Image Tag Accessibility Attributes dialog box, then click **OK**.

   The spacer image is a 30-pixel transparent square. It is used to insert 30 pixels of horizontal space between the two images.

3. Select the map_small image, click the **Browse for File button** next to the Link text box, navigate to the assets folder in the drive and folder where you store your Data Files, click **map_large.jpg**, then click **OK**.

   The small map image now links to the large map image, so viewers can click the small version to view the large version.

4. Click to place the insertion point after the last paragraph, insert a paragraph break, type **Click the map below to view a larger image.**, then compare your screen to Figure 29.

5. Save your work, then preview the page in your browser.

6. Click the **small map image** to view the large map image in a separate window, use the Back button to return to the about_us page, then close the browser.

You inserted a small image on the page and linked it to a larger image. You also used a spacer image to insert some horizontal space between the two images.

Figure 29 *The about_us page with an image linking to a larger image*

Link text box

Small map image links to large map image

Both map images are copied to the assets folder

DREAMWEAVER 4-26

Adding Images

Figure 30 *Copying the favicon.ico file in the data files folder*

Paste the starfish.ico file in the striped_umbrella site root folder

Figure 31 *Adding code to link the favicon*

Type this code above the <title> tag

Figure 32 *Viewing a favicon in the Firefox browser*

Starfish favicon

Insert a favicon on a page

1. Open Windows Explorer (Win) or Finder (Mac), then browse to the chapter_4 folder in the drive and folder where your Data Files are stored.

2. Right-click the file **starfish.ico**, copy it, browse to your site root folder, then paste the **starfish.ico** file into the site root folder, as shown in Figure 30, then close Windows Explorer (Win) or Finder (Mac).

3. Switch to Code view in Dreamweaver, insert a blank line above the line of code for the page title, then insert this code directly above the <title> tag: `<link rel="shortcut icon" href="starfish.ico" type="image/x-icon" />` as shown in Figure 31.

4. Save your work, then preview the about_us page in the browser.

   The favicon will appear in the address bar right before the page title and on the page tab in browsers that use tabbed pages, as shown in Figure 32.

   TIP Internet Explorer may not display the favicon until the website is published to a server.

5. Copy the code for the favicon link, then paste it into the code for the index and spa pages.

6. Save your work, close all open pages, then exit Dreamweaver.

You copied a favicon to the site root folder, then added code to the About Us page to direct browsers to display the favicon in the title bar when the page is viewed in a browser. Then you copied the code to link the favicon to the index and spa pages.

Lesson 4   Add Graphic Enhancements

DREAMWEAVER 4-27

SKILLS REVIEW

Insert and align images.

1. Open the Blooms & Bulbs website, open dw4_2.html from the drive and folder where you store your Data Files, then save it as **plants.html** in the Blooms & Bulbs website, overwriting the existing plants.html file. Do not update links.
2. Close dw4_2.html, then verify that the path of the Blooms & Bulbs banner on the plants page is set correctly to the assets folder in the blooms site root folder.
3. Verify that the Accessibility preferences will prompt you to add alternate text to images is set.
4. Insert an image placeholder to the left of the words "Who can resist" with the following settings: Name: **rose_bud**; Width: **300 pixels**; Height: **207 pixels**; Alternate text: **Rose bud on bird bath**.
5. Use the Browse for file button next to the Src text box on the Property inspector to replace the image placeholder with the rose_bud.jpg file from the assets folder in the drive and folder where you store your Data Files.
6. Use Bridge to insert the rose_bloom.jpg file, from the assets folder in the drive and folder where you store your Data Files, in front of the words "For ease of growing" and add **Rose bloom** as alternate text.
7. Insert the two_roses.jpg file from the assets folder in the drive and folder where you store your Data Files in front of the words "The Candy Cane" and add **Candy Cane Floribunda** as alternate text.
8. Refresh the Files panel to verify that all three images were copied to the assets folder.
9. Attach the blooms_styles.css file to the plants page, then add a new class rule named **img_left_float** that adds a left float property and value in the Box category.
10. Add another class rule named **img_right_float** that adds a right float property and value to the style sheet.
11. Apply the img_left_float rule to the rose_bud image.
12. Apply the img_right_float rule to the rose_bloom image.
13. Apply the img_left_float rule to the two_roses image.
14. Save your work, then open the tips page.
15. Click to select the butterfly image under the banner, then apply the img_float_left rule to it.

Enhance an image and use alternate text.

1. Use the HTML Property inspector to apply the Heading 1 format to the heading at the top of the plants page and the body_text rule to the rest of the text on the page. (*Hint*: Use the Class text box to select the body_text rule from the list.)
2. Edit the img_left_float rule to add a border to all sides of an image with the following settings: Top=solid; Width=thin; Color=#333.
3. Edit the Box Margin property to add a 10 px margin to the right side only, then save your changes.
4. Repeat Step 2 to add the same border to the img_right_float rule.
5. Edit the Box Margin property of the img_right_float rule to add a 10 px margin to the left side only.

Figure 33 *Completed Skills Review*

SKILLS REVIEW
(CONTINUED)

6. Save your work, preview it in the browser, then compare your screen to Figure 33.

Insert a background image and perform site maintenance.

1. Insert the lady_in_red.jpg file as a background image from the assets folder where you store your Data Files.
2. Save your work.
3. Preview the web page in your browser, then close your browser.
4. Remove the lady_in_red.jpg file from the background.
5. Open the Assets panel, view the images, then refresh the Files list.
6. Use the Files panel to delete the lady_in_red.jpg file from the list of images.
7. Refresh the Assets panel, then verify that the lady_in_red.jpg file has been removed from the website.
8. View the colors used in the site in the Assets panel.
9. Save your work.

Add graphic enhancements.

1. Select the two_roses image on the plants page.
2. Use the Link text box on the Property inspector to link the two_roses image to the two_roses_large.jpg file in the assets folder where you store your Data Files.
3. Add the sentences **You must see a close-up of these beauties! Click the image on the left to enlarge them**. at the end of the last paragraph.

TIP To make sure your insertion point is inside the body_text tag so the formatting will be applied, place the insertion point in front of the period at the end of the sentence in Design view, press the right arrow key to move the insertion point after the period, then add the new sentence. Another option is to place the insertion point right before the ending body_text tag in Code view, then switch to Design view to add the new sentence.

4. Save your work, preview the page in the browser, then click the two_roses image to view the larger version of the image.
5. Use the Back button to return to the plants page, then close the browser.
6. Open Windows Explorer (Win) or Finder (Mac), browse to the folder where you store your Data Files, then copy the file flower.ico.
7. Paste the file flower.ico in the blooms site root folder.
8. Close Windows Explorer (Win) or Finder (Mac), then switch to Code view for the plants page.
9. Insert a blank line above the title tag, then type this code directly above the <title> tag:
   ```
   <link rel="shortcut icon" href="flower.ico" type="image/x-icon" />
   ```
10. Verify that you entered the code correctly, copy the new line of code, then switch back to Design view.
11. Paste the same code you typed in step 9 to the index and tips pages, then save all files.
12. Preview the page in the browser, compare your screen to Figure 34, then close all open pages.

Figure 34 *Completed Skills Review*

PROJECT BUILDER 1

Use Figure 35 as a guide to continue your work on the TripSmart website that you began in Project Builder 1 in Chapter 1, and continued to work on in Chapters 2 and 3. You are now ready to begin work on the destinations page that showcases one of the featured tours to the Galápagos. You want to include some colorful pictures on the page.

1. Open the TripSmart website.
2. Open dw4_3.html from the drive and folder where you store your Data Files and save it in the tripsmart site root folder as **tours.html**, overwriting the existing tours.html file and not updating the links. Close the dw4_3.html file.
3. Verify that the path for the banner is correctly set to the assets folder of the TripSmart website.
4. Attach the tripsmart_styles.css file.
5. Apply the Heading 1 format to the "Destination: The Galápagos" heading.
6. Insert iguana_and_lizard from the assets folder in the drive and folder where you store your Data Files to the left of the sentence beginning "We have a really special", then add appropriate alternate text.
7. Insert blue_footed_booby.jpg from the assets folder in the drive and folder where you store your Data Files to the left of the sentence beginning "After arriving at Baltra's", then add appropriate alternate text.
8. Create one or more new rules in the tripsmart_styles.css file to add alignment, spacing, and borders of your choice.
9. If you would like, use the existing rules in the style sheet to add any additional formatting to the page to enhance the appearance.
10. View your colors in the Assets panel and see if your color choices work well together. If they don't, consider replacing them with different colors.
11. Copy the file airplane.ico from the folder where you store your data files to your site root folder.
12. Add appropriate code to the head content to link the favicon to the page, then copy the code to the index and newsletter pages.
13. Save your work, then preview the tours, index, and newsletter pages in your browser.
14. Close your browser, then close all open files.

Figure 35 *Sample Project Builder 1*

PROJECT BUILDER 2

In this exercise, you continue your work on the Carolyne's Creations website that you started in Project Builder 2 in Chapter 1, and continued to build in Chapters 2 and 3. You are now ready to add a new page to the website that will display featured items in the kitchen shop. Figure 36 shows a possible solution for this exercise. Your finished page will look different if you choose different formatting options.

1. Open the Carolyne's Creations website.
2. Open dw4_4.html from the drive and folder where you store your Data Files, save it to the site root folder as **shop.html**, overwriting the existing file and not updating the links.
3. Insert peruvian_glass.jpg from the assets folder in the drive and folder where you store your Data Files, in a location of your choice on the page, adding alternate text when prompted.
4. Attach the cc_styles.css file to the page, then add a rule to the style sheet that adds alignment and spacing to the Peruvian glass image.
5. Apply the nav_bar rule to the navigation links, the Heading 1 format to the page heading "June Special: Peruvian Glasses", and the body_text rule to the paragraphs of text if necessary.
6. Link the peruvian_glass image to the file brunch.jpg from the assets folder where you store your Data Files, then enter some descriptive text on the page to prompt viewers to click on the peruvian_glass image.
7. Save the shop page, then preview it in the browser.
8. Close your browser, then close all open pages.

Figure 36 *Sample Project Builder 2*

DESIGN PROJECT

Patsy Broers is working on a team project to design a website for her high school drama department. She has been assigned the task of gathering images to add interest and color.

1. Connect to the Internet, then navigate to the William J. Clinton Presidential Center website at www.clintonpresidentialcenter.org, shown in Figure 37.
2. Do you see a favicon used on the page?
3. Are any of the images on the page used as links to other images or pages?
4. Is a background image used for any of the page objects?
5. How do the images, horizontal and vertical spacing, color, and text work together to create an attractive and interesting experience for viewers?

Figure 37 *Design Project*
Courtesy of the William J. Clinton Presidential Center

PORTFOLIO PROJECT

In this assignment, you will continue to work on the website that you started in Chapter 1, and continued to build in Chapters 2 and 3. No Data Files are supplied. You are building this site from chapter to chapter, so you must do each Portfolio Project assignment in each chapter to complete your website.

You continue building your website by inserting appropriate images on a page and enhancing them for maximum effect.

1. Consult your wireframe and decide which page to create and develop for this chapter.
2. Plan the page content and make a sketch of the layout. Your sketch should include several images and a background color or image.
3. Create the page using your sketch for guidance.
4. Access the images you gathered, and place them on the page so that the page matches the sketch you created in Step 2. Add a background image if you want, and appropriate alternate text for each image.
5. Create rules in your style sheet to position and format your images.
6. Identify any files in the Assets panel that are currently not used in the site. Decide which of these assets should be removed, then delete these files.
7. Preview the new page in a browser, then check for page layout problems and broken links. Make any necessary corrections in Dreamweaver, then preview the page again in the browser. Repeat this process until you are satisfied with the way the page looks in the browser.
8. Use the checklist in Figure 38 to check all the pages in your site.
9. Close the browser, then close the open pages.

Figure 38 *Portfolio Project checklist*

Website Checklist
1. Does each page have a page title?
2. Does the home page have a description and keywords?
3. Does the home page contain contact information?
4. Does the home page have a last updated statement that will automatically update when the page is saved?
5. Do all paths for links and images work correctly?
6. Do all images have alternate text?
7. Are there any unnecessary files you can delete from the assets folder?
8. Is there a style sheet with at least two rules?
9. Did you apply the rules to all text?
10. Did you use rules to position and format images?
11. Do all pages look good using at least two different browsers?

ADOBE DREAMWEAVER CS6

CHAPTER 5

WORKING WITH LINKS AND NAVIGATION

1. Create external and internal links
2. Create internal links to named anchors
3. Create, modify, and copy a Spry menu bar
4. Create an image map
5. Manage website links
6. Incorporate Web 2.0 technology

CHAPTER 5
WORKING WITH LINKS AND NAVIGATION

Introduction

What makes websites so powerful are the links, or hyperlinks, that connect one page to another within a website or to any page on the Web. Although you can enhance a website with graphics, animations, movies, and other features to make it visually attractive, the links you include are a site's most essential components. Links that connect the pages within a site are important because they help users navigate between the pages of the site. If it's important to keep users within your site, link only to pages within your website and avoid including links to external sites. For example, most e-commerce sites only link to other pages in their own site to discourage shoppers from leaving.

In this chapter, you will create links to other pages in The Striped Umbrella website and to other sites on the Web. You will insert a Spry menu bar, and check the site links to make sure they all work correctly. You will also learn about Web 2.0 and social networking, an area of the Internet that has exploded in recent years. **Social networking** refers to the grouping of individual web users who connect and interact with other users in online communities. **Online communities**, or virtual communities, are social websites you can join, such as Facebook and Twitter, where you can communicate with others by posting messages or media content such as images or videos. You will learn about how you can connect your website to these communities.

Understanding Internal and External Links

Web pages contain two types of links: internal links and external links. **Internal links** are links to web pages within the same website, and **external links** are links to web pages in other websites or to email addresses. Both internal and external links have two important parts that work together. The first part of a link is displayed on a web page, for example, text, an image, or a button that is used for a link. The second part of a link is the **path**, or the name and location of the web page or file that users click to open the target for the link. Setting and maintaining the correct paths for all of your links is essential to avoid having broken links in your site, which can cause a user to leave the site.

TOOLS YOU'LL USE

Named Anchor button

Anchor name

Spry Menu Bar button

DREAMWEAVER 5-3

LESSON 1

Create External and INTERNAL LINKS

What You'll Do

In this lesson, you will create external links on The Striped Umbrella activities page that link to websites related to area attractions. You will also create internal links to other pages within The Striped Umbrella website.

Creating External Links

If one of the objectives of a site is to provide users with additional research sources for information not provided within the site, external links are one way to meet that objective. To create an external link, first select the text or object that you want to serve as a link, then type the absolute path to the destination web page in the Link text box in the Property inspector. An **absolute path** is a path used for external links that includes the complete address for the destination page, including the protocol (such as http://) and the complete **URL** (Uniform Resource Locator), or address, of the destination page. When necessary, the web page filename and folder hierarchy are also part of an absolute path. Figure 1 shows an example of an absolute path showing the protocol, URL, and path, which in this case is a single folder name. Paths can contain several folder levels and a file name, depending on how the destination page is stored on the server. An example of the code for the external link to the United States Army website would be <a href="http://www.army.mil"> The United States Army website</a>.

Creating Internal Links

Each page in a website usually focuses on an individual information category or topic. You should make sure that the home page provides links to each major page in the site, and that all pages in the site contain numerous internal links so that users can move easily from page to page. To create an internal link, you first select the text element or image that you want to use to make a link, and then use the Browse

Figure 1 *An example of an absolute path*

Protocol | Website URL | Path (folder name)

http://www.army.mil/news/

for File button next to the Link text box in the HTML Property inspector to specify the relative path to the destination page. A **relative path** is a type of path that references web pages and media files within the same website. Relative paths include the filename and folder location of a file. An example for the code for a relative internal link would be <a href="news.html"> News</a>.

Figure 2 shows an example of a relative path. Table 1 describes absolute and relative paths. Relative paths can either be site-root relative or document-relative. The internal links that you will create in this lesson will be document-relative. You can also use the Point to File button in the HTML Property inspector to select the file you want to link to, or drag the file you want to use for the link from the Files panel into the Link text box in the Property inspector.

You should take great care in managing your internal links to make sure they work correctly and are timely and relevant to the page content. Design the navigation structure of your website so that users are never more than a few clicks away from the page they are seeking.

Figure 2 *An example of a relative path*

Folder name   Filename

src="images/parade.jpg"

TABLE 1: DESCRIPTION OF ABSOLUTE AND RELATIVE PATHS

Type of path	Description	Examples
Absolute path	Used for external links and specifies protocol, URL, and filename of the destination page	http://www.yahoo.com/recreation
Relative path	Used for internal links and specifies location of file relative to the current page	spa.html or assets/heron.gif
Root-relative path	Used for internal links when publishing to a server that contains many websites or where the website is so large it requires more than one server	/striped_umbrella/activities.html
Document-relative path	Used in most cases for internal links and specifies the location of a file relative to the current page	cafe.html or assets/heron.gif

© Cengage Learning 2013

Create an external link

1. Open The Striped Umbrella website, open dw5_1.html from the drive and folder where you store your Chapter 5 Data Files, then save it as **activities.html** in the striped_umbrella local site folder, overwriting the existing activities page, but not updating links.
2. Close the dw5_1.html page, attach the **su_styles.css** file, then apply the **body_text rule** to the paragraphs of text on the page (not to the menu bar).
3. Select the first broken image link, click the **Browse for File button** next to the Src text box, then select **family_sunset.jpg** in the Data Files assets folder to save the image in your assets folder.
4. Click the image, then use the Property inspector to apply the **img_left_float** rule, as shown in Figure 3.
5. Repeat Step 3 for the second broken image link, linking it to two_dolphins_small.jpg, apply the **img_right_float** rule then refresh the Files panel if necessary.

    The two new files are copied into the assets folder, as shown in Figure 4.
6. Scroll down, then select the text "Blue Angels" in the first line of the second to last paragraph.

(continued)

Figure 3 *Saving an image file in the assets folder*

Broken image is replaced when file is saved in the site assets folder

Image is saved in site assets folder

img_left_float rule applied

Figure 4 *Assets panel with two new images added*

Two images added to the website

DREAMWEAVER 5-6

Working with Links and Navigation

Figure 5 *Creating an external link to the Blue Angels website*

[Screenshot showing Dreamweaver interface with labels: HTML button, Text for link, URL for link]

7. Click the **HTML button** in the Property inspector to switch to the HTML Property inspector if necessary, click in the Link text box, type **http://www.blueangels.navy.mil**, press [**Enter**] (Win) or [**return**] (Mac), click on the page to deselect the link, then compare your screen to Figure 5.

8. Repeat Steps 6 and 7 to create a link for the USS Alabama site in the next paragraph: **http://www.ussalabama.com**.

9. Save your work, preview the page in your browser, test all the links to make sure they work, then close your browser.

TIP You must have an active Internet connection to test the external links. If clicking a link does not open a page, make sure you typed the URL correctly in the Link text box.

You opened The Striped Umbrella website, replaced the existing activities page, attached the su_styles.css file, applied the body_text rule to the text, then imported images into the site. You then applied a rule to each image to set the alignment and spacing. You added two external links to other sites, then tested each link in your browser.

Typing URLs

Typing URLs in the Link text box in the Property inspector can be tedious. When you need to type a long and complex URL, it is easy to make mistakes and create a broken link. You can avoid such mistakes by copying and pasting the URL from the Address text box (Internet Explorer) or Location bar (Mozilla Firefox) to the Link text box in the Property inspector. Copying and pasting a URL ensures that the URL is entered correctly.

Create an internal link

1. Select the text "fishing excursions" in the third paragraph.
2. Click the **Browse for File button** next to the Link text box in the HTML Property inspector, navigate to the site root folder, then double-click **fishing.html** in the Select File dialog box to set the relative path to the fishing page.

   The filename fishing.html appears in the Link text box in the Property inspector, as shown in Figure 6. (The link is deselected in the figure for readability.)

   TIP Pressing [F4] will hide or redisplay all panels, including the Property inspector and the panels on the right side of the screen.

3. Select the text "dolphin cruises" in the same sentence.
4. Click the **Browse for File button** next to the Link text box in the HTML Property inspector, then double-click **cruises.html** in the Select File dialog box to specify the relative path to the cruises page.

   The words "dolphin cruises" are now a link to the cruises page.

5. Save your work, preview the page in your browser, verify that the internal links work correctly, then close your browser.

   The fishing and cruises pages do not have page content yet, but serve as placeholders until they do.

You created two internal links on the activities page, then tested the links in your browser.

Figure 6 *Creating an internal link on the activities page*

Relative link to fishing.html *Text to be used for link* *Browse for File button*

Using Case-Sensitive Links

When you hear that text is "case sensitive," it means that the text will be treated differently when it is typed using uppercase letters rather than lowercase letters, or vice-versa. With some operating systems, such as Windows, it doesn't matter which case you use when you enter URLs. However, with other systems, such as UNIX, it does matter. To be sure that your links will work with all systems, use lowercase letters for all URLs. This is another good reason to select and copy a URL from the browser address bar, and then paste it in the Link text box or Dreamweaver code when creating an external link. You won't have to worry about missing a case change.

DREAMWEAVER 5-8   *Working with Links and Navigation*

Figure 7 *Assets panel with three external links*

Three external links, including the email link.

View links in the Assets panel

1. Click the Assets panel tab to view the Assets panel.
2. Click the **URLs button** in the Assets panel.
3. Click the **Refresh Site List button**.

   Three links appear in the Assets panel: one external link for the email link on the home page and two external links, to the Blue Angels and USS Alabama websites on the activities page, as shown in Figure 7. Notice that the internal links do not appear in the Assets panel. The Assets panel shows the links for the entire site, not just for the open page.
4. Click the **Files panel tab** to view the Files panel.
5. Close the activities page.

You viewed the external links on the activities page in the Assets panel.

LESSON 2

Create Internal Links
TO NAMED ANCHORS

What You'll Do

In this lesson, you will insert four named anchors on the spa page: one for the top of the page and three for each of the spa services lists. You will then create internal links to each named anchor.

Inserting Named Anchors

Some web pages have so much content that users must scroll repeatedly to get to the bottom of the page and then back up to the top of the page. To make it easier for users to navigate to specific areas of a page without scrolling, you can use a combination of internal links and named anchors. A **named anchor** is a specific location on a web page that has a descriptive name. Named anchors act as targets for internal links and make it easy for users to jump to a particular place on the same page quickly. A **target** is the location on a web page that a browser displays when users click an internal link. For example, you can insert a named anchor called "top" at the top of a web page, and then create a link to it from the bottom of the page.

You can also insert named anchors in strategic places on a web page, such as at the beginning of paragraph headings. The Neighbor's Mill website shown in Figure 8 uses a named anchor at the top of each page with a text link at the bottom of each page that links to it.

This gives users a way to quickly return to the top of a page after they have scrolled down through the page content.

You insert a named anchor using the Named Anchor button in the Common category on the Insert panel. You then enter the name of the anchor in the Named Anchor dialog box. You should choose short names that describe the named anchor location on the page. In Dreamweaver, named anchors appear on a web page as yellow anchor icons in Design view. Selected anchors appear as blue icons. You can show or hide named anchor icons by clicking View on the Menu bar, pointing to Visual Aids, and then clicking Invisible Elements.

Creating Internal Links to Named Anchors

Once you create a named anchor, you can create an internal link to it using one of two methods. You can select the text or image on the page that you want to use to make a link, and then drag the Point to File button from

DREAMWEAVER 5-10

Working with Links and Navigation

the Property inspector to the named anchor icon on the page. Or, you can select the text or image to which you want to use to make a link, then type # followed by the named anchor name (such as "#top") in the Link text box in the Property inspector.

QUICK TIP

To avoid possible errors, you should create a named anchor before you create a link to it.

Figure 8 *Neighbor's Mill website with named anchors*

Neighbor's Mill website used with permission from Mike and Karin Nabors – www.neighborsmill.com

Named anchor location

Text link to named anchor

Lesson 2   Create Internal Links to Named Anchors

DREAMWEAVER 5-11

Insert a named anchor

1. Open the spa page, click the **banner image** to select it, then press [←] to place the insertion point to the left of the banner.
2. Click **View** on the Menu bar, point to **Visual Aids,** then verify that Invisible Elements is checked.

   TIP If there is no check mark next to Invisible Elements, this feature is turned off. Click Invisible Elements to turn this feature on.

3. Select the Common category on the Insert panel if necessary.
4. Click **Named Anchor** on the Insert panel to open the Named Anchor dialog box, type **top** in the Anchor name text box, compare your screen with Figure 9, then click **OK**.

   An anchor icon now appears before The Striped Umbrella banner. Depending on your window size, the anchor icon might appear above the banner or to the left of the banner.

   TIP Use lowercase letters, no spaces, and no special characters in named anchor names. You should also avoid using a number as the first character in a named anchor name.

   (continued)

Figure 9 *Named Anchor dialog box*

Name of new named anchor

Using Visual Aids

The Visual Aids submenu on the View menu gives you several choices for displaying page elements in Design View, such as named anchor icons. Named anchor icons are considered invisible elements. When you check the Invisible Elements option, you will see the named anchor icons on the page. The icons do not appear when the page is viewed in a browser. Turning on visual aids makes it easier to edit the page. Other options in the Visual Aids menu are Fluid Grid Layout Guides, CSS Layout Backgrounds, CSS Layout Box Model, CSS Layout Outlines, AP Element Outlines, Table Widths, Table Borders, Frame Borders, and Image Maps. The Hide All option hides all of these page elements. In later chapters, as you work with each page object that these refer to, you will see the advantages of displaying them. The CSS options allow you to see the formatting properties for CSS layout blocks such as the outline, background color, and margins.

Figure 10 *Named anchors on the spa page*

Named anchor icons

Selected named anchor icon

Name of selected named anchor

5. Scroll down to the list of massages, click to the left of the Massages heading, then insert a named anchor named **massages**.
6. Insert named anchors to the left of the Facials and Body Treatments headings using the following names: **facials** and **body_treatments**.

   Your screen should resemble Figure 10.

You created four named anchors on the spa page, one at top of the page, and three that will help users quickly access the Spa Services headings on the page.

Lesson 2 Create Internal Links to Named Anchors

DREAMWEAVER 5-13

Create an internal link to a named anchor

1. Select the word "Massages" to the right of The Sea Spa logo, then drag the **Point to File button** from the Property inspector to the anchor next to the massages heading, as shown in Figure 11.

   The word "Massages" is now linked to the Massages named anchor. When users click the word "Massages" at the top of the page, the browser will display the Massages heading at the top of the browser window. The Link text box on the Property inspector now reads #massages.

   TIP The name of a named anchor is always preceded by a pound (#) sign in the Link text box in the Property inspector.

2. Create internal links for Facials and Body Treatments to the right of The Sea Spa logo by first selecting each of these words or phrases, then dragging the **Point to File button** to the appropriate named anchor icon.

   The words "Facials" and "Body Treatments" are now links that connect to the Facials and Body Treatments headings.

   TIP Once you select the text on the page you want to link, you might need to scroll down to view the named anchor on the screen. Once you see the named anchor on your screen, you can drag the Point to File button on top of it. You can also move the pointer to the edge of the page window (still in the cream area of the page) to scroll the page.

   (continued)

Figure 11 *Dragging the Point to File button to a named anchor*

Point to File icon dragged to named anchor

Text to link to named anchor

Named anchor name preceded by # sign

Point to File button

DREAMWEAVER 5-14

Working with Links and Navigation

Figure 12 *Spa page with internal links to named anchors*

Internal links to named anchors

3. Scroll down to the bottom of the page, then place the insertion point at the end of the last sentence on the page.
4. Press [**Enter**] (Win) or [**return**] (Mac) twice to insert two paragraph breaks, then type **Return to top of page**.
5. Place the insertion point to the left of the text "Return to top of page," then click the **Remove Blockquote button** to move the text to the left margin, if necessary.
6. Apply the body_text rule to "Return to top of page" if necessary.
7. Select the text "Return to top of page", scroll to the top of the page, then use the Point to File button on the HTML Property inspector to link the text to the anchor named top.
8. Save your work, preview the page in your browser, as shown in Figure 12, then test the links to each named anchor, using the Back button to return to the links.

   When you click the Body Treatments link in the browser, the associated named anchor may appear in the middle of the page instead of at the top. This happens because the spa page is not long enough to position this named anchor at the top of the page.
9. Close your browser.

You created internal links to the named anchors next to the Spa Services headings and to the top of the spa page. You then previewed the page in your browser and tested each link.

Lesson 2   Create Internal Links to Named Anchors

DREAMWEAVER 5-15

LESSON 3

Create, Modify, and
COPY A SPRY MENU BAR

What You'll Do

In this lesson, you will create a menu bar on the spa page that can be used to link to each main page in the website. The menu bar will have five elements: Home, About Us, Cafe, Spa, and Activities. You will also copy the new menu bar to other pages in the website. On each page you will modify the appropriate element state to reflect the current page.

Creating a Spry Menu Bar

To make your website more visually appealing, you can add special effects. For example, you can create a menu bar with rollover images rather than with plain text links. One way to do this is to insert a Spry menu bar. A **Spry menu bar** is one of the pre-set widgets available in Dreamweaver that creates a dynamic, user-friendly menu bar that is easy to insert and customize. A **widget** is a piece of code that allows a user to interact with a program, such as clicking a menu item to open a page. Other examples of widgets are interactive buttons, pop-up windows, and progress indicators. **Spry**, or **Spry framework**, is open source code developed by Adobe Systems to help designers quickly incorporate dynamic content on their web pages. To insert a Spry menu bar, click Insert on the Menu bar, point to Layout Objects, then click Spry Menu Bar. The Insert Spry Menu Bar dialog box appears. You use this dialog box to specify the appearance of the menu bar and each link, called an **item**. When you first insert a Spry menu bar, Dreamweaver automatically assigns it four menu items, some of which have submenu items. It you want your menu bar to display a different number of menu items and submenu items, you can add new ones and delete the ones you do not need.

You can add special effects for menu bar items by changing the characteristics for each item's state. A **state** is the condition of the item relative to the mouse pointer. You can create a rollover effect for each menu item by using different background and text colors for each state to represent how the menu item appears when the users move their mouse over it or away from it. You can also create special effects for web page links. The NOAA (National Oceanic and Atmospheric Administration) website shown in Figure 13 uses several different types of links: plain text links, links created as list items, and links created with images.

When you insert a menu bar on a web page using the Insert Spry Menu Bar command, Dreamweaver automatically adds JavaScript code and CSS styles to the page to make the interaction work with the menu bar items. Dreamweaver also creates a SpryAssets folder and adds it to the local site folder. The SpryAssets folder stores the newly created files that make the menu function correctly in the browser. When a user views a web page with one of these menu bars, the files that run the menu functions are stored on the user's, or client's, computer. One of the new HTML5 tags is the <nav> tag. The <nav> tag is used to designate a section of a page with navigation links. Although links do not have to be placed within <nav> tags, doing so will help provide accessibility. This is another example of content used by screen readers.

There are other methods that you can use to create a menu bar with images, such as an image map. You will learn about image maps in Lesson 4.

Copying and Modifying a Menu Bar

After you create a menu bar, you can save time by copying and pasting it to the other main pages in your site. Make sure you place the menu bar in the same position on each page. This practice ensures that the menu bar will look the same on each page, making it much easier for users to navigate to all the pages in your website. If you are even one line or one pixel off, the menu bar will appear to "jump" as it changes position from page to page. When you learn to use templates, you can create a main page template with a menu bar, then base the rest of your pages on the template. This makes it easy to provide continuity across the site and is easier to update when changes are needed.

Figure 13 *NOAA website*
NOAA website - www.noaa.gov

Plain text links

Links created as list items

Images used for links

Images used for links

Lesson 3   Create, Modify, and Copy a Spry Menu Bar

DREAMWEAVER 5-17

Create a Spry menu bar

1. Create a new Tag rule in the su_styles.css style sheet to modify the img tag with the following setting: in the Block Category, set the Vertical-align to **bottom**.

   This new rule will keep a vertical gap from appearing between the banner and our new menu bar.

2. Select the banner on the spa page, then press [→].

   The insertion point is now positioned between the banner and the spa logo.

3. Click the **Spry** category on the Insert panel, then click **Spry Menu Bar**.

   TIP The Spry Menu Bar button is also in the Layout category on the Insert panel.

4. Click to select the **Horizontal** layout in the Spry Menu Bar dialog box to specify that the menu bar be placed horizontally on the page, if necessary, as shown in Figure 14, then click **OK**.

   Your new menu bar containing four items appears under the banner. The menu bar is selected and the Property inspector shows its properties. Each button contains placeholder text, such as Item 1.

5. Type **Menu** in the Menu Bar text box, replacing the placeholder text, on the Property inspector, then notice that Item 1 is selected in the Item column (first column on the left) in the Property inspector.

   Now you are ready to rename the first item, delete its submenu items, and choose the file you want this item to link to.

6. Select Item 1 in the Text text box on the right side of the Property inspector, type **Home**, select Item 1.1 in the first submenu column (second column) in the Property inspector, as shown in Figure 15, then click the **Remove menu item**

   (continued)

Figure 14 *Spry Menu Bar dialog box*

Horizontal layout option

Figure 15 *Property inspector with Menu Bar properties*

Menu Bar text box — Home menu item — Item 1.1 — Click Remove menu Item button to delete submenu Item 1.1 — Text text box

Understanding the Web Accessibility Initiative - Accessible Rich Internet Applications Suite

The Web Accessibility Initiative Accessible Rich Internet Applications Suite (WAI-ARIA) is a resource for applying best practices when adding advanced user interface controls to a website. Functions such as drag-and-drop or browsing through a menu can be difficult for users who rely on assistive devices to navigate a site. WAI-ARIA, at w3.org/TR/wai-aria/, provides guidelines and techniques for planning and implementing accessible content. It also provides presentations, handouts, and tutorials for developers who are interested in learning how to provide content that all users can easily navigate, such as providing alternative keyboard navigation for web objects primarily designed to function using mouse clicks. The information offered through WAI-ARIA is developed by the Protocols and Formats Working Group (PFWG), a part of the World Wide Web Consortium (W3C).

Figure 16 *Home item on the Menu Bar*

Submenu items have been deleted

Click Browse for File button to select index.html

Figure 17 *The Spry Menu Bar on the spa page*

Spry Menu Bar label

Item 1 is renamed "Home"

button ![-] above the first submenu column to delete the submenu item 1.1.

7. Click the **Remove menu item button** ![-] two more times to delete the submenu Item 1.2 and Item 1.3.

   The three submenu items would have appeared as a drop-down menu under the Home menu, but the Home link does not require a submenu, so they can be deleted.

   TIP You can add submenu items by clicking the Add menu item button ![+].

8. Click the **Browse for File button** next to the Link text box on the Property inspector, then double-click the file **index.html**, as shown in Figure 16.

   The Home item is now linked to the index page.

9. Switch to Code view, click to place the insertion point after the ending </ul> tag, switch back to Design view, enter a paragraph break, enter a line break, compare your screen to Figure 17, save your file, then click **OK** to close the Copy Dependent Files dialog box.

   A SpryAssets folder and six files are copied to the site root folder. These are dependent files necessary for the SpryMenu bar. If you don't see them listed, refresh the Files panel.

   TIP If you see a space between the banner and the menu bar, go to Code view to look for <p> tags around the banner. If you see them, delete them.

You used the Insert Spry Menu Bar dialog box to create a menu bar for the spa page and renamed the first item "Home." You deleted the placeholder submenu items under the Home menu item.

Lesson 3 *Create, Modify, and Copy a Spry Menu Bar*

DREAMWEAVER 5-19

Add items to a menu bar

1. Click the Spry Menu Bar tab to select it, click **Item 2** in the first column under the Home item in the Property inspector, then replace the text "Item 2" in the Text text box with **About Us**.
2. Click the **Browse for File button** next to the Link text box, then double-click **about_us.html** in the local site folder to link the About Us menu item to the about_us page.
3. Repeat Steps 1 and 2 to rename Item 3 **Sand Crab Cafe** and link it to the cafe.html page.
4. Delete each submenu item under the Sand Crab Cafe item, clicking **OK** to close the warning box that asks if you want to also remove the submenus, or children menus, under the submenu item.
5. Repeat Steps 1 and 2 to rename Item 4 **The Sea Spa** and link it to the spa.html page.
6. With The Sea Spa menu item selected in the Property inspector, click the **Add menu item button** + above the first column to add an additional menu item, then name it **Activities** and link it to the activities.html page.
7. With the Activities menu item selected, click the **Add menu item button** + above the *second* column to add a submenu item named **Cruises** and link it to the cruises.html page.
8. Repeat Step 7 to add another submenu item named **Fishing** that is linked to the fishing.html page.
9. Save your work, click **OK**, then compare your screen to Figure 18.

TIP If you accidentally created menus, instead of submenus, for Cruises and Fishing, delete them and try again, selecting Activities and adding the items to the second column.

You completed The Striped Umbrella menu bar by adding four more elements to it, each of which contains links to four pages in the site. You then added two submenus under the Activities menu item.

DREAMWEAVER 5-20

Figure 18 *Menu bar with all menu and submenu items in place*

Menu item names   Submenu item names   Link to fishing page   Submenu items

Inserting a Fireworks Menu Bar

Another option for adding a menu bar to your page is to create a menu bar in Fireworks and import it onto an open page in Dreamweaver. To do this you first create a menu bar in Fireworks and export the file to a Dreamweaver local site folder. This file contains the HTML code that defines the menu bar properties. Next, open the page you want to insert it on in Dreamweaver, then use the Insert, Image objects, Fireworks HTML command to place the HTML code on the page. You can also use Dreamweaver to import rollover images and buttons created in Fireworks.

Working with Links and Navigation

Figure 19 *Settings for ul.MenuBarHorizontal rule*

Font-size = 14 px   Font-family = "Trebuchet MS", Arial, Helvetica, sans-serif   Select ul.MenuBarHorizontal rule

Use CSS to format a menu bar

1. Click the **All button** in the CSS Styles panel if necessary, click the **plus sign** next to SpryMenuBarHorizontal.css in the CSS Styles panel, select the rule ul.MenuBarHorizontal, then click the **Edit Rule button** to open the CSS Rule Definition for ul.MenuBarHorizontal in SpryMenuBarHorizontal.css dialog box.

   The SpryMenuBarHorizontal.css style sheet, which was automatically created when you inserted the Spry menu bar, contains properties for the way the menu items will appear in the browser. In that style sheet, the ul.MenuBarHorizontal rule determines the global settings, including the font family, font size, and font alignment, for all the menu and submenu items, regardless of whether the mouse is placed over them.

   TIP You can also use the Properties pane in the CSS Styles panel to modify style properties.

2. Click the **Type** category, click the **Font-family** list arrow, then click **Trebuchet MS, Arial, Helvetica, sans-serif.**

3. Click the **Font-size** list arrow, click **14**, click the **Font size unit of measure list arrow**, then click **px** as shown in Figure 19, then click **OK**.

   Next, you set the width and height for each menu item button by modifying the ul.MenuBarHorizontal li rule. Recall that the <li> tag is the HTML code for list item. The Spry menu bar is built using unordered list items for each menu item. This rule sets the properties that determine the appearance of the menu items.

   (continued)

Lesson 3   Create, Modify, and Copy a Spry Menu Bar

4. Select the rule **ul.MenuBarHorizontal li** in the CSS Styles panel, then click the **Edit Rule button** to open the CSS Rule Definition for ul.MenuBarHorizontal li in SpryMenuBarHorizontal.css dialog box.

5. Click the **Box** category, click the **Width** text box, replace the current value with **190**, click the **Width unit of measure list arrow,** then click **px**.

TIP To calculate the width for each menu item, divide the number of pixels of the banner width by the number of menu items.

6. Click the **Height text box**, type **25**, verify that px is the unit of measure, then compare your screen to Figure 20.

The menu bar items will be spread across the page to equal the width of the banner. Next, you'll edit the rule that defines the properties of each menu item button when the mouse is not positioned over them.

7. Click in the Block category, change the Text-align value to **center**, then click **OK**.

8. Click the **ul.MenuBarHorizontal a** rule in the CSS Styles panel, then click the **Edit Rule button** to open the CSS Rule Definition for ul.MenuBarHorizontal a in SpryMenuBarHorizontal.css dialog box .

See Table 3 for a summary of the rules applied to the the Spry menu bar.

TIP If you want to understand the function of each rule in the SpryMenuBarHorizontal.css style sheet, click the SpryMenuBarHorizontal.css button in the Related files toolbar and take a few minutes to read the comments for each rule. Click the Show Design View button to return to Design view.

(continued)

DREAMWEAVER 5-22

Figure 20 *Add properties to the ul.MenuBarHorizontal li rule*

Width = 190 px
Box Category
Height = 25 px

TABLE 3: SUMMARY OF EDITING STEPS FOR CSS MENU BAR RULES

CSS Rule	What We Did
ul.MenuBarHorizontal	We changed the Font-family and Font-size for the menu bar.
ul.MenuBarHorizontal li	We changed the Box Width, Box Height, and Text-align properties for each menu item.
ul.MenuBarHorizontal a	We changed the Type color and Background color for all menu items when the mouse is not positioned over them in the browser.
ul.MenuBarHorizontal a.MenuBarItemHover, ul.MenuBarHorizontal a.MenuBarItemSubmenuHover, ul.MenuBarHorizontal a.MenuBarSubmenuVisible	We changed the Type color and Background color for all menu items when the mouse is positioned over them in the browser.
ul.MenuBarHorizontal ul li	We changed the width and height of the submenu items to make them match the dimensions of the menu items.
ul.MenuBar Horizontal ul	We changed the Box width to prevent a space between the main menu item and the first submenu item.

© Cengage Learning 2013

Working with Links and Navigation

Figure 21 *Setting the menu item appearance when the mouse will not be over them*

Menu buttons will have a blue background with white text when the mouse is not positioned over them

Select a shade of blue from the banner

9. Click the **Type** category, type **#FFF** in the Color text box, click the **Background** category, click the **Background-color color picker**, use the eyedropper to select a blue shade from the banner, as shown in Figure 21, then click **OK**.

   The menu items will have a blue background with white text when the mouse is not positioned over them. Now you are ready to set the colors the menu bar items will be when users point to (hover their mouse over) a menu item that has submenus. This rule is the longest one in the style sheet, because it includes properties that determine the appearance of menu items with submenus, both when the mouse is hovering over them and when the mouse is not hovering over them.

10. Click the longest rule name, **ul.MenuBarHorizontal a.MenuBarItemHover, ul.MenuBarHorizontal a.MenuBarItemSubmenuHover, ul.MenuBarHorizontal a.MenuBarSubmenuVisible** in the CSS Styles panel, click the **Edit Rule button** to open the rule definition dialog box, click the **Type** category, type **#630** in the Color text box, click the **Background** category, use the eyedropper to select a shade of sand from the banner for the Background color, then click **OK**.

    The menu and submenu items will have a sand background with brown text when the mouse is positioned over them in the browser.

    (continued)

Lesson 3 Create, Modify, and Copy a Spry Menu Bar

DREAMWEAVER 5-23

TIP To locate the longest rule, place your mouse over each rule name to see the extended names. You will quickly spot the longest name! You can also widen the CSS Styles panel temporarily to see the entire names.

11. Select the rule **ul.MenuBarHorizontal ul li** in the CSS Styles panel, then click the **Edit Rule button** to open the CSS Rule Definition for ul.MenuBarHorizontal ul li in SpryMenuBarHorizontal.css dialog box.

    You will now edit the rule that determines the width and height of the submenu items to make them match the size of the menu items.

12. Click the **Box** category, delete the default Box Width, then click **OK**.

    By removing the default settings, the submenu items will be the same width as the main menu items.

13. Select the rule **ul.MenuBarHorizontal ul** in the CSS Styles panel, click the **Edit Rule button**, click the **Box** category, change the Box width to **190px**, then click **OK**.

    This setting will prevent a space between a main menu item and the first submenu item.

14. Save all files, preview your page in the browser, compare your screen to Figure 22, test each link to ensure that each works correctly, then close the browser.

    The cafe, cruises, and fishing pages are still blank. Use the Back button after you click these links to return to pages with content.

    As you roll the mouse over each menu and submenu item, the background and text colors change. Because the colors you used

    (continued)

Figure 22 *Spa page in the browser with the mouse over the Activities item*

Submenu items are the same size as the menu items now

Menu item appearance when the mouse is placed over it

DREAMWEAVER 5-24

Working with Links and Navigation

Figure 23 *Selecting the menu bar on the spa page*

Click tab to select the menu bar

Figure 24 *The activities page with the completed menu bar*

for the backgrounds are from the banner, the buttons complement the banner.

You edited the properties of five rules in the style sheet that set the appearance of the menu bar on the page.

Copy and paste a menu bar

1. Verify that Invisible Elements is turned on, then click the **Spry Menu Bar: Menu tab** above the top left corner of the menu bar, as shown in Figure 23.
2. Click **Edit** on the Menu bar, then click **Copy**.
3. Double-click **activities.html** on the Files panel to open the activities page.
4. Select the original menu bar on the page, click **Edit** on the Menu bar, click **Paste**, click to the right of the menu bar, enter a line break, delete the horizontal rule under the menu bar (you can click the far right side of it to select it) compare your screen to Figure 24, then save the page.
5. Open the index page, delete the existing menu bar, paste the new menu bar, add two line breaks between the menu bar and horizontal rule, delete the horizontal rule, then save and close the index page.
6. Open the about_us page, replace the existing menu bar with the new menu bar, add a line break between the menu bar and horizontal rule, delete the horizontal rule, then save your work.
7. Preview the about_us page in your browser, test the menu bar on the home, about_us, spa, and activities pages, then close your browser. Close all open pages except the activities page.

You copied the menu bar on the spa page to three additional pages in The Striped Umbrella website.

Lesson 3   Create, Modify, and Copy a Spry Menu Bar

DREAMWEAVER 5-25

LESSON 4

Create an
IMAGE MAP

What You'll Do

In this lesson, you will create an image map by placing a hotspot on The Striped Umbrella banner on the activities page that will link to the home page.

Understanding Image Maps

Another way to create links for web pages is to combine them with images by creating an image map. An **image map** is an image that has one or more hotspots placed on top of it. A **hotspot** is a clickable area on an image that, when the user clicks it, links to a different location on the page or to another web page. For example, see the National Park Service website shown in Figure 25. When you click a state, you link to information about national parks in that state.

You can create hotspots by first selecting the image on which you want to place a hotspot, and then using one of the hotspot tools in the Property inspector to define its shape.

There are several ways to create image maps to make them user-friendly and accessible. One way is to be sure to include alternate text for each hotspot. Another is to draw the hotspot boundaries a little larger than they need to be to cover the area you want to set as a link. This allows users a little leeway when they place their mouse over the hotspot by creating a larger target area for them. Always assign a unique name for each image map.

Dreamweaver hotspot tools make creating image maps a snap. In addition to the Rectangle Hotspot Tool, you can create any shape you need using the Circle Hotspot Tool and the Polygon Hotspot Tool. For instance, on a map of the United States, you can draw an outline around each state with the Polygon Hotspot Tool and then make each state "clickable." You can easily change and rearrange hotspots on the image. Use the Pointer Hotspot Tool to select the hotspot you would like to edit. You can drag one of the hotspot selector handles to change its size or shape. You can also move the hotspot by dragging it to a new position on the image. It is a good idea to limit the number of complex hotspots in an image because the code can become too lengthy for the page to download in a reasonable length of time.

Figure 25 *Viewing an image map on the National Park Service website*
National Park Service website – www.nps.gov

Clicking on an individual state links to information about parks in that state

To view the hotspot, move the pointer over a state. Then press and hold the mouse button

Lesson 4   Create an Image Map

DREAMWEAVER 5-27

Create an image map

1. Select the banner on the activities page, then click the **Rectangle Hotspot Tool** in the Property inspector.

2. Drag the **pointer** to create a rectangle over the text "The Striped Umbrella" in the banner, as shown in Figure 26, then click **OK** to close the dialog box that reminds you to supply alternate text for the hotspot.

   TIP To adjust the shape of a hotspot, click the Pointer Hotspot Tool in the Property inspector, then drag a sizing handle on the hotspot.

3. Drag the **Point to File button** next to the Link text box in the Property inspector to the index.html file on the Files panel to link the hotspot to the index page.

4. Replace the default text "Map" with **Home** in the Map text box in the Property inspector to give the image map a unique name.

5. Click the **Target list arrow** in the Property inspector, then click **_top**.

   When the hotspot is clicked, the _top option opens the home page in the same window. See Table 2 for an explanation of the four target options.

6. Type **Link to home page** in the Alt text box in the Property inspector, as shown in Figure 27, then press **[Enter]** (Win) or **[return]** (Mac).

7. Save your work, preview the page in your browser, then place the pointer over the image map.

   (continued)

Figure 26 *A hotspot drawn on the banner*

Hotspot

Rectangle Hotspot Tool

TABLE 2: OPTIONS IN THE TARGET LIST

Target	Result
_blank	Displays the destination page in a separate browser window
new	Displays the destination page in a new tab (CSS3)
_parent	Displays the destination page in the parent frameset (replaces the frameset)
_self	Displays the destination page in the same frame or window
_top	Displays the destination page in the whole browser window

© Cengage Learning 2013

DREAMWEAVER 5-28

Working with Links and Navigation

Figure 27 *Hotspot properties*

- Image map name
- Target for hotspot
- Link to index page
- Alternate text for the hotspot

Figure 28 *Preview of the image map on the activities page in the browser*

- Space has been added and needs to be removed
- When pointer is over the hotspot, the link appears in the bottom-left corner of the screen
- Pointing finger indicates pointer is over the link hotspot

As you place the pointer over the hotspot, the pointer turns to a pointing finger, indicating that it is a link, as shown in Figure 28. Notice that there is now a space between the banner and the menu bar. The code for the image map added a line break between the two, which caused the space to appear.

8. **Return to Dreamweaver, switch to Code view and locate the <br> code between the ending </map> tag and the code that begins the menu bar.**

9. **Delete the <br> code.**

   The space is removed. Refer to the What You'll Do figure at the beginning of this lesson to see the completed page with the space removed.

10. **While still in Code view, locate the code for the banner, then add this code inside the <img> tags: style="border:0".**

    For example: "<img style="border:0" src="assets/su_banner.gif"....../>. As long as you type it between the beginning and ending image tags, it will work correctly. This code will prevent a border from appearing around the banner in Internet Explorer.

11. **Return to Design view, save your file, then preview the page in the browser.**

12. **Click the link to test it, close the browser, then close all open pages.**

You created an image map on the banner of the activities page using the Rectangle Hotspot Tool. You then linked the hotspot to the home page and removed a line break that was added with the image map code.

Lesson 4   Create an Image Map

DREAMWEAVER 5-29

LESSON 5

Manage WEBSITE LINKS

What You'll Do

In this lesson, you will use some Dreamweaver reporting features to check The Striped Umbrella website for broken links and orphaned files.

Managing Website Links

Because the World Wide Web changes constantly, websites might be up one day and down the next. If a website changes server locations or goes down due to technical difficulties or a power failure, the links to it become broken. Broken links, like misspelled words on a web page, indicate that a website is not being maintained diligently.

Checking links to make sure they work is an ongoing and crucial task you need to perform on a regular basis. You must check external links manually by reviewing your website in a browser and clicking each link to make sure it works correctly. The Check Links Sitewide feature is a helpful tool for managing internal links. You can use it to check your entire website for the total number of links and the number of links that are broken, external, or orphaned, and then view the results in the Link Checker panel. **Orphaned files** are files that are not linked to any pages in the website.

> **DESIGNTIP**
>
> **Using Good Navigation Design**
>
> As you work on the navigation structure for a website, you should try to limit the number of links on each page to no more than is necessary. Too many links may confuse users of your website. You should also design links so that users can reach the information they want within a few clicks. If finding information takes more than three or four clicks, the user may become discouraged or "lost" in the site. It's a good idea to provide visual clues on each page to let users know where they are, much like a "You are here" marker on a store directory at the mall, or a breadcrumbs trail. A **breadcrumbs trail** is a list of links that provides a path from the initial page you opened in a website to the page that you are currently viewing. Many websites provide a list of all the site's pages, called a **site map**. A site map is similar to an index. It lets users see how the information is divided between the pages and helps them locate the information they need quickly.

Figure 29 *Link Checker panel displaying external links*

List of external links — Results list for all categories — Show list arrow

Figure 30 *Link Checker panel displaying one orphaned file*

One orphaned file listed — Show list arrow

Figure 31 *Assets panel displaying links*

URLs button

External links for The Striped Umbrella website

Manage website links

1. Click **Site** on the Menu bar, point to **Advanced**, then click **Recreate Site Cache**.

2. Click **Site** on the Menu bar, then click **Check Links Sitewide**.

    The Results tab group opens, with the Link Checker panel in front. By default, the Link Checker panel initially lists any broken internal links found in the website. The Striped Umbrella website has no broken links.

3. Click the **Show list arrow** in the Link Checker panel, click **External Links**, then compare your screen to Figure 29.

4. Click the **Show list arrow**, then click **Orphaned Files** to view the orphaned files in the Link Checker panel, as shown in Figure 30.

    The Striped Umbrella website has one orphaned file, water.jpg. You may use this file later, so you leave it in the assets folder.

5. Right-click (Win) or Control-click (Mac) in an empty area of the Results tab group title bar, then click **Close Tab Group**.

6. Display the Assets panel if necessary, then click the **URLs button** in the Assets panel if necessary to display the list of links in the website.

    The Assets panel displays the external links used in the website, as shown in Figure 31.

You used the Link Checker panel to check for broken links, external links, and orphaned files in The Striped Umbrella website. You also viewed the external links in the Assets panel.

Update a page

1. Open dw5_2.html from the drive and folder where you store your Data Files, then save it as **fishing.html** in the striped_umbrella local site root folder, overwriting the existing fishing page, but not updating the links.

2. Click the broken link image placeholder, click the **Browse for File button** next to the Src text box in the Property inspector, browse to the drive and folder where you store your Data Files, open the assets folder, then select the file **fisherman.jpg** to copy the file to the striped_umbrella assets folder.

3. Deselect the image placeholder and the image appears, as shown in Figure 32.

    The text is automatically updated with the body_text style. The code was already in place on the page linking su_styles.css to the file. The Spry menu bar was also updated using the link to the SpryMenuBarHorizontal.css file.

4. Save and close the fishing page, then close the dw5_2.html page.

5. Open dw5_3.html from the drive and folder where you store your Data Files, then save it as **cruises.html** in the striped_umbrella local site folder, overwriting the existing cruises page, but not updating the links.

(continued)

Figure 32 *Fishing page updated*

Testing Your Website Against the Wireframe

Another test you should run regularly is a comparison of how your developing website pages are meeting the specifications of your wireframe prototype. Compare each completed page against its corresponding wireframe to make sure that all page elements have been placed in their proper locations on the page. Verify that all specified links have been included and test them to make sure that they work correctly. You might also consider hiring site-usability testers to test your site navigation. A site usability test provides impartial feedback on how intuitive and user-friendly your site is to use.

Figure 33 *Cruises page updated*

6. Click the broken link image placeholder, click the **Browse for File button** next to the Src text box in the Property inspector, then browse to the drive and folder where you store your Data Files, open the assets folder, then select the file boats.jpg to copy the file to the striped_umbrella assets folder.

TIP If you have trouble selecting the placeholder, click the middle of the placeholder to select it.

7. Deselect the image placeholder and the image will appear as shown in Figure 33.

   The text is automatically updated with the body_text style. The code was already in place on the page linking su_styles.css to the file. The Spry menu bar was also updated as the SpryMenuBarHorizontal.css rules were applied.

8. Save your work if necessary.

9. Preview each page in the browser, close the browser, then close all open pages.

You added content to two previously blank pages in the website and previewed each page to check for consistent layout.

POWER USER SHORTCUTS

To do this:	Use this shortcut:
Close a file	[Ctrl][W] (Win) or ⌘[W] (Mac)
Close all files	[Ctrl][Shift][W] (Win) or ⌘[Shift][W] (Mac)
Print code	[Ctrl][P] (Win) or ⌘[P] (Mac)
Check page links	[Shift][F8] (Win) or [fn][shift][F8] (Mac)
Undo	[Ctrl][Z], [Alt][BkSp] (Win) or ⌘[Z], [option][delete] (Mac)
Redo	[Ctrl][Y], [Ctrl][Shift][Z] (Win) or ⌘[Y], ⌘[Shift][Z] (Mac)
Refresh Design view	[F5]
Hide all visual aids	[Ctrl][Shift][I] (Win) or ⌘[Shift][I] (Mac)
Insert a named anchor	[Ctrl][Alt][A] (Win) or ⌘[option][A] (Mac)
Make a link	[Ctrl][L] (Win) or ⌘[L] (Mac)
Remove a link	[Ctrl][Shift][L] (Win) or ⌘[Shift][L] (Mac)
Check links sitewide	[Ctrl][F8] (Win) or [fn]⌘[F8] (Mac)
Show Files tab group	[F8] (Win) or ⌘[Shift][F] (Mac)

© Cengage Learning 2013

Lesson 5 Manage Website Links

LESSON 6

Incorporate Web 2.0 TECHNOLOGY

What You'll Do

Peace Corps website – www.peacecorps.gov

In this lesson, you will explore some of the Web 2.0 applications that can be used to engage website users.

What Exactly Is Web 2.0?

The term **Web 2.0** describes the evolution of web applications that facilitate and promote information sharing among Internet users. These applications not only reside on computers, but on cell phones, in cars, on portable GPS devices, and in game devices. **GPS (Global Positioning System)** devices are used to track your position through a global satellite navigation system, and are popular to use for driving directions, hiking, and map making. Web 2.0 applications do not simply display information for users to read passively; they allow users to actively contribute to the content.

RSS feeds are another easy way to share information with users. **RSS** stands for **Really Simple Syndication**. Websites use **RSS feeds** to distribute news stories, information about upcoming events, and announcements. Web users can subscribe to RSS feeds to receive regular releases of information from a site. Users can download and play these digitally broadcasted files called **podcasts (Programming On Demand)** using devices such as computers or MP3 players. Many news organizations and educational institutions publish both audio and video podcasts. Video podcasts are referred to as **vodcasts** or **vidcasts**.

Web 2.0 also includes social networking. **Social networking** refers to any web-based service that facilitates social interaction among users. Examples of social networking sites include **Facebook**, **Pinterest**, and **Match.com**. These sites allow users to set up profile pages and post information on them for others to view. Facebook pages often contain lots of text, images, and videos. Pinterest is an online pinboard for sharing crafts, recipes, and other items of interest.

A wiki is another example of a Web 2.0 application. The term **wiki** (named for the Hawaiian word for "quick") refers to a site where a user can use simple editing tools to contribute and edit the page content in a site. A good example is **Wikipedia**, an online encyclopedia. Wikipedia allows users to post new information and edit existing information on any topic. Although people have different opinions about the academic integrity of the information on Wikipedia, Wikipedia is a rich source of information. Proponents argue that its many active and vigilant users maintain its information integrity.

Working with Links and Navigation

Blogs (web logs) are another example of a Web 2.0 application. **Blogs** are websites where the website owner regularly posts commentaries and opinions on various topics. Content can consist of text, video, or images. Users can respond to the postings and read postings by other users. **Twitter** is a website where users can post short messages, called **tweets**. Twitter is considered a blog or a micro blog, because you cannot enter more than 140 characters in each post. To use Twitter, you must first join by creating a free account. Then you can post messages about yourself, "follow" other people's tweets, and invite others to "follow" you. **Tumblr** is another popular blog where you can post and share text, photos, music, and videos.

There are many video sharing applications such as Skype, Google Video Chat, and YouTube. **Skype** and **Google Video Chat** are free applications that you use to communicate live with other people through video conferencing, using a high-speed Internet connection and a web camera, called a **web cam**. **YouTube** is a website where you can upload and share videos. To upload videos, you need to register with the site.

So how do these various Web 2.0 components relate to the process of creating websites? Most websites today engage their users in one or more of these applications. The Peace Corps website, shown in Figure 34, has links to Facebook, Twitter, YouTube, and RSS Feeds. When you are designing a site, one of the decisions you must make is not if, but how you will incorporate Web 2.0 technology to fully engage your users. To incorporate one of these applications into your website, first register to set up an account on the social networking site, then place a link on one of your site's web pages (usually the home page) that links to each social networking site and opens your page. For example, if your Twitter account is located at twitter.com/your_name, add this link to your home page using the Twitter logo as a graphic link. You can download social networking sites' logos from their websites. Some applications specify how you should refer to and link to their site.

Using the applications that are a part of Web 2.0 with your website can bring your site from simply presenting information on pages for users to read to facilitating a compelling dialog between the users and the site. They will no longer be just "users," but active participants.

Web 3.0 will be the next generation of the Web. With Web 3.0, browsers will be able to handle multiple searches simultaneously. For instance, you could search for a recent Oscar best picture nominee and sushi restaurant in the vicinity of the theater where it is playing. The new iPhones come with a personal assistant you can "talk" with, rather than typing in searches. Browsers may soon be able to do this, too. The more information that is stored from your past searches, the more they will get to "know" you and be able to give responses that fit your profile.

Figure 34 *Viewing social networking links on the Peace Corps website*
Peace Corps website – www.peacecorps.gov

Links to Facebook, Twitter, Flickr, YouTube, Tumblr, LinkedIn

SKILLS REVIEW

Create external and internal links.

1. Open the Blooms & Bulbs website.
2. Open dw5_4.html from the drive and folder where you store your Data Files, then save it as **newsletter.html** in the Blooms & Bulbs website, overwriting the existing file without updating the links. Close dw5_4.html.
3. Verify that the banner path is set correctly to the assets folder in the website and correct it, if it is not, then browse to the drive and folder where you store your Chapter 5 Data Files assets folder and copy the ruby_grass, trees, and plants broken images to the site assets folder.
4. Add a new tag selector rule to the blooms_styles.css file that modifies the <h2> tag as follows: Font-family: Arial, Helvetica, sans-serif; Font-size: 16px; Font-weight: Bold; Color: #030.
5. Modify the <h1> rule to change the Font-size to 18px, then add a new tag selector rule to the blooms_styles.css file that modifies the <h3> tag as follows: Font-family: Arial, Helvetica, sans-serif; Font-size: 16px; Color: #030.
6. Apply the img_left_float rule to the ruby_grass and plants images.
7. Apply the img_right_float rule to the trees image.
8. Scroll to the bottom of the page, then link the National Gardening Association text to http://www.garden.org.
9. Link the Organic Gardening text to http://www.organicgardening.com.
10. Link the Southern Living text to http://www.southernliving.com/southern.
11. Save all files, then preview the page in your browser, verifying that each link works correctly.
12. Close your browser, returning to the newsletter page in Dreamweaver.
13. Scroll to the paragraph about gardening issues, select the gardening tips text in the last sentence, then link the selected text to the tips.html file in the blooms site root folder.
14. Change the page title to read **Gardening Matters**, then save your work.
15. Open the plants page and add a new paragraph to the bottom of the page: **In addition to these marvelous roses, we have many annuals, perennials, and water plants that have just arrived**.
16. Apply the body_text rule to the new paragraph if necessary.
17. Link the "annuals" text to the annuals.html file, link the "perennials" text to the perennials.html file, and the "water plants" text to the water_plants.html file.
18. Save your work, test the links in your browser, then close your browser. (*Hint*: These pages do not have content yet, but are serving as placeholders.)

Create internal links to named anchors.

1. Show Invisible Elements, if necessary.
2. Click the Common category in the Insert panel.
3. Switch to the newsletter page, then insert a named anchor in front of the Grass heading named **grass**.
4. Insert a named anchor in front of the Trees heading named **trees**.
5. Insert a named anchor in front of the Plants heading named **plants**.
6. Use the Point to File button in the Property inspector to create a link from the word "grass" in the Gardening Issues paragraph to the anchor named "grass."
7. Create a link from the word "trees" in the Gardening Issues paragraph to the anchor named "trees."
8. Create a link from the word "plants" in the Gardening Issues paragraph to the anchor named "plants."
9. Save your work, view the page in your browser, test all the links to make sure they work, then close your browser.

Create, modify, and copy a Spry menu bar.

1. Delete the horizontal rule under the banner, select the banner, press the right arrow key, enter a line break, click the Spry category on the Insert panel, then click Spry Menu Bar to insert a horizontal Spry menu bar at the top of the newsletter page below the banner and above the Gardening Matters heading. Add two line breaks to separate the menu bar from the heading.
2. Select the Menu bar, select Item 1 in the Property inspector, remove the three submenu items under Item 1, type **Home** in the Text text box, then browse to link the Home menu item to the **index.html** file.
3. Select Item 2, then replace the text name with **Newsletter** and link it to the **newsletter.html** file.
4. Repeat Step 3 to rename Item 3 **Plants** and link it to the **plants.html** file.
5. Select the submenu Item 3.1, rename it **Annuals**, link it to the **annuals.html** file, then delete the submenu items under the Annuals submenu item.
6. Repeat Step 5 to rename Item 3.2 **Perennials**, then link it to the **perennials.html** file.
7. Repeat Step 5 to rename Item 3.3 **Water Plants**, then link it to the **water_plants.html** file.
8. Select the Item 4 menu item, rename it **Tips**, then link it to the **tips.html** file.

SKILLS REVIEW
(CONTINUED)

9. Add a new menu item named **Workshops**, then link it to the **workshops.html** file.
10. Edit the ul.MenuBarHorizontal rule to change the Font-family to **Verdana, Geneva, sans-serif**, and the Font-size to **14 px**.
11. Edit the ul.MenuBarHorizontal li to set the Text-align to **Center**, the Box width to **190 px** and the Box height to **25 px**.
12. Edit the ul.MenuBarHorizontal a rule to change the Type color to **#030** and the background color to **#99F**.
13. Edit the ul.MenuBarHorizontal a.MenuBarItemHover, ul.MenuBarHorizontal a.MenuBarItemSubmenuHover ul.MenuBarHorizontal a.MenuBarSubmenuVisible rule (the longest one) to change the Type color to **#FFC** and the background color to one of the light green colors in the banner.
14. Save all files, copying dependent files, test each link in the browser to make sure the links work correctly, then close the browser.
15. Add a new rule to the blooms_styles.css file to modify the <img> tag by setting the vertical alignment to bottom.
16. Select and copy the menu bar, then open the home page.
17. Delete the current menu bar and horizontal rule on the home page, and paste the new menu bar under the banner with a line break between them. Remove any space between the banner and menu bar if necessary. (*Hint*: If you see space between the banner and the menu bar, go to Code view and check to make sure that you used a <br> tag between the banner and the menu bar.)

Figure 35 *Completed Skills Review*

Working with Links and Navigation

DREAMWEAVER 5-37

SKILLS REVIEW
(CONTINUED)

18. Save and close the page, switch to the plants page, then paste the menu bar on the page in the same position under the banner.
19. Add a two line breaks between the menu bar and the first heading, then save and close the page.
20. Open the tips page and repeat Steps 18 and 19 to add the menu bar and any additional spacing to the page.
21. Save and close the tips page.
22. Save your work, preview all the pages in your browser, compare your newsletter page to Figure 35, test all the links, then close your browser.

Create an image map.
1. On the newsletter page, use the Rectangle Hotspot Tool to draw an image map across the name "Blooms & Bulbs", on the banner that will link to the home page.
2. Name the image map **home** and set the target to _top.
3. Add the alternate text **Link to home page**, save the page, then preview it in the browser to test the link.
4. Close the browser, then switch to Code view.
5. Add the following code to the <img> tag for the banner: **style="border:0"**, return to Design view, then save your work.
6. If you still see a space between the banner and the menu bar, go to Code view and remove the break tag after the code for the image map.

Manage website links.
1. Use the Link Checker panel to view and fix broken links and orphaned files in the Blooms & Bulbs website. (*Hint*: Remember to recreate your site cache if you see any. That usually fixes them.)
2. Open dw5_5.html from the drive and folder where you store your Data Files, then save it as **annuals.html**, replacing the original file. Do not update links, but save the file coleus.jpg from the Chapter 5 Data Files assets folder to the assets folder of the website. Close dw5_5.html.
3. Apply the img_left_float to the coleus image.
4. Repeat Steps 2 and 3 using dw5_6.html to replace perennials.html, saving the fiber_optic_grass.jpg file in the assets folder and using dw5_7.html to replace water_plants.html, saving the water_lily.jpg file in the assets folder.
5. Save your work, then close all open pages.

PROJECT BUILDER 1

Use Figure 36 as a guide to continue your work on the TripSmart website, which you began in Project Builder 1 in Chapter 1 and developed in the previous chapters. You have been asked to create a new page for the website that lists helpful links for customers. You will also add content to the destinations, peru, and galapagos pages.

1. Open the TripSmart website.
2. Open dw5_8.html from the drive and folder where you store your Data Files, then save it as **services.html** in the TripSmart website root folder, replacing the existing file and not updating links. Close dw5_8.html.
3. Verify that the TripSmart banner is in the assets folder of the local site folder.
4. Apply the paragraph_text rule to the paragraphs of text and the list_term rule to the four main paragraph headings.
5. Create named anchors named **reservations**, **outfitters**, **tours**, and **links** in front of the respective headings on the page, then link each named anchor to "Reservations," "Travel Outfitters," "Escorted Tours," and "Helpful Links in Travel Planning" in the first paragraph, as shown in Figure 36.
6. Link the text "on-line catalog" in the Travel Outfitters paragraph to the catalog.html page.
7. Link the text "CNN Travel Channel" under the heading Helpful Links in Travel Planning to http://www.cnn.com/TRAVEL.
8. Repeat Step 7 to create links for the rest of the websites listed:

U.S. Department of State: http://travel.state.gov
Yahoo! Currency Converter: http://finance.yahoo.com/currency-converter
The Weather Channel: http://www.weather.com

Figure 36 *Sample Project Builder 1*

PROJECT BUILDER 1
(CONTINUED)

9. Save the services page, preview the page in the browser to test each link, then open the index page.
10. Replace the menu bar on the home page with a horizontal Spry menu bar, using formatting of your choice, but using MenuBar as the menu ID. The menu bar should contain the following elements: **Home**, **Catalog**, **Services**, **Tours**, and **Newsletter**. Figure 37 shows one example of a possible menu bar. Create two submenu items for the peru and galapagos pages under the tours menu item, then delete all other submenu items.
11. Test the menu bar links in the browser, then close the browser and correct any errors you find.
12. Copy the menu bar, then place it on each completed page of the website.
13. Save each page, then check for broken links and orphaned files.
14. Open the tours.html file in your local site folder and save it as **galapagos.html**, overwriting the existing file, then close the file.
15. Open dw5_9.html from the drive and folder where you store your Data Files, then save it as **peru.html**, overwriting the existing file. Do not update links, but save the machu_picchu_from_high.jpg and llama.jpg files from the data files folder in the assets folder of the website, apply a rule to set the float for each image, then save and close the file. Close dw5_9.html.
16. Open dw5_10.html from the driver and folder where you store your Data Files, then save the file as **tours.html**, overwriting the existing file. Do not update links, but save the sea_lions_in_surf.jpg and machu_picchu_ruins.jpg files from the data files folder in the assets folder of the website and apply a rule to set the float for each image. Close dw5_10.html.
17. Link the text "Galápagos" in the second sentence of the first paragraph on the tours page to the galapagos.html file.
18. Link the text "Peru" in the first sentence in the second paragraph on the tours page to the peru.html file.
19. Add a rule to the tripsmart_styles.css file to modify the <img> tag by setting the vertical alignment to bottom.
20. Save all files and preview them in the browser, checking to see that all links work and all pages have a consistent look.
21. Compare your tours page to Figure 37, close your browser, then close all open pages.

Figure 37 *Sample Project Builder 1*

PROJECT BUILDER 2

You are continuing your work on the Carolyne's Creations website, which you started in Project Builder 2 in Chapter 1 and developed in the previous chapters. Chef Carolyne has asked you to create a page describing her cooking classes offered every month. You will create the content for that page and individual pages describing the children's classes and the adult classes. Refer to Figures 38, 39, and 40 for possible solutions.

1. Open the Carolyne's Creations website.
2. Open dw5_11.html from the drive and folder where you store your Data Files, save it as **classes.html** in the local site folder of the Carolyne's Creations website, overwriting the existing file and not updating the links. Close dw5_11.html.
3. Select the broken banner image, browse to the data files folder, then select the new banner, cc_banner_with_text.jpg, then verify that it was saved to the site assets folder. Notice that styles have already been applied to the page text because the data file included a relative link to the style sheet.
4. Select the text "adults' class" in the last paragraph, then link it to the adults.html page. (*Hint*: This page has not been developed yet.)
5. Select the text "children's class" in the last paragraph and link it to the children.html page. (*Hint*: This page has not been developed yet.)
6. Create an e-mail link from the text "Sign me up!" that links to **carolyne@carolynescreations.com**.
7. Insert the image file fish.jpg from the assets folder where you store your Data Files at the beginning of the second paragraph, add appropriate alternate text, then choose your own alignment and formatting settings.
8. Add the image file children_cooking.jpg from the assets folder where you store your Data Files at the beginning of the third paragraph, then choose your own image rule alignment and formatting settings.
9. Check the rest of the pages with images and adjust your image rules if necessary to improve the appearance of each page.
10. Create hot spots on the black bar at the bottom of the new banner that was imported with the data file, cc_banner_with_text.jpg, that link each menu item with its corresponding page. (*Hint*: Remember to include alternate text and a target for each menu item.)
11. Compare your work to Figure 38 for a possible solution, copy the new banner, then save and close the file.
12. Open dw5_12.html from the drive and folder where you store your Data Files, then save it as **children.html**, overwriting the existing file and not updating links. Save the image cookies_oven.jpg from the assets folder where you store your Data Files to the website assets folder. Close dw5_12.html.

Figure 38 *Completed Project Builder 2*

Working with Links and Navigation

DREAMWEAVER 5-41

PROJECT BUILDER 2
(CONTINUED)

13. Paste your new banner on the children.html page, replacing the previous banner, compare your work to Figure 39 for a possible solution, then save and close the file.
14. Repeat Steps 12 and 13 to open the dw5_13.html file and save it as **adults.html**, overwriting the existing file and saving the file peruvian_appetizers.jpg from the folder where you save your data files in the assets folder, then use alignment settings of your choice. Replace the banner with your new banner, compare your work to Figure 40 for a possible solution, then save and close the files.
15. Open the index page and delete the menu bar and horizontal rule.
16. Replace the banner with your new banner.
17. Copy the new banner with the menu bar to each completed page, deleting existing menu bars and banners.
18. Save all the pages, then check for broken links and orphaned files. You will see one orphaned file, the original version of the banner. Delete this file.
19. Apply a rule from the style sheet to any text or image that is not formatted with a style. (Remember to add an inline style to each page to prevent a border from appearing in Internet Explorer.)
20. Preview all the pages in your browser, check to make sure the links work correctly, close your browser, then close all open pages.

Figure 39 *Completed Project Builder 2*

Figure 40 *Completed Project Builder 2*

DREAMWEAVER 5-42

Working with Links and Navigation

DESIGN PROJECT

Sherrill Simmons is a university English instructor. She would like to find new ways to engage her students through her university website. She decided to explore incorporating podcasts, FaceBook, and Twitter. She spends several hours looking at other websites to help her get started.

1. Connect to the Internet, then navigate to the Federal Bureau of Investigation website at fbi.gov.
2. Browse through the site and locate the link to "Podcasts & Radio." What are the options they have provided for their users to download and listen to them?

Figure 41 *Design Project*
The Federal Bureau of Investigation website – www.fbi.gov

Working with Links and Navigation

DREAMWEAVER 5-43

DESIGN PROJECT
(CONTINUED)

3. Navigate to the U.S. Navy website at navy.mil, as shown in Figure 42.
4. Describe how the Navy is using Web 2.0 technology. What do you think their purpose might be for incorporating each application?
5. Which Web 2.0 applications would you include on your website if you were Sherrill?
6. Describe how you would use each one of them to engage her students.

Figure 42 *Design Project*
The United States Navy website — www.navy.mil

PORTFOLIO PROJECT

In this assignment, you will continue to work on the website that you started in Chapter 1 and developed in the previous chapters.

You will continue building your website by designing and completing a page with a menu bar. After creating the menu bar, you will copy it to each completed page in the website. In addition to the menu bar, you will add several external links and several internal links to other pages as well as to named anchors. You will also link text to a named anchor. After you complete this work, you will check for broken links and orphaned files.

1. Consult your wireframe to decide which page or pages you would like to develop in this chapter. Decide how to design and where to place the menu bar, named anchors, and any additional page elements you decide to use. Decide which reports should be run on the website to check for accuracy.
2. Research websites that could be included on one or more of your pages as external links of interest to your users. Create a list of the external links you want to use. Using your wireframe as a guide, decide where each external link should be placed in the site.
3. Add the external links to existing pages or create any additional pages that contain external links.
4. Create named anchors for key locations on the page, such as the top of the page, then link appropriate text on the page to them.
5. Decide on a design for a menu bar that will be used on all pages of the website.
6. Create the menu bar and copy it to all finished pages on the website.
7. Think of a good place to incorporate an image map, then add it to a page.
8. Decide on at least one Web 2.0 application that you might like to incorporate and determine how and on what page they would be included.
9. Use the Link Checker panel to check for broken links and orphaned files.
10. Use the checklist in Figure 43 to make sure your website is complete, save your work, then close all open pages.

Figure 43 *Portfolio Project checklist*

> **Website Checklist**
> 1. Do all pages have a page title?
> 2. Does the home page have a description and keywords?
> 3. Does the home page contain contact information?
> 4. Does every page in the website have consistent navigation links?
> 5. Does the home page have a last updated statement that will automatically update when the page is saved?
> 6. Do all paths for links and images work correctly?
> 7. Do all images have alternate text?
> 8. Are there any unnecessary files that you can delete from the assets folder?
> 9. Is there a style sheet with at least two styles?
> 10. Did you apply the style sheet to all page content?
> 11. Does at least one page contain links to one or more named anchors?
> 12. Does at least one page contain either a named anchor or an internal link?
> 13. Do all pages look good using at least two different browsers?
> 14. Did you incorporate at least one Web 2.0 technology?

ADOBE DREAMWEAVER CS6

CHAPTER 6 POSITIONING OBJECTS
WITH CSS AND TABLES

1. Create a page using CSS layouts
2. Add content to CSS layout blocks
3. Edit and format CSS layout blocks
4. Create a table
5. Resize, split, and merge cells
6. Insert and align images in table cells
7. Insert text and format cell content

CHAPTER 6: POSITIONING OBJECTS WITH CSS AND TABLES

Introduction

To create an organized, attractive web page, you need precise control of the position of page elements. CSS page layouts can provide this control. **CSS page layouts** consist of containers formatted with CSS rules into which you place page content. These containers can accommodate images, blocks of text, Flash movies, or any other page element. The appearance and position of the containers are set through the use of HTML tags known as **div tags**. Using div tags, you can position elements next to each other as well as on top of each other.

Another option for controlling the placement of page elements is through the use of tables. **Tables** are placeholders made up of small boxes called **cells**, into which you can insert text and graphics. Cells in a table are arranged horizontally in **rows** and vertically in **columns**. Using tables on a web page gives you control over the placement of each object on the page, similar to the way CSS blocks control placement. In this chapter, you use a predesigned CSS page layout with div tags to place text and graphics on a page. You then add a table to one of the CSS blocks on the page.

Using Div Tags Versus Tables for Page Layout

Div tags and tables both enable you to control the appearance of content in your web pages. Unlike tables, div tags let you stack your information, allowing for one piece of information to be visible at a time. Tables are static, which makes it difficult to change them quickly as need arises. Div tags can be dynamic, changing in response to variables such as a mouse click. You can create dynamic div tags using JavaScript **behaviors**, simple action scripts that let you incorporate interactivity by modifying content based on variables like user actions. For example, you could add a JavaScript behavior to text in a div tag to make it become larger or smaller when the pointer is over it.

Designers previously used tables to position content on web pages. Since the inception of CSS, designers have moved to positioning most page content with CSS layouts. However, tables are still used for some layout purposes, such as arranging tabular data on a page. As a designer, you should become familiar with the tools that are available to you, including CSS and tables, then decide which tool meets current standards and is best suited for the current design challenge.

TOOLS YOU'LL USE

DREAMWEAVER 6-3

LESSON 1

Create a Page
USING CSS LAYOUTS

What You'll Do

In this lesson, you will create a new page based on a predesigned CSS layout to become the new cafe page for the website.

Understanding Div Tags

Div tags are HTML tags that define how areas of content are formatted or positioned on a web page. For example, when you center an image on a page or inside a table cell, Dreamweaver automatically inserts a div tag in the HTML code. In addition to using div tags to align page elements, designers also use them to assign background colors or borders to content blocks, CSS styles to text, and many other properties to page elements. One type of div tag is an AP div tag. AP stands for absolutely positioned, so an **AP div tag** creates a container that has a specified, fixed position on a web page. The resulting container that an AP div tag creates on a page is called an **AP element**.

Using CSS Page Layouts

Because building a web page using div tags can be tedious for beginning designers, Dreamweaver CS6 provides 18 predesigned layouts that are available in the New Document dialog box, as shown in Figure 1.

New to CS6 are the two HTML5 layouts. These give you the option of creating HTML pages based on either 2-column or 3-column layouts. These layouts include new HTML tags to support semantic markup such as <section>, <header>, <footer>, <article>, and <aside>. You can use these layouts to create web pages with attractive and consistent layouts.

There are two types of CSS layouts: fixed and liquid. A **fixed layout** expresses all widths in pixels and remains the same size regardless of the size of the browser window. A **liquid layout** expresses all widths in percents and changes size depending on the size of the browser window.

Predesigned CSS layouts contain div tags that control the placement of page content using placeholders. Each div tag container has placeholder text that appears until you replace it with your own content. Because div tags use CSS for formatting and positioning, designers prefer them for building web page content. When you use the Dreamweaver predesigned layouts, you can be sure that your pages will appear with a consistent design when viewed in all browsers. Once you become more comfortable using the predesigned layouts, you will begin to build your own CSS-based pages from scratch.

QUICK TIP

The Browser Compatibility Check feature flags code that might present a CSS rendering issue in some browsers by underlining code in green. To see this feature, switch to Code view and browse through the code.

Viewing CSS Layout Blocks

As you design your page layouts using div tags, you can use Design view to see and adjust CSS content blocks. In Design view, text or images that have been aligned or positioned using div tags have a dotted border, as shown in Figure 2. In the Visual Aids list on the View menu, you can display selected features of div tag elements, such as CSS Layout Backgrounds, CSS Layout Box Model, CSS Layout Outlines, and AP Element Outlines. The CSS Layout Box Model displays the padding and margins of a block element.

QUICK TIP

Windows users should set their display settings to 100% to match the figures. This setting is found in the Display section in the Control Panel.

Figure 2 *CSS blocks defined by dotted borders*

Figure 1 *New Document dialog box*

HTML5 layouts

Preview of selected layout

Predesigned div tag layouts

Dotted-line borders surround the CSS blocks

Using Tracing Images for Page Design

Another design option for creating a page layout is to use a tracing image. A **tracing image** is an image that is placed in the background of a document. By adjusting the transparency (opacity) of the image, you can then use it to create page elements on top of it, similar to the way you would place a piece of tracing paper on top of a drawing and trace over it. To insert a tracing image, Use the Modify, Page Properties, Tracing Image dialog box or the View, Tracing Image, Load command. Browse to select the image you want to use for the tracing image, then adjust the transparency as desired. The tracing image serves as a guide or pattern. You can delete it after you complete your design.

Lesson 1 Create a Page Using CSS Layouts

Create a page with a CSS layout

1. Open The Striped Umbrella website.
2. Click **File** on the Menu bar, click **New**, verify that Blank Page is highlighted in the first column of the New Document dialog box, click **HTML** in the Page Type column if necessary, then click **HTML 5: 2 column fixed**, **right sidebar**, **header and footer** in the Layout column, as shown in Figure 3.

   A fixed layout remains the same size regardless of the size of the browser window.

3. Click the **Attach Style Sheet button** in the bottom-right corner of the dialog box, then click **Browse** in the Attach External Style Sheet dialog box.

   The Select Style Sheet File dialog box opens.

4. Select the **su_styles.css** external style sheet in the Select Style Sheet File dialog box, then click **OK** to close the Select Style Sheet File dialog box.

   If a dialog box opens reminding you to save your file before a document-relative path can be created, click OK to close the dialog box.

   TIP Dreamweaver has an option in the New Document dialog box to enable **InContext Editing**, or **ICE**, as shown in Figure 3. This feature sets up editable regions on web pages that users can change while viewing the page in a browser. See page 6-10 for more information.

5. Verify that the Link option is selected in the Attach External Style Sheet dialog box, then click **OK** to close the Attach External Style Sheet dialog box.

   (continued)

Figure 3 *Predesigned CSS layout selected for new page*

Blank Page option selected

HTML Page Type

HTML 5: 2 column fixed, left sidebar, header and footer Layout

Enable InContext Editing check box

Attach Style Sheet button

Using XML and XSL to Create and Format Web Page Content

You can also create information containers on your web pages using XML, Extensible Markup Language, and XSL, Extensible Stylesheet Language. **XML** is a language that you use to structure blocks of information, similar to HTML. It uses similar opening and closing tags and the nested tag structure that HTML documents use. However, XML tags do not determine how the information is formatted, which is handled using XSL. **XSL** is similar to CSS; the XSL stylesheet information formats the containers created by XML. Once the XML structure and XSL styles are in place, **XSLT**, **Extensible Stylesheet Language Transformations**, interprets the code in the XSL file to transform an XML document, much like style sheet files transform HTML files from an unformatted file to a formatted file. XSL transformations can be written as client-side or server-side transformations. To create XML documents, use the XML page type in the New Document dialog box.

Figure 4 *The su_styles.css file is attached to the new page*

- Enable InContext Editing option
- Create button
- su_styles.css file is attached
- Layout CSS list arrow

Figure 5 *New page based on CSS layout*

- Blocks of content based on CSS layout
- Attached su_styles.css file
- Rules in new external style sheet based on CSS layout choice

The su_styles.css file is attached to the new page, as shown in Figure 4. The next time you create a new page, the style sheet will be selected automatically.

6. Click the **Layout CSS list arrow**, click **Create New File** (if it's not already selected), then click **Create** in the New Document dialog box.

7. Verify that the site root folder appears in the Save in text box, then click **Save** to close the Save Style Sheet File As dialog box.

A new two-column HTML5 page opens based on the predesigned CSS layout you chose. It has CSS content blocks arranged in two columns, one as a sidebar on the right side, as well as a header and footer. Placeholder text appears in each of the blocks, as shown in Figure 5. You will replace the text with content for The Striped Umbrella website. The CSS blocks each have a different color background to help you see how the blocks are arranged on the page. This new page will replace the blank cafe page.

8. Expand the new style sheet, HTML5_twoColFixRHdr.css, in the CSS Styles panel, if necessary, so you can see the new rules.

Notice that you have two sets of styles now: the external style sheet su_styles.css; and the external style sheet HTML5_twoColFixRHdr.css, with the rules that define the CSS blocks on the page.

9. Save the file as **cafe.html**, overwriting the existing blank cafe page.

You created a new page based on a predesigned CSS layout with the attached style sheet for The Striped Umbrella website and a new external style sheet that defines the rules for the CSS layout. You then saved the new file as cafe.html, overwriting the existing blank cafe page.

Lesson 1 Create a Page Using CSS Layouts

DREAMWEAVER 6-7

LESSON 2

Add Content to CSS
LAYOUT BLOCKS

What You'll Do

In this lesson, you will copy the menu bar and banner from the index page and paste it into the new page. You will add text and images for the new cafe page you are creating, then overwrite the old cafe page with this new one.

Understanding Div Tag Content

As you learned in Lesson 1, a div tag is a container that formats blocks of information on a web page, such as background colors, images, links, tables, and text. Once you have created a layout using div tags, you are ready to insert and format text. As with formatting text on a web page, you should use CSS styles to format text in div tags. You can also add all other properties such as text indents, padding, margins, and background color using CSS styles.

In this lesson, you use a CSS layout to create a new cafe page that arranges the content into defined areas on the page.

Using Dreamweaver New Page Options

You can use either the Welcome Screen or the New command on the File menu to create several different types of pages. The predesigned CSS page layouts make it easy to design accessible web pages based on Cascading Style Sheets, without an advanced level of expertise in writing HTML code. Predesigned templates are another time-saving feature that promotes consistency across a website. Fluid Grid layouts, CSS Style Sheets, and Sample Pages are a few of the other options. It is worth the time to explore each category to understand what is available to you as a designer. Once you have selected a page layout, you can customize it to suit your client's content and design needs.

Understanding CSS Code

When you view a page based on a predesigned CSS layout in Code view, you see helpful comments that explain sections of the code, as shown in Figure 6. The comments are in gray to differentiate them from the rest of the code. The CSS rules can reside in the Head section of a page or in an external style sheet. The code for a CSS container begins with the class, or name of the rule, and is followed by rule properties. For example, in Figure 6, the container described on line 45 begins with the class name .container, which is followed by three properties and values: width: 960 px; background: #FFF; and margin: 0 auto. The code that links the rules to the content is located in the body section.

Figure 6 *Code view for CSS in head content*

Comments in gray text

Rule name preceded by period

Rule properties

```
34   /* ~~ This fixed width container surrounds all other blocks ~~ */
35   .container {
36       width: 960px;
37       background-color: #FFFFFF;
38       margin: 0 auto; /* the auto value on the sides, coupled with the width, centers the layout */
39   }
40   /* ~~ The header is not given a width. It will extend the full width of your layout. ~~ */
41   header {
42       background-color: #ADB96E;
43   }
44   /* ~~ These are the columns for the layout. ~~
45   
46   1) Padding is only placed on the top and/or bottom of the block elements. The elements within these blocks have padding on
        their sides. This saves you from any "box model math". Keep in mind, if you add any side padding or border to the block
        itself, it will be added to the width you define to create the *total* width. You may also choose to remove the padding on
        the element in the block element and place a second block element within it with no width and the padding necessary for
        your design.
47   
48   2) No margin has been given to the columns since they are all floated. If you must add margin, avoid placing it on the
        side you're floating toward (for example: a right margin on a block set to float right). Many times, padding can be used
        instead. For blocks where this rule must be broken, you should add a "display:inline" declaration to the block element's
        rule to tame a bug where some versions of Internet Explorer double the margin.
49   
50   3) Since classes can be used multiple times in a document (and an element can also have multiple classes applied), the
        columns have been assigned class names instead of IDs. For example, two sidebar blocks could be stacked if necessary.
        These can very easily be changed to IDs if that's your preference, as long as you'll only be using them once per document.
51   
52   4) If you prefer your nav on the left instead of the right, simply float these columns the opposite direction (all left
        instead of all right) and they'll render in reverse order. There's no need to move the blocks around in the HTML source.
53   
54   */
55   .sidebar1 {
56       float: right;
```

Lesson 2 Add Content to CSS Layout Blocks **DREAMWEAVER 6-9**

Add text to a CSS container

1. Skim through the placeholder text to read the instructions included in them, then select all content between the Header and Footer in the main section (content block) of the page through the last paragraph describing the backgrounds, as shown in Figure 7, then press **[Delete]**.

   TIP Before you delete placeholder text, it is a good idea to read it. The placeholder text has helpful information that helps you to understand the way the page is designed. It gives you pointers for the best way to replace the placeholder text with your text.

2. Change to the HTML Property inspector if necessary, click the **Format list arrow**, then click **Paragraph**.

   This deletes the remaining H1 tag in the block.

3. Import the Word document **cafe.doc** from the drive and folder where you store your Data Files (Win) or copy and paste it (Mac) in the blank container.

4. Click **Commands** on the Menu bar, click **Clean Up Word HTML**, click **OK**, then click **OK** in the dialog box that appears.

   (continued)

Figure 7 *Text selected in content block of new page*

Using Adobe Business Catalyst for InContext Editing

Adobe Business Catalyst is a hosted application for setting up and maintaining an online business. It has an editing component called InContext Editing (ICE) that is available through Dreamweaver. **InContext Editing** allows a page developer to designate regions on a page that can be edited by users while they are viewing a page in a browser. This is great because it does not require a web editing program or any prior knowledge of HTML. Users simply log in to InContext Editing while a page is open in a browser, make their edits, then save the page. To use this feature, the developer checks the Enable InContext Editing check box in the New Document dialog box, then designates the regions of a page that will be available for editing by others.

Figure 8 *Text selected in sidebar1 block in Code view*

```
15      <a href="#"><img src="" alt="Insert Logo Here" width="180" height="90" id="Insert_logo" style="background-color: #C6D580;
        display:block;" /></a>
16      </header>
17      <div class="sidebar1">
18         <ul class="nav">
19            <li><a href="#">Link one</a></li>
20            <li><a href="#">Link two</a></li>
21            <li><a href="#">Link three</a></li>
22            <li><a href="#">Link four</a></li>
23         </ul>
24         <aside>
25            <p> The above links demonstrate a basic navigational structure using an unordered list styled with CSS. Use this as a
        starting point and modify the properties to produce your own unique look. If you require flyout menus, create your own using a
        Spry menu, a menu widget from Adobe's Exchange or a variety of other javascript or CSS solutions.</p>
26            <p>If you would like the navigation along the top, simply move the ul to the top of the page and recreate the styling.</p
        >
27         </aside>
28      <!-- end .sidebar1 --></div>
```

Beginning tag for sidebar1

Ending tag for sidebar1

Figure 9 *Text pasted into Content block and typed into sidebar1 block and footer block of new page*

Insert_logo (180 x 90)

The Sand Crab Cafe is located in The Club House and has three dining areas: The Terrace, Beach 25, and The Cabana. The Terrace is outdoor dining with a breathtaking view of the Gulf, especially at sunset. Beach 25 is casual, indoor dining on the second floor. The Cabana is poolside.

Reservations are recommended for Beach 25 (our main dining room) during the peak summer season. Call 555-594-9458, extension 55.

Copyright 2002 - 2015 The Striped Umbrella

5. Switch to Code view, select the code between the beginning and end of the <div class="sidebar1"> tag, as shown in Figure 8, then press **[Delete]** to delete the placeholder text.

   Be careful not to delete the beginning and ending div tags.

6. Return to Design view, then type **Reservations are recommended for Beach 25 (our main dining room) during the peak summer season. Call 555-594-9458: extension 55.** at the insertion point.

7. Delete all of the text in the footer block, then type **Copyright 2002 - 2015 The Striped Umbrella** as shown in Figure 9, then save your work.

You imported text and typed text in the CSS blocks, replacing the placeholder text in the body, sidebar, and footer.

Add images to a CSS block

1. Open the Striped Umbrella index page and copy both the banner and the menu bar.

   TIP You might find it easier to copy the banner and menu bar separately. If you copy them together, click in front of the banner, hold down the Shift key, then click under the menu bar to select both the banner and the menu bar.

2. Switch back to the cafe page, click the **placeholder logo image**, paste the banner and menu bar into the header section of the page, then insert two line breaks and a paragraph break after the menu bar. (If you have trouble adding the paragraph break, go to Code view and enter <p> </p> after the closing header tag.).

   TIP Press [Ctrl][Tab] (Win) or ⌘ ['] (Mac) to switch between two open pages.

3. Close the index page.

4. Place the insertion point immediately in front of the word "Reservations", insert a paragraph break, press [↑], insert **cafe_logo.gif** from the drive and folder where you store your Data Files, then type **Sand Crab Cafe logo** as the alternate text in the Image Tag Accessibility Attributes dialog box and click **OK** to close the dialog box.

5. Select the **crab logo** if necessary, press [←], then enter a line break in front of the logo.

6. Place the insertion point after the period after the word "poolside" in the body text, insert a paragraph break, insert **cafe_photo.jpg** from the drive and folder where you store your Data Files, then type **Sand Crab Cafe photo** as the alternate text. See Figure 10.

(continued)

Figure 10 *Images added to header, sidebar 1, and content blocks*

The Evolution of HTML5

HTML has been in existence since the early 1990s, but it wasn't until 1997 that the then current version, HTML4, became a W3C recommendation. Many HTML4 attributes such as body background, align, cell padding, and hspace are now added using CSS3. HTML5 introduced new ways to add interactivity and tags that support semantic markup, such as the <nav> tag used for navigation links. In Chapter 3 you learned about using semantic markup to incorporate meaning with your HTML markup. Other semantic HTML5 tags include <header>, <footer>, <article>, <audio>, <section>, and <video>. HTML5 is still a work in progress, but most modern browsers support it. HTML5 also introduces markup for Web applications (apps), an exploding sector of Web development.

Figure 11 *Images placed on page*

Insertion point is in content block

HTML Property inspector displays content (class name) in the Class text box

7. Deselect the image, click the **HTML Property inspector button** if necessary to switch to the HTML Property inspector, then click to place the insertion point in the content CSS block above the cafe_photo image.

   Notice that the Class text box in the HTML Property inspector shows the class to be "content", as shown in Figure 11.

8. Click to place the insertion point in the sidebar1 block.

   The Property inspector displays the class rule assigned to the block.

9. Save your work, preview the page in the browser to verify that there is no gap between the banner and the menu bar, then return to Dreamweaver.

You copied the banner and menu bar from the index page, pasted it onto the new cafe page, then added the cafe logo and photo to the page.

Lesson 2 Add Content to CSS Layout Blocks

DREAMWEAVER 6-13

LESSON 3

Edit and Format CSS LAYOUT BLOCKS

What You'll Do

In this lesson, you will center the two images you have added to the page. You will then view the div tag properties and edit the background colors. You will also change the body background color.

Editing Content in CSS Layout Blocks

It is unlikely that you will find a predesigned CSS page layout that is exactly what you have in mind for your website. However, once you have created a page with a predesigned CSS layout, it is easy to modify the individual rule properties to change content formatting or placement to better fit your needs. For example, you can easily change the properties to fit the color scheme of your website.

To change rule properties, click the plus sign next to the style sheet name, if necessary, to see the rules listed in each section, as shown in Figure 12, and then select the rule you want to modify. The properties and values for the selected rule appear in the Properties pane, where you can modify them. If you have multiple style sheets, you can use either style sheet or a combination to format the page content.

Figure 12 *Viewing the CSS Styles panel*

External style sheet the developer created

External style sheet for predefined CSS layout

Style sheet for Spry menu bar (saved in SpryAssets folder)

DREAMWEAVER 6-14

Positioning Objects with CSS and Tables

Figure 13 *Adjusting alignment in layout blocks*

Logo and text are centered within this block and text breaks more logically

Insertion of transparent spacer image indents club_house image

Using the Adobe CSS Advisor for Cross-Browser Rendering Issues

You can use the **Browser Compatibility Check (BCC)** feature to check for problems in the HTML code for CSS features that may render differently in multiple browsers. It flags and rates code on three levels: an error that could cause a serious display problem; an error that probably won't cause a serious display problem; or a warning that it has found code that is unsupported, but won't cause a serious display problem. Each bug is linked to the CSS Advisor, a part of the Adobe website, that offers solutions for that particular bug and other helpful information for resolving any issues with your pages. To check for browser compatibility, click File, point to Check Page, and then click Browser Compatibility or click the Check browser compatibility button on the Document toolbar.

Edit block properties to align content

1. Place the insertion point in front of the cafe logo.

   Notice that the class rule for this block is named .sidebar1.

2. Click the **.sidebar1 rule** in the CSS Styles panel, click the **Edit Rule button**, click the **Block category** in the CSS Rule definition for .sidebar1 dialog box, click the **Text-align list arrow**, then click **center**.

   The logo and text will now be centered in the left sidebar.

3. Click the **Box Category**, change the Float from right to left, then click **OK**.

   The sidebar moves to the left side of the page.

4. Edit the sidebar text to match Figure 13 by deleting "(our main dining room)" and by using line breaks to divide up the lines of text.

   Now the lines of text break in more logical places.

5. Click in front of the club_house image, click **Insert** on the Menu bar, click **Image**, browse to your website assets folder, then double-click **spacer_30px.gif**.

6. Add the alternate text **Spacer image**, change to Live view, then compare your screen to Figure 13.

   The club_house image is indented from the left side of the CSS layout block by 30 pixels.

   (continued)

7. Move the pointer over the left border of the content block (the block containing the cafe description and picture), click the **red border** to select the block (the border turns blue after it is selected), then move the pointer inside the block and hover until the floating window shown in Figure 14 appears.

The properties of the div tag appear in a floating window. The Property inspector displays the div tag class name.

TIP   You can change the border color of div tags when the mouse is positioned over them in the Preferences dialog box. Select the Highlighting category, then click the Mouse-Over color box and select a different color. You can also disable highlighting by deselecting the Show check box for Mouse-Over.

8. Save your work.

You centered the logo and the reservations text, and indented the cafe_photo image. You then edited the sidebar text to make it flow more smoothly, then viewed the properties of the div tag.

Figure 14   *Viewing the class properties*

Border for div block

Properties of class

Class rule assigned to div tag

Viewing Options for CSS Layout Blocks

You can view your layout blocks in Design view in several ways. You can choose to show or hide outlines, temporarily assign different background colors to each individual layout block, or view the **CSS Layout Box Model** (padding, margins, borders, etc.) of a selected layout. To change these options, use the View > Visual Aids menu, and then select or deselect the CSS Layout Backgrounds, CSS Layout Box Model, or CSS Layout Outlines menu choice. You can also use the Visual Aids button on the Document toolbar.

Figure 15 *Editing the body Font-family property*

Figure 16 *The cafe page with edited body Font-family property*

Edit type properties in CSS layout blocks

1. Select the **body rule** in the HTML5_twoColFixRtHdr .css file CSS Styles panel, click the **Edit Rule button**, then click the **Type category** in the CSS Rule definition for body dialog box.
2. Click the **Font-family list arrow**, then click **Arial, Helvetica, sans-serif,** as shown in Figure 15.
3. Click **OK** to close the dialog box, compare your screen to Figure 16, then save your work.

The new font family property is applied to the text on the page. The Font-family property in the body rule determines the font family for all text on the page unless another one is specified for a different container, such as the footer, with an external style or a different internal style. The body is a **parent container**, a container with other tags falling between its opening and closing tags. **Child containers** are containers whose code resides inside a parent container. All HTML tags for page content are inside the body tags. So unless a different font is specified in a different container, each child container inherits the properties from the parent container.

You leave the rest of the type properties with the default CSS settings. This page uses the settings from the HTML5_twoColFixRtHdr.css external style sheet, but this style sheet is not attached to the rest of the pages in the site, so until it is, you still need the body_text and body rules from the su_styles.css style sheet to use to format the other pages.

You changed the font-family property in the body that determines the font family for all text on the page.

Lesson 3 Edit and Format CSS Layout Blocks

DREAMWEAVER 6-17

Edit CSS layout block properties

1. Click the **header rule** in the CSS Styles panel to select it, then click the **Show only set properties button**.

   The value for the background property appears in the Properties pane. The header block has background color of #ADB96E, a muted green color.

2. Click the **background text box** to place the insertion point, replace #ADB96E with **#FFF**, press **[Enter]** (Win) or **[return]** (Mac), and compare your screen to Figure 17.

   TIP You may have to adjust the size of your CSS Styles panel to view both panes.

   The header background color changes to white.

3. With the header rule still selected, click the **Edit Rule button**, click the **Box category**, type **5** in the Top Margin text box, verify that the Same for all check box is checked, as shown in Figure 18, then click **OK**.

   You can edit rule properties in either the CSS Styles Properties pane or by opening the CSS Rule definition dialog box. With the header margins set, the banner will now appear more centered on the page.

   TIP The top margin will appear wider because the banner has a transparent background that makes the top margin look wider (to make room for the top of the umbrella). The bottom margin will appear wider than it is because there are two line breaks under the banner.

   (continued)

Figure 17 *Editing the properties of the header rule*

Figure 18 *Editing the properties of the header rule*

Figure 19 *The four layout blocks now have a white background*

5px margin is applied to header

The four blocks have the same background color

Copyright statement is centered in footer

4. Repeat Step 2 to change the background color in the footer rule to #FFF and the background color in the sidebar1 rule to #FFF.

   The header, footer, and sidebar1 background colors are now white.

   TIP You only need to use the abbreviated hexadecimal color code, such as #FFF, when specifying colors. However, in the Dreamweaver predesigned CSS layouts, the color codes are shown with the full 6-character codes. Either code works. You can also specify colors by their names. For example, the color magenta can be specified as "magenta", #FF00FF or #F0F

5. Edit the footer rule to change the Text-align block property to center.

6. Save your work, then compare your screen to Figure 19.

You changed the margin width of a CSS layout block, changed the background color of three CSS layout blocks to white, then centered the footer.

NEW **Using a Fluid Grid Layout**

Dreamweaver has a new type of predesigned layout available as a choice in the New Document dialog box called a Fluid Grid Layout. The **Fluid Grid Layout** is a system for designing layouts that will adapt to three different screen sizes: Mobile, Tablet, and Desktop. By using percentages to set page and page element dimensions, the design will expand or contract to fit the dimensions of the device being used to view the page. The Fluid Grid Layout produces an HTML5 document type. When you create a new page based on a fluid grid, two style sheets will be created: a boilerplate.css file and one that you assign a name. If you plan to use a fluid grid layout, take some time to study the style sheet code and the comments embedded in the page source code before you begin adding page content.

Lesson 3 Edit and Format CSS Layout Blocks

Edit page properties

1. Select the **container rule** in the CSS Styles panel.
2. Open the CSS Rule definition for .container dialog box, then click the **Border category**.

   A border around the page sets it off from the extra space around it when it is viewed in a browser.
3. Click the **Top list arrow** in the Style column, then click **solid**.
4. Click the **Width list arrow** in the first text box in the Width column, then click **thin**.
5. Click the first **Color text box** in the Color column, type **#033**, press **Tab**, compare your screen to Figure 20, then click **OK**.
6. Click the **body rule** in the HTML5_twoColFixRtHdr.css style sheet in the CSS Styles panel, then open the CSS Rule definition for body dialog box.
7. Click the **Background category** if necessary, change the Background-color text box to **#FFF**, then click **OK**.

(continued)

Figure 20 *Adding a border to the container*

Figure 21 *Viewing the cafe page in the browser*

Border appears around page in browser

8. Use the Document toolbar to add the page title **The Striped Umbrella Sand Crab Cafe** to the page.
9. Save your work, preview the page in your browser, compare your screen to Figure 21, then close the browser.

You added a border to the page.

Lesson 3 Edit and Format CSS Layout Blocks

DREAMWEAVER 6-21

LESSON 4

Create
A TABLE

What You'll Do

In this lesson, you will create a table for the cafe page in The Striped Umbrella website to provide a grid for the cafe hours.

Understanding Table Modes

Now that you have learned how CSS can act as containers to hold information in place on web pages, let's look at tables as another layout tool. Tables are great when you need a grid layout on a page for a list of data. To create a table, click the Table button on the Insert panel. When the Layout category of the Insert panel is displayed, you can choose between two modes that give you different ways to view your table: Standard mode or Expanded Tables mode. Expanded Tables mode adds extra space between cells, which makes it easier to select small cells. Click the appropriate button on the Insert panel after selecting a table on the page.

Creating a Table

To create a table in Standard mode, click the Table button on the Insert panel to open the Table dialog box. You can enter values for the number of rows and columns in the Table dialog box, but the rest of the table properties should be assigned using CSS. If you only plan to use one table design in a site, you can create a rule to modify the <table> tag and save it in your website style sheet. You then use this rule to add formatting options to the table such as adding a border or table width. The **border** is the outline or frame around the table and is measured in pixels. The table width can be specified in units of measure such as pixels, or as a percentage. When the table width is specified as a percentage, the table width expands to fill up its container (the browser window, a CSS container, or another table). Table width is set using the Width property in the Box category of the relevant CSS style.

To align a table on a page or within a CSS layout block, use a Float property in the Box category. A table placed inside another table is called a **nested table**. **Cell padding** is the distance between the cell content and the **cell walls**, the lines inside the cell borders. **Cell spacing** is the distance between cells. Neither cell padding or cell spacing is supported by HTML5, however, so it's better to address spacing issues by assigning styles.

Positioning Objects with CSS and Tables

Before you create a table, you should include in your wireframe a plan for it that shows its location on the page and the placement of text and graphics in its cells. You should also decide whether to include borders around the tables. Setting the border value to 0 causes the table borders to be invisible. Users will not realize that you used a table unless they look at the code.

Using Expanded Tables Mode

Expanded Tables mode is a feature that allows you to change to a table view with expanded table borders and temporary cell padding and cell spacing. This mode makes it easier to actually see how many rows and columns you have in your table. Often, especially after splitting empty cells, it is difficult to place the insertion point precisely in a table cell. Expanded Tables mode allows you to see each cell clearly. However, most of the time, you will want to work in Standard mode to maintain the WYSIWYG environment. **WYSIWYG** is the acronym for What You See Is What You Get, and means that your page should look the same in the browser as it does in the web editor.

Setting Table Accessibility Preferences

You can make a table more accessible to visually impaired users by adding a table caption and a table header that screen readers can read. A **table caption** appears at the top of a table and describes the table contents. **Table headers** are another way to provide information about table content. Table headers can be placed at the top of columns. They are automatically centered and bold and are used by screen readers to help users identify the table content. Table captions and headers are created with the Table dialog box.

Formatting Tables with HTML5 and CSS3

Many of the HTML codes used to format tables in HTML4 are now considered to be **deprecated**, or no longer within the current standard and in danger of becoming obsolete. As you design web pages, it is best to avoid using deprecated tags because eventually they will cause problems when they are no longer supported by newer browsers. Deprecated HTML4 table tags include summary, cellpadding, cellspacing, align, width, and bgcolor. Rather than format tables using the Table dialog box or the Property inspector, use CSS to create rules that modify table properties and content. You can either add properties to the <table> tag itself or create new class rules that you can then assign to specific tables. Use the HTML5 tags <th> and <caption>. The table header <th> tag is a type of cell that contains header information, such as column headings, that identify the content of the data cells below them. The <caption> tag is the caption, or title, of a table and describes the table content. These tags provide greater accessibility, because they are used by screen readers. They also add value as semantic markup because they help to label and describe table content.

Create a table

1. Click to place the insertion point to the right of the cafe photo.
2. Click **Table** in the Common category on the Insert panel.
   The Table dialog box opens.
3. Type **5** in the Rows text box, type **3** in the Columns text box, delete any value previously left in the Table width, Border thickness, Cell padding, or Cell spacing text boxes, then click the **Top** Header.

   TIP It is better to add more rows than you think you need when you create your table. After they are filled with content, it is easier to delete rows than to add rows if you decide later to split or merge cells in the table.

4. In the Caption text box, type **The Sand Crab Cafe Hours**, compare your screen to Figure 22, then click **OK**.

   The table appears very small because the width for the table has not yet been set. You will define a new table CSS rule to use to format the table.

5. Click the **Insert panel list arrow**, click **Layout**, click the **Expanded Tables mode button** [Expanded], click **OK** in the Getting Started in Expanded Tables Mode dialog box if necessary, then compare your screen to Figure 23.

(continued)

Figure 22 *Table dialog box*

- Rows text box
- Columns text box
- Verify that these text boxes are empty
- Top Header
- Caption text box

Figure 23 *Expanded Tables mode*

- Standard mode button
- Expanded Tables mode button
- Expanded Tables mode displays more space between cells for easier editing
- Click "exit" to return to Standard mode

Figure 24 *Property inspector showing properties of selected table*

Selected table

DESIGN TIP

Setting Table Widths

If you have a large table of complex data, it is wise to set the width of the table in pixels. This ensures that the table will remain one size and not resize itself proportionately if the browser window size is changed. This will also keep the print the same size so the data will always be large enough to be readable. For example, if the width of a table is set to slightly less than 800, the table will stretch across the whole width of a browser window set at a resolution of 800 x 600. The same table would be the same size on a screen set at 1024 x 768 and therefore would not stretch across the entire screen. Be aware, however, that if you set the width of your table to 800 pixels, your table will be too wide to print the entire width of the page, and part of the right side of the page will be cut off. If you are designing a table layout for a page that you expect viewers to print, you should make your table narrower to fit on a printed page. If you set a table width as a percentage, however, the table would resize itself proportionately in any browser window, regardless of the resolution.

The Expanded Tables mode makes it easier to see individual cells and select and edit tables.

6. Click the **Standard mode button** Standard to return to Standard mode.

TIP You can also return to Standard mode by clicking [exit] in the blue bar below the Document toolbar.

You created a table on the cafe page that will display the cafe hours with five rows and three columns. You used a top header and added a table caption that will be read by screen readers.

Set table properties

1. Click the **New CSS Rule button** in the CSS Styles panel, choose **Tag (redefines an HTML element)** in the Class text box, type **table** in the Selector Name text box, if necessary, then save the rule in the su_styles.css style sheet.

   This rule will format the only table in the website.

2. Click the **Box Category**, type **600** in the Width text box, verify that **px** is the unit of measure, change the Float to **left**, then click **OK**.

   The <table> rule modified the table by setting the width and alignment on the page, as shown in Figure 24.

You modified the table rule by adding table width and float properties.

Lesson 4 Create a Table

LESSON 5

Resize, Split, AND MERGE CELLS

What You'll Do

In this lesson, you will set the width of the table cells to be split across the table in predetermined widths. You will then split one cell. You will also merge some cells to provide space for the table header.

To create HTML5-compliant table coding, you should resize tables, rows, and cells using Cascading Style Sheets. If you only have one table in your site, you can modify the <table> tag by assigning properties and values to set the table width. If you have multiple tables, you can create a new class rule for each table and format each individually using class rule properties. This will allow you to use multiple tables with differing widths. When you first create a table, the columns are created with equal widths. To widen a column and meet HTML5 standards, use the column group tag <colgroup> to set properties for an entire column or the column tag <col> to set properties for an individual cell.

Sometimes you want to adjust the cells in a table by splitting or merging them. To **split** a cell means to divide it into multiple rows or columns. To **merge** cells means to combine multiple cells into one cell. Using split and merged cells gives you more flexibility and control in placing page elements in a table and can help you create a more visually exciting layout. When you merge cells, the HTML tag used to describe the merged cell changes from a width size tag to a

Adding or Deleting a Row

As you add new content to your table, you might find that you have too many or too few rows or columns. You can add or delete one row or column at a time or several at once. You use commands on the Modify menu to add and delete table rows and columns. When you add a new column or row, you must first select the existing column or row to which the new column or row will be adjacent. The Insert Rows or Columns dialog box lets you choose how many rows or columns you want to insert or delete, and where you want them placed in relation to the selected row or column. The new column or row will have the same formatting and number of cells as the selected column or row. After you have split and merged cells, it can be challenging to add or delete rows. You can also use the shortcut menu or keyboard shortcuts to add or delete rows.

column span or row span tag. For example, <td colspan="2"> is the code for two cells that have been merged into one cell that spans two columns.

QUICK TIP
You can split merged cells and merge split cells.

Understanding Table Tags

When formatting a table, it is important to understand the basic HTML table tags. The tags for creating a table are <table> </table>. The tags to create table rows are <tr></tr>. The tags used to create table data cells are <td></td>. The tags used to create table header cells are <th> </th>. Dreamweaver places the < > code into each empty table cell at the time you create it. The < > code represents a nonbreaking space, or a space that a browser will display on the page. Some browsers collapse an empty cell, which can ruin the look of a table. The nonbreaking space holds the cell until you place content in it, when at that time it is automatically removed.

DESIGN TIP

Using Nested Tables
A nested table is a table inside a table. To create a nested table, you place the insertion point in the cell where you want to insert the nested table, then click the Table button on the Insert panel. A nested table is a separate table that can be formatted differently from the table in which it is placed. Nested tables are useful when you want part of your table data to have visible borders and part to have invisible borders. For example, you can nest a table with red borders inside a table with invisible borders. You need to plan carefully when you insert nested tables. It is easy to get carried away and insert too many nested tables, which makes it more difficult to apply formatting and rearrange table elements. Before you insert a nested table, consider whether you could achieve the same result by adding rows and columns or by splitting cells.

Split cells

1. Click inside the first cell in the last row, then click **<td>** in the tag selector.

TIP You can click the cell tag <td> (the HTML tag for that cell) on the tag selector to select the corresponding cell in the table. You can also just place the insertion point inside the cell before you begin Step 2.

2. Click the **Splits cell into rows or columns button** in the Property inspector.

3. Click the **Split cell into Rows option button** (if necessary), type **2** in the Number of rows text box (if necessary), as shown in Figure 25, click **OK**, then click in the cell to deselect it.

   The cell is split, as shown in Figure 26.

TIP To create a new row at the end of a table, place the insertion point in the last cell, then press [Tab].

You split a cell into two rows.

Figure 25 *Splitting a cell into two rows*

Splits cell into rows or columns button   *Selected cell*   *Number of rows text box*

Figure 26 *Splitting one cell into two rows*

Two cells split from one cell

DREAMWEAVER 6-28

Positioning Objects with CSS and Tables

Figure 27 *Merging selected cells into one cell*

Merges selected cells using spans button

Resulting merged cell

Figure 28 *Code for merged cells*

colspan tag

Nonbreaking spaces

Merge cells

1. Click to set the insertion point in the first cell in the top row, then drag to the right to select the three cells in the top row.

2. Click the **Merges selected cells using spans button** in the Property inspector.

   The three cells are merged into one cell, as shown in Figure 27. This merged cell will act as a table header. Descriptive text in this cell will spread across the table width.

   TIP You can only merge cells that are adjacent to each other.

3. Click the **Show Code view button** Code, then view the code for the merged cells, as shown in Figure 28.

   Notice the table tags denoting the column span (th colspan="3") and the nonbreaking spaces ( ) inserted in the empty cells.

4. Click the **Show Design view button** Design, select and merge the first cells in rows 2, 3, 4, and 5 in the left column, then save your work.

You merged three cells in the first row to make room for the table header. You then merged four cells in the left column to make room for an image.

Lesson 5 Resize, Split, and Merge Cells

DREAMWEAVER 6-29

LESSON 6

Insert and Align
IMAGES IN TABLE CELLS

What You'll Do

In this lesson, you will insert an image of a chocolate cake in the left column of the table. After placing the image, you will align it within the cell.

Inserting Images in Table Cells

You can insert images in the cells of a table using the Image command in the Images menu on the Insert panel. If you already have images saved in your website that you would like to insert in a table, you can drag them from the Assets panel into the table cells. When you add a large image to a cell, the cell expands to accommodate the inserted image. If you select the Show attributes when inserting Images check box in the Accessibility category of the Preferences dialog box, the Image Tag Accessibility Attributes dialog box opens after you insert an Image, prompting you to enter alternate text. Figure 29 shows the USHorse.biz website, which uses several tables for page layout and contains images in its table cells. Notice that some images appear in cells by themselves, and some appear in cells containing text or other graphics. Some cells have a light background, and some have a darker background.

Aligning Images in Table Cells

You can align images both horizontally and vertically within a cell. With HTML5, it's best to align an image by creating a rule with alignment settings, then apply the rule to the image content. For example, if you have inserted an image in a table cell, you can create a Class rule in your style sheet called something like img_table_cell, then assign a center-align property to the rule.

After saving the rule, select the image, then apply the img_table_cell rule to it. It will then center-align itself within the table cell.

Another way to align content in table cells that is HTML5 compliant is to add a style to the individual cell tag that sets the cell alignment. For example, add the code "style=text-align:center" to the cell tag for the cell you want to modify to center the cell's contents.

Figure 29 *USHorse.biz website*
USHorse.biz website used with permission from USHorse.biz – www.ushorse.biz.com

Insert images in table cells

1. Click in the merged cells in the left column of the table (under the merged cell in the top row) to place the insertion point.
2. Insert **chocolate_cake.jpg** from the drive and folder where you store your Data Files, then type **Chocolate Grand Marnier Cake** for the alternate text.

   TIP You may see some extra space around the image, but this will be corrected later.

3. Compare your screen to Figure 30.
4. Refresh the Files panel and verify that the new image was copied to The Striped Umbrella website assets folder.
5. Save your work, then preview the page in your browser.
6. Close your browser.

You inserted an image into a table cell on the cafe page.

Figure 30 *Image inserted into table cell*

chocolate_cake.jpg

Using Rulers, Grids, and Guides for Positioning Page Content

To help you position your page content, the View menu offers grids and guides. **Grids** provide a graph paper-like view of a page. Horizontal and vertical lines fill the page when this option is turned on. You can edit the line colors, the distance between them, whether they are composed of lines or dots, and whether or not objects "snap" to them. **Guides** are horizontal or vertical lines that you drag onto the page from the rulers. You can edit both the colors of the guides and the color of the distance, a feature that shows you the distance between two guides. You can lock the guides so you don't accidentally move them and you can set them either to snap to page elements or have page elements snap to them. To display grids or guides, click View on the Menu bar, point to Grid, then click Show Grid or point to Guides and then click Show Guides.

DREAMWEAVER 6-32

Positioning Objects with CSS and Tables

Figure 31 *Aligning image in cell by editing a <td> rule*

```
47    <table>
48      <caption>
49        The Sand Crab Cafe Hours
50      </caption>
51      <tr>
52        <th colspan="3" scope="col"> </th>
53      </tr>
54      <tr>
55        <td rowspan="4" style="text-align:center"><img src="assets/chocolate_cake.jpg" width="110" height="84"
    alt="Chocolate Grand Marnier Cake"></td>
56        <td> </td>
57        <td> </td>
58      </tr>
59      <tr>
60        <td> </td>
61        <td> </td>
62      </tr>
63      <tr>
```

Code to assign an align style

Align graphics in table cells

1. Click to the right side of the **chocolate_cake image** in the same cell to place the insertion point.

2. Switch to Code view, then place the insertion point right after the tag "<td rowspan="4"".

   You'll add a style to this table cell tag to center-align its contents.

3. Press the **Spacebar** to enter a space, then type **style="text-align:center"** as shown in Figure 31.

   TIP Notice how the Code Hints feature offers suggestions as you type code in Code view. If the suggestion matches your needs, press [Tab] to accept it.

4. Return to Design view, then save your work.

5. Preview the page in your browser, view the aligned image, then close your browser.

   Don't be concerned if your cell width has increased. This will be corrected as content is added to the other cells.

You center-aligned cell content by editing the cell <td> rule.

Working with Div Tags

Div tags are used to format blocks of content, similar to the way <p> tags are used to format paragraphs of text. However, div tags are more flexible because they can act as containers for any type of block content. They are convenient for centering content on a page or applying color to an area of a web page. Div tags combine easily with Cascading Style Sheets for formatting and positioning. When you align a page element Dreamweaver automatically adds a div tag. Div tags are frequently used in style sheets to specify formatting attributes.

Lesson 6   Insert and Align Images in Table Cells

DREAMWEAVER 6-33

LESSON 7

Insert Text and Format
CELL CONTENT

What You'll Do

In this lesson, you will type the cafe hours in the table. You will also format the text to enhance its appearance on the page. Last, you will add formatting to some of the cells and cell content.

Inserting Text in a Table

You can enter text in a table either by typing it in a cell, copying it from another source and pasting it into a cell, or importing it from another program. Once you place text in a table cell, you can format it to make it more readable and more visually appealing on the page.

Formatting Cell Content

To format the contents of a cell, select the cell contents, then apply formatting to it. For example, you can select an image in a cell and add properties such as a font, font size, or background color by using a class rule. Or, you can select text in a cell and use the Blockquote or Remove Blockquote buttons in the HTML Property inspector to move the text farther away from or closer to the cell walls.

If a cell contains multiple objects of the same type, such as text, you can format each item individually by applying different CSS rules to each one.

Formatting Cells

Formatting a cell is different from formatting a cell's contents. Formatting a cell can include setting properties that visually enhance the cell's appearance, such as setting a cell width and assigning a background color. To format a cell with code that is HTML5 compliant, use tags to define a column group style <colgroup>, which will format all cells in a particular column. You can also use the column tag <col> to apply formatting styles to singular cells. Once you have created your styles, you add them to the code for the appropriate columns or cells you wish to format.

QUICK TIP
Although you can set some table and cell properties using the Property inspector, strive to use CSS Styles for all formatting tasks.

Figure 32 *Typing text into cells*

Text typed into cells

Importing and Exporting Data from Tables

You can import and export tabular data into and out of Dreamweaver. Tabular data is data that is arranged in columns and rows and separated by a **delimiter**: a comma, tab, colon, semicolon, or similar character. **Importing** means to bring data created in another software program into Dreamweaver, and **exporting** means to save data created in Dreamweaver in a special file format that can be opened by other programs. Files that are imported into Dreamweaver must be saved as delimited files. **Delimited files** are database, word processing, or spreadsheet files that have been saved as text files with delimiters such as tabs or commas separating the data. Programs such as Microsoft Access and Microsoft Excel offer many file formats for saving files. To import a delimited file, click File on the Menu bar, point to Import, then click Tabular Data. The Import Tabular Data dialog box opens, offering you formatting options for the imported table. To export a table that you created in Dreamweaver, click File on the Menu bar, point to Export, then click Table. The Export Table dialog box opens, letting you choose the type of delimiter you want for the delimited file.

Insert text

1. Click in the cell below the chocolate cake photo, type **Chocolate**, press **[Shift][Enter]** (Win) or **[shift][return]** (Mac), type **Grand Marnier**, press **[Shift][Enter]** (Win) or **[shift][return]** (Mac), then type **Cake**.

   TIP If you can't see the last lines you typed, toggle Live view, or resize your screen to refresh it.

2. Click in the top row of the table to place the insertion point, then type **Our individual dining area hours are listed below**.

   The text is automatically bolded because you selected the top row header when you created the table. A table's header row is bold by default.

3. Merge the two bottom-right cells in the last row, then enter the cafe dining area names, hours, and room service information as shown in Figure 32. Use a line break after the first line of text in the last cell.

   The type in the table has inherited the Font-family property from the body tag properties.

You entered text in the table to provide information about the dining room hours.

Lesson 7 Insert Text and Format Cell Content

DREAMWEAVER 6-35

Format cell content

1. Click the **New CSS Rule button** to create a new class style called **feature_item** in the su_styles.css style sheet file.

   The CSS Rule Definition for .feature_item in su_styles.css dialog box opens.

2. In the Type category, leave the Font-family text box blank, set the Font-size to **12**, the Font-weight to **bold**, the Color to **#003**, then click **OK** to close the dialog box.

   You'll use this rule to format the name of the featured dessert.

3. Either click in the text or select **Chocolate Grand Marnier Cake** under the cake image, click the **CSS button** on the Property inspector, then apply the **feature_item rule** to the text.

   Your screen should resemble Figure 33. Because the only property values you set for the feature_item rule were for the font size, font weight, and color, the font family value was inherited from the parent body tag and is the same as the rest of the text on the page.

You created a new rule in the su_styles.css style sheet and used it to format text in a table cell.

Figure 33 *Formatting text using a Class rule*

feature_item rule applied

The rest of the text on the page has inherited the font properties from the body tab

POWER USER SHORTCUTS	
To do this:	**Use this shortcut:**
Insert table	[Ctrl][Alt][T] (Win) or ⌘[option][T] (Mac)
Select a cell	[Ctrl][A] (Win) or ⌘[A] (Mac)
Merge cells	[Ctrl][Alt][M] (Win) or ⌘[option][M] (Mac)
Split cell	[Ctrl][Alt][S] (Win) or ⌘[option][S] (Mac)
Insert row	[Ctrl][M] (Win) or ⌘[M] (Mac)
Insert column	[Ctrl][Shift][A] (Win) or ⌘[Shift][A] (Mac)
Delete row	[Ctrl][Shift][M] (Win) or ⌘[Shift][M] (Mac)
Delete column	[Ctrl][Shift][-] (Win) or ⌘[Shift][-] (Mac)
Increase column span	[Ctrl][Shift][]] (Win) or ⌘[Shift][]] (Mac)
Decrease column span	[Ctrl][Shift][[] (Win) or ⌘[Shift][[] (Mac)

© Cengage Learning 2013

Figure 34 *Adding a property to a <td> tag*

Cake text is centered in cell

Figure 35 *Adding style code to a <td> tag*

```
62          </tr>
63          <tr>
64              <td>The Cabana</td>
65              <td>10:00 a.m. - 7:00 p.m.</td>
66          </tr>
67          <tr>
68              <td colspan="2" rowspan="2" style="text-align:center">Room service is available from 6:00 a.m. - 12:00 a.m.<br>
69                  Please call extension 54 to place an order.</td>
70          </tr>
71          <tr>
72              <td class="feature_item">Chocolate<br>
73                  Grand Marnier<br>
74                  Cake</td>
```

Cake text is centered in cell

Format cells

1. Click to place the insertion point in the cell with the cake text.

   Notice that the feature_item rule is applied to the text. You will modify the feature_item rule to add an alignment value.

2. Click the **feature_item** rule in the CSS Styles panel, then click the **Edit Rule button**.

3. Click the **Block Category**, click the **Text-align list** arrow, click **center**, then click **OK**.

   The cake text is now centered in the cell, as shown in Figure 34.

4. Place the insertion point in the cell with the cake image, then switch to Code view.

   Next you will align the contents of the cell describing room service. Since there is not a separate rule applied to this text, you modify the cell tag code to align the cell contents.

5. Copy the code **style="text-align:center"**, then paste it in the line of code for the cell with the room service text, as shown in Figure 35.

(continued)

Lesson 7 Insert Text and Format Cell Content

6. Return to Design view, compare your screen to Figure 36, then save your work.

   The room service text is centered in the cell.

You formatted table cells by applying a rule and modifying a cell tag's code.

Figure 36 *Editing a rule*

Room service text is centered in cell

Figure 37 *Placing horizontal rules in the table*

Horizontal rules added

Modify cell content

1. Click after the word "cake" in the bottom left cell, then press **[Tab]**.

   Pressing the Tab key while the insertion point is in the last cell of the table creates a new row. Even though it looks like the cell with the room service information is the last cell, it is not because of the merged cells.

2. Merge the cells in the new row, click in the merged cells, click **Insert** on the Menu bar, point to **HTML**, then click **Horizontal Rule**.

3. Click in front of the table header, insert another horizontal rule, then save your work.

4. Switch to Live view, compare your table to Figure 37, then turn off Live view.

You added two horizontal rules to the table to set the table off from the rest of the page.

Using Inherited Properties to Format Cell Content

If a table is inside a CSS layout, you can simply let the properties from the existing CSS rules format the content, rather than applying additional rules. This is called **inheritance**. When a tag is placed, or **nested**, inside another tag (the parent tag), the properties from the parent tag are inherited by any tags nested within that tag. For example, if you set the Font-family property in the body tag, all content on the page inherits and displays that same font family unless you specify otherwise.

Lesson 7 Insert Text and Format Cell Content

Check layout

1. Click the **Visual Aids button** on the Document toolbar, then click **Hide All Visual Aids**.

    As shown in Figure 38, the borders around the table cells, and CSS blocks are all hidden, allowing you to see more clearly how the table will look in the browser. Visual aids are helpful while you are editing and formatting a page. However, turning them off is a quick way to see how the page will appear in the browser without having to open it in the browser window.

2. Repeat Step 1 to show the visual aids again.

    TIP You can also click the Live View button on the Document toolbar to see how the page will look in the browser. Turn Live View off by clicking it again.

3. Save your work, preview the cafe page in the browser, then close the browser.

4. Edit the body rule in the su_styles.css file to change the background color to **#FFFFFF**.

    Now all of the pages in the site will have the same background color.

5. Save your work.

You used the Hide All Visual Aids command to hide the table borders and layout block outlines, then showed them again.

Figure 38 *Hiding visual aids*

Live View button   *Visual aids button*

Dotted lines showing div tag borders are hidden

DREAMWEAVER 6-40

Positioning Objects with CSS and Tables

Figure 39 *Validating HTML5 markup*

Search	Reference	Validation	Browser Compatibility	Link Checker	Site Reports	FTP Log	Server Debug
	File/URL		Line	Description			
	😕 cafe.html			No errors or warnings found. [HTML5]			

Current document validation complete [0 Errors, 0 Warnings, 0 Hidden]

W3C validation button

Validate HTML5 markup

1. Click **Window** on the Menu bar, point to **Results**, then click **Validation**.
2. Click the **W3C Validation button**, then click **Validate Current Document (W3C)**.
3. Click **OK** to close the W3C Validator Notification dialog box.

    The Results panel shows no errors or warnings found, as shown in Figure 39.

    TIP You can also click the W3C Validation button in the Document toolbar to validate your document.

4. Click the **panel options button**, then click **Close Tab Group**.

    The Results panel closes.

    TIP If you see any errors or warnings listed, refer to the line number that corresponds to each error, then check your code to locate and correct the error.

NEW Validating Your Pages Against HTML5 Standards

One of the tests you should run on your web pages is to validate your page code against current HTML5 standards. Dreamweaver provides a quick way to test each page with the Validation panel in the Results panel group. When you click the Validate Current Document (W3C) button, Dreamweaver connects to the W3C server, submits the page code, and records the results in the Validation panel. If you want to test your pages against other versions of HTML, click Validate Current Document (W3C), click Settings, then choose the additional version or versions of HTML you would like to use for validation. The live validation service is new in Dreamweaver 5.5. Previously, the code was validated using internal documentation.

Lesson 7 Insert Text and Format Cell Content

SKILLS REVIEW

Create a page using CSS layouts.
1. Open the Blooms & Bulbs website, then create a new blank HTML5 page with the 2 column fixed, right sidebar, header and footer style, and link the blooms_styles.css file to the page. Save the HTML5_twoColFixRtHdr.css file in the blooms site root folder.
2. Save the file as **workshops.html**, overwriting the existing workshops page.

Add content to CSS layout blocks.
1. Open the index page, then copy the banner and menu bar. (*Hint*: Select the banner, hold down the Shift key, then click right under the menu bar to select the menu bar and the banner together.)
2. Close the index page, then on the workshops page, delete the logo placeholder in the header, then paste the banner and menu bar in the header block. (*Hint*: If you have trouble copying and pasting the banner and menu bar together, try copying and pasting them separately.) Enter a paragraph break after the menu bar.
3. Delete the footer placeholder text, then type **Copyright 2001 - 2015 Blooms & Bulbs** in the footer block.
4. Delete the placeholder content from the content block.
5. Type **New Composting Workshop!**, enter a paragraph break, import the text composting.doc from the drive and folder where you store you Data Files, then use the Commands > Clean up Word HTML command.
6. Enter a paragraph break after the inserted text, then insert the chives.jpg from the drive and folder where you store your Data Files. Add the alternate text **Even chives can be beautiful** to the image when prompted.
7. Save your work.

Edit and format CSS layout blocks.
1. Select the footer rule in the CSS Styles panel, then edit its Text-align property in the Block category to center the content.
2. Select the heading "New Composting Workshop!" and format it using the Heading 1 tag if necessary.
3. Select the header rule in the CSS Styles panel and change its background color to **#FFF**.
4. Repeat Step 3 to change the background color of the sidebar1 rule to **#FFF** and the footer rule to **#AFA19E**.
5. Edit the header rule so that the header has a 5-pixel margin on all sides.
6. Edit the body rule to change the Font-size to 14 pixels.
7. Edit the sidebar1 rule Float to left.
8. Use the Blockquote button to indent the chives image.
9. Save your work.

Create a table.
1. Delete the placeholder text in the sidebar, then insert a table with the following settings: Rows: **8**, Columns: **2**, and Header: **Top**.
2. Edit the sidebar1 rule to center-align the contents.
3. Add the page title **Blooms & Bulbs workshops** then save your work.
4. Create a new rule to modify the table tag in the blooms_styles.css file and set the table box width to 175 pixels.

Resize, split, and merge cells.
1. Merge the two cells in the first row.
2. Merge the two cells in the last row.
3. Save your work.

Insert and align images in table cells.
1. Use the Insert panel to insert gardening_gloves.gif in the last row of the table. You can find this image in the assets folder where you store your Data Files. Add the alternate text **Gardening gloves** to the image when prompted.
2. Save your work.

Insert text and format cell content.
1. Type **Currently Scheduled Workshops** in the merged cell in the first row, using a line break after the word "Scheduled".
2. Type the names and dates for the workshops from Figure 40 in each row of the table.
3. Edit the table rule to center-align the contents.
4. Save your work, preview the page in your browser, then close your browser.
5. Validate the workshops page for HTML5 compliance, correct any errors or warnings found, then save and close all open pages.

SKILLS REVIEW
(CONTINUED)

Figure 40 *Completed Skills Review*

PROJECT BUILDER 1

In this exercise, you continue your work on the TripSmart website that you began in Project Builder 1 in Chapter 1 and developed in the previous chapters. You are ready to begin work on a page featuring a catalog item. You plan to use a CSS layout with a table to place the information on the page.

1. Open the TripSmart website.
2. Create a new page based on the HTML5: 3 column fixed, header and footer CSS page layout, attach the tripsmart_styles.css file, save the new HTML5_thrColFixHdr.css file in the site root folder, then save the file as **catalog.html**, replacing the placeholder catalog page in the website.
3. Open the index page, delete the horizontal rule, copy the banner and menu bar, then switch to the catalog page.
4. Delete the logo image placeholder in the header, paste the banner and menu bar in the header block, then add a paragraph break.
5. Replace the placeholder text in the footer with the website copyright statement from the index page, then edit the footer rule in the HTML5_thrColFixHdr.css style sheet to center align the content, and set the background color to #FFF.
6. Edit the header rule so its background is #FFF and all margins to 5 px.
7. Edit the body style in the HTML5_thrColFixHdr.css style sheet to change the Font-family to Arial, Helvetica, sans-serif, the Font-size to 14 pixels, and the background color to white.
8. Save your work.
9. Delete the placeholder content in the center body section, then type **This Week's Featured Catalog Item**. Enter a paragraph break, then import the Word document, walking sticks.doc and use the Clean Up Word HTML command after importing it.
10. Delete the placeholder text in the first column including the links, and type **These are the lengths available for order:**
11. Delete the placeholder text in the third column then type **Special Shipping Offer**, enter a paragraph break, type **Order two or more walking sticks this week and your shipping is free. Enter the code twosticks when you check out to receive free shipping**, then apply the Heading 2 Paragraph format to the Special Shipping Offer text.
12. Create a new Tag rule in the tripsmart_styles.css style sheet that modifies the Heading 2 tag as follows: Font-family: Arial, Helvetica, sans-serif; Font-size: 16 pixels; Type Color: #54572C.
13. Create a new Class rule called **centered_text** in the tripsmart.css style sheet and set the Text-align property to center. Select the Special Shipping Offer text and apply the centered_text rule.
14. Enter a paragraph break after the heading in the second column, then insert the image walking_stick.jpg from the drive and folder where you store you Chapter 6 data files. Add appropriate alternate text.
15. Use settings of your choice to create a new class rule named catalog_images in the tripsmart_styles.css file that will add a border around the image, set the float to left, and add a margin to all sides. Apply your new rule to the walking stick image.
16. Edit the sidebar1 rule and the aside rule to set the background colors to #FFF.
17. Edit the footer rule to add a top border.
18. Edit the container rule to add a border around all sides.
19. Edit the content rule to change the width to 580 pixels, 10-pixel padding for all sides, and the file tripsmart_gradient.jpg from the drive and folder where you store your Chapter 6 data files for a background image.
20. Insert a table under the text "These are the lengths available for order" with the following settings: Rows: **8**, Columns: **2**, Header: **Top**.
21. Type the text for the table using the information in the table in Figure 41.
22. Create a rule in the tripsmart_styles.css file to modify the table tag as follows: Box Width: 175 px; Border solid, Border Width: thin; Border Color: #BABD9F, Text-align: center.
23. Add the page title **TripSmart - Serving all your travel needs**.
24. Add the heading **Walking sticks** above the walking stick paragraph, apply the Heading 2 format, then adjust your spacing if necessary.
25. Save your work, validate the page code for HTML5, then correct any warnings or errors that you find.
26. Open the services page and copy the line of code that inserts the favicon on the page (the code right above the title tag in the head content), then paste it in the code on the catalog page right above the code for the title.
27. Save your work, preview the page in the browser and compare your screen to Figure 41, close the browser, then close all open pages.

PROJECT BUILDER 1
(CONTINUED)

Figure 41 *Sample Project Builder 1*

PROJECT BUILDER 2

Use Figure 42 as a guide to continue your work on the Carolyne's Creations website that you started in Chapter 1 and developed in the previous chapters. You are now ready to begin work on a page showcasing the company's catering services. You decide to use an HTML5 layout and add a small table.

1. Open the Carolyne's Creations website, then create a new page based on the HTML5: 2 column fixed, right sidebar, header and footer layout, attach the cc_styles.css file, and save the page as **catering.html**, overwriting the existing page.
2. Copy the banner that includes the menu bar from one of the other pages, then paste it on the page, replacing the logo placeholder.
3. Delete the placeholder text in both the sidebar and content sections, then type **Special Treats for Valentine's Day** in the content block. You can import the text for the paragraph that follows using the marshmallows.doc file in your Chapter 6 Data Files folder. (Remember to clean up the Word HTML.)
4. Insert a table in the sidebar block to with the following settings: Rows: 5, Columns: 2, and Header: Top.
5. Create a new Tag rule in the cc_styles.css file to modify the table tag with the following settings: Width: 175, Text-align: center; Float: left, Font-size: 12px., then enter the data for the table using the table data in Figure 42.
6. Insert the file marshmallows.jpg from the drive and folder where you store your Chapter 6 Data Files at the end of the paragraph.
7. Assign the Heading 1 format to the page heading "Special Treats for Valentine's Day" if necessary.
8. Assign the Heading 2 tag to the text above the table "Marshmallow Options".
9. Edit the header rule to add a solid, 5 pixel border for each side and a background color of #333333.
10. Replace the footer content with a copyright statement, then edit the footer rule to set the text alignment to center.
11. Add the page title **Carolyne's Creations Catering Services**.
12. Create a new rule in the cc_styles.css style sheet named **centered_text** and use it to center the text "Marshmallow Options" above the table.
13. Edit the header rule Block text-align property to center the banner.
14. Save your work then use the Validation panel to test your page for HTML5 compliance. Correct any errors or warnings that are listed.
15. Make any adjustments of your choice to the layout to improve the page appearance.
16. Add the phrase **Call 24 hours in advance to ensure the availability of your choice**. under the Marshmallow Options table, then apply a rule to format the text.
17. Save your work, preview the page in your browser, then close all open files.

PROJECT BUILDER 2
(CONTINUED)

Figure 42 *Sample Project Builder 2*

Special Treats for Valentine's Day

Remember that we have lots of small items (in addition to complete party fare) that our catering staff can provide. One of our most popular items this season has been our delicious home-made marshmallows. These confectionary delights are made with our own homemade vanilla and are dusted with powdered sugar. They make wonderful gourmet s'mores, but are at their best floating on top of a cup of rich hot cocoa.

Marshmallow Options

Flavor	Price
Vanilla	$6.00 doz
Chocolate	$7.00 doz
Peppermint	$8.00 doz
Swirl	$8.00 doz

Call 24 hours in advance to ensure the availability of your choice.

Copyright 2001 - 2015

DESIGN PROJECT

Jon Bishop is opening a new restaurant and wants to launch his restaurant website two weeks before his opening. He has hired you to create the site and has asked for several design proposals. You begin by looking at some restaurant sites with pleasing designs.

1. Connect to the Internet, then go to jamesatthemill.com, as shown in Figure 43.
2. How are CSS styles used in this site?
3. How are CSS styles used to prevent an overload of information in one area of the screen?
4. View the source code for the page and locate the html tags that control the CSS layout on the page.
5. Use the Reference panel in Dreamweaver to look up the code used in this site to place the content on the page. (*Hint*: To do this, make note of a tag that you don't understand, then open the Reference panel and find that tag in the Tag list in the Reference panel. Select it from the list and read the description in the Reference panel.)
6. Do you see any tables on the page? If so, how are they used?

Figure 43 *Design Project*
James at the Mill website used with permission from Miles James — www.jamesatthemill.com

PORTFOLIO PROJECT

For this assignment, you continue to work on the portfolio project that you have been developing since Chapter 1. No Data Files are supplied. You are building this website from chapter to chapter, so you must do each Portfolio Project assignment in each chapter to complete your website.

You continue building your website by designing and completing a page that uses a CSS layout for page design.

1. Consult your wireframe to decide which page to create and develop for this chapter. Draw a sketch of the page to show how you plan to use CSS to lay out the content.
2. Create the new page for the site using one of the predesigned CSS layouts.
3. Add text, background images, and background colors to each container.
4. Create the navigation links that will allow you to add this page to your site.
5. Update the other pages of your site so that each page includes a link to this new page.
6. Add images in the containers (where appropriate), making sure to align them attractively.
7. Review the checklist in Figure 44 and make any necessary changes.
8. Save your work, preview the page in your browser, make any necessary modifications to improve the page appearance, close your browser, then close all open pages.

Figure 44 *Portfolio Project checklist*

Website Checklist
1. Do all pages have a page title?
2. Do all navigation links work correctly?
3. Did you validate your code for at least one level of HTML?
4. Did you use a CSS predefined page layout for at least one page?
5. Do your pages look the same in at least two current browsers?
6. Does all content in your CSS containers appear correctly?

ADOBE DREAMWEAVER CS6

CHAPTER 7

MANAGING A WEB
SERVER AND FILES

1. Perform website maintenance
2. Publish a website and transfer files
3. Check files out and in
4. Cloak files
5. Import and export a site definition
6. Evaluate web content for legal use
7. Present a website to a client

CHAPTER 7
MANAGING A WEB SERVER AND FILES

Once you have created all the pages of your website, finalized all the content, and performed site maintenance, you are ready to publish your site to a remote server so the rest of the world can access it. In this chapter, you start by running some reports to make sure the links in your site work properly and that any orphaned files are removed. Next, you set up a connection to the remote site for The Striped Umbrella website. You then transfer files to the remote site and learn how to keep them up to date. You also check out a file so that it is not available to other team members while you are editing it and you learn how to cloak files. When a file is **cloaked**, it is excluded from certain processes, such as being transferred to the remote site. Next, you export the site definition file from The Striped Umbrella website so that other designers can import the site. Finally, you research important copyright issues that affect all websites, and learn how to present your work to a client.

Preparing to Publish a Site

Before you publish a site, it is extremely important that you test it to make sure the content is accurate and up to date and that everything is functioning properly. When viewing pages over the Internet, users find it frustrating to click a link that doesn't work or to wait for pages that load slowly because of large graphics and animations. Remember that the typical user has a short attention span and limited patience.

Before you publish your site, be sure to use the Link Checker panel to check for broken links and orphaned files. Make sure that all image paths are correct and that all images load quickly and have alternate text. Verify that all pages have titles. View the pages in at least two different browsers and different versions of the same browser to ensure that everything works correctly. The more frequently you test, the better the chance that your users will have a positive experience at your site and want to return. Finally, before you publish your pages, verify that all content is original to the website, has been obtained legally, and is used properly without violating the copyright of someone else's work.

TOOLS YOU'LL USE

LESSON 1

Perform WEBSITE MAINTENANCE

What You'll Do

In this lesson, you will use Dreamweaver site management tools to check for broken links, orphaned files, and missing alternate text. You will also validate your markup to locate CSS3 and HTML5 errors. You will then evaluate and correct any problems that you find.

Maintaining a Website

As you add pages, links, and content to a website, it can quickly become difficult to manage. It's easier to find and correct errors as you go, rather than waiting until the end of the design phase. It's important to perform maintenance tasks frequently to make sure your website operates smoothly and remains "clean." You have already learned about some of the tools described in the following paragraphs. Although it is important to use them as you create and modify your pages, it is also important to run them at periodic intervals after publishing your website to make sure it is always error-free.

Using the Assets Panel

You should use the Assets panel to check the list of images and colors used in your website. If you see images listed that are not being used, you should move them to a storage folder outside the website until you need them. You should also make note of any non-websafe colors. This is much less of an issue today than in the past, but it doesn't hurt to evaluate any non-websafe colors you find to determine whether slight variations in the way the colors are rendered could cause contrast problems, especially with mobile devices.

Checking Links Sitewide

Before and after you publish your website, you should use the Link Checker panel to make sure all internal links are working. If the Link Checker panel displays any broken links, repair them. If the Link Checker panel displays any orphaned files, evaluate whether to delete them or link them with existing pages. To delete a file that you decide not to use, select it in the Files panel, then press [Delete] or right-click the file, click Edit, then click Delete. You should also check all external links by testing them in a browser to make sure that all links find the intended website.

Using Site Reports

You can use the Reports command in the Site menu to generate five different HTML reports that can help you maintain your website. You choose the type of report you want to run in the Reports dialog box, shown in Figure 1. You can specify whether to generate the report for the current document, the entire current local site, selected files in the site, or a selected folder. You can also generate workflow reports

DREAMWEAVER 7-4

Managing a Web Server and Files

to see files that have been checked out by others or recently modified or you can view the Design Notes attached to files.

Design Notes are separate files in a website that contain additional information about a page file or a graphic file. If several designers are working collaboratively to design a site, they can record notes to exchange information with other design team members about the status of a file. Design Notes are also a good place to store information about the source files for graphics, such as Flash or Fireworks files.

Validating Markup

Because there are now several different languages used for developing web pages, it's important to ensure that the various language versions are compatible. To address this need, Dreamweaver can validate markup. To **validate markup**, Dreamweaver submits the files to the W3C Validation Service to search through the code to look for errors that could occur with different language versions, such as XHTML or HTML5. To validate code for a page, click the W3C Validation button on the Document toolbar or use the Window > Results > Validation command to open the Validation panel. A new feature beginning with Dreamweaver CS5.5 sends the page code to the live W3C site to be validated. The Results tab group displaying the Validation panel opens and lists any pages with errors, the line numbers where the errors occur, and an explanation of the errors. You should also submit your CSS files for CSS validation to the W3C Validation Service at jigsaw.w3.org/css-validator.

Testing Pages

Finally, you should test your website using many different types and versions of browsers, platforms, and screen resolutions. You can use the Check browser compatibility button on the Document toolbar to check for issues with your site pages that might cause problems when they are viewed using certain browsers. Examples can include the rendering of square bullets, table borders, horizontal rules, or CSS AP elements. If you find such issues, you can choose to change your pages to eliminate the problems. The Results Tab group's Browser Compatibility panel includes a URL that you can visit to find the solutions to identified problems. You should test every link to make sure it connects to a valid, active website. Adobe has an application called **Adobe BrowserLab** that is a useful tool for cross-browser and cross-platform compatibility testing. Adobe BrowserLab is an online service, so you can access it from any computer with an Internet connection. Go to browserlab.adobe.com to learn more about using Adobe BrowserLab.

If, in your testing, you find any pages that download slowly, reduce their size to improve performance. Consider optimizing graphics by cropping or resizing images, reducing the number of media files, or streamlining the page code.

As part of your ongoing site testing, you should present the web pages at strategic times in the development process to your team members and to your clients for feedback and evaluation. Analyze all feedback on the website objectively, incorporating both the positive and the negative comments to help you make improvements to the site and meet the clients' expectations and goals.

Figure 1 *Reports dialog box*

— Report on list arrow
— Scope of report choices

Check for broken links

1. Open The Striped Umbrella website.
2. Show the Files panel, if necessary.
3. Click **Site** on the Menu bar, point to **Advanced**, then click **Recreate Site Cache**.

   It is a good idea to recreate the site cache to force Dreamweaver to refresh the file listing before running reports.

4. Click **Site** on the Menu bar, then click **Check Links Sitewide**.

   No broken links are listed in the Link Checker panel of the Results Tab Group, as shown in Figure 2.

You verified that there are no broken links in the website.

Check for orphaned files

1. On the Link Checker panel, click the **Show list arrow**, then click **Orphaned Files**.

   There is one orphaned file, water.jpg, as shown in Figure 3. You may decide to use this image for a background later, so you leave it in the local site folder for now.

2. Close the Results Tab Group.

You found one orphaned file in the website, but decided to leave it there for now.

Figure 2 *Link Checker panel displaying no broken links*

No broken links listed

Figure 3 *Link Checker panel displaying one orphaned file*

Summary   One orphaned file listed

Validating Accessibility Standards

There are many accessibility issues to consider to ensure that your website conforms to current accessibility standards. HTML Reports provide an easy way to check for missing alternate text, missing page titles, and improper markup. You can run HTML Reports on the current document, selected files, or the entire local site.

Figure 4 *Reports dialog box with Untitled Documents option selected*

Figure 5 *Results panel showing the spa page without a page title*

The spa page does not have a page title

Untitled Documents check box

Report on list arrow

Figure 6 *Reports dialog box with Missing Alt Text option selected*

Missing Alt Text check box

Figure 7 *Site Reports panel displaying no missing alt text*

No pages have missing alt text tags

Check for untitled documents

1. Click **Site** on the Menu bar, then click **Reports** to open the Reports dialog box.
2. Click the **Report on list arrow**, click **Entire Current Local Site**, click the **Untitled Documents check box**, as shown in Figure 4, then click **Run**.

   The Site Reports panel opens in the Results Tab Group, and shows that the spa page does not have a page title, as shown in Figure 5.
3. Open the spa page, add the page title **The Striped Umbrella Sea Spa**, save and close the page, then repeat Steps 1 and 2 to run the report again.

   All files now have page titles.

You ran a report for untitled documents, and added a page title to the page found without one.

Check for missing alternate text

1. Using Figure 6 as a guide, run another report that checks the entire current local site for missing alternate text.

   There are no images with missing alternate text, as shown in Figure 7.
2. Close the Results Tab Group, then close all open pages.

You ran a report to check for missing alternate text in the entire site.

Lesson 1 Perform Website Maintenance

DREAMWEAVER 7-7

Validate for HTML5 standards

1. Open the cafe page (the only page built using HTML5).
2. Click the **W3C Validation button** on the Document toolbar, as shown in Figure 8, click **Validate Current Document (W3C)**, then click **OK** to close the W3C Validator Notification dialog box.

   The Validation panel shows no errors or warnings for HTML5, as shown in Figure 9.
3. Close the Results Tab Group, then close the cafe page.

You validated the cafe page against HTML5 markup standards and no errors or warnings were found.

Figure 8 *Validating the cafe page for HTML5 markup*

Validate Current Document (W3C) command

W3C Validation button

Figure 9 *Validation panel with no errors or warnings found*

The café page has no errors or warnings listed

Figure 10 *Submitting a style sheet for validation*
Courtesy of w3.org

By file upload tab

Path and name of file to be validated

CSS level 3

Check button

Figure 11 *W3C validation results for su_styles.css file*
Courtesy of w3.org

Results show no errors found

Lesson 1 Perform Website Maintenance

Validate CSS

1. Open your browser and go to **jigsaw.w3.org/css-validator**.

    The CSS Validation Service provides a fast way to validate the code in your style sheets to be sure they are compliant with the most current published CSS standards.

2. Click the **By file upload tab**, click the **Browse button** next to the Local CSS file text box, navigate to your website's local site folder, double-click to select **su_styles.css**, click **More Options**, then click **CSS level 3**, as shown in Figure 10.

3. Click **Check**, then view the validation results, as shown in Figure 11.

    There are no errors listed in the su_styles.css file.

4. Close the browser and return to Dreamweaver.

You submitted the main style sheet for validation and found that it met CSS3 standards.

DREAMWEAVER 7-9

Enable Design Notes

1. Click **Site** on the Menu bar, click **Manage Sites**, verify that The Striped Umbrella site is selected, click the **Edit the currently selected site button**, click **Advanced Settings**, then click **Design Notes**.

2. Click the **Maintain Design Notes check box** to select it, if necessary, as shown in Figure 12.

   When this option is selected, designers can record notes about a page in a separate file linked to the page. For instance, a Design Note for the index.html file would be saved in a file named index.html.mno. Dreamweaver creates a folder named _notes and saves all Design Notes in that folder. This folder does not appear in the Files panel, but it is visible in the local site folder in Windows Explorer (Win) or Finder (Mac).

3. Click **File View Columns**, then click **Notes** in the Name column.

4. Click the **Edit existing Column button**, click the **Options**. **Show check box** to select it, if necessary, then click **Save**.

   The Notes row now displays the word "Show" in the Show column, as shown in Figure 13, indicating that the Notes column will be visible in the Files panel.

5. Click **Save** to close the Site Setup for The Striped Umbrella dialog box, then click **Done** in the Manage Sites dialog box.

You set the preference to use Design Notes in the website. You also set the option to display the Notes column in the Files panel.

Figure 12 *Design Notes setting in the Site Setup for The Striped Umbrella*

Figure 13 *Showing the Notes column in the Site Setup for The Striped Umbrella*

DREAMWEAVER 7-10

Managing a Web Server and Files

Figure 14 *Design Notes dialog box*

Status list arrow

Current date and note added

Show when file is opened checkbox

Insert date icon

Associate a Design Note with a file

1. Open the activities page, click **File** on the Menu bar, click **Design Notes**, then click the **Basic info tab**, if necessary.

   The Design Notes dialog box opens. You can enter a note related to the open file in the text box. You can also assign the note a status, insert today's date, and indicate if the note appears whenever the file is opened.

2. Click the **Insert date button** above the Notes text box on the right.

   The current date is added to the Notes text box.

3. Click under the date, then type **Add video demonstrating how to use an umbrella anchor.** in the Notes text box.

4. Click the **Status list arrow**, then click **needs attention**.

5. Click the **Show when file is opened** check box to select it, as shown in Figure 14, then click **OK**.

6. Click the **Refresh button** on the Files panel.

   An icon appears next to the activities page in the Notes column in the Files panel, indicating that there is a Design Note attached to the file.

You added a Design Note to the activities page with the current date and a status indicator. The note opens each time the file is opened.

Using Version Cue to Manage Assets

Another way to collaborate with team members is through Adobe Version Cue, a workgroup collaboration system that is included in Adobe Creative Suite 6. You can manage security, back up data, and use metadata to search files. **Metadata** includes information about a file such as keywords, descriptions, and copyright information. Adobe Bridge also organizes files with metadata.

Lesson 1 Perform Website Maintenance

DREAMWEAVER 7-11

Edit a Design Note

1. Click **File** on the Menu bar, then click **Design Notes** to open the Design Note associated with the activities page.

   TIP You can also right-click (Win) or [control]-click (Mac) the filename in the Files panel, shown in Figure 15, then click Design Notes to open the Design Note. You can also double-click the Note icon to open a Design Note.

2. Edit the note by adding the sentence **Ask Sam Geren to send the file**. after the existing text in the Notes section, then click **OK** to close it.

   Dreamweaver created a file named activities.html.mno in a new folder called _notes in the local site folder. This folder and file do not appear in the Files panel unless you have selected the option to show hidden files and folders. To show hidden files, click the Files Panel options button, then click View, Show hidden files. However, you can switch to Windows Explorer (Win) or Finder (Mac) to see them without selecting this option. When you select the option to Enable Upload Design Notes for sharing, you can share the notes with team members working with you on the site.

3. Right-click (Win) or [control]-click (Mac) **activities.html** in the Files panel, then click **Explore** (Win) or **Reveal in Finder** (Mac).

   (continued)

Figure 15 *Files panel with Notes icon displayed*

Notes icon for activities file

Deleting a Design Note

There are two steps to deleting a Design Note that you don't need anymore. The first step is to delete the Design Note file. To delete a Design Note, right-click the filename in the Files panel that is associated with the Design Note you want to delete, and then click Explore (Win) or Reveal in Finder (Mac) to open your file management system. Open the _notes folder, delete the .mno file in the files list, and then close Explorer (Win) or Finder (Mac). The second step is done in Dreamweaver: Click Site on the Menu bar, click Manage Sites, click Edit the currently selected site button, click Advanced Settings, then select the Design Notes category. Confirm that Maintain Design Notes is still selected, then click the Clean up Design Notes button. (*Note*: Don't do this if you deselect Maintain Design Notes first or it will delete all of your Design Notes!) The Design Notes icon will be removed from the Notes column in the Files panel.

Figure 16 *Windows Explorer displaying the _notes folder and file*

Notes file in _notes folder

Figure 17 *Code for the activities.html.mno file*

```
<?xml version="1.0" encoding="utf-8" ?>
<info>
    <infoitem key="notes" value="2/24/2012: &#xD;Add video demonstrating how to use an umbrella anchor. Ask Sam Geren to send the file." />
    <infoitem key="status" value="needs attention" />
    <infoitem key="showOnOpen" value="true" />
</info>
```

4. Double-click the **_notes** folder to open it, then double-click the file **activities.html.mno**, shown in Figure 16, to open the file in Dreamweaver.

   The notes file opens in Code view in Dreamweaver, as shown in Figure 17.

5. Read the file, close it, close Explorer (Win) or Finder (Mac), then close the activities page.

You opened the Design Notes dialog box and edited the note in the Notes text box. Next, you viewed the .mno file that Dreamweaver created when you added the Design Note.

Lesson 1 Perform Website Maintenance

LESSON 2

Publish a Website
AND TRANSFER FILES

What You'll Do

In this lesson, you will set up remote access to either an FTP folder or a local/network folder for The Striped Umbrella website. You will also view a website on a remote server, upload files to it, and synchronize the files.

Defining a Remote Site

As you learned in Chapter 1, publishing a site means transferring a copy of all the site's files to a web server. A **web server** is a computer with software that enables it to host websites and is connected to the Internet with an IP (Internet Protocol) address so that it is available on the Internet. Before you can publish a site to a web server, you must first define the remote site by specifying the Servers settings in the Site Setup dialog box as shown in Figure 18. You can specify remote settings when you first create a new site and define the local site folder (as you did in Chapter 1 when you defined the remote access settings for The Striped Umbrella website). Or you can do it after you have completed all of your pages and are confident that your site is ready for public viewing. To specify the remote settings for a site, click the Add new Server button in the Site Setup

Figure 18 *Accessing the server settings in the Site Setup dialog box*

Servers tab

Add new Server button

Managing a Web Server and Files

dialog box, then add your server name, and choose a connection setting, which specifies the type of server you will use. You can set up multiple servers with Dreamweaver. You can set up a server for testing purposes only and a server for the live website. The most common connection setting is FTP (File Transfer Protocol). If you choose FTP, you need to specify a server address and folder name on the FTP site where you want to store your remote site root folder. You can also use **Secure FTP (SFTP)**, which lets you encrypt file transfers to protect your files, user names, and passwords. To use SFTP, select SFTP on the Connect using list in the site setup dialog box. You also need to enter login and password information. Figure 19 shows an example of FTP settings in the Add new server dialog box.

QUICK TIP

If you do not have access to an FTP site, you can publish a site to a local/network folder. This is referred to as a **LAN**, or a Local Area Network. Use the alternate steps provided in this lesson to publish your site to a local/network folder.

Viewing a Remote Site

Once you have set up a remote server, you can then view the remote folder in the Files panel by choosing Remote server from the View list. If your remote site is located on an FTP server, Dreamweaver will connect to it. You will see the File Activity dialog box showing the progress of the connection. You can also use the Connect to Remote Server button on the Files panel toolbar to connect to the remote site. If you defined your site on a local/network folder, then you don't need to use the Connect Remote Server button; the local site folder and any files and folders it contains appear in the Files panel when you switch to Remote server view.

Transferring Files to and from a Remote Site

After you set up a remote site, you need to **upload**, or copy, your files from the local version of your site to the remote host. To do this, view the site in Local view, select the files you want to upload, and then click the Put File(s) button on the Files panel toolbar. The Put File(s) button includes the name of the server

Figure 19 Viewing remote server settings

User login information to access remote server

Folder on FTP site where site will be published

Server name
Connection method
FTP site location

Lesson 2 Publish a Website and Transfer Files

DREAMWEAVER 7-15

in the tooltip. Once you click this button, a copy of the files is transferred to the remote site. To view the uploaded files, switch to Remote server in the Files panel. Or, you can expand the Files panel to view both the Remote Site and the Local Site panes by clicking the Expand to show local and remote sites button in the Files panel.

If a file you select for uploading requires additional files, such as graphics, a dialog box opens after you click the Put File(s) button and asks if you want those files (known as **dependent files**) to be uploaded. By clicking Yes, all dependent files for the selected page will be uploaded to the appropriate folder in the remote site. If a file that you want to upload is located in a folder in the local site, the folder will automatically be transferred to the remote site.

QUICK TIP
To upload an entire site to a remote host, select the local site folder, then click the Put File(s) button.

If you are developing or maintaining a website in a group environment, there might be times when you want to transfer or **download** files that other team members have created from the remote site to your local site. To do this, switch to Remote Server in the Files panel, select the files you want to download, then click the Get File(s) button on the Files panel toolbar. The Get File(s) button includes the name of the server in the tooltip.

Synchronizing Files

To keep a website up to date—especially one that contains several pages and involves several team members—you need to update and replace files. Team members might make changes to pages on the local version of the site or make additions to the remote site. If many people are involved in maintaining a site, or if you are constantly making changes to the pages, ensuring that both the local and remote sites have the most up-to-date files could get confusing. Luckily, you can use the Synchronize command to keep things straight. The **Synchronize command** instructs Dreamweaver to compare the dates of the saved files in both versions of the site, then transfers only copies of files that have changed. To synchronize files, use the Synchronize Files dialog box, shown in Figure 20. You can synchronize an entire site or only selected files. You can also specify whether to upload newer files to the remote site, download newer files from the remote site, or both.

Figure 20 *Synchronize Files dialog box*

Instructs Dreamweaver to synchronize all files in the site

Understanding Dreamweaver Connection Options for Transferring Files

The connection types with which you are probably the most familiar are FTP and Local/Network. Other connection types that you can use with Dreamweaver include Microsoft Visual SafeSource (VSS), WebDav, and RDS. **VSS** is used only with the Windows operating system with Microsoft Visual SafeSource Client version 6. **WebDav** stands for Web-based Distributed Authoring and Versioning. This type of connection is used with the WebDav protocol. An example would be a website residing on an Apache web server. The **Apache web server** is a public domain, open source web server that is available using several different operating systems including UNIX and Windows. **RDS** stands for Remote Development Services, and is used with web servers using Cold Fusion.

DREAMWEAVER 7-16   Managing a Web Server and Files

Figure 21 *FTP settings specified in the Site Setup for The Striped Umbrella dialog box*

Callouts on figure:
- Servers option
- Type password here
- Web URL
- Test button
- Type address of FTP server here
- Type username here
- Type folder where website files will be stored on FTP site

Comparing Two Files for Differences in Content

There are situations where it would be helpful to be able to compare the contents of two files, such as a local file and the remote version of the same file; or an original file and the same file that has been saved with a different name. Once the two files are compared and differences are detected, you can merge the information in the files. A good time to compare files is before you upload them to a remote server to prevent accidentally writing over a file with more recent information. To compare files, you must first locate and install a third-party file comparison utility, or "dif" tool, such as Araxis Merge or Beyond Compare. (Dreamweaver does not have a file comparison tool included as part of the software, so you need to download one.) If you are not familiar with these tools, find one using your favorite search engine.

After installing the file comparison utility, use the Preferences command on the Edit menu to open the Preferences dialog box, then select the File Compare category. Next, browse to select the application you want to use to compare files. After you have set your Preferences, click the Compare with Remote Server command on the File menu to compare an open file with the remote version.

Lesson 2 Publish a Website and Transfer Files

Set up a web server connection on an FTP site

NOTE: Complete these steps only if you know you can store The Striped Umbrella files on an FTP site and you know the login and password information. If you do not have access to an FTP site, complete the exercise called Set up a web server connection to a local or network folder on Page 7-18.

1. Click **Site** on the Menu bar, then click **Manage Sites**.
2. Click **The Striped Umbrella** in the Manage Sites dialog box, if necessary, then click the **Edit currently selected site button** .
3. Click **Servers** in the Site Setup dialog box, click the **Add new Server** button , type your server name, click the **Connect using list arrow**, click **FTP** if necessary, then compare your screen to Figure 21.
4. Enter the FTP Address, Username, Password, Root Directory, and Web URL information in the dialog box.

TIP You must have file and folder permissions to use FTP. The server administrator can give you this and also tell you the folder name and location you should use to publish your files.

5. Click the **Test button** to test the connection to the remote site.
6. If the connection is successful, click **Save** to close the dialog box; if it is not successful, verify that you have the correct settings, then repeat Step 5.
7. Click **Save** to close the open dialog box, click **Save** to close the Site Setup dialog box, then click **Done** to close the Manage Sites dialog box.

You set up remote access information for The Striped Umbrella website using FTP settings.

DREAMWEAVER 7-17

Set up a web server connection to a local or network folder

NOTE: Complete these steps if you do not have the ability to post files to an FTP site and could not complete the previous set of steps.

1. Using Windows Explorer (Win) or Finder (Mac), create a new folder on your hard drive or on a shared drive named **su_yourlastname** (e.g., if your last name is Jones, name the folder **su_jones**).
2. Switch back to Dreamweaver, open The Striped Umbrella website, then open the Manage Sites dialog box.
3. Click **The Striped Umbrella**, then click the **Edit the currently selected site button** to open the Site Setup for The Striped Umbrella dialog box.

   TIP You can also double-click the site name in the Site Name box in the Files panel to open the Site Setup dialog box.

4. Click **Servers**, then click the **Add new Server button** .
5. Type **SU Remote** for the Server Name, click the **Connect using list arrow**, then click **Local/Network**.
6. Click the **Browse button** next to the Server Folder text box to open the Browse For Folder dialog box, navigate to and double-click the folder you created in Step 1, then click **Select**.
7. Compare your screen to Figure 22, click **Save**, click **Save** to close the Site Setup dialog box, click **Save** to close the dialog box, then click **Done**.

You created a new folder and specified it as the remote location for The Striped Umbrella website, then set up remote access to a local or network folder.

Figure 22 *Local/Network settings in the Site Setup for The Striped Umbrella dialog box*

Local or network drive and folder where remote site will be published (your drive may differ and the folder name should end with your last name)

Local/Network setting selected

Testing Your Site's Usability

Once you have at least a prototype of the website ready to evaluate, it is a good idea to conduct a site usability test. This is a process that involves asking unbiased people, who are not connected to the design process, to use and evaluate the site. A comprehensive usability test includes pre-test questions, participant tasks, a post-test interview, and a post-test survey. This provides much-needed information as to how usable the site is to those unfamiliar with it. Typical questions include: "What are your overall impressions?"; "What do you like the best and the least about the site?"; and "How easy is it to navigate inside the site?" For more information, go to w3.org and search for "site usability test."

Figure 23 *Connecting to the remote site*

- Connect to Remote Server button
- Remote folder name
- Remote server selected
- Expand to show local and remote sites button

Figure 24 *Viewing the local and remote site folders*

- Remote folder
- Disconnect from Remote Server button
- Local site folder
- Collapse to show only local or remote site button

View a website on a remote server

1. Click the **View list arrow** in the Files panel, click **Remote server**, then compare your screen to Figure 23.

   If you set your remote access to be a local or network folder, then the su_yourlastname folder appears in the Files panel. If your remote access is set to an FTP site, Dreamweaver connects to the host server and displays the remote folders and file.

2. Click the **Expand to show local and remote sites button** on the Files panel to view both the Remote Site and Local Files panes. The su_yourlastname folder appears in the Remote Site portion of the expanded Files panel, as shown in Figure 24.

   TIP If you don't see your remote site files, click the Disconnect from Remote Server button or the Refresh button. If you don't see two panes, one with the remote site files and one with the local files, drag the panel border to enlarge the panel.

   When the Files panel is expanded to show both the local and remote sites, the Expand to show local and remote sites button becomes the Collapse to show only local or remote site button. and the Connect to Remote Server button becomes the Disconnect from Remote Server button.

You used the Files panel to set the view for The Striped Umbrella site to Remote view. You then connected to the remote server to view the remote folder you created earlier.

Lesson 2 Publish a Website and Transfer Files

DREAMWEAVER 7-19

Upload files to a remote server

1. Click the **about_us.html file**, then click the **Put file(s) to "Remote Server" button** ⇧ on the Files panel toolbar.

   Notice that the Put File(s) to "Remote Server" button screentip includes the name of the remote server you are using. The Dependent Files dialog box opens, asking if you want to include dependent files.

2. Click **Yes**.

   The about_us file, the style sheet files, the Spry assets files, and the image files used in the about_us page are copied to the remote server. The Background File Activity dialog box appears and flashes the names of each file as they are uploaded.

3. Expand the assets folder and the SpryAssets folder in the remote site if necessary, then compare your screen to Figure 25.

   The remote site now contains the about_us page as well as the Spry files, the image files, and the external style sheet files, all of which are needed by the about_us page.

TIP You might need to expand the su_yourlastname folder in order to view the uploaded files and folders.

You used the Put File(s) button to upload the about_us file and all files that are dependent files of the about_us page.

Figure 25 *Remote view of the site after uploading the about_us page*

about us page and its dependent files in remote site

Local site files

Continuing to Work While Transferring Files to a Remote Server

During the process of uploading files to a remote server, there are many Dreamweaver functions that you can continue to use while you wait. For example, you can create a new site, create a new page, edit a page, add files and folders, and run reports. However, there are some functions that you cannot use while transferring files, many of which involve accessing files on the remote server or using Check In/Check Out.

Figure 26 *Synchronize Files dialog box*

Figure 27 *Files that need to be uploaded to the remote site*

Synchronize files

1. Click the **Collapse to show only local or remote site button**, change to Local view, then open each page in the website in Code view and locate those that are missing the link to the website favicon in the line above the code for the page title.
2. Open the index page, if necessary, then copy the code in the head content that links the favicon to the page.
3. Paste the favicon link to each of the pages you identified in Step 1, then save and close each page.
4. Click the **Synchronize button** on the Files panel toolbar to open the Synchronize with Remote Server dialog box.
5. Click the **Synchronize list arrow**, then click **Entire 'The Striped Umbrella' Site**.
6. Click the **Direction list arrow**, click **Put newer files to remote** if necessary, then compare your screen to Figure 26.
7. Click **Preview**.

    The Background File Activity dialog box might appear and flash the names of all the files from the local version of the site that need to be uploaded to the remote site. The Synchronize dialog box, shown in Figure 27, opens and lists all the files that need to be uploaded to the remote site.

8. Click **OK**.

    All the files from the local The Striped Umbrella site are copied to the remote version of the site. If you expand the Files panel, you will notice that the remote folders are yellow (Win) or blue (Mac) and the local folders are green.

You synchronized The Striped Umbrella website files to copy all remaining files from the local site folder to the remote site folder.

Lesson 2   Publish a Website and Transfer Files

DREAMWEAVER 7-21

LESSON 3

Check Files
OUT AND IN

What You'll Do

In this lesson, you will use the Site Setup dialog box to enable the Check Out feature. You will then check out the cafe page, make a change to it, and then check it back in.

Managing a Website with a Team

When you work on a large website, chances are that many people will be involved in keeping the site up to date. Different individuals will need to make changes or additions to different pages of the site by adding or deleting content, changing graphics, updating information, and so on. If everyone had access to the pages at the same time, problems could arise. For instance, what if you and another team member both made edits to the same page at the same time? If you post your edited version of the file to the site after the other team member posts his edited version of the same file, the file that you upload will overwrite his version and none of his changes will be incorporated. Fortunately, you can avoid this scenario by using Dreamweaver's collaboration tools.

Checking Out and Checking In Files

Checking files in and out is similar to checking library books in and out or video/DVD rentals. No one else can access the same copy that you have checked out. Using Dreamweaver's Check Out feature ensures that team members cannot overwrite each other's pages. When this feature is enabled, only one person can work on a file at a time. To check out a file, click the file you want to work on in the Files panel, and then click the Check Out File(s) button on the Files panel toolbar. Files that you have checked out are marked with green check marks in the Files panel. Files that have been checked in are marked with padlock icons.

After you finish editing a checked-out file, you need to save and close the file, and then click the Check In button to check the file back in and make it available to other users. When a file is checked in, you cannot make edits to it unless you check it out again. Figure 28 shows the Check Out File(s) and Check In buttons on the Files panel toolbar.

Enabling the Check Out Feature

To use the Check Out feature with a team of people, you must first enable it. To turn on this feature, check the Enable file check-out check box in the Remote Server section of the Servers Advanced tab in the Site Setup dialog box. If you do not want to use this feature, you should turn it off so you won't have to check files out every time you open them.

Using Subversion Control

Another file management tool is Subversion control. A remote SVN (Apache Subversion) repository is used to maintain current and historical versions of your website files. It is used in a team environment to move, copy, and delete shared files. You can protect files from being accessed using the svn:ignore property to create a list of files that are to be ignored in a directory.

Figure 28 *Check Out File(s) and Check In buttons on the Files Panel toolbar*

Activate the Enable file check-out feature

1. Change to expanded view in the Files panel, click **Site** on the Menu bar, click **Manage Sites** to open the Manage Sites dialog box, click **The Striped Umbrella** in the list, then click the **Edit the currently selected site button** to open the Site Setup for The Striped Umbrella dialog box.
2. Click **Servers**, select your remote server, click the **Edit existing Server button**, click the **Advanced tab**, then click the **Enable file check-out check box** to select it.
3. Check the **Check out files when opening check box** to select it, if necessary.
4. Type your name in the Check-out Name text box.
5. Type your email address in the Email Address text box.
6. Compare your screen to Figure 29, click **Save** to close the open dialog box, click **Save** to close the Site Setup for The Striped Umbrella dialog box, then click **Done** to close the Manage Sites dialog box. Your dialog box will differ from the figure if you are using FTP access.

You used the Site Definition for The Striped Umbrella dialog box to enable the Check Out feature, which tells team members when you are working with a site file.

Figure 29 *Enabling the Check Out feature*

Click to enable the Check Out feature

Type your e-mail address here

Type your name here

Figure 30 *Files panel in Local view after checking out cafe page*

Dependent files have padlock icon

Check mark indicates file is checked out

Check out a file

1. Click the **cafe page** in the Local Files list in the Files panel to select it.
2. Click the **Check Out File(s) button** on the Files panel toolbar.

   The Dependent Files dialog box appears, asking if you want to include all files that are needed for the cafe page.

3. Click **Yes**, expand the assets and SpryAssets folders if necessary in the local site files, click the **Collapse to show only local or remote site button**, click the **View list arrow**, click **Local view** if necessary, then compare your screen to Figure 30.

   The cafe file has a check mark next to it indicating you have checked it out. The dependent files have a padlock icon, indicating that they cannot be changed as long as the cafe file is checked out.

You checked out the cafe page so that no one else can use it while you work on it.

Lesson 3   Check Files Out and In

DREAMWEAVER 7-25

Check in a file

1. Open the cafe page, change the closing hour for The Cabana in the table to **8:00 p.m.**, then save your changes.
2. Close the cafe page, then click the **cafe page** in the Files panel to select it.
3. Click the **Check In button** on the Files panel toolbar.

   The Dependent Files dialog box opens, asking if you want to include dependent files.
4. Click **Yes**, click another file in the Files panel to deselect the cafe page, then compare your screen to Figure 31.

   A padlock icon appears instead of a green check mark next to the cafe page on the Files panel. The padlock icon indicated that the file is read-only now and cannot be edited unless it is checked out.

You made a content change on the cafe page, then checked in the cafe page, making it available for others to check it out.

Figure 31 *Files panel after checking in cafe page*

Dependent files are also locked

Padlock icon indicates file is read-only and cannot be edited unless it is checked out

DREAMWEAVER 7-26

Managing a Web Server and Files

Figure 32 *Files panel after turning off the read-only feature*

All files are now unlocked

Edit site preferences

1. Click **Site** on the Menu bar, click **Manage Sites** to open the Manage Sites dialog box, click **The Striped Umbrella** in the list, then click the **Edit the currently selected site button** to open the Site Setup for The Striped Umbrella dialog box.

2. Click **Servers**, select your remote server, click the **Edit existing Server button**, click the **Advanced tab**, then click the **Enable file check-out check box** to deselect it.

   Now that you understand how to use this feature, it will be easier to have this option turned off so that each time you open a page you will not have to check it out the next time you use it.

3. Click **Save** to close the open dialog box, click **Save** to close the Site Setup dialog box, then click **Done** to close the Manage Sites dialog box.

4. Right-click the **local site folder** in the Files panel, then click **Turn off Read Only** (Win) or **Unlock** (Mac).

   All files are writeable now and the padlock icons have disappeared, as shown in Figure 32.

You disabled the Enable file check-out feature and then turned off the Read-only feature for all site files.

Lesson 3 Check Files Out and In

DREAMWEAVER 7-27

LESSON 4

Cloak
FILES

What You'll Do

In this lesson, you will cloak the assets folder so that it is excluded from various operations, such as the Put, Get, Check In, and Check Out commands. You will also use the Site Setup dialog box to cloak all .gif files in the site.

Understanding Cloaking Files

There may be times when you want to exclude a particular file or files from being uploaded to a server. For instance, suppose you have a page that is not quite finished and needs more work before it is ready to be viewed by others. You can exclude such files by **cloaking** them, which marks them for exclusion from several commands, including Put, Get, Synchronize, Check In, and Check Out. Cloaked files are also excluded from site-wide operations, such as checking for links or updating a template or library item. You can cloak a folder or specify a type of file to cloak throughout the site.

QUICK TIP

By default, the cloaking feature is enabled. However, if for some reason it is not turned on, open the Site Setup dialog box, click Advanced Settings, click Cloaking, then click the Enable Cloaking check box.

Cloaking a Folder

In addition to cloaking a file or group of files, you might also want to cloak an entire folder. For example, if you are not concerned with replacing outdated image files, you might want to cloak the assets folder of a website to save time when synchronizing files. To cloak a folder, select the folder, click the Files

DREAMWEAVER 7-28

Managing a Web Server and Files

panel Options button, point to Site, point to Cloaking, and then click Cloak. The folder you cloaked and all the files it contains appear with red slashes across them, as shown in Figure 33. To uncloak a folder, click the Panel options button on the Files panel, point to Site, point to Cloaking, and then click Uncloak.

> **QUICK TIP**
>
> To uncloak all files in a site, click the Files Panel options button, point to Site, point to Cloaking, then click Uncloak All.

Cloaking Selected File Types

There may be times when you want to cloak a particular type of file, such as a .jpg file. To cloak a particular file type, open the Site Setup dialog box, click Advanced, click Cloaking, click the Cloak files ending with check box, and then type a file extension in the text box below the check box. All files throughout the site that have the specified file extension will be cloaked.

Figure 33 *Cloaked assets folder in the Files panel*

Lesson 4 Cloak Files

DREAMWEAVER 7-29

Cloak and uncloak a folder

1. Verify that Local view is displayed in the Files panel, then open the Manage Sites dialog box.
2. Click **The Striped Umbrella** if necessary, click the **Edit the currently selected site button** to open the Site Setup for The Striped Umbrella dialog box, click **Advanced Settings**, click **Cloaking**, verify that the Enable Cloaking check box is checked, click **Save**, then click **Done**.
3. Click the **assets folder** in the Files panel, click the **Files Panel options button**, point to **Site**, point to **Cloaking**, click **Cloak**, then compare your screen to Figure 34.

   A red slash now appears on top of the assets folder in the Files panel, indicating that all files in the assets folder are cloaked and will be excluded from putting, getting, checking in, checking out, and many other operations.

   TIP You can also cloak a folder by right-clicking (Win) or [control]-clicking (Mac) the folder, pointing to Cloaking, then clicking Cloak.

4. Right-click (Win) or [control]-click (Mac) the **assets folder**, point to **Cloaking**, then click **Uncloak**.

   The assets folder and all the files it contains no longer appear with red slashes across them, indicating they are no longer cloaked.

You cloaked the assets folder so that this folder and all the files it contains would be excluded from many operations, including uploading and downloading files. You then uncloaked the assets folder.

Figure 34 *Assets folder after cloaking*

Red slashes indicate folder and files in it are cloaked

Figure 35 *Specifying a file type to cloak*

Specify file type to cloak here

Figure 36 *Assets folder in Files panel after cloaking .gif files*

All .gif files are cloaked

Assets folder is not cloaked

Cloak selected file types

1. Right-click (Win) or [control]-click (Mac) the **assets folder** in the Files panel, point to **Cloaking**, then click **Settings** to open the Site Setup for The Striped Umbrella dialog box with the Cloaking category selected.

2. Click the **Cloak files ending with check box**, select the text in the text box that appears, type **.gif** in the text box, then compare your screen to Figure 35.

3. Click **Save**.

   A dialog box opens, indicating that the site cache will be recreated.

4. Click **OK**, expand the assets folder if necessary, then compare your screen to Figure 36.

   All of the .gif files in the assets folder appear with red slashes across them, indicating that they are cloaked. Notice that the assets folder is not cloaked.

5. Click the **local site folder** in the Files panel, right-click, point to **Cloaking**, click **Uncloak All**, then click **Yes** to close the warning message.

   All files are uncloaked now and will not be excluded from any site commands.

You cloaked all the .gif files in The Striped Umbrella website. You then uncloaked all files.

Lesson 4 Cloak Files

DREAMWEAVER 7-31

LESSON 5

Import and Export
A SITE DEFINITION

What You'll Do

In this lesson, you will export the site definition file for The Striped Umbrella website. You will then import The Striped Umbrella website.

Exporting a Site Definition

When you work on a website for a long time, it's likely that at some point you will want to move it to another machine or share it with other collaborators who will help you maintain it. When you move a site, you need to move its site definition. The **site definition** for a website contains important information about the site, including its URL, preferences that you've specified, and other secure information, such as login and password information. You can use the Export command to export the site definition file to another location. The Export command creates a file with an .ste file extension. To do this, open the Manage Sites dialog box, click the site you want to export, and then click Export currently selected site. Because the site definition file contains password information that you will want to keep secret from other site users, you should never save the site definition file in the website. Instead, save it in an external folder.

Importing a Site Definition

If you want to be able to access the site settings in a website that someone else has created, you can import the site definition file once you have the necessary .ste file. To do this, click Import Site in the Manage Sites dialog box to open the Import Site dialog box, navigate to the .ste file you want to import, then click Open.

Figure 37 *Saving The Striped Umbrella.ste file in the su_site_definition folder*

Export a site definition

1. Use Windows Explorer (Win) or Finder (Mac) to create two new folders on your hard drive or external drive named **su_site_definition**.

2. Switch back to Dreamweaver, open the Manage Sites dialog box, click **The Striped Umbrella**, then click the **Export the currently selected site(s) button** to open the Export Site dialog box.

TIP If you see a message asking if you are exporting the site to back up your settings or to share your settings with other users, choose the Back up my settings option, then click OK.

3. Navigate to and double-click to open the **su_site_definition folder** that you created in Step 1, as shown in Figure 37, click **Save**, then click **Done**.

You used the Export command to create the site definition file and saved it in the su_site_definition folder.

Lesson 5 Import and Export a Site Definition

DREAMWEAVER 7-33

Import a site definition

1. Open the Manage Sites dialog box, click **The Striped Umbrella**, then click **Import Site** to open the Import Site dialog box.
2. Navigate to the su_site_definition folder, compare your screen to Figure 38, select **The Striped Umbrella.ste**, then click **Open**.

   A dialog box opens and says that a site named The Striped Umbrella already exists. It will name the imported site The Striped Umbrella 2 so that it has a different name.
3. Click **OK**.
4. Click **The Striped Umbrella 2** if necessary, click the **Edit the currently selected site(s) button** , then compare your screen to Figure 39.

   The settings show that The Striped Umbrella 2 site has the same local site folder and default images folder as The Striped Umbrella site. Both of these settings are specified in The Striped Umbrella.ste file that you imported. Importing a site in this way makes it possible for multiple users with different computers to work on the same site.

   TIP Make sure you know who is responsible for which files to keep from overwriting the wrong files when they are published. The Synchronize Files and Check In/Check Out features are good procedures to use with multiple designers.
5. Click **Save**, click **OK** to close the warning message, then click **Done**.

   TIP If a dialog box opens warning that the local site folder chosen is the same as the folder for the site "The Striped Umbrella," click OK. Remember that you only import the site settings when you import a site definition. You are not importing any of the website files.

You imported The Striped Umbrella.ste file and created a new site, The Striped Umbrella 2.

Figure 38 *Import Site dialog box*

Figure 39 *Site Definition for The Striped Umbrella 2 dialog box*

Name of imported site

Figure 40 *Viewing The Striped Umbrella 2 website files*

View the imported site

1. Click the **Expand to show local and remote sites button** on the Files panel toolbar to expand the Files panel.
2. Expand the local site folder in the Local Files pane to view the contents, if necessary.
3. Click the **Refresh button** to view the files in the Remote Site pane.

   As shown in Figure 40, the site is identical to the original The Striped Umbrella site, except the name has been changed to The Striped Umbrella 2.

   TIP If you don't see your remote site files, click the Connect to Remote Server button.

4. Click the **Collapse to show only local or remote site button** to collapse the Files panel.
5. Open the Manage Sites dialog box, verify that The Striped Umbrella 2 site is selected, click the **Delete the currently selected site(s) button**, click **Yes** in the warning dialog box, then click **Done** to delete The Striped Umbrella 2 website.

   This does not delete all of the files that were created; it only removes the site from Dreamweaver's site management list.

6. Close all open pages, then close Dreamweaver.

You viewed the expanded Files panel for The Striped Umbrella 2 website, then deleted The Striped Umbrella 2 website.

POWER USER SHORTCUTS

To do this:	Use this shortcut:
Get	[Ctrl][Shift][D] (Win) or ⌘ [Shift][D] (Mac)
Check Out	[Ctrl][Alt][Shift][D] (Win) or ⌘ [opt] [Shift][D] (Mac)
Put	[Ctrl][Shift][U] (Win) or ⌘ [Shift][U] (Mac)
Check In	[Ctrl][Alt][Shift][U] (Win) or ⌘ [opt] [Shift][U] (Mac)
Check Links	[Shift][F8] (Win) or [fn][shift][F8] (Mac)
Check Links Sitewide	[Ctrl][F8] (Win) or [fn] ⌘ [F8] (Mac)

© Cengage Learning 2013

LESSON 6

Evaluate Web Content
FOR LEGAL USE

What You'll Do

Library of Congress website — www.loc.gov

▶ *In this lesson, you will examine copyright issues in the context of using content gathered from sources such as the Internet.*

Can I Use Downloaded Media?

The Internet has made it possible to locate compelling and media-rich content to use in websites. A person who has learned to craft searches can locate a multitude of interesting material, such as graphics, animations, sounds, and text. But just because you can find it easily does not mean that you can use it however you want or under any circumstance. Learning about copyright law can help you decide whether or how to use content created and published by someone other than yourself.

Understanding Intellectual Property

Intellectual property is a product resulting from human creativity. It can include inventions, movies, songs, designs, clothing, and so on.

The purpose of copyright law is to promote progress in society, not expressly to protect the rights of copyright owners. However, the vast majority of work you might want to download and use in a project is protected by either copyright or trademark law.

Copyright protects the particular and tangible *expression* of an idea, not the idea itself. If you wrote a story using the idea of aliens crashing in Roswell, New Mexico, no one could copy or use your story without permission. However, anyone could write a story using a similar plot or characters—the *idea* of aliens crashing in Roswell is not copyright-protected. Generally, copyright lasts for the life of the author plus 70 years.

Trademark protects an image, word, slogan, symbol, or design used to identify goods or services. For example, the Nike swoosh, Disney characters, or the shape of a classic Coca-Cola bottle are works protected by trademark. Trademark protection lasts for 10 years with 10-year renewal terms, lasting indefinitely provided the trademark is in active use.

What Exactly Does the Copyright Owner Own?

Copyright attaches to a work as soon as you create it; you do not have to register it with the U.S. Copyright Office. A copyright owner has a "bundle" of six rights, consisting of:

1) reproduction (including downloading)
2) creation of **derivative works** (for example, a movie version of a book)
3) distribution to the public

DREAMWEAVER 7-36

Managing a Web Server and Files

4) public performance
5) public display
6) public performance by digital audio transmission of sound recordings

By default, only a copyright holder can create a derivative work of his or her original by transforming or adapting it.

Understanding Fair Use

The law builds in limitations to copyright protection. One limitation to copyright is **fair use**. Fair use allows limited use of copyright-protected work. For example, you could excerpt short passages of a film or song for a class project or parody a television show. Determining if fair use applies to a work depends on the *purpose* of its use, the *nature* of the copyrighted work, *how much* you want to copy, and the *effect* on the market or value of the work. However, there is no clear formula on what constitutes fair use. It is always decided on a case-by-case basis.

How Do I Use Work Properly?

Being a student doesn't mean you can use any amount of any work for class. On the other hand, the very nature of education means you need to be able to use or reference different work in your studies. There are many situations that allow you to use protected work.

In addition to applying a fair use argument, you can obtain permission, pay a fee, use work that does not have copyright protection, or use work that has a flexible copyright license, where the owner has given the public permission to use the work in certain ways. For more information about open-access licensing, visit creativecommons.org. Work that is no longer protected by copyright is in the **public domain**; anyone can use it however they wish for any purpose. In general, the photos and other media on Federal government websites are in the public domain.

Understanding Licensing Agreements

Before you decide whether to use media you find on a website, you must decide whether you can comply with its licensing agreement.

Figure 41 *Library of Congress home page*
Library of Congress website – www.loc.gov

A **licensing agreement** is the permission given by a copyright holder that conveys the right to use the copyright holder's work under certain conditions.

Websites have rules that govern how a user may use its text and media, known as **terms of use**. Figures 41, 42, and 43 are great examples of clear terms of use for the Library of Congress website.

A site's terms of use do not override your right to apply fair use. Also, someone cannot compile public domain images in a website and then claim they own them or dictate how

Link to legal information regarding the use of content on the website

Lesson 6 Evaluate Web Content For Legal Use

the images can be used. Conversely, someone can erroneously state in their terms of use that you can use work on the site freely, but they may not know the work's copyright status. The burden is on you to research the veracity of anyone claiming you can use work.

Obtaining Permission or a License

The **permissions process** is specific to what you want to use (text, photographs, music, trademarks, merchandise, and so on) and how you want to use it (school term paper, personal website, fabric pattern). How you want to use the work determines the level and scope of permissions you need to secure. The fundamentals, however, are the same. Your request should contain the following:

- Your full name, address, and complete contact information.
- A specific description of your intended use. Sometimes including a sketch, storyboard, wireframe, or link to a website is helpful.
- A signature line for the copyright holder.
- A target date when you would like the copyright holder to respond. This can be important if you're working under deadline.

Posting a Copyright Notice

The familiar © symbol or "Copyright" is no longer required to indicate copyright, nor does it automatically register your work, but it does serve a useful purpose. When you post

Figure 42 *Library of Congress website legal page*
Library of Congress website – www.loc.gov

or publish it, you are stating clearly to those who may not know anything about copyright law that this work is claimed by you and is not in the public domain. Your case is made even stronger if someone violates your copyright

DREAMWEAVER 7-38

Managing a Web Server and Files

and your notice is clearly visible. That way, a violator can never claim ignorance of the law as an excuse for infringing. Common notification styles include:

Copyright 2015
Cengage Learning
or
© 2015 Cengage Learning

Giving proper attribution for text excerpts is a must; giving attribution for media is excellent practice, but is never a substitute for applying a fair use argument, buying a license, or simply getting permission.

You must provide proper citation for materials you incorporate into your own work, such as the following:

References
Waxer, Barbara M., and Baum, Marsha L. 2006. *Internet Surf and Turf—The Essential Guide to Copyright, Fair Use, and Finding Media*. Boston: Thomson Course Technology.

This expectation applies even to unsigned material and material that does not display the copyright symbol (©). Moreover, the expectation applies just as certainly to ideas you summarize or paraphrase as to words you quote verbatim.

Guidelines have been written by the American Psychological Association (APA) to establish an editorial style to be used to present written material. These guidelines include the way citations are referenced. Here's a list of the elements that make up an APA-style citation of web-based resources:

- Author's name (if known)
- Date of publication or last revision (if known), in parentheses
- Title of document
- Title of complete work or website (if applicable), underlined
- URL
- Date of access, in parentheses

Following is an example of how you would reference the APA Home page on the Reference page of your paper:

APA Style.org. (Retrieved August 22, 2014), from APA Online website: http://www.apastyle.org/electext.html.

There are APA styles that are used for other sources of text such as magazines, journals, newspaper articles, blogs, and email messages. Here's a list of the elements that make up an APA-style citation of images, sounds, or video:

- Name of the researching organization
- Date of publication
- Caption or description
- Brief explanation of what type of data is there and in what form it appears (shown in brackets)
- Project name and retrieval information.

Another set of guidelines used by many schools and university and commercial presses is the Modern Language Association (MLA) style. For more information, go to mla.org.

Figure 43 *Library of Congress website copyright information*
Library of Congress website – www.loc.gov

About Copyright and the Collections

Whenever possible, the Library of Congress provides factual information about copyright owners and related matters in the catalog records, finding aids and other texts that accompany collections. As a publicly supported institution, the Library generally does not own rights in its collections. Therefore, it does not charge permission fees for use of such material and generally does not grant or deny permission to publish or otherwise distribute material in its collections. Permission and possible fees may be required from the copyright owner independently of the Library. It is the researcher's obligation to determine and satisfy copyright or other use restrictions when publishing or otherwise distributing materials found in the Library's collections. Transmission or reproduction of protected items beyond that allowed by fair use requires the written permission of the copyright owners. Researchers must make their own assessments of rights in light of their intended use.

If you have any more information about an item you've seen on our website or if you are the copyright owner and believe our website has not properly attributed your work to you or has used it without permission, we want to hear from you. Please contact OGC@loc.gov with your contact information and a link to the relevant content.

View more information about copyright law from the U.S. Copyright Office »

Lesson 6 Evaluate Web Content For Legal Use

LESSON 7

Present a
WEBSITE TO A CLIENT

What You'll Do

Copyright © 2008, 2012 WireframeSketcher.com

In this lesson, you will explore options for presenting a website to a client at the completion of a project.

Are You Ready to Present Your Work?

Before you present a website to a client as a finished project, you should do a final check on some important items. First, do all your final design and development decisions reflect your client's goals and requirements? Does the website not only fulfill your client's goals and requirements, but those of the intended audience as well? Second, did you follow good web development practices? Did you check your pages against your wireframes as you developed them? Did you check each page against current accessibility standards? Did you run all necessary technical tests, such as validating the code, and searching for missing alternate text or missing page titles? Did you verify that all external and internal links work correctly? Third, did your final delivery date and budget meet the timeframe and budget you originally promised the client?

If you find that you did spend more time on the site than you expected to, determine if it was because you underestimated the amount of work it would take, ran into unforeseen technical problems, or because the client changed the requirements or increased the scope of the project as it went along. If you underestimated the project or ran into unexpected difficulties from causes other than the client, you usually cannot expect the client to make up the difference without a prior agreement. No client wants surprises at the end of a project, so it's best to communicate frequently and let the client know the status of all site elements as you go.

If the client changes the project scope, make sure you discuss the implication of this with the client. Ideally, you have made the client aware of any schedule or budget changes at the time they began to occur, and the client expects that your estimate will grow by a predictable, agreed-upon amount.

Client communication, both at the beginning of a project and throughout a project, is critical to a successful web design and a solid customer relationship. In building a house, a good architect makes an effort to get to know and understand a new client before beginning a house design. The design must be functional and meet the client's checklist of requirements, but it must also fit the client's personality and taste. The final structure must continue to meet those needs; the same is true of a website.

Some clients have a difficult time looking at architectural drawings and visualizing what the home will look like, so architects use different methods to communicate their design. Some use scale mockups, 3-D renderings, or photos of similarly styled homes to help the client visualize what their home will look like when completed. Web designers use similar strategies. You may be capable of building a great website, but you must communicate with the client from the beginning of the project to set and satisfy client expectations. Without this mutual understanding, the project's successful completion will be at risk. It is much less expensive to make changes and adjustments at the beginning of a project, and as changes occur, rather than close to completion. Communication is key.

What Is the Best Way to Present Your Work?

Ideally, you presented some form of prototype of the website at the beginning of the development process. You may have chosen to use low-fidelity wireframes such as one created in Microsoft PowerPoint or Adobe Photoshop. Or you may have used a high-fidelity wireframe that is interactive and multidimensional such as OverSight, ProtoShare, or WireframeSketcher, as shown in Figure 44. To communicate with your client and ensure a mutual understanding of the project, you could also use **BaseCamp**, a web-based project collaboration tool that many companies use. There is a monthly fee for using it, based on the number of projects you are running and your storage needs. You can use BaseCamp throughout the project cycle, not just at the end. To present the final project, consider publishing the site to a server and sending the client a link to view the completed website. Creating PDFs of the site and sending them to the client for approval is another possible method.

Figure 44 *WireframeSketcher website*
Copyright © 2008, 2012 WireframeSketcher.com

Another communication option is to invite the client to your office and do a full walkthrough of the site with them, which offers them a chance to ask questions. This is probably one of the best options if it is feasible. If you have taken the time to build a relationship of trust over the project, neither side should expect unpleasant surprises at the end.

SKILLS REVIEW

Perform website maintenance.

1. Open the Blooms & Bulbs website, then re-create the site cache.
2. Use the Link Checker panel to check for broken links, then fix any broken links that appear.
3. Use the Link Checker to check for orphaned files. If any orphaned files appear in the report, take steps to link them to appropriate pages or remove them.
4. Use the Assets panel to check for non-websafe colors. Evaluate any non-websafe colors you find to see if they affect your page content.
5. Run an Untitled Documents report for the entire local site. If the report lists any pages that have no titles, add page titles to the untitled pages, and edit any titles if they seem incomplete. Run the report again to verify that all pages have page titles.
6. Run a report to look for missing alternate text. Add alternate text to any graphics that need it, then run the report again to verify that all images contain alternate text.
7. Submit the blooms_styles.css file for CSS3 validation and correct any errors that are found.
8. Validate the workshops page for HTML5 markup and correct any errors that are found.
9. Verify that the Design Notes preference is enabled and add a Design Note to the workshops page as follows: **Shoot a video of the hanging baskets class to add to the page**. Add the status **needs attention**, add the current date, and check the Show when file is opened option.

Publish a website and transfer files.

1. Set up web server access for the Blooms & Bulbs website on an FTP server or a local/network server (whichever is available to you) using blooms_yourlastname as the remote folder name.
2. View the Blooms & Bulbs remote site in the Files panel.
3. Upload the water_lily.jpg file to the remote site, then view the remote site.
4. Add the code that links the favicon to the head content of any pages in the site that do not have it.
5. Synchronize all files in the Blooms & Bulbs website, so that all files from the local site are uploaded to the remote site.

Check files out and in.

1. Enable the Enable file check-out feature.
2. Check out the plants page and all dependent pages.
3. Open the plants page, change the heading to "Featured Spring Plants: Roses!", then save the file.
4. Check in the plants page and all dependent files.
5. Disable the Enable file check-out feature.
6. Turn off read only (Win) or Unlock (Mac) for the entire site.

Cloak files.

1. Verify that cloaking is enabled in the Blooms & Bulbs website.
2. Cloak the assets folder, then uncloak it.
3. Cloak all the .jpg files in the Blooms & Bulbs website, then expand the assets folder if necessary to view the cloaked files in the Files panel.
4. Uncloak the .jpg files.

Import and export a site definition.

1. Create a new folder named **blooms_site_definition** on your hard drive or external drive.
2. Export the Blooms & Bulbs site definition to the blooms_site_definition folder.
3. Import the Blooms & Bulbs site definition to create a new site called **Blooms & Bulbs 2**.
4. Make sure that all files from the Blooms & Bulbs website appear in the Files panel for the imported site, then compare your screen to Figure 45.
5. Remove the Blooms & Bulbs 2 site.
6. Close all open files.

SKILLS REVIEW
(CONTINUED)

Figure 45 *Completed Skills Review*

Managing a Web Server and Files

DREAMWEAVER 7-43

PROJECT BUILDER 1

In this Project Builder, you publish the TripSmart website that you have developed throughout this book to a local/network folder. Thomas Howard, the owner, has asked that you publish the site to a local folder as a backup location. You first run several reports on the site, specify the remote settings for the site, upload files to the remote site, check files out and in, and cloak files. Finally, you export and import the site definition.

1. Use the TripSmart website that you began in Project Builder 1 in Chapter 1 and developed in previous chapters.
2. Use the Link Checker panel to check for broken links, then fix any broken links that appear.
3. Use the Link Checker to check for orphaned files. If any orphaned files appear in the report, take steps to link them to appropriate pages or remove them.
4. Use the Assets panel to check for non-websafe colors. If you find any, evaluate whether or not they pose a problem for any of the pages.
5. Run an Untitled Documents report for the entire local site. If the report lists any pages that lack titles, add page titles to the untitled pages. Run the report again to verify that all pages have page titles.
6. Run a report to look for missing alternate text. Add alternate text to any graphics that need it, then run the report again to verify that all images contain alternate text.
7. Submit the tripsmart_styles.css file for CSS3 validation and correct any errors that are found.
8. Validate the catalog page for HTML5 markup and correct any errors that are found.
9. Enable the Design Notes preference, if necessary, and add a design note to the tours page as follows: **Add content and a video of the Galapagos sea lions**. Add the current date, the status **needs attention** and check the Show when file is opened option.
10. If you did not do so in Project Builder 1 in Chapter 1, use the Site Definition dialog box to set up web server access for a remote site using a local or network folder.
11. Upload the index page and all dependent files to the remote site.
12. View the remote site to make sure that all files uploaded correctly.
13. Add the code that links the favicon to the head content of any pages in the site that do not have it.
14. Synchronize the files so that all other files on the local TripSmart site are uploaded to the remote site.
15. Enable the Enable file check-out feature.
16. Check out the index page in the local site and all dependent files.
17. Open the index page, close the index page, then check in the index page and all dependent pages.
18. Disable the Enable file check-out feature, then turn off the read-only status (Win) or unlock (Mac) for the entire site.
19. Cloak all .jpg files in the website.
20. Export the site definition to a new folder named **tripsmart_site_definition**.
21. Import the TripSmart.ste file to create a new site named TripSmart 2.
22. Expand the assets folder in the Files panel if necessary, then compare your screen to Figure 46.
23. Remove the TripSmart 2 site.
24. Uncloak all files in the TripSmart site, then close any open files.

Figure 46 *Sample completed Project Builder 1*

PROJECT BUILDER 2

In this Project Builder, you finish your work on the Carolyne's Creations website. You are ready to publish the website to a remote server and transfer all the files from the local site to the remote site. First, you run several reports to make sure the website is in good shape. Next, you enable the Enable file check-out feature so that other staff members may collaborate on the site. Finally, you export and import the site definition file.

1. Use the Carolyne's Creations website that you began in Project Builder 1 in Chapter 1 and developed in previous chapters.
2. If you did not do so in Project Builder 2 in Chapter 1, use the Site Definition dialog box to set up web server access for a remote site using either an FTP site or a local or network folder.
3. Run reports for broken links and orphaned files, correcting any errors that you find.
4. Run reports for untitled documents and missing alt text, correcting any errors that you find.
5. Submit the cc_styles.css file for CSS3 validation and correct any errors that are found.
6. Validate the catering page for HTML5 markup and correct any errors that are found.
7. Upload the classes.html page and all dependent files to the remote site.
8. View the remote site to make sure that all files uploaded correctly.
9. Synchronize the files so that all other files on the local Carolyne's Creations site are uploaded to the remote site.
10. Enable the Enable file check-out feature.
11. Check out the classes page and all its dependent files.
12. Open the classes page, then change the price of the adult class to **$45.00**.
13. Save your changes, close the page, then check in the classes page and all dependent pages.
14. Disable the Enable file check-out feature, then turn off read only for the entire site.
15. Export the site definition to a new folder named **cc_site_definition**.
16. Import the Carolyne's Creations.ste file to create a new site named Carolyne's Creations 2.
17. Expand the local site folder in the Files panel if necessary, compare your screen to Figure 47, then remove the Carolyne's Creations2 site.

Figure 47 *Sample completed Project Builder 2*

DESIGN PROJECT

Throughout this book you have used Dreamweaver to create and develop several websites that contain different elements, many of which are found in popular commercial websites. For instance, Figure 48 shows the National Park Service website, which contains photos and information on all the national parks in the United States. This website contains many types of interactive elements, such as image maps and rollovers—all of which you learned to create in this book.

1. Connect to the Internet, then go to the National Park Service website at nps.gov.
2. Spend some time exploring the pages of this site to familiarize yourself with its elements.
3. Type a list of all the elements in this site that you have learned how to create in this book. After each item, write a short description of where and how the element is used in the site.
4. Click the link for the Site Index in the menu bar at the bottom of the page. Describe the information provided with the site index.
5. Click the Accessibility link, then click the Text Sizes links and describe how the page appearance changes as you click each option. How do you think this feature adds to the page accessibility?
6. Print the home page and one or two other pages that contain some of the elements you described and attach it to your list.

Figure 48 *Design Project*
National Park website – www.nps.gov

Managing a Web Server and Files

PORTFOLIO PROJECT

In this project, you will finish your work on the website that you created and developed throughout this book. You publish your site to a remote server or local or network folder.

1. Before you begin the process of publishing your website to a remote server, make sure that it is ready for public viewing. Use Figure 49 to assist you in making sure your website is complete. If you find problems, make the necessary changes to finalize the site.
2. Decide where to publish your site. The folder where you will publish your site can be either an FTP site or a local/network folder. If you are publishing to an FTP site, be sure to write down all the information you will need to publish to the site, including the URL of the FTP host, the directory on the FTP server where you will publish your local site folder, and the login and password information.
3. Use the Site Setup dialog box to specify the remote settings for the site using the information that was decided upon in Step 2.
4. Transfer one of the pages and its dependent files to the remote site, then view the remote site to make sure the appropriate files were transferred.
5. Synchronize the files so that all the remaining local pages and dependent files are uploaded to the remote site.
6. Enable the Enable file check-out feature.
7. Check out one of the pages. Open the checked-out page, make a change to it, save the change, close the page, then check the page back in.
8. Cloak a particular file type.
9. Export the site definition for the site to a new folder on your hard drive or on an external drive.
10. Close any open pages, then exit Dreamweaver.

Figure 49 *Portfolio Project*

```
                    Website Checklist
 1. Are you satisfied with the content and appearance of every page?
 2. Are all paths for all links and images correct?
 3. Does each page have a title?
 4. Does the stylesheet pass CSS3 validation?
 5. Do all images have appropriate alternate text?
 6. Have you eliminated any orphaned files?
 7. Have you deleted any unnecessary files?
 8. Have you viewed all pages using at least two different browsers?
 9. Does the home page have keywords and a description?
10. Is all text based on a CSS style?
```

ADOBE DREAMWEAVER CS6

CHAPTER 8 USING STYLES AND STYLE SHEETS
FOR DESIGN

1. Create and use embedded styles
2. Modify embedded styles
3. Use CSS3 and Media Queries
4. Work with conflicting styles

CHAPTER 8: USING STYLES AND STYLE SHEETS FOR DESIGN

Introduction

In Chapter 3, you learned how to create, apply, and edit Cascading Style Sheets. Using CSS is the best and most powerful way to ensure that all elements in a website are formatted consistently. The advantage of using CSS is that all of your formatting rules can be kept in a separate or **external style sheet** file, so that you can change the appearance of every page to which the style sheet is attached by modifying the style sheet file. For example, suppose your external style sheet contains a style called headings that is applied to all top-level headings in all your website pages. If you want to change the heading color to blue, you simply change that rule's color value to blue, and all headings in the website are updated instantly. This type of rule that affects all website content is called a **global CSS rule**. Because style sheets separate the formatting from the content, all pages in the site are formatted automatically from the style sheet information without affecting the content itself.

You can also create **embedded styles**, which are internal styles whose code is located within the head section of the HTML code of a web page. The advantage of embedded styles is that you can use them to override an external style. For instance, if all headings in your website are blue because the external style applied to them specifies blue as the color value, you could change the color of one of those headings to a different color by creating and applying an embedded style that specifies a different color as the color attribute. Embedded styles are a choice you make when you use a Dreamweaver CSS predesigned layout to format the div tags on each page. You can choose to save the styles in an external style sheet or in a document. However, in general, you should use embedded styles for small formatting changes or for content that needs specific formatting, rather than to format all the pages of a website. Keeping formatting rules in a separate file from the web page content reduces the overall file sizes of your pages. As you develop your site's content, it's good practice to format most of your page content using external style sheets, rather than embedded styles in individual pages.

In this chapter, you back up your site files, and then import a redesigned Striped Umbrella website. Each page has been redesigned using CSS for page layout to provide consistency. You will use this new site for the rest of the book. You then create and apply embedded styles and work with external style sheets to format the pages in the site.

TOOLS YOU'LL USE

LESSON 1

Create and Use
EMBEDDED STYLES

What You'll Do

In this lesson, you will replace your Striped Umbrella files by importing a revised website. Next, you will create and apply an embedded style to the home page.

Understanding Embedded Styles

In Chapter 3, you learned how to create and use an external style sheet to apply consistent formatting to website elements. Recall that an external style sheet is a separate file with a .css extension that contains a collection of rules that create styles to format web page elements. Because you can apply external style sheets to multiple pages, they are a great tool to help ensure consistent formatting globally, across all pages of a website. For instance, you can set link properties, background colors, and text properties to appear uniformly on all pages. However, you might want to create a rule that is used only on a single page in your site. You can do this using an **embedded style**, a style whose code is embedded in the head section of an individual page. Embedded styles do not format website content globally. If both an external style and embedded style are applied to a single element, the embedded style overrides the external style.

There is also a type of style similar to an embedded style called an inline style. Like an embedded style, the **inline style** is part of the individual page code, but it is written in the body section, rather than the head section. Inline styles refer to a specific instance of a tag. ID selector types (as opposed to class, tag, or compound types) can only be used once on each page. For example, <p id="footer"> would apply the footer style to one paragraph. Inline style rule names are preceded by a # sign. To apply an inline style to a page element, use the ID list arrow on the HTML Property inspector. For a summary of the differences between external, embedded, and inline styles, see Table 1.

Creating and Applying Embedded Styles

To create an embedded style, you use the New CSS Rule button in the CSS Styles panel to open the New CSS Rule dialog box, shown in Figure 1. You use this dialog box to create both embedded styles as well as styles that are added to external style sheets. To specify the new style as an embedded style, click the (This document only) option in the Rule Definition section. If you click the (New Style Sheet File) option, you need to name and save a new CSS external style sheet file

DREAMWEAVER 8-4

Using Styles and Style Sheets for Design

using the Save Style Sheet File As dialog box. You also have the choice of creating a new style in an existing style sheet, such as the one you have already created for The Striped Umbrella website. So you can create a new style that is an embedded style, an external style saved in a new external style sheet file, or an external style added to an existing external style sheet file.

You use the New CSS Rule dialog box to create a **class style** (also known as a **custom style**), which contains a combination of formatting attributes that can be applied to a block of text or other page elements. When you name a class style, you begin the name with a period (.).

Figure 1 *New CSS Rule dialog box*

TABLE 1: SUMMARY OF STYLE TYPES

Style Type	What it Formats	Style is stored in	Created using this selection in New CSS Ruled box	Apply this style using	Notes
External Style	Multiple pages	Separate file with a .css extension	Rule Definition: New Style Sheet File or choose an existing style sheet file	HTML Property inspector: Class list OR CSS Property inspector: Targeted Rule list	Used for global formatting
Embedded Style	Elements on one page	In page head section code	Rule Definition: This document only	HTML Property inspector: Class list OR CSS Property inspector: Targeted Rule list	Overrides external style
Inline Style	A specific instance of a tag	In page body section code	(Type it in the page code in the body section)	It is applied after you type it	Use only once per page; refers to a specific instance of a tag; name is preceded by #

© Cengage Learning 2013

Lesson 1   Create and Use Embedded Styles

DREAMWEAVER 8-5

QUICK TIP

If you don't type a period at the beginning of a class style name, Dreamweaver automatically adds it for you.

After you name the rule and click OK, the CSS Rule definition dialog box opens with settings for the Type category displayed, as shown in Figure 2. This dialog box contains nine different categories whose settings you can define. To specify the settings for a category, click the category, then enter the settings. When you finish specifying settings for all of the desired categories, click OK.

Once you create a class style, it appears in the CSS Styles panel. It also appears as a choice in the Class list in the HTML Property inspector

Figure 2 *CSS Rule Definition for .contact_info style*

Choose a category to see property options for that category

DREAMWEAVER 8-6

Using Styles and Style Sheets for Design

or in the Targeted Rule list in the CSS Property inspector. To apply a class style to a web page element, select the element, then click the style from the Class list in the HTML Property inspector or the Targeted Rule list in the CSS Property inspector. For a summary of the differences between the various selector types, see Table 2.

QUICK TIP

Most browsers read style sheets. A browser that cannot read style sheets ignores the styles and renders the affected page elements with default settings.

TABLE 2: SUMMARY OF SELECTOR TYPES

Selector type	What it does	Style is stored in	Select this in New CSS Rule dialog box	Apply using	Notes
Class	Formats any HTML element	External style sheet file or as an inline style	Selector Type: Class	HTML Property inspector: Class list or CSS Property Inspector: Targeted Rule list	Begins with a period (.); most versatile type, can be used multiple times
ID	Formats one element	External style sheet file or as an inline style	Selector Type: ID	HTML Property inspector: ID list	Begins with a # sign, used once per page, used for div tags
Tag	Redefines an HTML tag	External style sheet file or as an inline style	Selector Type: Tag	(Automatically applied when the tag is used on a page)	Rule name is the tag itself
Compound	Formats a selection	External style sheet file or as an inline style	Selector Type: Compound	(Automatically applied to the relevant page elements)	Begins with a # sign, combines two or more styles in nested tags

© Cengage Learning 2013

Replace the folder for The Striped Umbrella website (Win)

1. Open Windows Explorer, navigate to the drive and folder where you store your striped_umbrella website, select the striped_umbrella folder, click **Organize**, then click **Copy**.
2. Navigate to a folder where you would like to store a backup of your original files, click **Organize**, then click **Paste**.

    TIP It is a good practice to make a backup copy of files in an offsite location before you delete them.

3. Navigate to the drive and folder where you store your Data Files for this chapter, so that the files appear in the right pane, select the striped_umbrella folder in the chapter_8 data folder as shown in Figure 3, click **Organize** on the toolbar, then click **Copy**.
4. Navigate to the drive and folder where you store your website files, select the original striped_umbrella folder, click **Organize**, click **Delete**, confirm the deletion when the confirmation dialog box opens, click **Organize**, then click **Paste**.

    The redesigned pages in the new folder replace the original folder. While your old files were useful for learning, you now know how to use many of the tools in Dreamweaver to create attractive, accessible pages. The new site files use CSS styles consistently for page formatting and more accurately reflect optimal site design principles.

5. Close Windows Explorer, then start Dreamweaver.
6. Open The Striped Umbrella website, and view the new files in the Files panel, as shown in Figure 4.

You copied your original files to a different folder as a backup before you replaced the folder with new, redesigned files for The Striped Umbrella website.

Figure 3 *Copying the striped_umbrella folder from the Data Files (Win)*

Copy command is on the Organize menu

Folder where you store your Data Files (your path will differ)

In Step 3, copy this folder

Figure 4 *The Files panel with the new files (Win)*

New files for The Striped Umbrella website

DREAMWEAVER 8-8

Using Styles and Style Sheets for Design

Figure 5 *Copying the striped_umbrella folder from the Data Files (Mac)*

Folder where you store your Data Files (your path will differ)

Figure 6 *The Files panel with the new files (Mac)*

New files for The Striped Umbrella website

Replace the folder for The Striped Umbrella website (Mac)

1. Open Finder, navigate to the drive and folder where you store your striped_umbrella website, select the striped_umbrella folder, click **Edit** on the menu bar, then click **Copy striped_umbrella**.

2. Click **File** on the Menu bar, click **New Finder Window** to open another instance of Finder, navigate to a folder where you would like to store your original files, click **Edit** on the menu bar, then click **Paste Item**.

   It is a good practice to make a backup copy of files in an offsite location before you delete them.

3. Navigate to the drive and folder where you store your Data Files for this chapter, select the striped_umbrella folder in the chapter_8 data_files folder as shown in Figure 5, click **Edit** on the menu bar, then click **Copy striped_umbrella**.

4. Navigate to the drive and folder where you store your website files, select the original striped_umbrella folder, right-click and select **Move to Trash**, click **Edit**, then click **Paste Item**.

   The redesigned pages in the new folder replace the original folder.

5. Close Finder, then start Dreamweaver.

6. Open The Striped Umbrella website, then verify that the new files are displayed in the Files panel, as shown in Figure 6.

TIP If you do not see the files listed in the Files panel, click the plus sign next to the site root folder.

You copied your original files to a different folder as a backup before you replaced the folder with new redesigned files for The Striped Umbrella website.

Lesson 1 Create and Use Embedded Styles

DREAMWEAVER 8-9

Create a class style

1. Open the index page in The Striped Umbrella website, expand the CSS Styles panel, then click the **Switch to All (Document) Mode button** [All] (if necessary).

   The new, redesigned home page is now based on a CSS layout. The CSS block elements are outlined with dotted borders.

2. Click the **New CSS Rule button** in the CSS Styles panel to open the New CSS Rule dialog box.

3. Click the **Selector Type list arrow**, click **Class (can apply to any HTML element)**, click in the **Selector Name text box**, type **contact_info**, click the **Rule Definition list arrow**, click **(This document only)**, then compare your screen to Figure 7.

4. Click **OK** to open the CSS Rule definition for .contact_info dialog box, and verify that the Type category is selected.

5. Set the Font family to **Arial**, **Helvetica**, **sans-serif**; set the Font-size to **small**; set the Font-style to **italic**; set the Color to **#003**, then compare your screen to Figure 8.

6. Click **OK**.

   The contact_info style appears in the CSS Styles panel.

   TIP If you do not see the contact_info style, click the plus sign (Win) or the triangle (Mac) next to <style> in the CSS Styles panel.

You created a new custom rule named contact_info and set the rule properties for it.

Figure 7 *New CSS Rule dialog box with settings for contact_info style*

Click to select the Class selector type

New rule name

Select this to specify an embedded style

Figure 8 *CSS Rule definition for .contact_info dialog box with Type settings*

DREAMWEAVER 8-10

Using Styles and Style Sheets for Design

Figure 9 *Applying the contact_info style using the Property inspector*

Text with contact_info rule applied

Class list arrow *Italic button*

Figure 10 *Viewing the embedded styles*

Embedded style sheet has one rule: contact_info

.contact_info rule

Apply a class style

1. Select the paragraph with The Striped Umbrella contact information.
2. Click the **Italic button** *I* in the HTML Property inspector to remove the italic formatting.

   You must remove manual formatting before applying a CSS style.
3. Click the **Class list arrow** in the Property inspector, click **None**, click the **Class list arrow**, click **contact_info**, deselect the text, then compare your results to Figure 9.

   Before applying a new style, you should remove any existing syles. The selected text is now smaller and gray, as specified by the contact_info rule.
4. Scroll down in the CSS Styles panel if necessary to view the contact_info rule, as shown in Figure 10.

   The contact_info rule appears in the CSS Styles panel, but not as a part of the su_styles.css style sheet. The contact_info rule is an embedded rule, listed in the CSS Styles panel under <style> rather than under su_styles.css.
5. Click **File**, then click **Save** to save your work.

You used the Property inspector to apply the contact_info rule to the contact information.

Lesson 1 Create and Use Embedded Styles

DREAMWEAVER 8-11

LESSON 2

Modify EMBEDDED STYLES

What You'll Do

In this lesson, you will modify the contact_info rule, redefine an HTML tag, edit an embedded rule, and then delete an embedded rule.

Editing Embedded Styles

To edit a rule, click the rule you want to edit in the CSS Styles panel, click the Edit Rule button in the CSS Styles panel, then use the CSS Rule Definition dialog box to change the settings as you wish, or simply enter the new settings in the CSS properties panel. Any changes that you make to the rule are automatically reflected on the page; all elements to which the rule is applied update to reflect the change.

Redefining HTML Tags

When you use the Property inspector to format a web page element, a predefined HTML tag is added to that element. You might want to change the definition of an HTML tag to add more "pizzazz" to elements that have that tag. For instance, perhaps you want all text that has the <em> tag, which is the tag used for italic formatting, to appear in bold purple. To change the definition of an HTML tag, click the Tag (redefines an HTML element) selector type in the New CSS Rule dialog box, click the Selector Name list arrow to view all available HTML tags, click the tag you want to redefine, then click OK to open the CSS Rule definition dialog box, where you specify the desired formatting settings. Once you save the rule and apply it, the tags you target will be formatted according to the new settings you specified.

Using the CSS Styles Panel

There are two modes in the CSS Styles panel: All mode and Current mode. When All mode is selected, style sheet rules appear in the top half of the panel, which is called the **All Rules pane**. When you click one of the rules, the bottom half, which is called the **Properties pane**, lists that rule's properties, as shown in Figure 11.

When Current mode is selected, the top half of the panel is called the **Summary for Selection pane**. When an object with a style is selected on an open web page, the Summary for Selection pane displays the properties for that style, as shown

DREAMWEAVER 8-12

Using Styles and Style Sheets for Design

in Figure 12. The bottom half of the CSS Styles panel is called the Properties pane in either mode. The small pane between the Summary for Selection pane and the Properties pane in Current mode is called the Rules pane. The **Rules pane** displays the location of the current selected rule in the open document.

> **QUICK TIP**
>
> To delete an embedded rule, click the rule you wish to delete, then click the Delete CSS Rule button in the CSS Styles panel.

Figure 11 CSS Styles panel in All mode

Figure 12 CSS Styles panel in Current mode

Lesson 2 Modify Embedded Styles

DREAMWEAVER 8-13

Modify a class style

1. Click the **contact_info rule** in the CSS Styles panel, then click the **Edit Rule button**.
2. Change the Color to **#000**, click **Apply**, then compare your screen to Figure 13.
3. Click **OK**, deselect the text if necessary, compare your screen to Figure 14, then save the index page.

   The text with the contact_info rule applied automatically changed to reflect the color change you made to the rule.

You changed the type color of the contact_info rule. You then saw this change reflected in text with the contact_info rule applied to it.

Figure 13 *CSS Rule definition for .contact_info dialog box with modified type setting*

Modified setting

Figure 14 *Viewing the contact information with the modified rule property*

Text with contact_info rule is now black

DREAMWEAVER 8-14

Using Styles and Style Sheets for Design

Figure 15 *Creating a new CSS Rule to redefine the hr HTML tag*

- Tag selector type
- hr tag is selected
- Location of rule definition
- Selector Name list arrow

Figure 16 *Redefining the hr HTML tag*

- Solid Top
- Thin Width
- Same for all check boxes
- Color is changed from the default color to blue

Redefine an HTML tag

1. Open the cafe page, then click the **New CSS Rule button** in the CSS Styles panel to open the New CSS Rule dialog box.

   TIP You can also click the Targeted Rule list box in the CSS Property inspector, click <New CSS Rule>, then click the Create or Change CSS Rule button (the Edit Rule button) to open the New CSS Rule dialog box.

2. Click the **Selector Type list arrow**, click the **Tag (redefines an HTML element)**, click the **Selector Name list arrow**, scroll down if necessary, click **hr**, click the **Rule Definition list arrow**, then click **(This document only)** if necessary, as shown in Figure 15.

   The hr tag is the tag that creates a horizontal rule.

   TIP To scroll quickly to the tags that begin with the letter h, type h after you click the Selector Name list arrow.

3. Click **OK** to open the CSS Rule definition for hr dialog box, click the **Border category**, set the Top style to **solid**, set the Width to **thin**, set the Color to **#006**, press **[Tab]**, compare your screen to Figure 16, make sure that each Same for all check box above each column is checked, then click **OK**.

   The horizontal rules on the page have changed to blue because the rule definition has changed the way a horizontal rule is rendered. The rules will look much better in the browser than they do in Design view.

4. Click the **Switch Design View to Live View button** on the Document toolbar, see the horizontal rules as they will appear in the browser, then click Live to return to Design view.

(continued)

Lesson 2 Modify Embedded Styles

DREAMWEAVER 8-15

5. Using Steps 1 through 3 as a guide, create a new embedded CSS rule that redefines the body HTML tag, by using the Background category rather than the Type category to set the page Background color to **#033**, as shown in Figure 17, then click **OK**.

   The page now has a dark gray background. (The page background is behind the CSS container with all of the page content. You may need to collapse your panels and scroll to see it.)

6. Switch to Code view, then scroll through the head section to view the code that changes the properties for the horizontal rule and the body tags, as shown in Figure 18.

   Because these are embedded styles, the code for the rules is embedded into the page in the head section of the code. The rule changing the background page color to dark gray overrode the white page background color that you defined earlier by using the Page Properties dialog box.

7. Scroll up or down in the code, if necessary, to find the code that links the external style sheet files, as shown in Figure 18.

   You cannot see the individual rule properties in the style sheets, because the files are linked, not embedded. If you open the individual style sheet files, however, you see the rules and properties listed.

TIP If you have two embedded styles, you can tell which style takes precedence by its position in the tag selector. Tags with greater precedence are positioned to the right of other tags in the tag selector.

You used the New CSS Rule dialog box to redefine the hr and body HTML tags. You also viewed the code for the new embedded styles and the code that links the external style sheet files.

Figure 17 *Redefining the body HTML tag*

Background category

Change the page background color to #033

Figure 18 *Viewing the code for embedded styles*

Links to three external style sheets

Code redefining the hr and body HTML tags is part of the head section

Figure 19 *Changing the border color property of the hr tag*

Select hr

Replace the color 006 with 003

Figure 20 *CSS Rules panel after deleting body rule*

body rule is removed

Delete CSS Rule button is only active if a rule or style sheet is selected

Lesson 2   Modify Embedded Styles

Edit an embedded style in the Properties pane

1. Switch to Design view, then view the external and embedded styles for the cafe page in the CSS Styles panel.
2. Click the **hr style** in the CSS Styles panel.

   The properties of the hr rule are displayed in the Properties pane.
3. Click to place the insertion point beside the border color number in the Properties pane, then replace color #006 with color **#003** to change the horizontal rule to a darker blue, press **[Enter]** (Win) or **[return]** (Mac), then compare your screen to Figure 19.

TIP You may have to resize your CSS Styles panel to see the contents of the Properties pane.

You used the CSS Styles panel to change the color settings for the hr embedded rule.

Delete an embedded style

1. Click the **body rule** at the bottom of the embedded rules list in the CSS Styles panel to select it.
2. Click the **Delete CSS Rule button** 🗑, then compare your screen to Figure 20.

   The body rule is removed from the CSS Styles panel. The page background changes back to white.

TIP You can also delete an embedded style by right-clicking (Win) or [control]-clicking (Mac) the rule in the CSS Styles panel, then clicking Delete.

3. Save your changes, then close the cafe page.

You used the CSS Styles panel to delete the body rule.

DREAMWEAVER 8-17

LESSON 3

Use CSS3 and MEDIA QUERIES

What You'll Do

Courtesy of w3.org

▶ *In this lesson, you will make formatting changes in the style sheet and see those changes reflected on pages. You will also add hyperlink styles and custom code to the su_styles style sheet. Finally, you will delete a style from the su_styles style sheet.*

Understanding CSS3 Features

You learned about Cascading Style Sheets, for years the preferred way to format web content, in Chapter 3. You also learned that CSS3 is the latest version of CSS being developed by the World Wide Web Consortium (W3C). CSS3 introduced improved coding techniques, such as new tags to insert audio and video objects, which you will learn about in Chapter 11. CSS3 is another step in the process of making web pages more accessible not only to users with limitations, but to all users.

One of the new features of CSS3 is the @font-face property, which allows developers to embed **WOFF (Web Open Font Format) fonts**. The @font-face property allows a browser to access and deliver a specified font from a server when a page is viewed in a browser. WOFF, developed by the Mozilla Foundation in concert with several other organizations, was proposed to the W3C in 2010 as a standard font format for all web browsers to use. When you use the @font-face property, a browser accesses the specified WOFF fonts using **font libraries**, collections of fonts such as typekit.com or google.com/webfonts.

Because WOFF is a compressed format, it allows WOFF-formatted content to download faster. Currently, the following browsers support the WOFF format: Firefox Version 3.6 and higher, Internet Explorer Version 9 and higher, Google Chrome Version 5 and higher, and Safari Version 5.1 and higher.

QUICK TIP

You can convert fonts to a WOFF format using Font Squirrel, a free online service at fontsquirrel.com/fontface/generator.

CSS3 and semantic coding work together to enhance the meaning of the content, while providing well-designed and accessible pages. Take advantage of style sheet properties to style text for the semantic web by using values such as "small" or "large" for font properties rather than a specific pixel value. Larger type implies more importance than smaller type. Applying heading formats to text is another easy way to indicate levels of importance among several headings on a page.

CSS3 also lets you round the corners of a div tag to set off content on a page, as shown in Figure 21. To add rounded corners to a div tag, add the following code to the content div properties, using values of your choice:

    -moz-border-radius: 10px;
    border-radius: 10px;

The first line of code targets the Mozilla Firefox browser to ensure that the corners display correctly. The second line is for all other browsers. This code creates four identical corners. You can also specify a different radius for each corner or a different shape for the corners. For instance, to create two rounded corners at the top with slightly different shapes, but square corners at the bottom, modify the code to:

border-radius: 21px 10px 0px 0px;

You can also use CSS3 to organize content by creating tabs, drop-down menus, and accordions. **Tabs** look similar to file folder tabs and are used for navigation above the top of page content. You click a tab to display information. **Accordions**, also used for navigation, are buttons that, when clicked, open up like an accordion to display information that drops down below the button. Clicking the button again closes it. These features do not require images or JavaScript to work, but incorporate the animation capabilities of CSS3.

NEW Using Media Queries and Fluid Grid Layouts

Today, it is no longer enough to design a web page that that looks and functions well only on a desktop monitor. Users will expect to be able to access your site using multiple mobile devices, such as tablets and mobile phones, so you'll have to design your pages so they display correctly on all of them. To do this,

you'll find Media Queries to be invaluable. **Media Queries**, a new feature introduced in Dreamweaver 5.5, are files that specify set parameters for displaying pages on separate devices, such as tablets or smartphones. Media Queries specify a different style sheet for each device: a style sheet for a desktop monitor, a style sheet for a tablet, and a style sheet for a cell phone. Dreamweaver has a function named Media Query that, like a traffic policeman, directs each device to the correct style sheet so the page will display correctly on that device. You can find the Media Queries command on the Multiscreen Preview menu, as shown in Figure 22. When you click the Multiscreen Preview command, you see the page content rendered on three different simulated screens such as a laptop, a cell phone, and a tablet.

QUICK TIP
The Media Queries command is also on the Modify menu.

Figure 21 *Example of a div with rounded corners*

Rounded corners on div

Figure 22 *Dreamweaver Media Queries dialog box*

Multiscreen Preview command

Media Queries command

Lesson 3 Use CSS3 and Media Queries

Figure 23 shows a page that has not been designed for multiple devices. Notice how you have to scroll horizontally to see the content. Figure 24 shows a page that has been designed for multiple devices. No scroll bars are required to view the content, since the page has been correctly sized for each device.

Another option for designing for multiple screen sizes is to use the Dreamweaver File > New > Fluid Grid Layout command to create a page layout with preset code for designing adaptive websites. **Adaptive websites** are websites that adjust or modify the page content to fit the user's needs and device type used to view the site. This grid contains three CSS layouts and typography presets based on a single fluid grid. You can save the styles Dreamweaver creates automatically in your existing style sheet.

Validating for CSS3 Standards

To make sure that your code is compliant with today's standards, you should validate the code before you publish your site. The W3C provides a free validation service for Web designers and developers. After you have used style sheets to format your content, you can upload your file to validate that your code is compliant with CSS3 standards by using the CSS Validation

Figure 23 *Multiscreen preview of a page not designed for multiple devices*

User will need to use scroll bars to read content on cell phone or tablet

Figure 24 *Multiscreen preview of a page designed for multiple devices*

User will not need to scroll to read content on cell phone or tablet

DREAMWEAVER 8-20

Using Styles and Style Sheets for Design

Service at jigsaw.w3.org/css-validator as shown in Figure 25. You can enter a URL, upload the file, or input the code directly. You can choose the CSS level you would like to use for validation: CSS level 1, level 2, level 2.1, or level 3. After you click the Check button, you will receive the results of the validation. You can request that the report submit both errors and warnings. Errors include code that will present a problem and warnings include code that could present problems. You can also specify the medium that the code will be checked against, for example: handheld, print, Braille, and TV.

Pages that have been validated can display either of the two icons shown in the results to prove that they are CSS3 compliant.

Testing Browser Compatibility with Adobe BrowserLab

Another way to test your pages for possible display issues is Adobe BrowserLab. **Adobe BrowserLab** is an online service that you can access through Dreamweaver to test your site with multiple browsers, without needing to have the browser programs installed on your computer. BrowserLab can alert you do possible display problems, like the one shown in Figure 26. BrowserLab shows that Internet Explorer 9 recognizes CSS3 rounded corners, but that Internet Explorer 8 does not. You can view two different browsers side by side or as onion skins, one on top of the other.

You use the Adobe BrowserLab panel to connect to BrowserLab. It provides online viewing, as well as diagnostic and comparison tools. You'll need an Adobe ID to access the service. There is no charge to create an Adobe ID, but there could be a charge for using Adobe BrowserLab.

Figure 25 *W3C CSS Validation Service*
Courtesy of w3.org

Figure 26 *The Adobe BrowserLab*
Copyright © 2012 Adobe Systems Incorporated. All rights reserved

Internet Explorer 9 shows rounded corners

Internet Explorer 8 does not recognize the rounded corners

Lesson 3 Use CSS3 and Media Queries

Add CSS3 tags for enhanced appearance

1. On the index page, click **HTML5_twoCol-FixRtHdr.css** on the Related files toolbar, then scroll in the code window to locate the .sidebar1 rule.

2. Place the insertion point at the end of the last property and value, which sets the border left style, press [Enter] (Win) or [Return] (Mac), then type the following code as shown in Figure 27.

   -moz-border-radius: 20px;

   border-radius: 20px;

   (continued)

Figure 27 *Entering code to add rounded corners to a div*

```
59  .sidebar1 {
60      float: left;
61      width: 180px;
62      background-color: #D9EFF4;
63      padding-bottom: 10px;
64      text-align: center;
65      border-top-style: none;
66      border-right-style: none;
67      border-bottom-style: none;
68      border-left-style: none;
69      -moz-border-radius:20px;
70      border-radius: 20px;
71  }
72  .content {
```

DESIGN TIP

Designing Media-Dependent Style Sheets

One challenge web designers have is to provide alternate versions of web pages that will display attractively on hand-held devices. Because of the vast difference in screen sizes, a page designed for viewing on a computer screen will not work well when viewed on a hand-held device, such as a smartphone. **Media-dependent style sheets** are tools for identifying the device being used and formatting the page appropriately. You can use one of two methods to identify a specific type of media that will be used to open a page: You can add code to an external style sheet such as "@media handheld" or "@media print," or you can add code to the head section of a document that specifies the target medium within the document language. For more information, go to w3.org and search for "media-dependent style sheets."

Figure 28 *Viewing the rounded div corners in Live view*

Div now has rounded corners

3. Save all files, preview the page with Live view, compare your screen to Figure 28, then return to Design view.

   The sidebar now appears with rounded corners to help set it off even more on the page.

   You added code to round the corners of the sidebar1 div.

Lesson 3   Use CSS3 and Media Queries

DREAMWEAVER 8-23

Modify CSS3 tags

1. Click the sidebar1 rule in the **HTML5_twoCol-FixRtHdr.css** in CSS Styles panel, then click the **Edit Rule button** .
2. Click the **Border** category, then change the Style Top to **solid**, the Width to **thin**, and the Color to **#39C** for all sides of the div.
3. Click the **Box** category, then change the Width to **175px**.

   This adjusts the box width slightly to make room for the border.
4. Click **OK**, then view the div in Live view, as shown in Figure 29.
5. Open the about_us page, switch to Code view, then scroll to locate the <div class="sidebar1"> tag.
6. Add the following code to the tag to read as follows: `<div class="sidebar1" style="height:700px">`.

   This embedded code lengthens the sidebar1 rule to more closely match the length of the content in the content div.
7. Save your work, then view the page in Live view.
8. Repeat steps 5 and 6 to set the length of each sidebar1 rule individually for the rest of the pages in the site, experimenting with the pixel settings until you are satisfied with the results.

Figure 29 *Viewing the modified div in Live view*

POWER USER SHORTCUTS

To do this:	Use this shortcut:
Collapse selection of code	[Ctrl][Shift][C] (Win) or ⌘ [shift][C] (Mac)
Collapse outside selection of code	[Ctrl][Alt][C] (Win) or ⌘ [option][C] (Mac)
Expand selection of code	[Ctrl[Shift][E] (Win) or ⌘ [shift][E] (Mac)
Collapse full tag	[Ctrl][Shift][J] (Win) or ⌘ [shift][J] (Mac)
Collapse outside full tag	[Ctrl][Alt][J] (Win) or ⌘ [option][J] (Mac)
Expand all (code)	[Ctrl][Alt][E] (Win) or ⌘ [option][E] (Mac)
Indent code	[Ctrl][Shift][>] (Win) or ⌘ [shift][>] (Mac)
Outdent code	[Ctrl][Shift][<] (Win) or ⌘ [shift][<] (Mac)
Balance braces	[Ctrl]['] (Win) or ⌘ ['] (Mac)
Go to line (of code)	[Ctrl][G] (Win) or ⌘ [,] (Mac)
Show code hints	[Ctrl][Spacebar] (Win) or [control][spacebar] (Mac)
Refresh code hints	[Ctrl][.] (Win) or [control][.] (Mac)

© Cengage Learning 2013

Figure 30 *Submitting a style sheet for validation*
Courtesy of w3.org

Profile list arrow   *Browse button*   *Check button*

Figure 31 *Validation report with no errors listed*
Courtesy of w3.org

Upload files for CSS3 validation

1. Open your browser and go to **jigsaw.w3.org/css-validator**.

   This site allows you to upload files for validation or enter a URL to check for validation.

2. Click the **By file upload tab**.

   You will submit the website main stylesheet.

3. Click **More Options**, click the **Profile list arrow**, then click **CSS level 3**, as shown in Figure 30.

4. Click the **Browse button**, browse to and select **su_styles.css**, then click the **Check button**.

   No errors are listed, as shown in Figure 31. If you see any errors displayed, read the documentation that cites the line number and nature of each error. Minimize the browser, then correct as necessary and resubmit the file until you do not have any errors.

5. Close the browser.

Lesson 3   Use CSS3 and Media Queries

DREAMWEAVER 8-25

LESSON 4

Work with
CONFLICTING STYLES

What You'll Do

In this lesson, you will learn the order of precedence as styles are applied to page content.

Understanding the Order of Precedence

When you have a mixture of embedded styles, external styles, and styles redefining HTML tags, you need to understand what happens when these styles conflict. First, you must understand the term "cascading" as applied to style sheets. **Cascading** refers to the way styles are ranked in order of precedence as they are applied to page elements. Style sheets originate from three sources: the author, who is the creator of the page and style sheet; the user, or person who is viewing the page; and the user agent, the software through which the page is delivered, such as a browser or a mobile device. All user agents have default style sheets that are used to read and display web pages.

The first order of precedence is to find declarations that specify and match the media type being used, such as a computer screen. For instance, if you are designing a page for a cell phone, you would use the rule "@media handheld" in the style sheet. For a page being viewed on a computer screen, you would use "@media screen" in the style sheet.

The second order of precedence is by importance and origin as follows:

1. user important declarations
2. author important declarations
3. author normal declarations
4. user normal declarations
5. user agent declarations

To be classified as an important declaration, the word "important" is included in the rule. For example: "p {font-size: 14 px ! important }" would take precedence over a p font-size tag without the important designation.

The third order of precedence is by specificity of the selector. More specific rules are applied when they are on an equal importance and origin with more general rules. The fourth and final order of precedence is by order specified in the code. Imported, or external style sheets, are considered to be before any internal styles.

When discussing the order of precedence of style types, pseudo-class styles are considered as normal class styles. **Pseudo class styles** refer to styles that determine the appearance of a page element when a certain condition resulting from information external to the

HTML source is met. For instance, a rule that sets the appearance of a link that has previously been clicked by a user might be:

a:visited {

   color: #999;

   text-decoration: underline

}

The color of the visited link in this example is specified as gray and underlined. The most common pseudo-class selectors are a:link, a:visited, a:hover, and a:active. For more information on Cascading Style Sheets, go to the W3C website at w3.org/TR/CSS1.

Using Tools to Manage Your Styles

There are several tools available to assist you in defining, modifying, and checking CSS rules. You have learned to use some of them such as the Code Navigator and Live View. The Browser Compatibility Check feature flags issues on a page that may present a problem when viewed in a particular browser. To use the Browser Compatibility Check feature, open a page you want to check, then use the File > Check Page > Browser Compatibility command to locate issues that may be a problem. Any issues Dreamweaver finds are listed in the Browser Compatibility Panel in the Results Panel Group with the line number and issue listed for each item it finds. You can modify the settings to add additional versions of browsers by clicking the arrow menu in the top left corner of the panel, then clicking Settings, as shown in Figure 32.

Another tool for managing your styles is Inspect mode. **Inspect mode** helps you to identify HTML elements and their associated styles. To access Inspect mode, go to Live view, click the Inspect button next to the Live Code button in the Document toolbar, then click Switch Now in the information bar that appears above the Document window. The Document window changes to Split view with Live view enabled. As you move the mouse pointer (hover) over a page element in Inspect mode, the element is highlighted in Design view in the right pane with the CSS box model attributes displayed in color. Different colors are used for the border, margin, padding, and content. The attributes of the highlighted element are also displayed in Code view in the left pane and in any related open panels, such as the CSS Styles panel.

QUICK TIP
If you click an element, you will turn off Inspect mode.

Another tool for managing your styles is Disable/Enable CSS. This feature allows you to disable a rule property in Design view so you can compare the effects of the affected page element with and without that property. To use this feature, select a rule property in the Properties pane in the CSS Styles panel, then click to the left of the property. The property will be disabled and an icon will appear beside it, as shown in Figure 33. Click the icon to enable the property.

Figure 33 *Disabling a rule property*

Figure 32 *Using the Browser Compatibility Check*

Click to add additional browsers for compatibility checking

Click to disable the rule property

Lesson 4 Work with Conflicting Styles

Compare conflicting styles

1. Open the body rule in the HTML5_twoCol-FixRtHdr.css file, change the font to Verdana, Geneva, sans-serif, then click **OK**.

    We are changing the font so the following steps will be easier for you to see what happens with conflicting styles. The body font properties were very close to the body_text properties.

2. Open the Activities page, select the first sentence on the page beginning "We have many . . .", click the **CSS button** on the Property inspector if necessary, click the **Targeted Rule list arrow**, click **<Remove Class>**, then deselect the text.

    When the body rule in the HTML5_twoCol-FixTrHdr.css style sheet is removed from the sentence, the font style from the body tag in the HTML5_twoColFixTrHdr.css style sheet is applied, as shown in Figure 34. Here, order of precedence is determined by specificity of the selector, which means that the selector closest in the code to an object it modifies will override any other selectors. The body_text rule is more specific than the body_text property in the body rule. The targeted rule text box shows all the heading tags grouped together separated by commas. To help to reduce the style sheet size, multiple selectors that share common properties and values can be grouped together. These are called **group selectors**.

3. Click **Edit** on the Menu bar, then click **Undo Apply <span>** (Win) or **Undo** (Mac) to apply the body_text style from the external style sheet again.

4. Edit the body rule to reassign the Arial, Helvetica, sans-serif font, then save your work.

You found that the external body_text style had precedence over the body style.

DREAMWEAVER 8-28

Figure 34 *Text with rule applied from redefined body tag*

Example of grouped selectors

The font in the first paragraph is now different from the rest of the page text

With no style applied, the font family is applied from the body tag

Using Styles and Style Sheets for Design

Figure 35 *Using the Browser Compatibility Check*

Browser Compatibility list arrow

No issues are detected

Panel options button

Figure 36 *Using the Browser Compatibility Check*

Minimum browser versions that will be used to verify page (your browsers and version numbers may differ)

Check for errors with Browser Compatibility Check

1. With the activities page open, click **File** on the Menu bar, point to **Check Page**, then click **Browser Compatibility**.

   The Browser Compatibility panel opens in the Results panel group and shows no compatibility errors, as shown in Figure 35.

2. Click the panel options button in the upper-right corner of the Browser Compatibility panel, then click **Settings**.

   The Target Browsers dialog box lists the names and versions of each browser that will be used to check the page for rendering issues, as shown in Figure 36. If you want to change the browser versions used for testing, click the version number next to each browser name, then select a different version.

3. Close the Target Browsers dialog box, close the Results Tab group, save and close all open files, then close Dreamweaver.

You checked the activities page for errors using the Browser Compatibility panel and found no errors. You then viewed the names and versions of the browsers that are currently set as the target browsers.

DESIGN**TIP**

Recognizing and Addressing Printing Issues

There are many factors that affect how a page will print compared to how it will appear in a browser window. While a page background color will appear in a browser window, it will not print unless the user selects the print option to print background colors. Although the width of the page in the browser window may fit on the screen, it could actually be too wide to print on a standard printer in portrait orientation. Also, table borders, horizontal rules, and divs may not print exactly how they look in a browser. Printing your pages to see how they actually appear will allow you to address most issues. You can also go to a site such as the World Wide Web Consortium (W3C) at w3.org to find the best solution for any printing problems you identify.

Lesson 4 Work with Conflicting Styles

DREAMWEAVER 8-29

SKILLS REVIEW

Create and use embedded styles.
1. Copy the Blooms & Bulbs local site root folder to a drive and folder where you want to store your original files.
2. Delete your original blooms local site root folder, then copy and paste the blooms folder from the chapter_8 Data Files folder to the same location where you stored your original folder.
3. Open Dreamweaver, open the Blooms & Bulbs website, then open the plants page.
4. Create a new embedded rule for the plants page that will redefine the horizontal rule tag.
5. In the Border category, set the Top style to solid, set the Top width to thin, set the Top color to #033; and in the Box category, set the Width to 400 px.
6. Insert a horizontal rule right after the third paragraph ending "to enlarge them". (*Hint*: If your horizontal rule does not appear as centered on the page, view it in Live view or the browser.)

Modify embedded styles.
1. Modify the horizontal rule settings to change the width to 500 px and add a top and bottom margin of 15px.
2. Save your changes, then preview the plants page in your browser, click each page link to check for appearance, then close your browser.
3. Open the index page, modify the table rule in the blooms_styles.css file to set the box width to 165px.

Use CSS3 and Media Queries.
1. Use the New CSS Rule dialog box to redefine the h4 tag in the blooms_styles.css file. Set the font-family to Arial, Helvetica, sans-serif and the font-size to medium.
2. Select the sidebar1 rule in the HTML5_twoColFixRtHdr.css in CSS Styles panel, then click the Edit Rule button.
3. In the Border category, then change the Style to solid, the Width to thin, and the Color to #724D6F for all sides.
4. In the Box category, change the Width to 165px and the margins to 5px, then close the dialog box. You have to adjust the box width slightly to make room for the border and margins.
5. Click HTML5_twoColFixRtHdr.css on the Related files toolbar, then scroll to locate the .sidebar1 rule.
6. Place the insertion point at the end of the last property and value, press [Enter] (Win) or [Return] (Mac), then type the following code:

   -moz-border-radius: 10px;
   border-radius: 20px;

7. Return to Design view, then switch to Code view for the index page.
8. Add the following code to the sidebar1 div tag: style="height:220px".
9. Save your work, view the page using Live view, then compare your page to Figure 37.
10. Repeat step 8 to modify each individual sidebar1 div tag for each page, experimenting with the pixel value to match the height of the content div as closely as possible.
11. Save your work, upload the blooms_styles.css page for CSS3 validation at jigsaw.w3.org/css-validator. If you see any errors listed, correct them and run the validation again.

Work with conflicting styles.
1. Select the copyright and last updated statement on the index page and remove the small_text rule.
2. Reapply the small_text rule.
3. Save and close the index page.
4. View each page in the browser and make any additional adjustments you would like to improve the appearance of each page.

SKILLS REVIEW
(CONTINUED)

Figure 37 *Completed Skills Review*

Blooms & Bulbs
HWY 43 SOUTH • ALVIN • TX 77511 • 555-248-0806

Home   Newsletter   Plants   Tips   Workshops

Blooms & Bulbs
Highway 43 South
Alvin, Texas 77511
555-248-0806
Customer Service

Welcome to Blooms & Bulbs

We carry a variety of plants and shrubs along with a large inventory of gardening supplies. Our four greenhouses are full of healthy young plants just waiting to be planted in your yard. We grow an amazing selection of annuals and perennials. We also stock a diverse selection of trees, shrubs, tropicals, water plants, and ground covers. Check out our garden ware for your garden accents or as gifts for your gardening friends. We are happy to deliver or ship your purchases.

Our staff includes a certified landscape architect, three landscape designers, and six master gardeners. We offer detailed landscape plans tailored to your location as well as planting and regular maintenance services. We have enjoyed serving Alvin and the surrounding area for twelve years now. Stop by and see us soon!

Copyright 2001 - 2015
Last updated on March 18, 2012

PROJECT BUILDER 1

In this Project Builder you will continue your work on the TripSmart website. You have decided to add a few more rules to the style sheet to improve some of the page formatting.

1. Copy your tripsmart folder to a different location for a backup copy, then replace your tripsmart folder with the new tripsmart folder from the drive and folder where you store your Chapter 8 Data Files.
2. Open the TripSmart website, then open the catalog page.
3. Create a new embedded rule that redefines the hr HTML tag using settings of your choice.
4. Add a horizontal rule above the contact information in the third column, using Figure 38 as a guide (your rule may have different characteristics).
5. Edit the hr style to change the color to a different color or length.
6. Convert the hr style to an external style in the tripsmart_styles.css styles file.
7. Open each page and add a horizontal rule below the contact information in the third column.
8. Open the HTML5_thrColFixHr.css file, then use Code view to add code to modify the corners of the content div with settings of your choice.
9. Save all files, then validate the tripsmart_styles.css file for CSS3 standards.
10. Preview the each page in your browser.
11. Close your browser, then close all open files.

Figure 38 *Sample Project Builder 1*

PROJECT BUILDER 2

In this Project Builder, you will continue your work on the Carolyne's Creations website that you started in Project Builder 2 in Chapter 1. You will continue to work on the page formatting to include all formatting with CSS styles.

1. Copy your cc folder to a different location for your backup copy, then replace your cc folder with the new cc folder from the drive and folder where you store your Chapter 8 Data Files.
2. Open the Carolyne's Creations website, then open the catering page.
3. Create a new class style in the cc_styles.css file called **prices**.
4. Select the settings of your choice for the prices rule that you will then use to format the prices for the four marshmallow flavors available.
5. Apply the prices rule to each of the four prices, save all files, then close the catering page.
6. Open the classes page, then create a new class style for this page only, named **class_name**, selecting formatting settings of your choice.
7. Remove the bold formatting from each class name, then apply the class_name rule to the Valentine Chocolate Extravaganza, Not So Traditional Thanksgiving, and Super Bowl Snacks text.
8. Convert the class_name rule to an external style in the cc_styles.css file.
9. Save your work, then preview the classes page in your browser. See Figure 39 for a possible solution.
10. Go to the W3C validation service, validate the cc_styles.css file for CSS Level 3, then correct any errors that you find.
11. Close your browser, then close all open files.

Figure 39 *Sample Project Builder 2*

Using Styles and Style Sheets for Design

DREAMWEAVER 8-33

DESIGN PROJECT

Most of today's leading websites use CSS to ensure consistent formatting and positioning of text and other elements. For instance, the United States Department of Justice website uses them. Figure 40 shows the Department of Justice home page.

1. Connect to the Internet, then go to the United States Department of Justice website at justice.gov.
2. Spend some time exploring the many pages of this site.
3. When you finish exploring all of the different pages, return to the home page. View the source code for the page.
4. Look in the head content area for code relating to the style sheet used. Read through the code and list five class names that you find on the page that are used for formatting page elements.
5. Close the Source window, then look at the home page. List any links that you find for social networking.

Figure 40 *Design Project*
United States Department of Justice website: www.justice.gov

PORTFOLIO PROJECT

In this assignment, you will continue to work on the website that you created in Chapters 1 through 7.

You will continue refining your site by using style sheets to format the text in your site consistently.

1. Write a plan in which you define styles for all of the text elements in your site. Your plan should include how you will use an external style sheet as well as embedded styles. You can use either the external style sheet you created in Chapter 3 or create a new one. Your plan should include at least one class rule, one rule that redefines an HTML tag, and one rule that uses a selector.
2. Attach the completed style sheet to all individual pages in the site.
3. Create and apply the embedded rules you identified in your plan.
4. Create and apply the rules that will be added to the external style sheet.
5. Review the pages and make sure that all text elements appear as they should and look appropriate. Use the checklist in Figure 41 to make sure you have completed everything according to the assignment.
6. Make any necessary changes.
7. Save your work, then close all open pages.

Figure 41 *Portfolio Project*

Website Checklist
1. Do all text elements in the site have a style applied to them?
2. Does your site have at least one embedded style?
3. Is the external style sheet attached to each page in the site?
4. Did you define and apply at least one class style, one style that redefines an HTML tag, and one style that uses a selector?
5. Are you happy with the overall appearance of each page?

ADOBE DREAMWEAVER CS6

CHAPTER 9 COLLECTING DATA
WITH FORMS

1. Plan and create a form
2. Edit and format a form
3. Work with form objects
4. Test and process a form

CHAPTER 9
COLLECTING DATA WITH FORMS

Introduction

Many websites have pages designed to collect information from users. You've likely seen such pages when ordering books online from Amazon.com or purchasing airline tickets from an airline website. Adding a form to a web page provides interactivity between your users and your business. To collect information from users, you add forms for them to fill out and send to a web server to be processed. Forms on a web page are no different from other forms you use in everyday life. Your bank checks are simple forms that ask for information: the date, the amount of the check, the name of the check's recipient, and your signature. A form on a web page consists of **form objects** such as text boxes or radio buttons into which users type information or from which they make selections. **Form labels** identify the form object by its function, such as a "First Name" label beside a text box that collects the user's first name.

In this chapter, you add a form to a page that provides a way for interested users to ask for more information about The Striped Umbrella resort. The form will also give them the opportunity to comment on the website and make helpful suggestions. Feedback is a vital part of a website and must be easy for a user to submit.

Using Forms to Collect Information

Forms are just one of the many different tools that web developers use to collect information from users. A simple form can consist of one form object and a button that submits information to a web server, such as a search text box that you fill out, and a button that you click to start the search. More complex forms can collect contact information, or allow students to take exams online and receive grades instantly. You can use forms to insert information into databases, or to find a specific record in a database. The range of uses for forms is limited only by your imagination.

All forms need to be connected to an application server that will process the information that the form collects. The application can store the form data in a database, or simply send it to you in an email message. You need to specify how you want the information used, stored, and processed.

TOOLS YOU'LL USE

Insert — Forms panel:
- Form
- Text Field
- Hidden Field
- Textarea
- Checkbox
- Checkbox Group
- Radio Button
- Radio Group
- Select (List/Menu)
- Jump Menu
- Image Field
- File Field
- Button
- Label
- Fieldset
- Spry Validation Text Field
- Spry Validation Textarea
- Spry Validation Checkbox
- Spry Validation Select
- Spry Validation Password
- Spry Validation Confirm
- Spry Validation Radio Group

Input Tag Accessibility Attributes dialog:
- ID: first_name
- Label:
- Style:
  - Attach label tag using 'for' attribute
  - Wrap with label tag
  - No label tag (selected)
- Position:
  - Before form item (selected)
  - After form item
- Access key: ___   Tab Index: ___

If you don't want to enter this information when inserting objects, change the Accessibility preferences.

Radio Group dialog:
- Name: newsletters
- Radio buttons: [+] [−]

Label	Value
Yes	positive
No	negative

- Lay out using:
  - Line breaks (
 tags) (selected)
  - Table

DREAMWEAVER 9-3

LESSON 1

Plan and CREATE A FORM

What You'll Do

In this lesson you will add a new form to a feedback page in The Striped Umbrella website.

Planning a Form

Before you use Dreamweaver to create a form, it's a good idea to write down the information you want to collect and the order in which you want to collect it. It's also a good idea to make a sketch of the form for your wireframe. Planning your form content at the beginning saves you from spending time organizing the information when you create the form in Dreamweaver. The Striped Umbrella website will contain a form for users to request more information, sign up for an electronic newsletter, and submit their comments about the website. Figure 1 shows a sketch of the form that you create in this chapter.

When planning your form content, you should organize the information in a logical order that will make sense to users. For instance, users expect to fill in their name before their address, because almost all forms, from your birth certificate to your IRS tax forms, request your name before your address, so you should follow this standard. Placing information in a different order will confuse your users.

People on the Internet are notoriously hurried and often provide only information that is required or that is located on the top half of the form. Therefore, it's a good idea to put the most important information at the top of your form. In fact, this is a good rule to follow for web pages in general. The most important information should be "above the fold" or on the part of the page that is visible before you have to scroll to see the rest. As with all pages, your forms should have good contrast between the color of the text and the color of the form background.

Creating Forms

Once you finish planning your form content, you are ready to create the form in Dreamweaver. To create a form object on a web page, use the Form button in the Forms category on the Insert panel. Clicking the Form button inserts a dashed red outline around the form area. But by itself, a form object can do nothing. To make your form usable, you need to configure it so that it "talks" to the scripts or email server and processes the information users enter. The form must have a script or program running "behind" it to process the information users enter so you can gather and use it.

Designers use two methods to process the information collected in a form: server-side scripting and client-side scripting. **Server-side scripting** uses applications that reside on your web server and interact with the form information collected. For example, when you order clothing from a retail website, the host web server stores and processes the item, size, color, price, shipping information, and credit card information. The most common types of server-side applications are **Common Gateway Interface (CGI)** scripts, **Cold Fusion** programs, **Java Server Page (JSP)**, and **Active Server Pages (ASP)** applications. **Client-side scripting** means that the user's computer processes the form. The script resides on the web page, rather than on the server. For example, a mortgage calculator that allows you to enter prices and interest rates to estimate mortgage payments processes the data on the user's computer. The most common types of scripts stored on a web page are created with a scripting language called **JavaScript**, or **Jscript**. Server-side applications and scripts collect the information from the form, process the information, and perform some sort of action depending on the information the form contains.

You can process form information several ways. The easiest and most common way is to have the information collected from the form and emailed to the contact person on the website. You can also have form data stored in a database to use at a later date. You can even have the application both collect the form data in a database and send it in an email message. You can also have the form data processed instead of stored. For instance, you can create a form that calculates item quantities and prices and provides a total cost to the user on the order page, without recording any subtotals in a database or email message. In this example, only the final order total would be stored in the database or sent in an email message.

You can also create forms that make changes to your web page based on information users enter. For example, you could create a form that asks users to select a background color for a web page. In this type of form, the information could be collected and sent to the processor. The processor could then compare the selected background color to the current background color and change the color if it is different from the user's selection.

Setting Form Properties

After you insert a form, use the Property inspector to specify the application that you want to process the form information and how you want it sent to the processing application. The **Action property** in the Property inspector specifies the application or script that will process the form data. Most of the time the Action property is the name and location of a CGI script, such as /cgi-bin/myscript.cgi; a Cold Fusion page, such as mypage.cfm; or an Active Server Page, such

Figure 1 *Sketch of the form you will add to the feedback page*

Lesson 1   Plan and Create a Form

DREAMWEAVER 9-5

as mypage.asp. Figure 2 shows the properties of a selected form.

The **Method property** specifies the **HyperText Transfer Protocol (HTTP)** used to send the form data to the web server. The **GET method** specifies that ASCII data collected in the form will be sent to the server appended to the URL or the file included in the Action property. For instance, if the Action property is set to /cgi-bin/myscript.cgi, then the data will be sent as a string of characters after the address, as follows: /cgi-bin/ myscript.cgi?a+collection+of+data+collected+by+the+form. Data sent with the GET method is usually limited to 8K or less, depending on the web browser. The **POST method** specifies that the form data should be sent to the processing script as a binary or encrypted file, allowing you to send data securely. When you specify the POST method, there is no limit to the amount of information that can be collected in the form, and the information is secure.

The **Form name property** specifies a unique name for the form. The name can be a string of any alphanumeric characters and cannot

Figure 2 *Form controls in the Property inspector*

include spaces. The **Target property** lets you specify the window in which you want the form data to be processed. For instance, the _blank target will open the form in a separate browser window.

Understanding CGI Scripts

CGI is one of the most popular tools used to collect form data. CGI allows a web browser to work directly with the programs that are running on the server and also makes it possible for a website to change in response to user input. CGI programs can be written in the computer languages Perl or C, depending on the type of server that is hosting your website. When a CGI script collects data from a web form, it passes the data to a program running on a web server, which in turn passes the data back to the user's web browser, which then makes changes to the website in response to the form data. The resulting data is then stored in a database or sent to an email server, which then sends the information in an email message to a designated recipient. Figure 3 illustrates how a CGI script processes information collected by a form.

Figure 3 *Illustration of CGI process on a web server*

Data is transferred through the Internet to the web server.

Web Browser
User types in data and the browser stores it until it is submitted to the server.

Web Server
Server finds the CGI Script and sends it with the raw data received from the web browser.

CGI Script
Collects data from server and processes it according to its programming.

Data collected OK?
- NO → Return error message to web browser, through the web server.
- YES ↓

Return data w/ email?
- YES → Format data, open mail server, create message, and send message to pre-specified address.
- NO ↓

Store data in database?
- YES → Sort order of data, open database, insert record into database, close, and save database contents.
- NO ↓

Adjust page appearance?
- YES → Identify adjustment to make, format JavaScript command, send command to browser, and implement.
- NO ↓

Other processing instructions are completed, and appropriate information is returned to the web browser through the web server.

Processed data is returned to the web browser from the web server. The browser then makes changes to the current page.

Lesson 1 Plan and Create a Form

Insert a form

1. Open The Striped Umbrella website, open the file dw9_1.html from the drive and folder where you store your Data Files, then save it as **feedback.html** in The Striped Umbrella website, but do not update links.

2. Close the dw9_1.html file, then click inside the content container on the feedback page to place the insertion point.

   TIP The content container top border is under the menu bar. Click right under it to place the insertion point in the correct location. To verify that it is the correct location, go to Code view and verify that the insertion point is between the <p> tags in the content container.

3. In Design view, select the Forms category on the Insert panel, then click the **Form button** to insert a new form on the page.

   A rectangle with a dashed red outline appears on the page, as shown in Figure 4. As you add form objects to the form, the form expands.

   TIP You can see the form only if Invisible Elements are turned on. To turn on Invisible Elements, click View on the Menu bar, point to Visual Aids, then click Invisible Elements.

You inserted a new form on the feedback page of The Striped Umbrella website.

Figure 4 *New form inserted on the feedback page*

Form outline

Form button

Figure 5 *Property inspector showing properties of selected form*

Form ID Name text box — Method specifying data transfer method — Method list arrow

Using CGI scripts

You can use CGI scripts to start and stop external programs or to specify that a page update automatically based on user input. You can also use them to create surveys, site search tools, and games. You can even use CGI to do basic tasks such as record entries to a guest book or count the number of people who have accessed a specific page of your site. CGI also lets you create dynamic web documents "on the fly" so that pages can be generated in response to preferences specified by the user. Although instructions for creating and modifying CGI scripts are not covered in this book, you can probably find a script by searching on the Internet.

Set form properties

1. Click the **Form tag (<form>)** in the tag selector on the status bar to select the form and display the form properties in the Property inspector.
2. Type **feedback** in the Form ID Name text box in the Property inspector.
3. Click the **Method list arrow** in the Property inspector, then click **POST** if necessary, as shown in Figure 5.

TIP Leave the Action and Target text boxes blank unless you have the information necessary to process the form. However, when you submit an HTML5 page for validation, the Results panel will list an error until you supply a form action.

4. Save your work.

You configured the form on the feedback page.

Lesson 1 Plan and Create a Form

DREAMWEAVER 9-9

LESSON 2

Edit and
FORMAT A FORM

What You'll Do

In this lesson, you will insert a table that will contain the form on the feedback page. You will also add and format form labels.

Using Tables to Lay Out a Form

Just as you can use CSS or tables to help place page elements on a web page, you can also use CSS or tables to help lay out forms. To make sure that your labels and form objects appear in the exact positions you want on a web page, you can place them on the page using layout options such as div tags, tables, and lists. When you use a table to lay out a form, you can place labels in the first column and place form objects in the second column, as shown in Figure 6.

Adding Labels to Form Objects

When you create a form, include form field labels so that users know what information you want them to enter in each field. Because labels play such an important part in identifying the information that the form collects, you need to make sure to use labels that make sense to your users. For example, First Name and Last Name are good form field labels, because users understand clearly what information they should enter. However, a label such as Top 6 Directory Name might

Using Fieldsets to Group Form Objects

If you are creating a long form on a web page, you might want to organize your form elements in sections to make it easier for users to fill out the form. You can use fieldsets to group similar form elements together. A **fieldset** is an HTML tag used to group related form elements together. You can have as many fieldsets on a page as you want. To create a fieldset, use the Fieldset button on the Insert panel.

confuse users and cause them to leave the field blank or enter incorrect information. If creating a simple and obvious label is not possible, then include a short paragraph that describes the information users should enter into the form field. Figure 7 shows clearly marked labels for each form field, as well as additional text providing directions or examples for the user to follow.

You can add labels to a form using one of two methods. You can simply type a label in the appropriate table cell or div or use the Label button in the Forms category on the Insert panel to link the label to the form object.

Using CSS to Format the Form

With CSS3, many of the tags used to position table content are deprecated. So if you use a table to position data in a form, you will need to create or modify CSS rules to format the labels and data fields, such as their horizontal and vertical alignment. If you have only one table in your site, you can simply add properties to the table tag. But if you have more than one table in your site and they have different dimensions, then you will need to format them separately, creating separate rules to format each one. If you only have one table and the rows and columns are of equal size and appearance, you can set row or column alignment or widths by modifying the row or column tags. If the rows and columns have different alignments or widths, you will have to create separate rules for each column or row.

Figure 6 *Website that uses tables to lay out a form*
U. S. Department of State website – www.state.gov

Figure 7 *Website with clear labels for form fields*
Social Security Administration website – www.ssa.gov

Lesson 2   Edit and Format a Form

DREAMWEAVER 9-11

Add a table to a form

1. Click to place the insertion point inside the form outline, as shown in Figure 8.
2. Select the Common category on the Insert panel, then click the **Table button**.
3. In the Table dialog box, set the Rows to **10**, Columns to **2**, delete any other settings that remain from previous tables, then click the **Top header option** in the Header section.

   TIP The Table dialog box will retain the settings from the last table you created, so be sure to remove all settings that you do not want to apply to the new table.

4. Compare your screen to Figure 9, then click **OK**.

   The table is currently formatted with the table rule in the su_styles.css file that you defined earlier for the cafe page. This rule specifies the table width.

   TIP Remember that there are several ways to apply styles in a table. You can apply styles by selecting text, clicking inside a paragraph, selecting a cell and applying a style to it, or applying a style to an HTML tag, such as a table tag.

You added a table to the form on the feedback page. The table will hold form objects.

Figure 8 *Placing the insertion point inside the form*

Insertion point placed inside form

Figure 9 *Setting table properties*

Rows=10

Top row header

Columns=2

Verify that these are blank

DREAMWEAVER 9-12

Collecting Data with Forms

Figure 10 *Typing labels in table cells*

Add form labels to table cells

1. Merge the top two cells in the first row of the table, then type **To request further information, please complete this form.** in the merged cells.

    Because you designated a header for this table, the top row text is automatically centered and bold. Screen readers use the header to assist users who have visual impairments to identify the table.

2. Click in the first cell in the fifth row, then type **I am interested in information about:**.

3. Press [↓], then type **I would like to receive your newsletters**.

4. Press [↓], type **I learned about you from:**, then press [↓].

5. Compare your screen to Figure 10.

You added a header and three form labels to table cells in the form.

Lesson 2 Edit and Format a Form

DREAMWEAVER 9-13

Add form labels using the Label button

1. Verify that the insertion point is in the cell below the one that contains the text "I learned about you from:".
2. Select the Forms category on the Insert panel, then click the **Label button**.

   The view changes to Code and Design view, as shown in Figure 11. The insertion point is positioned in the Code view pane between the tags <label> and </label>, which were added when you clicked the Label button.

   TIP You may need to scroll down in the Design pane to see the cell.

3. Type **Comments:**, then click the **Refresh button** in the Property inspector.

   The label appears in the table cell in the Design view pane.

4. Compare your screen to Figure 12, click the **Show Design view button**, then save your work.

You added a new label to the form on the feedback page using the Label button.

Figure 11 *Adding a label to a form using the Label button*

Insertion point between Label tags in Code view

Label button

Figure 12 *New label added using the Label button*

New label

DREAMWEAVER 9-14

Collecting Data with Forms

Figure 13 *Table formatted with new form_table rule and <td> rule*

form_table rule applied to table

Create a rule for the form table

1. Create a new class selector rule in the su_styles.css file named **form_table** with the following property: Box Width: **625px**.
2. Select the **<table> tag** in the Tag Selector, then use the Class list box to apply the form_table rule.

   The table is now wider, which will allow the labels in the first column to all appear on one line without wrapping after more form objects are added.
3. Create a new tag selector rule that modifies the <td> tag in the su_styles.css file with the following property: Block Vertical-align: **top**.

   The text in each cell is now aligned at the top of the cell, which will be more apparent as you add longer text labels and larger text fields to some of the table cells.
4. Compare your screen to Figure 13, then save your work.

You created a new rule to format the table and a new rule to format the table cells.

Lesson 2 Edit and Format a Form

DREAMWEAVER 9-15

LESSON 3

Work with
FORM OBJECTS

What You'll Do

In this lesson, you will add form objects to the form on the feedback page.

Understanding Form Objects

A form provides a structure in which you can place form objects. Form objects—which are also called **form elements**, **form controls**, **form inputs**, or **form fields**—are the form components such as check boxes, text boxes, and radio buttons that allow users to provide information and interact with the website. You can use form objects in any combination to collect the information you need. Figure 14 shows a form that contains a variety of form objects.

Text fields are the most common type of form object and are used for collecting a string of characters, such as a name, address, password, or email address. Use the Text Field button on the Insert panel to insert a text field. You can specify single-line or multi-line text fields.

A **text area field** is a text field that can store several lines of text. You can use text area fields to collect comments, descriptions of problems, long answers to questions, or even a résumé. Use the Textarea button on the Insert panel to insert a text area.

You can use **check boxes** to create a list of options from which a user can make multiple selections. For instance, you could add a series of check boxes listing hobbies and ask users to select the ones that interest them. A group of check boxes is called a **check box group**.

You can use **radio buttons** to provide a list of options from which only one selection can be made. A group of radio buttons is called a **radio group**. Each radio group you create allows only one selection from within that group. You could use radio groups to ask users to select their annual salary range, their age group, or the T-shirt color they want to order. You could also use a radio group for users to answer a yes or no question. To insert a radio group, use the Radio Group button in the Forms category on the Insert panel.

You can insert a **menu** or **list** on a form using the Select(List/Menu) button on the Insert panel. You use menus when you want a user to select a single option from a list of choices. You use lists when you want a user to select one or more options from a list of choices. Menus are often used to provide navigation on a website, while lists are commonly used in order forms to let users choose from a list of possibilities. Menus must be opened to see all of the options they contain, whereas lists display some of their options all of the time. When you create a list, you need to specify the number of lines that will be visible on the screen by setting a value for the Height property in the Property inspector.

Using **hidden fields** makes it possible to provide information to the web server and form-processing script without the user knowing that the information is being sent. For instance, you could add a hidden field that tells the server who should receive an email message and what the subject of the message should be. You can also use hidden fields to collect information that a user does not enter and cannot see on the screen. For instance, you can use a hidden field to send you the user's browser type or IP address.

You can insert an **image field** into a form using the Image Field button on the Insert panel. You can use image fields to create buttons that contain custom graphics.

If you want your users to upload files to your web server, you can insert a **file field**. You could insert a file field to let your users upload sample files to your website or to post photos to your website's photo gallery.

All forms must include a **Submit button**, which users click to transfer the form data to the web server. You can also insert a **Reset button**, which lets users clear data from a form and reset it to its default values, or a **custom button** to trigger an action that you specify on the page. You can insert a Submit, Reset, or custom button using the Button button on the Insert panel. Place Submit and Reset buttons at the bottom of the form. You can also add a security challenge, as shown in Figure 14, to prevent automated programs from using the form.

Jump menus are navigational menus that let users go quickly to different pages in your site or to different sites on the Internet. You can create jump menus quickly and easily by using the Jump Menu button in the Forms category on the Insert panel.

When you insert a form object in a form, you use the Property inspector to specify a unique name for it. You can also use the Property inspector to set other appropriate properties for the object, such as the number of lines or characters you want the object to display.

Setting Form Object Attributes

As you place a control on a form, you usually need to add a label. You can place a form label either before or after it by typing it directly on the form. This is a good idea if you need more than a word or two for a form label.

Figure 14 *Website form with several form objects*
Federal Bureau of Investigation website — www.tips.fbi.gov

For instance, "Please explain the problem you are experiencing." would need to be typed on the form next to a text box. If, however, you only need the words "Yes" and "No" beside two radio buttons, you can add the labels "Yes" and "No" using a form attribute called a **label tag**. You can add a label tag before or after the form object using the Input Tag Accessibility Attributes dialog box. Label tags provide good accessibility for your form objects, as they clearly identify each form object and are read with screen readers.

Using Dreamweaver Exchange

To obtain form controls designed for creating specific types of forms, such as online tests and surveys, you can visit the Adobe Marketplace & Exchange (adobe.com/cfusion/exchange/), shown in Figure 15, a central storage location for program extensions, also known as **add-ons**. You can search the site by using keywords in a standard Search text box. You can also search for items featured by their staff, and for the most recent, most popular, and most highly rated.

Figure 15 *Using Adobe Marketplace & Exchange*
Adobe product screen shot reprinted with permission from Adobe Systems Incorporated — www.adobe.com

Click to visit Dreamweaver Exchange

Figure 16 *Input Tag Accessibility Attributes dialog box*

Select No label tag option

Figure 17 *Property inspector showing properties of selected text field*

ID   Char width = 40   Max chars = 100   Single line option button   New text field   Text Field button

Lesson 3   Work with Form Objects

Insert single-line text fields

1. Place the insertion point in the first cell under the header, then type **First Name**.

2. Press **[Tab]**, then click the **Text Field button** on the Insert panel to open the Input Tag Accessibility Attributes dialog box.

TIP The Input Tag Accessibility Attributes dialog box does not appear if you do not have the accessibility preference set for adding form objects.

3. Type **first_name** in the ID text box, click the **No label tag option button** in the Style section, as shown in Figure 16, then click **OK**.

TIP You can also type the text field name in the TextField text box in the Property inspector.

4. Type **40** in the Char width text box in the Property inspector.

   This specifies that 40 characters will be visible inside this text field when displayed in a browser.

5. Type **100** in the Max chars text box in the Property inspector.

   This specifies that a user can type no more than 100 characters in this field.

6. Click the **Single line option button** in the Property inspector if necessary, then compare your screen to Figure 17.

7. Repeat Steps 1 through 6 to create another label and single-line text field under the First Name label and text field, typing **Last Name** as the label in the first column and **last_name** for the text field.

(continued)

DREAMWEAVER 9-19

8. Repeat Steps 1 through 6 to create another label and single-line text field under the Last Name label and text field, using **Email** for the label and **email** for the TextField name.
9. Save your changes, preview the page in your browser, compare your screen to Figure 18, then close your browser.

You added three single-line text fields to the form, then previewed the page in your browser.

Figure 18 *Form with single-line text fields added*

DREAMWEAVER 9-20

Collecting Data with Forms

Figure 19 *Property inspector with properties of selected text area displayed*

Char width=50
Num lines=4
Multi line option button
New multiple-line text field
Textarea button

Insert a multiple-line text field

1. Click in the cell to the right of the Comments: label.
2. Click the **Textarea button** on the Insert panel, type **comments** in the ID text box, click the **No label tag option button** in the Input Tag Accessibility Attributes dialog box if necessary, then click **OK**.
3. Verify that the Multi line option button is selected in the Property inspector.
4. Type **50** in the Char width text box in the Property inspector.

   This specifies that 50 characters will be visible inside this text field when the page is displayed in a browser.
5. Type **4** in the Num lines text box in the Property inspector, as shown in Figure 19.

   This specifies that the text box will display four lines of text.

You added a multiple-line text field to the form.

Lesson 3   Work with Form Objects

DREAMWEAVER 9-21

Insert a Checkbox Group

1. Place the insertion point in the empty table cell to the right of "I am interested in information about:".

   This field will use a form label tag that is added when the form control is added.

2. Click the **Checkbox Group button** on the Insert panel.

3. Type **brochures** in the Name text box, click **Checkbox** in the first row of the Label column to select it, type **Fishing**, press **[Tab]**, then type **fishing** in the value column.

4. Click **Checkbox** in the second row of the Label column to select it, type **Cruises**, press **[Tab]**, type **cruises** in the value column, click the **Line breaks option button** if necessary, compare your screen to Figure 20, then click **OK**.

5. Click the **Fishing** check box to select it, compare your screen to Figure 21, click the **Unchecked option button** after Initial state in the Property inspector if necessary, then save your work.

   The check box will appear unchecked by default. If the user clicks it, a check mark will appear in the box.

(continued)

Figure 20 *Checkbox Group dialog box*

- Checkbox Group name
- Checkbox labels
- Lay out using Line breaks option
- Checkbox values

Figure 21 *Property inspector with check box properties displayed*

- Checkbox Group name = brochures
- Checked value = fishing
- Initial state = Unchecked
- Fishing checkbox

DREAMWEAVER 9-22

Collecting Data with Forms

Figure 22 *Feedback page in browser with check boxes added to the form*

6. Repeat Step 5 to verify that the check box for the Cruises option's initial state is Unchecked.
7. Preview the page in your browser, compare your screen to Figure 22, then close your browser.

You added two check boxes in a check box group to the form that will let users request more information about fishing and cruises.

Lesson 3 Work with Form Objects

DREAMWEAVER 9-23

Add radio groups to a form

1. Click in the empty table cell to the right of "I would like to receive your newsletters."
2. Click the **Radio Group button** on the Insert panel to open the Radio Group dialog box.
3. Type **newsletters** in the Name text box.
4. Click the **first instance of Radio** in the Label column of the Radio Group dialog box to select it, then type **Yes**.
5. Press **[Tab]** or click the **first instance of Radio** in the Value column to select it, then type **positive**.

   You named the first radio button Yes and set positive as the value that will be sent to your script or program when the form is processed when users click this check box.

6. Press **[Tab]** or click the **second instance of Radio** to add another radio button named **No** with a value of **negative**.
7. Click the **Line breaks (
 tags) option button**, if necessary, to select it.

   TIP If the Table option button is selected, then the radio buttons will appear in a separate table within the currently selected table.

8. Compare your screen with Figure 23, then click **OK** to close the Radio Group dialog box.

(continued)

Figure 23 *Radio Group dialog box*

Radio button labels

*Line breaks (
 tags) option button*

Collecting Data with Forms

Figure 24 *Feedback page with new radio group*

Radio group

9. Save your work, preview the page in your browser, compare your screen to Figure 24, then close your browser.

TIP To create radio buttons that are not part of a radio group, click the Radio Button button on the Insert panel.

You added a radio group that will let users answer whether or not they would like to receive The Striped Umbrella newsletters.

Lesson 3 Work with Form Objects

DREAMWEAVER 9-25

Add a menu

1. Click in the cell to the right of the text "I learned about you from:".
2. Click the **Select (List/Menu) button** on the Insert panel, click the **No label tag option button** in Style section of the Input Tag Accessibility Attributes dialog box, then click **OK**.
3. Type **reference** in the Select text box in the Property inspector.
4. Verify that the Menu option button in the Type section is selected in the Property inspector, as shown in Figure 25, then click the **List Values button** to open the List Values dialog box.
5. Click below the Item Label column heading if necessary, type **Select from list:**, then press **[Tab]**.
6. Type **none** in the Value column.

   This value will be sent to the processing program when a user accidentally skips this menu. If one of the real choices was in the top position, it might return false positives when users really did not select it, but just skipped it. This is a clue to users that they have not made a choice yet, but will not penalize them if they accidentally skip over this form control.

   (continued)

Figure 25 *Property inspector showing properties of selected List/Menu*

Menu option button   *List Values button*

Using Secure Forms

If you plan to include a form on your website, it is important to consider the sensitivity of the information that users transmit using the form. If they will enter confidential information such as credit card numbers or social security numbers, you should set up a secure form that protects the information from being harvested by unauthorized people. One way to do this is to place your forms on a secure server. SSL, which stands for **Secure Socket Layer**, is the industry standard for viewing and sending confidential information over the Internet by encrypting the data. Notice the next time that you place an order over the Internet that the *http* protocol changes to the *https* protocol when you open the page that contains the credit card form control. The https protocol stands for **Hypertext Transfer Protocol Secure**. You can create secure forms with plug-ins or services that are available commercially. Search the Internet for "Secure online forms" to locate the many companies that offer this service. WebAssist, a company listed in the Adobe Dreamweaver Exchange, offers a product called CSS Form Builder that allows you to build secure CSS forms. For more information, visit the Adobe Market Place & Exchange at adobe.com/cfusion/exchange/.

Figure 26 *List Values dialog box*

Add button

New item labels

Click to reorder list items

Values of new items

Figure 27 *Feedback page with menu*

Completed menu

7. Press **[Tab]**, type **From a friend** as a new Item Label, then type **friend** in the Value column.
8. Use the **Add button** to add the following three Item Labels: **Internet search**, **Magazine ad**, and **Television ad**, setting the Values as **internet**, **magazine**, and **tv**.

TIP You can also press [Tab] after entering an entry in the Value column to add a new item label.

9. Compare your screen to Figure 26, then click **OK**.
10. Save your work, preview the page in your browser, click the **list arrow** to view the menu, compare your screen to Figure 27, then close your browser.

You added a menu to the form on the feedback page.

Lesson 3 Work with Form Objects

DREAMWEAVER 9-27

Insert a hidden field

1. Click to the left of the First Name label at the top of the form to place the insertion point.
2. Click the **Hidden Field button** on the Insert panel.

   A Hidden Field icon appears at the insertion point.

   TIP If you do not see the Hidden Field icon, click View on the Menu bar, point to Visual Aids, then click Invisible Elements.

3. Type **required** in the HiddenField text box in the Property inspector, then type **first_name**, **last_name**, **email** in the Value text box, as shown in Figure 28.

   Typing first_name, last_name, email in the Value text box specifies that users must enter text in the First Name, Last Name, and Email fields before the script can process the form. The field names you type in the Value text box must match those in your form exactly.

4. Save your work.

You added a hidden field to the form that will let users know if they neglect to complete the fields for their first name, last name, and email address.

Figure 28 *Property inspector showing properties of selected hidden field*

HiddenField text box   Values   Hidden field icon   Hidden Field button

DREAMWEAVER 9-28

Collecting Data with Forms

Figure 29 *New Submit and Reset buttons added to form*

Button name text box | Value text box | Reset form action | Submit button | Reset button | Button button

Add Submit and Reset buttons

1. Click in the **second cell** of the second to last row of the table.

2. Click the **Button button** on the Insert panel, type **Submit** in the ID text box, click the **No label tag option button** in the Input Tag Accessibility Attributes dialog box if necessary, then click **OK**.

3. Verify that the Submit form option button is selected next to Action in the Property inspector.

    When a user clicks the Submit button, the information in the form will be sent to the processing script.

4. Verify that "Submit" is the name in the Value text box and in the Button name text box in the Property inspector.

5. Click to the right of the Submit button on the form, insert a space, then click the **Button button** on the Insert panel, click the **No label tag option button** in the Input Tag Accessibility Attributes dialog box if necessary, click **OK**.

6. Click the **Reset form option button** in the Property inspector, verify that the Value text box and Button name text box are set to Reset, then compare your screen to Figure 29.

    When a user clicks the Reset button, the form removes any information typed by the user.

7. Save your work.

You added a Submit button and a Reset button to the form.

Lesson 3 Work with Form Objects

DREAMWEAVER 9-29

LESSON 4

Test and PROCESS A FORM

What You'll Do

In this lesson, you will check the spelling on the feedback page and create a link to the feedback page on the about_us page. You will then open the about_us page in your browser, click the feedback link, then test the form and reset it.

Creating User-Friendly Forms

After you create a form, you should test it to make sure that it works correctly and is easy to use. Verify that the fields are arranged to provide a logical flow of information, so the user is not confused about where to go next when completing the form. Make sure that there is enough contrast between the form text and the table background so the text is readable.

When a form contains several required fields (fields that must be filled out before the form can be processed), it is a good idea to provide visual clues such as a different font color or other notation that label these fields as required fields. Often, you see an asterisk next to a required field with a corresponding note at either the top or the bottom of the form explaining that all fields marked with asterisks are required fields. This encourages users to initially complete these fields rather than attempt to submit the form and then receive an error message asking them to complete required fields that have been left blank. Using a different font color for the asterisks and notes is an easy way to call attention to them and make them stand out on the page.

When you are finished with your form, you should always have several people test it before you publish it. Then make any necessary changes based on any testing feedback that you receive and test it one final time.

Figure 30 *Adding visual clues for required fields*

First column height is extended   *Hint for user*   *Asterisks added after labels*

Using a Testing Server and Live View to Test Dynamic Content

When a web page contains content that allows the user to interact with the page by clicking or typing, and then responds to this input in some way, the page is said to contain **dynamic content**. A form is an excellent example of dynamic content, because as the user fills out the form, feedback can be returned, such as the availability of window seats on a particular airplane flight or whether or not certain colors or sizes of clothing items are available for purchase. This exchange of information is made possible through the use of a database, as you learned in Lesson 1. Once a form is developed and a database is tied to it, you should set up a **testing server** to evaluate how the form works and the data is processed. Your local computer or your remote server can serve as a testing server. You set up a testing server by filling out the relevant information in the Testing Server section of the Site Definition dialog box. You can also test your dynamic data in Design view by using Live View. **Live View** is a choice on the View menu that lets you add, edit, or delete dynamic content or server behaviors. You can use the Switch Design View to Live View button on the Document toolbar to change to Live View. The opposite of dynamic content is static content. **Static content** refers to page content that does not change or allow user interaction.

Lesson 4   Test and Process a Form

Check spelling and create visual clues for required fields

1. Click **Commands** on the Menu bar, click **Check Spelling** to check the spelling on the form.
2. Correct any spelling errors you find, then close the Check Spelling dialog box.
3. Click after the text First Name, then type * (an **asterisk**).

   The asterisk gives users a clue that this is a required field.
4. Place an asterisk after the words "Last Name" and "Email."
5. Merge the two cells in the last row, then type *****Required fields** in the merged field.
6. Edit the sidebar1 rule to add the following properties: Box Height: **400px**, Padding Top: **20px**.

   These properties add some space between the text and the top of the column and increase the div height.
7. Compare your screen to Figure 30, save your work, preview the page in the browser, close the browser, then close the feedback page.

You checked the spelling on the feedback page, then added asterisks to the required fields on the page. Next, you typed text explaining what the asterisks mean and edited the sidebar1 rule.

DREAMWEAVER 9-31

Link a file

1. Open the **about_us** page and click to place the insertion point after the last sentence on the page.
2. Enter a paragraph break then type **Please give us your feedback so that we may make your next stay the best vacation ever!**
3. Select the word "feedback," then use the **Point to File button** on the HTML Property inspector to link the feedback text to the feedback page.
4. Compare your screen with Figure 31, save your work, then preview the page in the browser.

(continued)

Figure 31 *Viewing the feedback link*

Link to feedback page

Using Spry Data Sets

One of the ways you can display data in a form is with a Spry data set. A **Spry data set** is a JavaScript object that stores data in rows and columns. You create a Spry data set in Dreamweaver and then write instructions to load the data from another source where the data is stored, such as an XML or HTML file. You can format the data to appear on a web page to your specifications. You create a Spry data set by using the Insert, Spry, Spry Data Set command on the Menu bar. This command opens the Spry Data Set dialog box, where you then specify the Data Type, Data Set Name, which tags to detect, and the Data File name and location.

Figure 32 *Testing the feedback page*

5. Click the **feedback link** to test it.

   The feedback page opens in a new window, as shown in Figure 32.

6. Test the form by filling it out, then clicking the **Reset button**.

   The Reset button clears the form, but the Submit button does not work because this form has not been set up to send information to a database. Linking to a database is beyond the scope of this book, but you can refer to the information on pages 9-5, 9-7, and 9-9 to learn more about CGI scripts.

7. Close the browser and close all open pages.

You created a link on the about_us page to link to the feedback form, and tested it in your browser.

Using Spry Validation Field Widgets

A **Spry widget** is a page element that enables user interaction on a web page. Spry widgets are stored within the **Spry framework**, a JavaScript library that provides access to reusable widgets that you can add to your pages. Some of the Spry widgets are fields that can be added to a form. These form fields are called **Spry Validation Field widgets**, which are fields that display valid or invalid states when text is being entered in a form on a web page. This instant feedback lets users correct their form before they try to submit it. Sometimes the widgets provide hints, such as the correct date format to use or the minimum number of characters required in a field. When a user does not enter the data correctly, an error message appears. To add a Spry Validation Field widget to a form, use the Insert, Spry, Spry Validation (field name) command, or select a button in the Spry category on the Insert panel. Spry widgets use a combination of CSS and JavaScript that work within the HTML code. The CSS code formats the widget and the JavaScript code makes it work.

Lesson 4 Test and Process a Form

DREAMWEAVER 9-33

SKILLS REVIEW

Plan and create a form.

1. Open the Blooms & Bulbs website.
2. Open the tips page.
3. Scroll to the bottom of the page, insert two paragraph breaks to end the ordered list after the last line of text, then insert a form.
4. Set the Method to POST in the Property inspector if necessary.
5. Name the form **submit_tips**.
6. Set the Target to _self.
7. Save your work.

Edit and format a form.

1. Insert a table within the form that contains 9 rows, 2 columns, and a Top header.
2. Create a new class rule in the blooms_styles.css file named tip_table with the following setting: Box Width: 600px.
3. Apply the tip_table rule to the new table.
4. Merge the cells in the top row and type **Submit Your Favorite Gardening Tip** in the newly merged cell.
5. Type **Email** in the first cell in the second row.
6. Type **Category** in the first cell in the third row.
7. Type **Subject** in the first cell in the fourth row.
8. Type **Description** in the first cell in the fifth row.
9. Merge the cells in the sixth row of the table, then insert the label **How long have you been gardening?** in the merged cell.
10. Merge both cells in the seventh row of the table, then insert the label **Receive notification when new tips are submitted?** in the resulting merged cell.
11. Save your work.

Work with form objects.

1. Click in the second cell of the second row. Insert a text field with no label tag, using the ID **email**. Set the Char width property to 30 and the Max chars property to 150. (*Hint*: The Input Tag Accessibility Attributes dialog box will not appear if you do not have the accessibility preference set for adding form objects.)
2. Click in the second cell of the fourth row, then insert a text field with no label tag and the ID **subject**. Set the Char width to 30 and the Max chars to 150.
3. Click in the second cell of the fifth row, then insert a textarea with no label tag and the ID **description**. Set the Char width to 40 and the Num lines to 5.
4. To the right of the "Receive notification when new tips are submitted?" label, insert a space and a check box with no label tag. Set the ID of the check box to **notification**, enter **yes** in the Checked value text box, then verify that the initial state is Unchecked.
5. To the right of the text "How long have you been gardening?" insert a radio group named **years_gardening**, that uses line breaks. It should contain the labels **1 to 5 years**, **5 to 10 years**, **Over 10 years** and the following corresponding values for each label: **1+**, **5+**, and **10+**.
6. Insert a Select (list/menu) with the ID **category** in the empty cell to the right of Category. Set the Type to Menu. Use the List Values dialog box to add the following item labels: **Select from list, Weed control, General growth**, and **Pest control**, and set the corresponding values for each to **none, weeds, growth**, and **pests**.
7. Insert a hidden field named **required** in the first cell of the eighth row that has the value **email**.
8. Insert a Submit button named **submit** in the second cell of the eighth row.
9. With your insertion point to the right of the Submit button, insert a Reset button named **reset** with the Reset form action.
10. Save your work.

SKILLS REVIEW
(CONTINUED)

Test and process a form.

1. Check the spelling on the page and correct any errors you find.
2. Type *(an asterisk) after the label Email.
3. Merge the cells in the last row, then type ***Required field** in the last row.
4. Add a border around the table.
5. Modify the tip_table rule to add a Box Left Margin of 50px.
6. Remove any extra space after the form, then save your work.
7. Preview the page in your browser, compare your form to Figure 33, then test the form by filling it out and using the Reset button.
8. Close your browser, then close all open pages.

Figure 33 *Completed Skills Review*

PROJECT BUILDER 1

In this exercise, you continue your work on the TripSmart website you created in Chapters 1 through 8. The owner, Thomas Howard, wants you to create a form to collect information from users who are interested in receiving more information on one or more of the featured trips.

1. Open the TripSmart website.
2. Open the tours page, cut the contact information, including the horizontal rule, from the third column and paste it at the end of the first column, apply the centered_text rule, add an <em> tag if necessary, then insert another horizontal rule above the contact information.
3. Insert a form named **information** at the top of the third column.
4. Specify the Method as POST, if necessary, and a target of _self.
5. Insert a table in the form that contains 8 rows, 1 column and a top Header.
6. In the top row, type **Please complete for more information on these tours.**.
7. Type **Email** in the second row, and **I am interested in:** in the fourth row.
8. Insert a single-line text field in the third row with the name **email**.
9. Set the Char width to 20 and the Max chars to 50 for the text field.
10. In the fifth row, insert a checkbox group with the name **tours**.
11. Use the Labels **Peru** and **Galapagos** with the values **peru** and **galapagos**.

PROJECT BUILDER 1
(CONTINUED)

12. Insert a Submit button and a Reset button in the seventh row.
13. Adjust your style sheet rules to fine-tune the placement of the form on the page.
14. Save your work, preview the page in your browser, test the form, compare your screen to Figure 34, close your browser, then close the tours page. (Your page will differ depending on the settings you have chosen.)

Figure 34 *Completed Project Builder 1*

PROJECT BUILDER 2

Use Figure 35 as a guide to continue your work on the Carolyne's Creations website you created in Project Builder 2 in Chapters 1 through 8. Chef Carolyne asked you to place a simple form on the catering page that allows customers to sign up for a class.

1. Open the Carolyne's Creations website.
2. Open the classes page.
3. Insert a form named **classes** at the top of the second column, right above the contact information with POST as the method and _self as the target.
4. Insert a table in the form that contains 11 rows, 1 column, and a top header.
5. In the top row, type **Class Registration**.
6. In the second row, type **Please select the class:**.
7. In the third row, insert a check box named **adult** with the ID **adult**. Wrap the label tag **Adult** after the check box.
8. In the fourth row, repeat Step 7 to add another check box with the name and ID **child** wrapped with the label tag **Child**.
9. In the fifth row, type **Please select the month:**.
10. In the sixth row, add a radio group named **month** with a button for **March** and a button for **April**.
11. In the seventh row, add a text field for a contact telephone number with a label tag identifying the text field before the text field.
12. In the eighth row, add a text field for the first name, using settings of your choice.
13. In the ninth row, add a text field for the last name, using settings of your choice.

PROJECT BUILDER 2
(CONTINUED)

14. Skip the tenth row, then add a Submit and Reset button in the eleventh row.
15. Add any additional formatting of your choice to the page, table, or form properties.
16. Save your work, preview the page in a browser, test the form, compare your screen to Figure 35, close your browser, then close the classes page.

Figure 35 *Completed Project Builder 2*

DESIGN PROJECT

Websites use many form objects to collect information from users. The form shown in Figure 36 is well organized and requests information that most people are comfortable giving over the Internet, such as name, address, and phone number. There are several helpful explanations that guide the user in filling out the form correctly to report an environmental violation.

1. Connect to the Internet, then navigate to the U.S. Environmental Protection Agency website, pictured in Figure 36, epa.gov. (The page in Figure 36 is at epa.gov/compliance/complaints/index.html.)
2. Does this site use forms to collect information? If so, identify each of the form objects used to create the form.
3. Is the form organized logically? Explain why or why not.
4. Locate the form action for each form. (*Hint*: To view the code of a page in a browser, click View on the menu bar of your browser, then click Source or Page Source.)
5. Do you see any hidden fields?
6. Are any of the forms secure?
7. Could the information in this form be collected with different types of form objects? If so, which form objects would you use?
8. Does the form use tables for page layout?
9. Does the form use labels for its fields? If so, were the labels created using the <label> element or with text labels in table cells? (*Hint*: Search the code for the form to look for <label> tags.)

Figure 36 *Design Project*
U. S. Environmental Protection Agency – www.epa.gov

DREAMWEAVER 9-40

Collecting Data with Forms

PORTFOLIO PROJECT

In this project, you continue to work on the website that you have been developing since Chapter 1.

You continue building your site by designing and completing a page that contains a form to collect visitor information as it relates to the topic of your site.

1. Review your wireframe. Choose a page to develop that will use a form to collect information.
2. Plan the content for the new page by making a list of the information that you will collect and the types of form objects you will use to collect that information. Plan to include at least one of every type of form object you learned about in the chapter. Be sure to specify how you will organize the form on the page.
3. Create the form and its contents.
4. Run a report that checks for broken links in the site. Correct any broken links that appear in the report.
5. Test the form by previewing it in a browser, entering information into it, and resetting it. Check to make sure the information gets to its specified location, whether that is a database or an email address.
6. Preview all the pages in a browser, then test all menus and links. Evaluate the pages for both content and layout.
7. Review the checklist shown in Figure 37. Make any modifications necessary to improve the form, the jump menu, or the page containing the form.
8. Close all open pages.

Figure 37 *Portfolio Project*

Website Checklist
1. Do all navigation links work?
2. Do all images appear correctly?
3. Do all form objects align correctly with their form labels?
4. Does the placement of the form objects appear in a logical order?
5. Does the most important information appear at the top of the form?
6. Did you test the form?
7. Are you happy with the overall appearance of each page?

ADOBE DREAMWEAVER CS6

CHAPTER 10 POSITIONING OBJECTS WITH AP DIVS

1. Insert an AP div
2. Set the position and size of an AP div
3. Add content to an AP div
4. Set AP div properties

CHAPTER 10
POSITIONING OBJECTS WITH AP DIVS

Introduction

You have learned how to control the position of text and graphic elements with precision on your web pages using CSS layout blocks. With **CSS layout blocks**, you use containers formatted with CSS to place content on web pages. These containers can hold images, blocks of text, Flash movies, or any other page elements. You set the appearance and position of these containers using HTML tags known as **div tags**. With div tags, you can position elements next to each other, as well as on top of each other in a stack. In this chapter, you will use another type of div called an AP div to place text and graphics on a page. AP stands for absolutely positioned. An **AP div tag** creates a div with a fixed position on a web page. When you create an AP div, Dreamweaver automatically creates a rule for it. The name of the rule begins with a pound sign (#) rather than a period. It is an ID type, not a class type.

Using AP Divs

AP divs let you control the appearance of elements on your web page. AP divs allow you to stack your information in a vertical pile, allowing for just one piece of information to be visible at a time. Browsers display AP divs as independent elements so you can easily change their contents or add or remove them without affecting the page flow. This makes them a good choice for page content that changes frequently or is based on certain conditions.

You can add behaviors to your AP divs with JavaScript. **JavaScript** is a program that is used to add interactivity to web pages. It is a **client-side script**, in which, as you learned in Chapter 9, the commands from the program are executed on the user's computer. This is the opposite of **server-side scripts**, which are executed on a web server. **Behaviors** are preset pieces of JavaScript code that you can attach to page elements, such as an AP div. A behavior instructs the page element to respond in a specific way when an event occurs, such as when the mouse pointer is positioned over the element. Behaviors are attached to page elements using **ActionScript**, a Flash scripting language developers use to add interactivity to movies, control objects, exchange data, and to create complex animations. You'll learn about adding behaviors in Chapter 11.

TOOLS YOU'LL USE

LESSON 1

Insert
AN AP DIV

What You'll Do

In this lesson, you will draw an AP div on The Striped Umbrella home page and set its properties using the Property inspector.

Understanding AP Elements

AP elements are page elements that are absolutely positioned, or assigned a fixed position on a web page. The most common AP element is an AP div. AP divs are created with AP div tags. In this chapter, we will use the term "AP element" when speaking in general about AP elements and "AP div" when specifically referring to AP divs. Using AP div tags, you can stack AP divs on top of each other and specify that only certain elements be visible at certain times or under conditions you specify. You can use AP divs to create special effects on a web page. For instance, you can use AP divs to build a whole image from individual pieces. You can then add code that will allow you to slide the pieces into their positions one at a time. You can also use AP divs to create dynamic pages that contain moving parts or objects that become visible or invisible, based on selections made by website users. Using AP divs to lay out a web page is like working with a stack of transparent sheets that you can stack on top of each other.

The National Parks Service page shown in Figure 1 uses divs to create interactive page content. When you place the pointer over one of the objects, it becomes selected and the spinning arrow points to it. When you move the pointer away from the object, it becomes deselected and the arrow moves away from it.

To insert an AP div, you can use the Draw AP Div button in the Layout Category on the Insert panel and drag to draw a rectangular shape anywhere on the page. You can also insert an AP div using the Layout Objects, AP Div command on the Insert menu. Specify the exact dimensions, color, and other attributes of a new AP div by changing the settings in the Preferences dialog box for all AP divs, or by setting rule properties for a specific AP div. After the AP div is in place, you can drag it to a different location on the page or edit the values in the L (left) or T (top) text boxes to change its position.

As you work with AP divs, it is often helpful to use guides to help you place and align the divs in consistent locations. A **guide** is a horizontal or vertical line that is used to position page content. You can add as many guides as you need to your web pages; the guides do not appear in the browser. To place a guide, drag the pointer from the horizontal or vertical ruler and release the mouse button when the guide is positioned in the correct location. A ScreenTip appears, telling you the exact position of the guide. You can use a guide to emulate a **fold line**, a term borrowed from newspapers. The fold line indicates where the paper is folded in half. The most important newspaper stories appear above the fold line. Similarly, you want the most important information on your page to appear above the "fold line," the portion of the screen that users can see without scrolling.

Using HTML Tags to Create AP Divs

Dreamweaver uses the <div> (division) tag to create an AP div. The default value for the first AP div on a page appears as <div id="apDiv1">. Dreamweaver assigns each additional AP div the next number in sequence. You can use either the Property inspector or the AP Elements panel to rename each AP div with a name that is relevant to its content. The styles for AP divs reside in the head content as part of the CSS code.

Understanding AP Div Content

An AP div is like a separate HTML document within a web page. It can contain the same types of elements that a page can, such as background colors, images, links, tables, and text. You can also set the contents of an AP div to work directly with a specified Dreamweaver behavior to make the page interact with a user in a certain way.

Formatting AP Divs

In using AP divs, it's best to use only as much content as fits in the container. If you add more information than the div can display at one time, you will need to use formatting controls to tell Dreamweaver how to handle the overflow. You can control the appearance of a selected AP div by changing the Clip, Visibility, and Overflow properties in the AP div rule.

The **Clip property** identifies the portion of an AP div's content that is visible in a web browser. By default, the clipping region matches the outside borders of the AP div, but you can change the amount that is visible by clipping one or all sides. For instance, if you set the L (left) Clip property to 10 pixels, then everything from the eleventh pixel to the right will appear in the browser. If you clip off 10 pixels from the right side, you will need to subtract 10 from the total width of the AP div and then type this value in the Clip R text box in the Property inspector. The clip setting can be applied only to AP divs that have an Overflow attribute set to a value other than visible.

The **Vis property** lets you control whether the selected AP div is visible. You can set the Vis property to default, visible, hidden, or **inherit**, which means that the visibility of the AP div is automatically inherited from its parent AP div or page.

The **Overflow property** specifies how to treat excess content that does not fit inside an AP div. You can make the content visible, hide the content, specify that scroll bars appear, or let the current AP div automatically deal with the extra content in the same manner as its parent AP div or page. However, some browsers do not support the overflow property.

Figure 1 *Using divs and Flash for placing interactive content*
National Park Service website — www.webrangers.us

Pointing to an object moves spinner so it points to that object

Draw an AP div

1. Open The Striped Umbrella website, open the index page, click **View** on the Menu bar, point to **Rulers**, then click **Show** to select this option if necessary.

   Rulers appear along the top and left side of the page and will help guide placement of page elements.

2. Place the mouse pointer on the horizontal ruler, then drag down to position a horizontal guide at approximately the **465 pixel mark** on the vertical ruler.

3. Select the Layout category on the Insert panel, then click the **Draw AP Div button**.

4. Using Figure 2 as a guide, drag a **rectangle** in the middle of the home page, and under the guide, that is approximately 250 pixels wide and 150 pixels tall.

   A new AP div appears on the page, but may not be selected. An AP div icon appears above the upper-left corner of the AP div.

   TIP You can also insert an AP div by clicking Insert on the Menu bar, pointing to Layout Objects, and then clicking AP Div.

5. Click the **AP div icon** above the AP div to select it, if necessary.

   TIP You can also select an AP div by clicking one of its borders or clicking the <div> tag in the tag selector.

You drew an AP div on the home page, then selected it.

Figure 2 *New AP div drawn on the home page*

Horizontal ruler

Vertical ruler

Horizontal guide

AP div icon

DREAMWEAVER 10-6

Positioning Objects with AP Divs

Figure 3 *Property inspector showing properties of selected AP div*

#girls rule

Properties for #girls rule (yours will differ slightly)

CSS-P Element ID text box

Overflow property

L, T, W, and H settings

Visible property

Selected AP div

Define an AP div

1. With the AP div selected, select **apDiv1** in the CSS-P Element text box in the Property inspector, type **girls**, then press **[Enter]** (Win) or **[return]** (Mac).

2. Verify that <div#girls> is selected in the Tag selector.

3. Click the **Overflow list arrow** in the Property inspector, then click **auto**.

4. Click the **Vis list arrow**, then click **visible**.

5. Compare your screen to Figure 3.

    The L, T, W, and H settings in the Property inspector specify the position and size of the AP div. Your settings will most likely differ from those shown in the figure because you probably drew your AP div with slightly different measurements.

6. Scroll down to view the new rule that has been defined in the CSS Styles panel called #girls.

    When you draw an AP div, Dreamweaver automatically creates a rule for it. As you make changes to the element properties, they appear in the Properties pane, when the rule is selected.

TIP You may see two different <style> sheets listed: one for the AP div rule and one for any other embedded rules.

7. Save your work.

You specified a name and other properties for the selected AP element. You viewed the new rule in the CSS Styles panel.

Lesson 1 Insert an AP Div

DREAMWEAVER 10-7

LESSON 2

Set the Position
AND SIZE OF AN AP DIV

What You'll Do

In this lesson, you will use the Property inspector to position and size AP divs on the home page of The Striped Umbrella website.

Understanding Absolute Positioning

To use AP divs, you must understand **absolute positioning**. The term "absolute" in this context means that the AP div will be locked in a fixed position on the page regardless of the size of the browser window. You position an AP div absolutely by specifying the distance between the upper-left corner of the AP div and the upper-left corner of the page or parent div in which it is contained. Figure 4 illustrates how an AP div keeps its position relative to the top left corner of a page as the page is scrolled.

AP divs have no impact on the location of other AP divs. In other words, if you insert an AP div, the page elements that follow it within the code will continue with the flow of the page, ignoring the presence of the AP div. This means you can create overlapping AP divs to create dynamic effects on a web page. To do this, you use JavaScript or CGI script to change the attributes associated with each AP div in response to actions by the user. For instance, an AP div could move or change its size when a user clicks or moves the mouse over a link on the page or in the AP div.

Setting Positioning Attributes

You can control the placement of AP divs by setting their attributes in the Property inspector or by editing the rule in the CSS Styles panel. These attributes work together to create an AP div that will hold its position on a page.

DREAMWEAVER 10-8

Positioning Objects with AP Divs

The **Left property (L)** specifies the distance between the left edge of an AP div and the left edge of the page or parent page element that contains it. The **Top property (T)** specifies the distance between the top edge of your AP div and the top edge of the page or the parent element that contains it.

The **Width (W)** and **Height (H) properties** specify the dimensions of the AP div, usually in pixels, although the AP div can be specified as a percentage of your screen dimension. For instance, you can specify that your AP div be 250 pixels by 250 pixels, or you can set it to 25% by 25%, which will create an AP div that is roughly 400 by 225 in a web browser on an 1600 × 900 resolution monitor.

Use the **Z-Index property** in the Property inspector to specify the vertical stacking order of AP divs on a page. If you think of the page itself as AP div 0, then any number higher than that will appear on top of the page. For instance, if you have three AP divs with the Z-Index values of 1, 2, and 3, then 1 will appear below 2 and 3, while 3 will always appear above 1 and 2. You can create a dynamic website by changing the Z-Index settings dynamically, as the user is viewing the page, using Dreamweaver's built-in JavaScript behaviors.

QUICK TIP
You cannot set Z-Index values below 0.

Figure 4 *Scrolling a page containing an AP div*

AP div moves up as page is scrolled up

Lesson 2 Set the Position and Size of an AP Div

DREAMWEAVER 10-9

Set the Left and Top positions of an AP div

1. Click the **AP div border** to select the AP div (if necessary).
2. Type **630px** in the L text box in the CSS-P Element section of the Property inspector, then press **[Tab]** (Win) or **[tab]** (Mac).

   The AP div moves automatically to the position you specified.

   TIP You can also drag a div by the div icon above the top-left corner of the div to reposition it.

3. Type **390px** in the T text box, then press **[Enter]** (Win) or **[return]** (Mac).
4. Save your work, then compare your screen to Figure 5.

   The div covers part of the text on the page now, but when the page is viewed in Live view or a browser, it will appear under the text.

   TIP The AP div may appear in a different position on your screen, depending on your screen size.

You adjusted the upper-left corner position of the AP div.

Figure 5 *AP div moved up and to the left on the page*

T = 390px   L = 630px   AP div moves according to new L and T properties   The width and height of your AP div may vary at this point

DREAMWEAVER 10-10

Positioning Objects with AP Divs

Figure 6 *AP div with width and height adjusted*

H = 179px *W = 250px* *AP div is resized, but stays in same position*

Set AP div height and width

1. Click the **AP div border** to select the AP div (if necessary).
2. Type **250px** in the W text box, then press **[Tab]**.

   The AP div automatically adjusts its width to the dimension you specified.
3. Type **179px** in the H text box, then press **[Tab]**.

   The AP div automatically adjusts to the height you specified. Notice that the upper-left corner stays in the same position.
4. Save your work, then compare your screen to Figure 6.

You adjusted the height and width of the AP div.

Lesson 2 Set the Position and Size of an AP Div

DREAMWEAVER 10-11

Set the Z-Index value for AP divs

1. Draw another AP div anywhere on the page, select it, then name it **white_ibis**.
2. Select the white_ibis AP div (if necessary), then adjust its size and position by setting the following properties in the Property inspector: L: **540px**, T: **470px**, W: **120px**, and H: **122px**.

   The new AP div is now positioned on top of the girls AP div, temporarily blocking part of it.

3. Select and change the Z-Index value of the white_ibis AP div to **2** in the Property inspector, if necessary, change the Overflow to **visible**, then change the Vis to **visible**, as shown in Figure 7.

   When an AP div is selected, it appears above other AP divs, regardless of its z-index value.

4. Repeat Steps 1 and 2 to draw another AP div on the page to the right of the girls AP div named **heron** with the following properties: L: **835px**, T: **460px**, W: **100px**, and H: **140px**, Overflow: **visible**, Vis: **visible**.

(continued)

Figure 7 *New white_ibis AP div appears to overlap the girls AP div*

Overflow = visible
New AP div name = white_ibis
Z index = 2
Vis = visible

DREAMWEAVER 10-12

Positioning Objects with AP Divs

Figure 8 *girls AP div selected on the page*

> Welcome to The Striped Umbrella — a full-service resort and spa just steps from the Gulf of Mexico and ten miles east of Crab Key, Florida. The Striped Umbrella has a variety of activities for adults and children. It is a perfect romantic getaway for two or a complete family vacation. Our activities include water sports, golf, shopping, and an award-winning spa.
>
> The restaurants at The Striped Umbrella are amazing. The Sand Crab Cafe can be enjoyed al fresco at The Terrace, poolside at The Cabana, and inside in The Dining Room. The Dining Room features fresh seafood and an extensive wine list. The Terrace offers more casual dining with sweeping views of the gulf and fabulous sunsets. The Cabana serves sandwiches, salads, and snacks around the pool area.
>
> The Striped Umbrella
> 25 Beachside Drive
> Ft. Eugene, Florida 33775
> 555-594-9458
> Club Manager

Come enjoy the best of both worlds, a secluded sandy beach populated with beautiful birds, yet a short drive down the road from world-class shopping, restaurants, and entertainment. Bring a good book and leave your laptop at the office. You won't want to go home!

girls AP div blocks some of the text on the page, but will appear correctly in a browser

5. Click the **girls AP div** to select it, by clicking its border or the AP div icon.
6. Change the Z-Index value of the girls AP div to **3**.

    The girls AP div will now be positioned in front of the other two AP divs in the browser.

7. Select the girls AP div if necessary.
8. Change the Z-Index value of the girls AP div back to **1** in the Property inspector, then save your work.

    Now the girls AP div will be positioned behind the other two AP divs in the browser.

9. Select the **girls AP div**, then compare your screen to Figure 8.

    The three AP divs are placed in position on the page. None of the AP divs has content yet. You can only see their outlines. The girls AP div looks like it overlaps paragraph text, but in the browser window it will appear slightly below it.

You added two new AP divs named white_ibis and heron to the home page, and specified their dimensions and position on the page using the Property inspector. You then adjusted their vertical stacking order.

Lesson 2   Set the Position and Size of an AP Div

LESSON 3

Add Content
TO AN AP DIV

What You'll Do

In this lesson, you will add a background image to an AP div. You will also insert an image on the other two AP divs and type text on an AP div.

Understanding AP Element Content

As you learned in Lesson 1, an AP div is like a separate document within a web page. It contains the same types of elements that any page would, such as background colors, images, links, tables, and text. If you want to add an image to an AP div, insert the image just as you would insert one on a page using the Insert panel. Figure 9 shows an AP div with an image placed inside it. If you want to be able to type on top of the image, insert the image as a background image for the AP div as shown in Figure 10.

If you add more content than the preset image size, the AP div will expand to display the content on your page in Dreamweaver.

However, when you preview the page in the browser, the amount displayed will depend on how you set your Overflow settings.

As on a web page, if you specify both a background color and a background image, the background image will override the background color. As the page is loading, the AP div background color may appear until the AP div background image finishes loading.

Also, as with formatting text on a web page, you should use CSS to format your text on an AP div. You can also add all other AP div properties such as text indent, padding, margins, and background color with styles.

DREAMWEAVER 10-14

Positioning Objects with AP Divs

Figure 9 *AP div with an inserted image*

Inserted image

Figure 10 *AP div with an image used as a background*

AP div with a background image and type added

Lesson 3 Add Content to an AP Div

DREAMWEAVER 10-15

Add an image to an AP div

1. Click inside the white_ibis AP div to place the insertion point there, click **Insert** on the Menu bar, click **Image**, browse to the drive and folder where you store your Data Files, open the assets folder, then double-click **white_ibis.jpg**. If a dialog box opens asking if you want to copy the image into your assets folder, click **Yes**.

   TIP Use care to place the insertion point inside the AP Div. It may take several attempts. You will see a long insertion point the height of the AP Div if you set it correctly.

2. Add **White Ibis** as the alternate text, then click **OK**.

   The image is inserted into the AP div, as shown in Figure 11. The Property inspector shows the properties of the selected image.

3. Select the white_ibis AP div, then compare your screen to Figure 12.

   The Property inspector now shows the properties of the AP div, as shown in Figure 12.

4. Save your work, preview the page in your web browser, then close the browser.

   TIP If your browser is not sized to the width of the window shown in Figure 14, your AP divs will not be positioned as shown. Remember you can also use Live View to preview your pages.

(continued)

Figure 11 *Image inserted into an AP div*

Property inspector shows image properties

white_ibis.jpg inserted into the AP Div

Figure 12 *Viewing the AP div properties*

Property inspector shows AP div properties

Vis property = visible

Selected AP div

DREAMWEAVER 10-16

Positioning Objects with AP Divs

Figure 13 *Second AP div with image inserted*

Image placed in heron AP div

Figure 14 *AP divs as they appear in a browser*

5. Click inside the heron AP div to set the insertion point.

    It may take you a few tries to set the insertion point. Try double-clicking or single-clicking right next to the left side of the AP div.

6. Select the **Common category** on the Insert panel, click the **Images list arrow**, then click **Image**.

7. Navigate to the drive and folder where you store your Data Files, open the assets folder, then double-click **heron.jpg**.

8. Type **Heron** in the Alternate text text box in the Image Tag Accessibility Attributes dialog box, click **OK**, then compare your screen to Figure 13.

9. Save your work, preview the page in your web browser, compare your screen to Figure 14, then close the browser.

    TIP If your browser window is not resized to the width of the window shown in Figure 14, your AP divs will not be positioned as shown.

You inserted images onto two AP divs on the home page.

Lesson 3 Add Content to an AP Div

DREAMWEAVER 10-17

Set a background image

1. Select the girls AP div, then click the **Browse for File button** next to the Bg image text box in the Property inspector to open the Select Image Source dialog box.

   Using the Bg image text box instead of the Insert panel inserts the image as a background on which you can easily enter text.

   TIP You can also change the background color of a div by using the Bg color text box.

2. Navigate to the drive and folder where you store your Data Files, open the assets folder, then click **two_girls.jpg**.

3. Click **OK** (Win) or **Choose** (Mac), then compare your screen to Figure 15.

4. Refresh the Files panel to verify that two_girls.jpg was copied to the assets folder of the website.

You added a background image to the girls AP div.

Figure 15 *Inserting a background image for an AP div*

Image is AP div background

Background image in the girls div

DREAMWEAVER 10-18

Positioning Objects with AP Divs

Figure 16 *Editing the #girls rule*

Type category
Block category

Font-size = small *Font-family = Verdana, Geneva, sans-serif* *Color = #FFFFFF* *Font-weight = bold*

Figure 17 *Index page with the formatted AP divs*

Add and format text on an AP div

1. Click inside the girls AP div to set the insertion point.
2. Type **beach walkers**.
3. Click the **#girls rule** in the CSS Styles panel, then click the **Edit Rule** button.
4. Click the **Type category**, as shown in Figure 16, change Font-family to **Verdana, Geneva, sans-serif**; Font-size to **small**; Font-weight to **bold**; and Color to **#FFFFFF**, then click **Apply**.
5. Click the **Block category**, change the Text-align setting to **left**, then click **OK**.

   The text changes to reflect the properties you have added to the girls rule. When you have text on an AP div, you should format the text using the AP div tag rule in the CSS Styles panel, rather than using the Property inspector, or the Property inspector will create an additional rule. It is more efficient to have all rule properties for a div tag in one rule.

6. Click to place the insertion point in front of the word "beach", click **Insert** on the Menu bar, point to **HTML**, point to **Special Characters**, then click **Non-Breaking Space**.
7. Repeat Step 6 to add another space in front of "beach".
8. Save your work, preview the page in your web browser, compare your screen to Figure 17, then close your browser.

You added text to the AP Div, and formatted it using the CSS Styles panel.

Lesson 3 Add Content to an AP Div

DREAMWEAVER 10-19

LESSON 4

Set AP Div
PROPERTIES

What You'll Do

In this lesson, you will use the AP Elements panel to change the name of an AP element, view and hide an AP element, and edit the rule properties.

Using the AP Elements Panel

You can use the **AP Elements panel** to control the visibility, name, and Z-Index order of all the AP elements on a web page. You can also use the AP Elements panel to see how an AP element is nested within the page structure and to change the nesting status of an AP element. **Nested AP elements** are those whose HTML code is included within another AP element's code. Nested AP elements can share common styles, with the child AP element inheriting the styles from the parent AP element. To change the nesting status of an AP element, drag it to a new location in the AP Elements panel. You can open the AP Elements panel using the Window menu, or click its tab in the CSS Styles tab group. The AP Elements panel is handy when you are trying to select an AP element on the bottom of a stack. Clicking the AP element name selects the AP element on the page. You can access the same information that is available in the AP Elements panel by selecting the AP element and viewing its settings in the Property inspector.

Using the AP Elements panel is the easiest way to change a series of AP element names, control AP element visibility while testing a site, and control the visible stacking order. The AP Elements panel also keeps track of all the AP elements on a page, making it easy to review the settings for each.

Setting AP Divs Relative to Containers

When you insert an AP div on a web page, its position is relative to the top left corner of the browser window. A problem arises when the page is viewed in different browser window sizes. Figures 18 and 19 compare what happens when default settings are used and a page is viewed in a wide and a narrower browser window. The AP divs shift to the right when the browser window is resized to a narrower width since the left values for the AP divs are relative to the top left corner of the browser window. To prevent this shifting, you can make the AP divs' positions relative to a parent container, such as a CSS div tag, rather than relative to the page in the browser window. This is a two-step process. First, set the Positioning property of the div tag you wish to use as the parent container to relative. Second, cut and paste the code for the AP divs after the beginning tag for the parent container. The AP divs are then placed on the page relative to the top left corner of the parent container and will remain in a fixed position no matter how wide or narrow the browser window.

Figure 18 *AP divs in narrow browser window*

AP div positions in narrow browser window

Figure 19 *AP divs in wider browser window*

AP div positions when browser window is resized

Lesson 4 Set AP Div Properties

DREAMWEAVER 10-21

Rename an AP element

1. Click **Window** on the Menu bar, then click **AP Elements,** or click **AP Elements** in the CSS Styles Tab group.

    The AP Elements panel appears in the CSS Styles Tab group.

2. Click **girls** on the AP Elements panel to select the girls AP element.

3. Double-click **girls** on the AP Elements panel to select its name.

4. Type **children**, press **[Enter]** (Win) or **[return]** (Mac), then compare your screen to Figure 20.

    The AP div is renamed.

TIP With the children AP div selected, it appears to be in front of the other two AP divs, but it is really behind it. When it is not selected, it appears in its actual position in back of the other two AP divs.

You used the AP Elements panel to change the name of one of the AP divs on the home page.

Figure 20 *Using the AP Elements panel to change an AP div name*

AP element names — heron, white_ibis, children

Z-index values — 3, 2, 1

These are the divs used to place the page content — Unnamed, Unnamed, Unnamed (1020), Unnamed, Unnamed

POWER USER SHORTCUTS

To do this:	Use this shortcut:
Hide all visual aids	[Ctrl][Shift][I] (Win) or ⌘[Shift][I] (Mac)
Show rulers	[Ctrl][Alt][R] (Win) or ⌘[Alt][R] (Mac)
Show Guides	[Ctrl][;] (Win) or ⌘[;] (Mac)
Lock Guides	[Ctrl][Alt][;] (Win) or ⌘[Alt][;] (Mac)
Snap to Guides	[Ctrl][Shift][;] (Win) or ⌘[Shift][;] (Mac)
Guides snap to elements	[Ctrl][Shift][/] (Win) or ⌘[Shift][/] (Mac)
Insert a non-breaking space	[Ctrl][Shift][Space] (Win) or ⌘[Shift][Space] (Mac)
View a guide's position	Point to a guide and press [Ctrl] (Win) or ⌘ (Mac) to see distance from both edges

© Cengage Learning 2013

DREAMWEAVER 10-22

Positioning Objects with AP Divs

Figure 21 *Using the AP Elements panel to hide the heron AP div*

Closed eye icon indicates that the heron AP div is hidden

heron AP div is hidden

Figure 22 *Using the AP Elements panel to make the heron AP div visible*

No eye icon lets AP div inherit its visibility from the index page (visible)

AP div is visible again because the index page is visible

Control AP div visibility

1. Click the **visibility column** twice for the heron AP div in the AP Elements panel, then compare your screen with Figure 21.

    The Closed eye icon appears, indicating that the heron AP div no longer appears in the document window.

2. Click the **Closed eye icon** on the heron AP div.

    Clicking the Closed eye icon makes the AP div visible. The Eye icon appears next to the heron element in the AP Elements panel.

3. Click the **Open eye icon** on the heron AP div.

    Now there is no icon by the heron AP div, as shown in Figure 22. Clicking the Open eye icon makes the AP div inherit the visibility status of its parent object. In this case, the parent object of the heron AP div is the index page. Because the home page is visible, the heron AP div is visible, too.

You used the AP Elements panel to change the visibility status of the heron AP div.

Lesson 4 Set AP Div Properties

Adjust the position of AP elements relative to a CSS container

1. Select the .container rule in the CSS Styles panel, click the **Edit rule button**, click the **Positioning category**, click the **Position list arrow**, then click **relative** if necessary.

2. Compare your screen to Figure 23, then click **OK**.

   To force your AP divs to remain in a fixed position in all sizes of browser windows, set a parent container to a relative position, and then move the AP div tags below the opening rule for that parent container.

3. Switch to Code view, then locate and select the three lines of code for the three AP divs, right under the closing container div tag, as shown in Figure 24.

   If you don't find the three AP divs in this location in the code, scan the code between the opening and closing body tags to locate them.

4. Cut the lines of code, paste them under the opening tag for the container rule, as shown in Figure 25, then refresh Code view.

5. Save your work, preview the page in your browser, then experiment by changing the width of your browser window.

   The AP divs remain in a fixed position on the page, rather than shifting as the window is resized.

You changed the position value for the container rule to relative. You then moved the code for the three AP divs to place them under the container tag so they will not shift their positions on the page when the browser window is resized.

Figure 23 *Changing the Positioning value for the container rule*

Positioning category

Position = relative

Figure 24 *Selecting the code for the three AP divs*

Code for the three AP divs

Figure 25 *Moving the code for the three AP divs*

The code for the three AP divs is moved under the container opening tag

Positioning Objects with AP Divs

Figure 26 *Adding a border to an AP element*

Figure 27 *The AP elements with borders*

Add borders to AP elements

1. Close the browser, return to Design view, then click **#children** in the CSS Styles panel.
2. Click the **Edit Rule button**, click the **Border** category, click the **Top list arrow** in the Style column, click **solid**, click the **Top list arrow** in the Width column, click **thin**, click in the top Color text box, then type **#5A6F81**.

   You leave each "Same for all" check box checked so the border will be consistent for each side.
3. Compare your screen to Figure 26, then click **OK**.
4. Repeat Steps 1 and 2 to add a border to the other two AP divs.
5. Save your work, preview the index page in the browser again and compare your screen to Figure 27, close all open pages, then exit Dreamweaver.

You added borders to each AP div.

Lesson 4 Set AP Div Properties

DREAMWEAVER 10-25

SKILLS REVIEW

Insert an AP div.

1. Open the Blooms & Bulbs website, then open the index page.
2. Use the Draw AP Div button to draw a rectangle about 1 inch tall by 1 inch wide on the bottom half of your page.
3. Name this AP div **bloom**.

Set the position and size of an AP div.

1. Select the bloom AP div if necessary, then set the Left property to **695px**.
2. Set the Top property to **425px**.
3. Set the Width property to **200px**.
4. Set the Height property to **143px**.
5. Set the Z-Index property to **1** (if necessary).
6. Create another AP div anywhere on the page about 200 pixels wide and 100 pixels high, select it, then name it **spring_is_here**.
7. Select the spring_is_here AP div if necessary, then adjust the size with the following settings: Left to **600px**; Top to **515px**; Width to **180px**; and Height to **45px**.
8. Change the background color of the spring_is_here AP div to a light tan.
9. Change the Z-Index value of the spring_is_here AP div to **2** if necessary.
10. Save your work.

Add content to an AP div.

1. Place the insertion point in the bloom AP div, then insert the image spring_bloom.jpg from the drive and folder where you store your Data Files, adding **Spring bloom** as the alternate text.
2. Set the bloom AP div tag Vis property to default if necessary.
3. Set the bloom AP div tag Overflow property to visible.
4. Place the insertion point in the spring_is_here AP div, then type **Spring is here!**
5. Insert a line break, then type **Come see our new arrivals!**
6. Edit the #spring_is_here rule to set the Font-family to Arial, Helvetica, sans-serif, the Font-size to small, the Font-weight to bold, the Color to #333, and the Text-align to center.
7. Save your work.

Set AP div properties.

1. Open the AP Elements panel (if necessary).
2. Use the AP Elements panel to change the spring_is_here AP div's name to **spring**.
3. Set the Vis property to visible.
4. On the web page, add a paragraph return after the last paragraph.
5. Save your work.

SKILLS REVIEW
(CONTINUED)

6. Select the #container rule in the CSS Styles panel and change the Position value to relative.
7. Switch to Code view and cut the code for the two AP div tags under the body tag.
8. Paste the code for the two AP div tags under the opening tag for the container rule, refresh Code view, then save your work and return to Design view.
9. Preview the page in your browser, compare your screen to Figure 28, close your browser, adjust the AP div positions (if necessary), then save and close the index page.

Figure 28 *Completed Skills Review*

Positioning Objects with AP Divs

DREAMWEAVER 10-27

PROJECT BUILDER 1

In this exercise, you will continue your work on the TripSmart website. The owner, Thomas Howard, wants you to create a small advertisement on the index page that gives a small preview of an upcoming tour to Scotland.

1. Open the TripSmart website, then open the index page.
2. Add two paragraph breaks after the last sentence in the content div.
3. Draw an AP div that is approximately one inch tall and one inch wide on the bottom of the page, then name it **castle**.
4. Set the Left property of the castle AP div tag to **700px** and the Top property to **340px**.
5. Set the Width property of the castle AP div tag to **250px**, the height to **200px**, and the Z-Index property to **1** if necessary.
6. Insert the image eilean_donan_castle.jpg from the drive and folder where your chapter_10 data files are stored into the castle AP div, adding appropriate alternate text.
7. Use the Property inspector to compare the dimensions of the castle image and the dimensions of the castle AP div, then adjust the width and height of the castle AP div so it fits the size of the eilean_donan_castle.jpg image.
8. Draw another AP div that is approximately 1 inch wide by one-half inches tall. Name it **scotland_tour** and assign it a background color of your choice.
9. In the new AP div, enter the text **Scotland: Castles and Kings**, enter a line break, type **Watch for our new tour coming soon!**, then refer to Figure 29 to adjust text properties in the scotland_tour div and the placement of the two AP divs on the page.
10. Use the CSS Styles panel to add borders of your choice to the #castle rule and the #scotland_tour rule.
11. Use the CSS Styles panel to set the position of the #container rule to relative.
12. Move the code for the two AP div tags below the opening tag for the container rule.
13. Save your work, preview the page in your browser, compare your screen to Figure 29, close your browser, make any spacing adjustments to improve the position or sizes of the AP divs, then save and close the index page.

PROJECT BUILDER 1
(CONTINUED)

Figure 29 *Sample Project Builder 1*

Positioning Objects with AP Divs

DREAMWEAVER 10-29

PROJECT BUILDER 2

Use Figure 30 as a guide to continue your work on the Carolyne's Creations website. You'll insert the logo on the index page that will straddle the right sidebar div and the footer div.

1. Open the Carolyne's Creations website, then open the index page.
2. Create an AP div on the page, then insert the file cc_logo.gif from the drive and folder where you store your Data Files folder in the AP div, adding appropriate alternate text.
3. Name the AP div **cc_logo**.
4. Adjust the size and position of the AP div with settings of your choice.
5. Make the appropriate adjustments to lock the position of the two AP divs on the page in any size browser window.
6. Save your work, preview the page in your browser, close your browser, then close the index page.

PROJECT BUILDER 2
(CONTINUED)

Figure 30 *Completed Project Builder 2*

DESIGN PROJECT

Gwen Gresham has recently been asked to redesign a website for a small business. She has decided to use CSS divs for her page layout. Because she has never developed a website with these features before, she decides to look at some other websites for ideas and inspiration.

1. Connect to the Internet, then go to the Weather Channel website at weather.com, as shown in Figure 31.
2. View the source code for the page and use the Edit, Find feature to locate div tags used in this site. (*Hint*: Use "div id" as the search string.)
3. View the source code for the page and locate the HTML tags that control the CSS page elements. (*Hint*: Use a CSS property such as "padding" or "top" as a search string.)
4. Do you see some div tags with either the dimensions or positions specified?

Figure 31 *Design Project*
This image was provided by the Weather Channel — www.weather.com

PORTFOLIO PROJECT

For this assignment, you will continue to work on the portfolio project that you have been developing since Chapter 1. There will be no Data Files supplied. You are building this website from chapter to chapter, so you must do each Portfolio Project assignment in each chapter to complete your website.

You will continue building your site by placing at least one AP div on a page.

1. Consult your wireframes to decide which page to develop for this chapter. Add a sketch to the wireframe to show how you will use AP divs on the page you have chosen.
2. Open the page and add the appropriate number of AP Divs to the page and configure them appropriately, making sure to name them and set the properties for each.
3. Add text, background images, and background colors to the AP divs.
4. Check to ensure that all AP divs are properly stacked using the Z-Index property.
5. Make the coding adjustments to lock the position of each AP div on the page when it is viewed with different browser sizes.
6. Review the checklist in Figure 32 and make any necessary modifications.
7. Save your work, preview the page in your browser, make any necessary modifications to make the page look good, close your browser, then close all open pages.

Figure 32 *Portfolio Project Checklist*

Website Checklist
1. Are all AP divs properly stacked with Z-index values assigned correctly?
2. Do all pages have page titles?
3. Do all navigation links work correctly?
4. Do your pages look acceptable in at least two different browsers and browser window sizes?
5. Do the APdivs hide any information on your pages?
6. Are you happy with the overall appearance of each page?

ADOBE DREAMWEAVER CS6

CHAPTER 11

ADDING MEDIA AND
INTERACTIVITY

1. Add and modify Flash objects
2. Add rollover images
3. Add behaviors
4. Add video
5. Add sound

CHAPTER 11
ADDING MEDIA AND INTERACTIVITY

Introduction

While a website with text and static images is adequate for presenting information, you can create a much richer user experience by adding movement and interactive elements. You can use Dreamweaver to add media objects created in other programs to the pages of your website. Some of the external media file types include Adobe Fireworks menu bars, rollover images, and buttons; video, sound, and animation; Flash Paper; Director and Shockwave movies and presentations; Java applets; ActiveX controls; server-side controls; and a variety of plug-ins. A **plug-in** (also called an **add-on**) is a small computer program that works with a host application such as a web browser to allow it to perform certain functions. For example, older web browsers usually don't come with the ability to play animations. So to play a Flash SWF file in a web browser, you would need to install the Adobe Flash Player plug-in. Newer browsers come with Flash Player preinstalled. To read Adobe PDF files, you need to install the Adobe Reader plug-in. Other players include Windows Media Player and RealPlayer by RealNetworks. Plug-ins allow you to extend the capabilities of the browser to display content, letting you create complex, interactive websites with media effects that can be viewed within the pages themselves. Then the pages don't have to load an external document player. In this chapter, you will use Dreamweaver to add media objects to The Striped Umbrella website and the means to allow them to play.

Understanding Media Objects

The term "media objects" has different meanings, depending on who you are talking to, and the industry in which they work. For our purposes, **media objects** are combinations of visual and audio effects and text that help make a website a fully engaging experience. Although this might be an open-ended definition, it is the experience you are striving for when you add video and audio elements to a web page. Think about the experience of watching a movie. You are engaged not just by the actors, but also by the sounds and special effects you experience. You want to create this same type of experience for your website users by adding media elements to your pages.

DREAMWEAVER 11-2

TOOLS YOU'LL USE

DREAMWEAVER 11-3

LESSON 1

Add and Modify FLASH OBJECTS

What You'll Do

In this lesson, you will insert and modify a Flash movie on the cafe page, and then play the movie both in Dreamweaver and in a browser.

Understanding Adobe Flash

Flash is a software program that allows you to create low-bandwidth, high-quality animations and interactive elements that you can place on your web pages. **Low-bandwidth** animations are animations that don't require a fast connection to work properly. These animations use a series of vector-based graphics that load quickly and merge with other graphics and sounds to create short movies. **Vector-based graphics** are scalable graphics that are built using mathematical formulas, rather than built with pixels. Figure 1 shows a web page that contains several Flash objects. Figure 2 shows the Flash program used to create Flash objects.

Once you create these short movies, you can place them on your web pages. Flash movies require Flash Player, a plug-in that is included in the latest versions of Internet Explorer, Mozilla Firefox, Safari, and Chrome, to view them. If you are using an older browser that does not support the version of Flash used to create your movie, you can download the latest Flash Player from the Adobe website, located at adobe.com. Almost all desktop Internet browsers worldwide use Flash Player. However, the mobile and touch-screen markets are not as supportive. Internet Explorer 10 Metro and Apple iOS devices do not support the Flash plug-in.

As HTML5 gains support across all browsers, you will want to use HTML5 tags to insert and format your media content. For example, the steps we will use to insert a Flash SWF file (named crabdance.swf) in this chapter work fine in all browsers that support the Flash plug-in. For those that don't, you use HTML5 media tags to insert the file: <object width="140" height="114" data="crabdance.swf"></object>. Flash movies inserted with the menu or Insert panel will work correctly, but will not pass HTML5 validation.

Inserting Flash Content

When you use the Insert panel to add Flash content to a web page, the code that links and runs the content (such as detecting the presence of Flash Player on the computer and directing the user to download the player if it is not found) is embedded into the page code. The original Flash file is stored as a separate file in the website root folder.

There are several types of Flash content that you can incorporate to enhance your users' experience as they view and interact with your website. A **Flash button** is a button made from a small, predefined Flash movie that you can insert on a web page to provide site navigation, either in place of or in addition to other types of hyperlinks, such as plain text links. You can assign Flash buttons a variety of behaviors in response to user actions, such as opening a different page in the browser when the mouse pointer is placed over it. Flash buttons have the .swf file extension.

Using Flash, you can also create Flash movies that include multimedia elements, such as audio files (both music and voiceovers), animated objects, scripted objects, clickable links, and just about any other animated or clickable object imaginable. You can use Flash movies to add content to your existing website or to create an entire website.

To add a Flash movie to a web page, click SWF from the Media menu in the Common category on the Insert panel to open the Select SWF dialog box, and then choose the Flash movie you want to insert. As with images, always add a title tag when inserting Flash content to provide accessibility. You also need to include code that will instruct the browser to check for and load Flash Player so the user can view the Flash content on the page. To view your Flash movies, you can either use Live view or preview them in a browser window. It is a kindness to your users to turn off the loop option for Flash movies unless you want the Flash content to play continuously while the page is being viewed. Content that plays continuously can be irritating to users when they do not have the controls to stop it.

Figure 1 *Website based on Flash*
NASA website—www.nasa.gov

Figure 2 *Adobe Flash CS6 workspace*

Lesson 1   Add and Modify Flash Objects

DREAMWEAVER 11-5

Insert Flash movies

1. Open the cafe page in The Striped Umbrella website.

2. Select the cafe logo on the left side of the page below the menu bar, then press **[Delete]** (Win) or **[delete]** (Mac).

3. Click the **Media list arrow** on the Common category of the Insert panel, then click **SWF**.

4. Navigate to the drive and folder where you store your Data Files, click **crabdance.swf**, click **OK** (Win) or **Open** (Mac), click **Yes** and then click **Save** to save the movie in the site root folder of the website, type **Crab logo animation** in the Title text box in the Object Tag Accessibility Attributes dialog box, then click **OK**. A Flash movie placeholder appears on the page, as shown in Figure 3.

   TIP If you already have a Flash file in your site root folder, you can drag and drop it from the Assets panel or Files panel instead of using the Insert panel or Insert menu.

5. Click the **Loop check box** on the Property inspector to deselect it.

   By turning off the Loop option, the file will play once in the browser, then stop.

You inserted a Flash movie on the cafe page of The Striped Umbrella website.

Figure 3 *Flash movie placeholder on the cafe page*

Properties of selected Flash movie

Loop check box   *Flash movie placeholder*

Collecting Flash Objects

Adobe and their devoted product users provide you with a variety of downloadable Flash objects that are available on the Adobe Exchange website, located at http://www.adobe.com/cfusion/exchange/?promoid=DIOCO. At this site, you can find collections of menus, transitions, image galleries, and just about anything else you might want. If you can't find exactly what you want, you can download a trial version of Flash to experiment with creating your own Flash objects. If you find that you will want to create Flash objects regularly, you can purchase the licensed version either as a separate program or as part of a suite of programs. There are many other websites that offer downloadable Flash objects; some of the objects are free and some are for purchase.

Figure 4 *Flash movie playing in Dreamweaver*

Flash movie playing

Click to stop movie

Figure 5 *Flash movie playing in the browser*

Lesson 1   Add and Modify Flash Objects

Play a Flash movie in Dreamweaver and in a browser

1. With the placeholder selected, click the **Play button** in the Property inspector to view the crabdance.swf movie, as shown in Figure 4, then click **Stop** (Win) or skip to Step 2 (Mac).

   TIP Mac users do not have a Play button in their Property inspector.

2. Save your work, then click **OK** to close the Copy Dependent Files dialog box.

   Two supporting files, expressInstall.swf and swfobject_modified.js, are copied to a new Scripts folder. These files are necessary for the movie to play in the browser correctly.

3. With the placeholder selected, enter the color value **#D9EFF4** in the Bg text box in the Property inspector.

   Since this is the color of the sidebar1 div, the crabdance animation background will now be the same color as the sidebar1 div background.

4. Save your file, preview the page in your browser, compare your screen to Figure 5, then close your browser.

   TIP If the movie did not play in Internet Explorer, click Tools on the menu bar, click Internet Options, click the Advanced tab, then click the Allow active content to run in files on My Computer under the Security category. If you are using a different browser or a version of Internet Explorer that is earlier than 8.0, look for a similar setting.

You played a Flash movie on the cafe page in The Striped Umbrella website in Dreamweaver and in your browser.

DREAMWEAVER 11-7

Modify a Flash file from Dreamweaver

1. To complete the steps in this lesson, you need the full Flash program (not Flash Player). If you don't have the full Flash program installed on your computer, you can go to the Adobe website at adobe.com to download a trial version or close the cafe page and skip to Lesson 2 on page 11-10.

2. Use Explorer (Win) or Finder (Mac) to copy the crabdance.fla source file from the Data Files folder to the site root folder of The Striped Umbrella website as shown in Figure 6.

   Even though you have the crabdance.swf file in your site root folder, you must copy the crabdance.fla source file to that location so you can make changes to it. After you change it, you have to republish it to recreate the .swf file to include your changes.

3. Close Explorer (Win) or Finder (Mac), then return to Dreamweaver.

4. With the Flash placeholder selected, click **Edit** in the Property inspector.

5. Click **crabdance.fla** in the striped_umbrella site root folder in the Locate FLA File dialog box, then click **Open**.

   The .swf file is a Flash Player file and cannot be edited. The .fla file is the editable Flash file. You must have this source file to edit the movie. After you select the .fla file, the file opens in Flash if Flash is installed on your computer.

   TIP If you receive a warning that one or more fonts used for this movie are not available, click Choose Substitute, then choose another font.

(continued)

Figure 6 *Selecting the crabdance.fla file*

The path for your site root folder

The crabdance.fla file is selected

Adding Media Objects Using HTML5 and Adobe Edge

Although Adobe Flash is still the premier tool used for creating animation, the development of HTML5 and CSS3 has given us new ways to incorporate motion and animation. HTML5 includes new tags for animation and video, such as the <audio> tag and the <video> tag, with attributes to set playback options such as autoplay, controls, looks, and src. CSS3 has new styles for enhancing the appearance of page objects, such as playback controls. **Adobe Edge**, an exciting new program, combines the new capabilities of HTML5, CSS3, and JavaScript, but uses a program interface similar to Flash. Like Flash, Adobe Edge has a stage, timeline, playhead, symbols, frames, and layers you can use to manipulate text, shapes, and images. Unlike Flash, Edge codes in **JSON (JavaScript Object Notation)**, a subset of JavaScript, rather than ActionScript. This means that Edge creates animation that is coded entirely with HTML and JavaScript, so browsers that support HTML5 will not need a plug-in to play the animations. Edge also integrates with font services such as TypeKit or FontSquirrel.

Figure 7 *Editing the Flash movie and returning to Dreamweaver*

Click Done to save the file and return to Dreamweaver

FPS text box

6. Click **12** next to FPS in the Properties panel, change the frame rate from 12 to **24** fps (frames per second) in the FPS text box, as shown in Figure 7, click **Done**, then close Flash.

   Flash automatically saves both the crabdance.fla file and the crabdance.swf file, then closes. (If the crabdance.fla file opens with an element selected, click in the gray area of the screen to deselect it. If an element is selected, you will not see the FPS text box.)

7. Switch back to Dreamweaver, preview the page in Live mode, then close the cafe page.

   Notice that the movie plays a little faster now. You changed the frames per second to a larger number, which had the effect of the movie playing faster.

You used the Edit button in the Property inspector to find and modify the Flash movie in Flash, then returned to Dreamweaver.

Lesson 1   Add and Modify Flash Objects

DREAMWEAVER 11-9

LESSON 2

Add Rollover IMAGES

What You'll Do

In this lesson, you will add two rollover images to the activities page of The Striped Umbrella website.

Understanding Rollover Images

A **rollover image** is an image that changes its appearance when the mouse pointer is placed over it in a browser. A rollover image actually consists of two images. The first image is the one that appears when the mouse pointer is not positioned over it, and the second image is the one that appears when the mouse pointer is positioned over it. Rollover images are often used to help create a feeling of action and excitement on a web page. For instance, suppose you are creating a website that promotes a series of dance classes. You could create a rollover image using two images of a dancer in two different poses. When a user places the mouse pointer over the image of the dancer in the first pose, the image would change to show the dancer in a different pose, creating a feeling of movement.

QUICK TIP

You can also add a link to a rollover image, so that the image will change only when the image is clicked.

Adding Rollover Images

You add rollover images to a web page using the Rollover Image command on the Images menu in the Common category shown in Figure 8. You specify both the original image and the rollover image in the Insert Rollover Image dialog box. The rollover image is the image that appears when the user moves (rolls) the mouse pointer over the original image. To prevent one of the images from changing size during the rollover, both images should be the same height and width. Another way to create a rollover image, button, or menu bar is to insert it as a Fireworks HTML file. After you

DREAMWEAVER 11-10

Adding Media and Interactivity

create and export the file from Fireworks, the code for the rollover is automatically inserted in the web page file. The Fireworks HTML command is also on the Images menu, as shown in Figure 8.

QUICK TIP

It's a good idea to select the Preload rollover image check box in the Insert Rollover Image dialog box to ensure that the rollover image appears without a delay.

You can also use rollover images to display an image associated with a text link. For instance, suppose you are creating a website for an upcoming election. You could create a web page that contains a list of candidates for the election and add a rollover image for each candidate's name that would result in a photograph of the candidate appearing when the mouse is placed over his or her name. You can also use this effect to make appropriate images appear when you point to different menu options. For instance, Figure 9 shows the Walton Arts Center website, which uses rollovers to display event details for a specific date on a calendar on its home page. It also uses rollover images for each social media button link. When a rollover image is inserted onto a page, Dreamweaver automatically adds two behaviors; a Swap Image behavior and a Swap Image Restore behavior. A **Swap Image behavior** is JavaScript code that directs the browser to display a different image when the mouse is rolled over an image on the page. A **Swap Image Restore** behavior restores the swapped image back to the original image.

Figure 8 *Images menu on the Insert panel*

Figure 9 *Walton Arts Center website using rollover images used to display menus*
Walton Arts Center website used by permission from Walton Arts Center—www.waltonartscenter.org

Add a rollover image

1. If you did not complete the Flash steps, close the cafe page; then open the activities page of The Striped Umbrella website.
2. Scroll down to find the image of the two dolphins, then delete it.
3. Click the **Images list arrow** in the Common group on the Insert panel, then click **Rollover Image**.
4. Type **dolphins** in the Image name text box.
5. Click **Browse** next to the Original image text box, browse to the drive and folder where you store your Data Files, open the assets folder, then double-click **one_dolphin.jpg**. (If a dialog box opens asking if you want to copy the file to the site, click Yes.)
6. Click **Browse** next to the Rollover image text box, then double-click the **two_dolphins.jpg** file from the drive and folder where you store your Data Files for the Rollover image text box. (If a dialog box opens asking if you want to copy the file to the site, click Yes.)
7. Type **Dolphins riding the surf** in the Alternate text text box, compare your screen to Figure 10, then click **OK**.
8. Select the image, apply the **img_right_float** rule, save your work, preview the page in your browser, move your mouse pointer over the dolphin image, then compare your screen to Figure 11.

   When you point to the image, the one_dolphin image is "swapped" with the two_dolphin image.

   (continued)

Figure 10 *Browsing to find the source files for the rollover image*

Figure 11 *Viewing the rollover image in the browser*

Image is swapped when you roll the mouse pointer over it

DREAMWEAVER 11-12

Adding Media and Interactivity

Figure 12 *Swap behavior code for rollover image*

```
65    <article class="content">
66        <p><span class="body_text"><img src="assets/family_sunset.jpg" alt="Family on sunset fishing trip" width=
      "350" height="235" class="img_left_float" />We have many activities for you to choose from, here at the  resort
      and in the surrounding area. </span></p>
67        <p class="body_text">Some of our visitors enjoy deep-sea fishing trips. We have a  small fleet of boats that
      will take you out for either a half or a full day. One of our most popular trips leaves late in the afternoon
      and stays out long enough to take in a beautiful Florida sunset on the way home. Of course,  you can also surf
      cast, right from the beach.</p>
68        <p class="body_text"><a href="#" class="img_right_float" onMouseOver=
      "MM_swapImage('dolphins','','assets/two_dolphins.jpg',1)" onMouseOut="MM_swapImgRestore()"><img src=
      "assets/one_dolphin.jpg" alt="Dolphins riding the surf" width="252" height="180" id="dolphins"></a>And don
      &rsquo;t forget our dolphin cruises. We have a unique  approach &mdash; two boats speed along, side by side,
      about 50 yards apart. The  dolphins love it because it generates a huge wake. You'll see them jumping  right
      between the boats! You can arrange for tickets for <a href="fishing.html">fishing excursions</a> or <a href=
      "cruises.html">dolphin cruises</a> at The Club House desk.</p>
69        <p>The famous <a href="http://www.blueangels.navy.mil">Blue Angels</a>, the nation&rsquo;s oldest flying
      aerobatic  team, are stationed at the Naval Air Station Pensacola, less than a one-hour  drive from The Striped
      Umbrella. You can watch the team practice at the Museum  of Naval Aviation viewing area, an unforgettable
      experience for all ages. Information  on dates and times is posted on their website, or you can call The Club
      House desk.</p>
```

Code for rollover image

TIP Remember to direct your browser to allow blocked content if the rollover does not work.

9. Close the browser.
10. Switch to Code view, then locate the code for the swap image behavior, shown in Figure 12.

    The code directs the browser to display the image with one dolphin "onmouseout"—when the mouse is not over the image. It directs the browser to display the image with two dolphins "onmouseover"—when the mouse is over the image.

TIP If your code is selected in Code view, that means the image is selected in Design view.

11. Return to Design view, then click the **Switch Design View to Live View button** [Live] and place your pointer over the dolphin image.

    Live view allows you to preview the swap image behavior as it will appear in the browser.

12. Click [Live] to turn off Live view.

You replaced an image with a rollover image on the activities page of The Striped Umbrella website, viewed the rollover in the browser and in Live view.

Lesson 2   Add Rollover Images

DREAMWEAVER 11-13

LESSON 3

Add
BEHAVIORS

What You'll Do

In this lesson, you will add an action that opens a browser window from the activities page of The Striped Umbrella website. You will then change the event for that action.

Adding Interactive Elements

You can make your web pages come alive by adding interactive elements to them. For instance, if you are creating a page about animals, you could attach an action to each picture that would result in a pop-up message with a description of the animal when the user rolls the mouse over it. You can add actions like this to elements by attaching behaviors to them. **Behaviors** are sets of instructions that you can attach to page elements that tell the page element to respond in a specific way when an event occurs, such as when the mouse pointer is positioned over the element. When you attach a behavior to an element, Dreamweaver generates the JavaScript code for the behavior and inserts it into your page code.

Using the Behaviors Panel

You can use the Behaviors panel located in the Tag Inspector panel group to insert a variety of JavaScript-based behaviors on a page. For instance, using the Behaviors panel, you can automate tasks, have items respond to user selections and mouse movements with pop-up menus, create games, go to a different URL, or add automatic dynamic effects to a web page. To insert a behavior, click the Add behavior button on the Behaviors panel to open the Actions menu, as shown in Figure 13, then select a behavior from the menu.

Understanding Actions and Events

Actions are triggered by events. For instance, if you want the user to see a page element slide across the page when the element is clicked, you would attach the Slide action using the onClick event to trigger the action. Other examples of events are onMouseOver and onLoad. The onMouseOver event will trigger an action when the mouse is placed over an object. The onLoad event will trigger an action when the page is first loaded in the browser window.

Using the Spry Framework

Some of the behaviors that you can add to web pages use a JavaScript library called the **Spry framework for AJAX**. **Asynchronous JavaScript and XML (AJAX)** is a method for developing interactive web pages that respond quickly to user input, such as clicking a map. In the library, you will find **spry widgets**, which are prebuilt components for adding interactivity to pages; and **spry effects**, which are screen effects such as fading and enlarging page elements. When you add a spry effect to a page element, Dreamweaver automatically adds a SpryAssets folder to the site root folder with the supporting files inside the folder.

Figure 13 *Behaviors panel with the Actions menu displayed*

Add a behavior

1. Open the file dw11_1.html from the drive and folder where you store your Data Files, then save it in the site root folder as **wildlife_message.html**, without updating links. Close the dw11_1.html page.
2. Select the family_sunset image on the activities page, click **Window** on the Menu bar, then click **Behaviors** to open the Tag Inspector panel.
3. Click the **Add behavior button** on the Behaviors panel toolbar to open the Actions menu, as shown in Figure 14, then click **Open Browser Window** to open the Open Browser Window dialog box.
4. Click **Browse** next to the URL to display text box to open the Select File dialog box, navigate to the site root folder if necessary, then double-click **wildlife_message.html**.
5. Type **300** in the Window width text box, type **300** in the Window height text box, type **message** in the Window name text box, compare your screen to Figure 15, then click **OK**.
6. Save your work, preview the page in your browser, test the Open Browser Window effect by clicking the family_sunset image, as shown in Figure 16, then close both browser windows.

TIP The pop-up window will not work if pop-up blocking is enabled in your browser. To disable pop-up blocking in Internet Explorer 9, click Tools on the Menu Bar, point to Pop-up Blocker, then click Turn Off Pop-up Blocker. In Firefox, click the Options button to tell the browser to display the wildlife_message page. If you are using the Google toolbar, you may also have to allow pop-ups.

You added an Open Browser Window effect to an image on the activities page of The Striped Umbrella website.

Figure 14 *Adding the Open Browser Window behavior to the family_sunset image*

Select family_sunset image   Click Open Browser Window

Figure 15 *Setting Open Browser Window options*

Figure 16 *Viewing the wildlife message in a browser*

DREAMWEAVER 11-16

Adding Media and Interactivity

Figure 17 *Viewing the edited window size for the behavior*

Figure 18 *Viewing the edited behavior*

onMouseOver action

Comparing the Behaviors and the Server Behaviors Panels

In addition to the Behaviors panel, Dreamweaver also features a Server Behaviors panel. Although the names are similar, the functions are not. You use the Behaviors panel to add JavaScript behaviors to page elements; use the Server Behaviors panel to add server behaviors, such as creating a login page or a page that is password protected. Building search pages to enable users to search a website for specific content is another server behavior that you can add with the Server Behaviors panel. After you have created a server behavior and enabled Dreamweaver to display live data, you can add, edit, or delete the server behavior while you are in Design view, but viewing the page in Live view. The Server Behaviors panel is in the Dynamic Content Tab group with the Databases, Bindings, and Components panels. The Databases panel is used to select the data source for dynamic data used with a page. The Bindings panel is used to define and edit dynamic content on a page. The Components panel is used to display information with ColdFusion components.

Edit a behavior

1. Right-click (Win) or [control]-click (Mac) the **right column** of the Open Browser Window action in the Behaviors panel, then click **Edit Behavior**.

   The Open Browser Window dialog box opens.

2. Change the window height to **250**, click **OK**, save your changes, preview the page in your browser, then click the **family_sunset image**.

   The browser window with the wildlife message is shorter in height, as shown in Figure 17.

3. Close the browser windows.

4. Click the **left column** of the Open Browser Window action in the Behaviors panel to display the events list arrow, click the **list arrow**, then click **onMouseOver**, as shown in Figure 18.

   This will change the event that triggers the action from clicking the image to simply placing the mouse over the image.

5. Save your work, open the page in the browser, then move the mouse over the family_sunset image.

   Now, simply placing the mouse over the image triggers the Open Browser Window event. (*Hint*: If you don't see the new window, disable the Google toolbar, or locate the option to allow pop-ups.)

6. Close the browser windows, close the Tag Inspector panel, then close the wildlife_message page. Leave the activities page open.

You edited the behavior in the Behaviors panel.

Lesson 3 Add Behaviors

DREAMWEAVER 11-17

LESSON 4

Add
VIDEO

What You'll Do

In this lesson, you will insert a video on the activities page.

Inserting Video

Another way to add rich media content to your web pages is to insert video files. Of the several available video formats, one of the most popular is the MP4 format. You can insert a video in Dreamweaver with the Insert, Media, Plugin command, but HTML5 introduced another way to add video with the <video> tag. The advantages of this method are numerous: it supports video in native formats; it is compatible with all browsers; and you can access the video controls using a keyboard. You can also include code to link multiple video formats to provide access for all browsers and make your videos searchable by search engines. To add video with the <video> tag, you add the tags in Code view. Other video formats that you can link or embed on a web page include **AVI (Audio Visual Interleave)**, the Microsoft standard for digital video, **FLV** (Adobe Flash video), **WebM** (an open, royalty-free media format sponsored by Google), **MOV** (Apple Quick Time), and **Ogg** (a free, open container format developed by the Xiph.Org Foundation). Currently, the MP4, WebM, and Ogg formats support the HTML5 <video> tag. However, not all browsers support all three formats, so it is a good idea to provide multiple file formats for your users to make sure that they will be able to play the video.

Figure 19 shows a page on the Federal Aviation Administration website that allows visitors to view educational videos on a number of topics. Users access playback controls with a **controller**. A controller appears as a graphic element called a **skin** placed over or below a video. Controls can include buttons or sliders to stop, start, and pause the video, control the sound level or mute the sound, or display a script of the video. After a user clicks the play button, the file begins downloading and starts to play as it downloads. A **progressive video download** will download the video to the user's computer, then allow the video to play before it has completely downloaded.

It will finish the download as the video plays, but the user will not notice that this is taking place. A **streaming video download** is similar to a progressive download, except streaming video uses buffers to gather the content as it downloads to ensure a smoother playback. A **buffer** is a temporary storage area on your hard drive that acts as a holding area for the video content as it is being played. Controllers can be coded to customize both the appearance of the skin and the controls that will be included. Used sparingly, video can be an effective way to add interest and depth to your web pages.

Figure 19 *Viewing a video in a browser*
Federal Aviation Administration website–www.faa.gov

Video window

Controls for video

Script for video is displayed when Closed caption option is selected

Closed caption option

Sound control

Lesson 4   Add Video

DREAMWEAVER 11-19

Add video

1. Using Windows Explorer (Win) or Finder (Mac), copy the file **umbrella_anchor_video.mp4** from the drive and folder where you store your Data Files, paste it into your Striped Umbrella site assets folder, then close Windows Explorer (Win) or Finder (Mac).

2. Open the about_us page, then click to place the insertion point under the last paragraph on the page.

   TIP You may not see the insertion point as clearly as you usually do. If it is easier for you, click at the end of the last paragraph and press [Enter].

3. Click the **Media list arrow** in the Common category on the Insert panel, then click **Plugin** to open the Select File dialog box.

4. Browse to your local site assets folder if necessary, then double-click **umbrella_anchor_video.mp4**.

   A placeholder for the movie appears on the page, as shown in Figure 20. You can only view the video in the browser or in Live view.

5. With the plug-in placeholder selected, change the W value in the Property inspector to **220**, and the H value to **200**, click the **Parameters button**, enter **autostart** for a Parameter and **false** for the Value, as shown in Figure 21, then click **OK**.

   The placeholder for the plug-in now fits the size of the video plus a little extra for the controls. The video will not start until the user clicks the Play button.

   (continued)

Figure 20 *Inserting a video on the about_us page*

Video placeholder inserted on page

Figure 21 *Editing the settings for the video*

W = 220   H = 200   New parameter = autostart   Parameters button   Value = false

Figure 22 *Viewing the video in a browser*

Play button becomes pause button while video is playing

POWER USER SHORTCUTS	
To do this:	**Use this shortcut:**
Enable Live view	[Alt][F11]
Exit Live view	[Alt][F11]
Insert a SWF file	[Ctrl][Alt][F] (Win) or ⌘ [Alt][F] (Mac)
Play a plug-in	(Select the placeholder) [Ctrl][Alt][P] (Win) or ⌘ [Alt][P] (Mac)
Stop a plug-in from playing	[Ctrl][Alt][X] (Win) or ⌘ [Alt][X] (Mac)
Play all plug-ins	[Ctrl][Alt][Shift][P] (Win) or ⌘ [Alt][Shift][P] (Mac)
Stop all plug-ins from playing	[Ctrl][Alt][Shift][X] (Win)

© Cengage Learning 2013

Lesson 4 Add Video

6. Place the insertion point to the right of the video placeholder image, type **See us at the front desk to pick up your complimentary Umbrella Anchor!** using line breaks as shown in Figure 22, then apply the **img_left_float** rule to the plug-in placeholder.

7. Select the sentence and apply the Heading 4 format to it, select the video placeholder, switch to Code view, then delete the ending </embed> tag from the code that embeds the video on the page.

   The code will work just fine without the </embed> tag; leaving it in the code will keep the page from passing HTML5 validation.

8. Return to Design view, save your work, preview the page in the browser, then compare your screen to Figure 22.

   You click the Play button ▶ to play the movie and the Stop button ■ to stop the movie.

TIP If your plugin is not working, check to see if you have a message asking if you will allow the plugin to run, and direct it to run.

9. Play the movie, then close the browser window.
10. Close the about_us page.

You inserted a video on the page, then viewed the page in your browser.

LESSON 5

Add
SOUND

What You'll Do

In this lesson, you will add a sound file to the activities page and modify the object parameters.

Adding Sound

There are several ways to incorporate sound into a website. Sound files are relatively small in file size and easy to add to a page. You can embed them as background sounds, embed them on a page with visible sound controls, link them to a page, or add them to a page with the new <audio> tags introduced with HTML5. A few audio file formats don't require a plug-in to play, such as the WAV (Waveform Extension) and AIF or AIFF (Audio Interchange File Format) file formats. Files that do require a plug-in are MP3 or MPEG (Motion Picture Experts Group) files, which can be played using QuickTime, Windows Media Player, or RealPlayer plug-ins.

Before you decide to add a sound to a page, think about the purpose you have in mind. Will the sound add to the rich media experience for your users? What devices will your users use to play the sound? Have you tested the audio file to make sure the sound quality is excellent? If you decide to use the <audio> tag, provide more than one file format, as all audio file formats are not supported by all browsers. File formats that are supported with the HTML5 <audio> tag are MP3, WAV, and OGG. The code to add an audio file with HTML5 is shown in Figure 23.

Figure 23 *Adding an audio file with HTML5*

```
<audio controls="controls">
    <source src="sound_file.ogg" type="audio/ogg" />
    <source src="sound_file.mp3" type="audio/mp3" />
    <source src="sound_file.wav" type="audio/wav" />
    Your device does not support the audio element.
</audio>
```

Using Controllers

The controller that appears on your page is determined by the tags used to add the sound file. Dreamweaver has a generic controller that you will see when you add a sound file in the following steps. The controller used with HTML5 looks a bit different. You can use CSS3 to change the appearance of a controller, but all controllers will have the basic play and pause buttons and a way to control the volume. Figure 24 shows a page on the Federal Aviation Administration website that provides audios of recordings made in control towers. When you click a link to play a recording, a new window opens with a controller that you use to play, pause, and adjust the volume of the recording.

Figure 24 *Playing an audio file on a web page*
Federal Aviation Administration website–www.faa.gov

Lists of audio files available

Pause/play button *Playhead indicates playback position* *Blue bar indicates how much of the file has been downloaded* *Volume control*

Lesson 5 Add Sound

DREAMWEAVER 11-23

Add sound

1. Use Windows Explorer (Win) or Finder (Mac) to copy the file **interviews.mp3** from the drive and folder where you store your Data Files to your website assets folder.

    This is an audio file with some guest comments.

2. On the activities page, add a paragraph break after the last paragraph, then type **Here are some comments from recent guests describing their favorite activities at The Striped Umbrella**.

3. Add another paragraph break, click **Insert** on the Menu bar, point to **Media**, click **Plugin**, browse to find the interviews.mp3 file in your website assets folder, then double-click **interviews.mp3**.

    A plug-in icon placeholder appears on the page, as shown in Figure 25.

4. Select the plug-in placeholder if necessary, then use the Property inspector to change the W value to **200** and the H value to **60**.

5. Click **Parameters** in the Property inspector, enter **autostart** for a Parameter and **false** for the Value, as shown in Figure 26, then click **OK**. (You may find that Chrome does not recognize the autostart parameter.)

(continued)

Figure 25 *Inserting an audio file on the activities page*

Plug-in icon placeholder inserted on page

Figure 26 *Editing the plug-in settings*

W = 200   H = 60   Parameters button   New parameter = autostart   Value = false

DREAMWEAVER 11-24

Adding Media and Interactivity

Figure 27 *Viewing the video in a browser*

Play button becomes pause button while video is playing

Figure 28 *Modifying the embed tag*

Delete ending embed tag

6. Save the activities page, preview it in your browser, then play the file, as shown in Figure 27.
7. Close the browser, then switch to Code view.
8. Scroll to locate the <embed> tag for the audio file, delete the ending </embed> tag at the end of the line, as shown in Figure 28, return to Design view, then save your work and close the page.

   The code will work just fine without the ending embed tag; leaving it there will keep the page from passing HTML5 validation.
9. Close Dreamweaver.

SKILLS REVIEW

Add and modify Flash objects.

1. Open the Blooms & Bulbs website, then open the workshops page.
2. Add a paragraph break after the last paragraph, then insert the garden_quote.swf Flash movie from the drive and folder where you store your Data Files at the insertion point, saving the file in the site root folder.
3. Type **Garden quote** as the Accessibility Attributes title, place the insertion point to the left of the placeholder, switch to Code view, then enter **style="margin-left:400px"** after the opening object tag (<object) to position the placeholder.
4. Return to Design view, play the garden_quote.swf movie in Dreamweaver, save your work, click OK to close the Dependent Files dialog box, preview the page in your browser, compare your screen to Figure 29, then close your browser.
5. Close the workshops page.

Add rollover images.

1. Open the tips page, then delete the butterfly graphic at the top of the page.
2. Verify that your insertion point is still at the beginning of the paragraph.
3. Insert a rollover image from the drive and folder where you store your Data Files by using the Images list arrow in the Common category on the Insert panel. Enter **butterfly_rollover** as the name, insert butterfly1.jpg from the drive and folder where you store your Data Files as the original image, butterfly2.jpg from the same location as the rollover image, then enter **Butterflies** as the alternate text.
4. Apply the img_left_float rule to the rollover image.
5. Save your work, preview the page in the browser to test the rollover, then close the tips page.

Add behaviors.

1. Open the water_plants page.
2. Select the water lily image, then use the Behaviors panel to add the Appear/Fade effect under the Effects menu that will fade from 100% to 50%, then select the Toggle Effect check box.

Figure 29 *Completed Skills Review*

3. Edit the behavior to use the onMouseOver action, then save your work. (*Hint*: Dreamweaver adds a new SpryAssets folder in the site with the SpryEffects.js supporting file.)
4. Preview the page in the browser or with Live view. (*Hint*: Place the mouse over the image to test the behavior. The image will alternate between 100% and 50% opacity each time you place the mouse over it.)
5. Close the browser or return to Design view, then close the water_plants page.

SKILLS REVIEW
(CONTINUED)

Add video.

1. Open the plants page, click right after the last sentence on the page (after "just arrived."), then insert a paragraph break.
2. In Windows Explorer (Win) or Finder (Mac), copy the hanging_baskets.mp4 file from the drive and folder where you store your Data Files to the Blooms and Bulbs site assets folder.
3. In Dreamweaver, insert the hanging_baskets.mp4 file at the insertion point location using the following settings: W=250, H=200, then add the parameter autostart and set the value to false.
4. After the last sentence on the page, type **Join us Saturday at 9:00 for a demonstration on hanging baskets**.
5. Place the insertion point to the left of the placeholder, switch to Code view, enter **style="margin-left:160px"** after the opening embed tag, then delete the ending embed tag and return to Design view.
6. Save all files, preview the page and play the movie in the browser, then compare your screen to Figure 30.
7. Close the browser, return to Design view, then close all open pages.

Figure 30 *Completed Skills Review*

Adding Media and Interactivity

DREAMWEAVER 11-27

SKILLS REVIEW (CONTINUED)

Add sound.

1. Copy the file seeds_audio.mp3 from the drive and folder where you save your Data Files to your website assets folder.
2. Open the tips page, place the insertion point after the last tip listed, enter two paragraph breaks, then type **Tip of the Week: Starting seeds for your vegetable garden**.
3. Enter a paragraph break, click Insert on the Menu bar, point to Media, click Plugin, then browse to and select the file seeds_audio.mp3.
4. Select the plug-in placeholder, then use the Property inspector to change the W value to 200 and the H value to 60.
5. Add a parameter to set autostart to false.
6. Delete the ending </embed> tag from the code for the audio file.
7. Save the tips page and test the audio file in the browser, comparing your screen to Figure 31.
8. Close the browser and close the tips page.

Figure 31 *Completed Skills Review*

PROJECT BUILDER 1

In this exercise, you will continue your work on the TripSmart website. You received a new video for the galapagos page and you insert it on the page. Use Figures 32 and 33 as guides as you develop your pages.

1. Open the TripSmart website, then open the galapagos page.
2. Copy the file sea_lions_video.mp4 from the drive and folder where you store your Data files to your local assets folder.
3. Insert the video after the last paragraph on the page, then delete the ending </embed> tag.
4. Type a short introduction to the video similar to the one in Figure 32.
5. Use the Property inspector to set the video placeholder width to 400 and the height to 240, then add a parameter to keep the video from playing automatically.
6. Add any additional settings to improve the appearance of the page, save your work, then preview the page in your browser.

Figure 32 *Sample Project Builder 1*

PROJECT BUILDER 1
(CONTINUED)

7. Play the video, close the browser, then close the galapagos page.
8. Open the file dw11_2.html from the drive and folder where you store your Data Files, then save it in the TripSmart site root folder as **galapagos_trip.html**. Do not update links.
9. Close the dw11_2.html page, then close the galapagos_trip.html page.
10. Open the galapagos page, then attach a behavior to the banner image that will open a new browser window when the banner image loads that displays the galapagos_trip.html file. Use 300 for the window width and 100 for the window height. Name the window **soldout**.
11. Save your work, preview the page in the browser to test the behavior, close the browser, then close all open pages.

Figure 33 *Sample Project Builder 1*

PROJECT BUILDER 2

Use Figure 34 as a guide to continue your work on the Carolyne's Creations website. You have decided to add an effect to the logo on the home page so it will move in some way when the page first loads. You also want to add a video to the adult cooking class page to showcase a Peruvian recipe.

1. Open the Carolyne's Creations website.
2. Open the index page.
3. Select the cc_logo AP element on the right side of the page, then attach a behavior and an action of your choice to it.
4. Switch to Live view to preview the behavior, turn off Live view, save and close the index page, then open the adults page.
5. Copy the video suspiro.mp4 from your Data Files folder to your site root folder; place the insertion point after the last paragraph, insert a new paragraph, then insert the video suspiro.mp4 from your site root folder, using settings of your choice for the video. (*Hint:* in Figure 34, the width is 225px and the height is 180px.)
6. Refer to the text in Figure 34 to add short descriptive text above the video, then add either an inline or external style to position the video on the page.
7. Apply styles where needed, make any other adjustments you wish, delete the closing </embed> tag, save your page, then preview the page in the browser.
8. Close the browser, then close all open pages.

Figure 34 *Sample Project Builder 2*

DESIGN PROJECT

Angie Wolf is an astronomer. She would like to design a website about planets, like the example shown in Figure 35. She would like her website to incorporate Flash elements, rollovers, and video and would like to use Dreamweaver to build the site.

1. Connect to the Internet and go to nasa.gov.
2. View the source code on several pages for the words "Flash" or "swf" to see if you see references to the use of Flash.
3. Which objects in the site are made with rollover images?
4. How has adding the Flash effects improved the appearance of this site?
5. Create a sketch of Angie's site that contains at least five pages. Indicate in your sketch what media elements you would insert in the site, including where you would add Flash objects, rollover images, and video.

Figure 35 *Design Project*
NASA website—www.nasa.gov

PORTFOLIO PROJECT

In this assignment, you will continue to work on the group website that you started in Chapter 1. There will be no Data Files supplied. You are building this site from chapter to chapter, so you must do each Portfolio Project assignment in each chapter to complete your site.

You will continue building your site by designing and completing a page that contains rich media content or by adding media content to existing pages. After completing your site, be sure to run appropriate reports to test the site.

1. Evaluate your wireframe, then choose a page, or series of pages, to develop in which you will include Flash objects as well as other media content, such as rollover images, video, and behaviors.
2. Plan the content for your new page so that the layout works well with both the new and old pages in your site. Sketch a plan for your wireframes for the media content you wish to add, showing which media elements you will use and where you will place them.
3. Create or find the media you identified in your sketch, choosing appropriate formatting.
4. Add the rollover images to the page.
5. Add a video, if possible, to the page.
6. Add a behavior to a page element, then specify the action you would like to use with it.
7. Run a report on your new page(s) to ensure that all links work correctly.
8. Preview the new page (or pages) in your browser and test all links. Evaluate your pages for content and layout. Use the checklist in Figure 36 to make sure your website is complete.
9. Make any modifications that are necessary to improve the page.

Figure 36 *Portfolio Project checklist*

```
                  Website Checklist
  1. Do your pages flow well together?
  2. Do all Flash movies play properly in the browser?
  3. Do all links work?
  4. Do all rollover images display properly?
  5. Do your video files load quickly and play correctly?
  6. Does the behavior assigned a page AP element respond correctly
     to the action assigned to it?
```

ADOBE DREAMWEAVER CS6

CHAPTER 12
CREATING AND USING TEMPLATES

1. Create templates with editable regions
2. Use templates to create pages
3. Use templates to update a site
4. Use advanced template options

CHAPTER 12
CREATING AND USING TEMPLATES

Introduction

When you create a website, it's important to make sure that each page has a unified look so that users know they are in your site, no matter what page they are viewing. For instance, you should make sure that common elements such as the menu bar and company banner appear in the same place on every page and that every page shares a basic design and color scheme. You have been using styles to provide continuity in your sites in previous chapters. Another way to make sure that every page in your site has a consistent appearance is by creating pages based on templates. A **template** is a special kind of page that contains both **locked regions**, which are areas on the page that cannot be modified by others who add content (content contributors), as well as other types of regions that they can change or edit. For instance, an **optional region** is an area in the template that content contributors can choose to show or hide, and an **editable region** is an area where template content contributors can add or change content.

Using templates not only ensures a consistent appearance throughout a website, but also saves considerable development time. Templates are especially helpful if you are working with a team to create the pages in your site. In this chapter, you will create a template from an existing page in The Striped Umbrella website and define editable regions in it.

Understanding How to Use Templates

The ideal process for using templates is for one person (the template author) to create a template that has locked regions containing the design elements common to every page in the site, as well as regions with content that content contributors can add or change. Once the template is fully developed, other team members can use it to create other site pages, adding appropriate content to the editable regions of each page. If the template author makes changes to the template, all pages to which the template is attached can be automatically updated to reflect those changes.

TOOLS YOU'LL USE

DREAMWEAVER 12-3

LESSON 1

Create Templates with
EDITABLE REGIONS

What You'll Do

In this lesson, you will create a template based on the cruises page of The Striped Umbrella website. You will then define editable regions in the template, edit content in one of the divs, and add links to the cruises and fishing pages.

Creating a Template from an Existing Page

If you have already created and designed a page that you think looks great, and you want to use the layout and design for other pages in your site, you can save the page as a template using the Save as Template command. Templates are saved with a .dwt extension and are stored in the Templates folder in the site root folder for your website. If your site does not have a Templates folder, Dreamweaver automatically creates one for you the first time you save a template. To view a list of templates in your site, open the Templates folder in the Files panel. To preview a template before opening it, open the Assets panel, click the Templates button on the Assets panel toolbar, and then click a template in the list. The template appears in the preview window above the templates list, as shown in Figure 1.

Defining Editable Regions

By default, when you save a template, all content on the page is locked, which means that no one else can add content or modify any part of the template to create new pages. If your template is going to be used effectively, you must have at least one editable region in it so that other content contributors can add content. You can specify a name for the region using the New Editable Region dialog box. Editable regions are outlined in blue on the template page, and the names of the editable regions appear in blue shaded boxes, as shown in Figure 2.

Defining Optional Regions

In addition to editable regions, you can also add optional regions to a template. An optional region is an area in a template that content contributors can choose to either show or hide. For instance, you could place an image in an optional region, so that content contributors can decide whether or not to show it on the page they are creating. An optional region's visibility is controlled by the conditional statement **if**. You can specify a page element as an optional region using the New Optional Region dialog box. You can name the region and specify whether to show or hide it by default. You access the Editable and Optional Region dialog boxes by clicking the Templates list arrow in the Common category of the Insert panel.

Defining Editable Optional Regions

If you want to give content contributors the ability to show or hide a page element, as well as make modifications to it, then you can define the element as an **editable optional region**. For instance, you might want to make an advertisement an editable optional region so that content contributors of the template can change its text and specify whether to show or hide it. Using the New Optional Region dialog box, you can name the region and specify whether to show or hide it by default.

Figure 1 *Template in Assets panel*

Assets panel
Preview of selected template
Templates button
List of templates available in this site

Figure 2 *Template with locked and editable regions*

Editable region label (all other regions are locked)
Blue outlines of editable region

Lesson 1   Create Templates with Editable Regions

Create a template from an existing page

1. Open Dreamweaver, open The Striped Umbrella website, then open the cruises page.
2. Click **File** on the Menu bar, then click **Save as Template** to open the Save As Template dialog box.
3. Verify that The Striped Umbrella is displayed in the Site text box, type **activities_pages** in the Save as text box, compare your screen to Figure 3, click **Save**, update the links, then click the **Refresh button** on the Files panel toolbar.

   The Templates folder, which contains the activities_pages template, appears in the Files panel.
4. Click the **plus sign** next to the Templates folder to display the activities_pages.dwt file.
5. Display the Assets panel, click the **Templates button** to view the list of templates in the site, then compare your Assets panel to Figure 4. Click the **Refresh button** if you don't see the template listed.

   TIP To create a template from scratch, click File on the Menu bar, click New to open the New Document dialog box, click Blank Template, click the type of template you want to create in the Template Type list, choose a layout from the Layout list, choose a document type, attach any existing style sheets you would like to use, then click Create.

6. Close the cruises page.

You created a template from the cruises page of The Striped Umbrella website.

Figure 3 *Save As Template dialog box*

Save as text box

Figure 4 *Assets panel showing saved template in The Striped Umbrella website*

Preview of activities_pages template

Templates button

activities_pages template

Refresh button

Figure 5 *New Editable Region dialog box*

Name of new editable region

Figure 6 *activities_pages template with editable region added*

Editable region label

Selected editable region is marked by blue outline

Templates list arrow

Create an editable region

1. Click to place the insertion point in the div with the boat graphic, then click the **<article.content> tag** in the tag selector to select all of the content in the div.

2. Select the **Common category** on the Insert panel, if necessary.

3. Click the **Templates list arrow** in the Common category, then click **Editable Region** to open the New Editable Region dialog box.

   TIP You can also press [Ctrl][Alt][V] (Win) or ⌘ [option][V] (Mac) to open the New Editable Region dialog box.

4. Type **contents** in the Name text box, as shown in Figure 5, click **OK**, click on the page to deselect the content, then compare your screen to Figure 6.

   A blue shaded box with the label "contents" appears above the top left corner of the div.

   TIP You must have Invisible Elements turned on to see the blue shaded box.

5. Save your work.

   TIP To remove an editable region from a template, select the editable region in the document window, click Modify on the Menu bar, point to Templates, then click Remove Template Markup.

You created one editable region in the activities_pages template.

Lesson 1   Create Templates with Editable Regions

Modify a template

1. Edit the text in the sidebar1 div by replacing the words "lunch for your day on the water." with "lunch and/or cold drinks for your day's activities." as shown in Figure 7.

   This text will now apply to activities that are not only on the water. Since this area of the page is not designated as an Editable Area, content contributors will not be able to change this content on pages based on this template unless they open the template itself.

2. Select and delete the copyright statement and last updated statement in the page footer, then type **Cruises**.

   Since this area of the page is not designated as an Editable Area either, content contributors will not be able to change this content on pages based on this template unless they open the template itself.

3. Press **[Spacebar]**, click **Insert** on the Menu bar, point to **HTML**, point to **Special Characters**, then click **Em-Dash**.

   (continued)

Figure 7 *Editing the activities_page template*

Edited text for sidebar div

DREAMWEAVER 12-8

Creating and Using Templates

Figure 8 *Links added to the activities_pages template*

Two links added to the template

4. Press **[Spacebar]**, then type **Fishing**.
5. Change to the HTML Property inspector if necessary, link the **Cruises text** to cruises.html, then link the **Fishing text** to fishing.html.

   Don't be concerned with the leading periods and slash before the link in the Link text box. They simply indicate that the template file is in a different folder from the cruises and fishing files.

6. Click **File** on the Menu bar, click **Save All**, then compare your screen to Figure 8.
7. Close the activities_pages template.

You edited the content in the div tag rule, then added links to the cruises and fishing pages.

Using InContext Editing

Another way to allow content contributors to modify web pages is through InContext Editing (ICE). **InContext Editing** is an online service that users can log into and be allowed to make changes to designated editable regions on a page while viewing it in a browser. This requires little knowledge of HTML or Dreamweaver. The commands to create editable regions are found in the InContext Editing category on the Insert panel. For more information, search either the Adobe Help files or the Adobe website at adobe.com.

Lesson 1 Create Templates with Editable Regions

DREAMWEAVER 12-9

LESSON 2

Use Templates
TO CREATE PAGES

What You'll Do

▶ In this lesson, you will use the activities_pages template to create a new page in The Striped Umbrella website. You will add content to the editable region, then apply the template to two existing pages in the website.

Creating Pages with Templates

There are many advantages to using a template to create a page. First, it saves a lot of time, because part of the content and format of your page is already set. Second, it ensures that the page you create matches the look and format of other pages in the site. You can create a page based on a template using many different methods. One way is to click File on the Menu bar, click New to open the New Document dialog box, click Page from Template, select the site and the template you want to use, and then click Create. Templates can be used only in the website that contains them.

QUICK TIP

You can also create a new page based on a template by right-clicking (Win) or [control]-clicking (Mac) a template in the Assets panel, and then clicking New from Template.

Modifying Editable Regions

When you create a new page that is based on a template, certain areas of the new page are locked. You can tell which areas are locked by the appearance of the mouse pointer. When positioned over a locked region, the mouse pointer appears in the shape of a circle with a line cutting through it, as shown in Figure 9. Editable regions are outlined in blue and marked with a shaded blue label.

Editing, deleting, or adding content in editable regions of a template-based page works just like it does on any other page. Simply select the element you want to modify and make your changes, or click in the editable region and insert the new content.

Creating Links in Template-Based Pages

When you add a link to a page that is based on a template, it is important to use document-relative links; otherwise, they will be broken links. The path to a link actually goes from the template file (not from the template-based page) to the linked page. To ensure that all of your links are document-relative, select the page element to which you want to add a link, and then drag the Point to File icon from the Property inspector to the page you want to link to in the Files panel, as shown in Figure 10.

Figure 9 *Working with a template-based page*

Notation that this page is based on the activities_pages template

Pointer positioned over a locked region

Lesson 2 Use Templates to Create Pages

Attaching a Template to an Existing Page

Sometimes you need to apply a template to a page that you have already created. For example, suppose you create a page for your department for your company's website, and then your manager tells you that it must be based on the template created by the marketing department. Before you attach a template to an existing page, you should delete any elements from your page that also appear in the template. For instance, if both your page and the template have a company logo, you should delete the logo on your page. If you don't delete it, the logo will appear twice. Once you delete the duplicate content on your page, attach the template by opening your page, selecting the template in the Assets panel, and clicking the Apply button in the Assets panel. When you do this, the Inconsistent Region Names dialog box opens, allowing you to specify in which regions of the template to place the document head and body content from your page. To detach a template from a page, open the page you want to detach from the template, click Modify on the Menu bar, point to Templates, then click Detach from Template.

QUICK TIP

You can also attach a template to an open page by dragging the template from the Assets panel to the Document window.

Figure 10 *Using the Point to File icon to specify a document-relative link*

Point to File icon

Figure 11 *New Document dialog box*

Page from Template option

Click to create new page based on activities_pages template

Update page when template changes check box

Create a new page based on a template

1. Click **File** on the Menu bar, click **New** to open the New Document dialog box, then click **Page from Template**.
2. Click **The Striped Umbrella** in the Site list box (if necessary), click **activities_pages** in the Template for Site "The Striped Umbrella" list box (if necessary), verify that the **Update page when template changes check box** is selected, compare your screen to Figure 11, then click **Create**.

    TIP You don't have to select the template name if there is only one listed. It will be selected automatically.

    A new untitled page opens with the activities_pages template applied to it. The current content serves as placeholder content.

3. Click **File** on the Menu bar, click **Save As** to open the Save As dialog box, type **golfing** in the File name text box, then click **Save**.

You created a new page in The Striped Umbrella website that is based on the activities_pages template. You then saved this page as golfing.html.

Lesson 2 Use Templates to Create Pages

DREAMWEAVER 12-13

Modify editable regions in a template

1. Select the boats image, delete it, insert golfer.jpg from the drive and folder where you store your Data Files at the insertion point (saving it to the site root folder), adding **Golfer swinging a club** as the alternate text.
2. Select and delete the existing text, use the File, Import, Word Document command to import **golf.doc** (Win) or copy and paste golf.doc (Mac) from the drive and folder where you store your Data Files, then clean up the Word HTML.

   If you see a message about making changes to locked regions, click Ignore. You only want to clean up the new text.
3. Enter a paragraph break after the paragraph, then insert the image ladies_group.jpg from the drive and folder where you store your Data Files, adding **Ladies' group** as the alternate text.
4. Select the golfer image, then apply the **img_left_float** rule.
5. Select the ladies_group image, apply the **img_right_float** rule, then compare your screen to Figure 12.

You replaced content from the editable region of a new golf page based on the activities_pages template. You then imported text to replace text in the content editable region, and applied rules to the new images.

Add a link

1. Select the text "The Sports Club" in the paragraph, then link the selected text to the file **about_us.html**, as shown in Figure 13.
2. Save and close the golfing.html page.

You linked a file to selected text.

Figure 12 *Golfing page with revised content in editable region*

Figure 13 *Linking to the about_us.html page*

Linked text

Link to about_us.html page

DREAMWEAVER 12-14

Creating and Using Templates

Figure 14 *New fishing page based on a template*

Convert existing pages to template-based pages

1. Open the fishing page.
2. Copy the paragraphs of text in the center of the page, then close the fishing page.
3. Create a new page based on the activities_pages template, replace the text in the template with the text you copied from the fishing page, then save the page as **fishing.html**, overwriting the original fishing.html page.
4. Delete the boat image and replace it with the **fisherman.jpg** image by dragging it from the assets folder to the beginning of the paragraph in the contents editable region, then add **Young fisherman** for the alternate text.
5. Select the fisherman image, then apply the **img_right_float** rule.
6. Save the file, compare your screen with Figure 14, then close the page.
7. Create a new page based on the activities_pages template, then save it as **cruises.html**, overwriting the original cruises page. You do not have to replace any of the content because this is the page that was used for the template.
8. Close the cruises page.

You created a new HTML page based on a template and replaced text and images in the page. You then made an existing page into a template-based page.

Lesson 2 Use Templates to Create Pages

DREAMWEAVER 12-15

LESSON 3

Use Templates
TO UPDATE A SITE

What You'll Do

▶ *In this lesson, you will make a change to the activities_pages template, then update the site so that all pages based on the template reflect the change.*

Making Changes to a Template

If you create a successful site that draws large numbers of faithful users, your site will probably enjoy a long life. However, a good website should be updated frequently to keep the content fresh and timely. Your company might decide to make new products or offer new services. After a relatively short time, a website can look dated, even with no changes in the company. When changes occur in your company, on a large or small scale, you will need to change your site's appearance and functionality. If your pages are based on a template or group of templates, you will have a much easier time making those changes.

You use the same skills to make changes to a template as you would when creating a template. Start by opening the template from the Files panel or Assets panel, then add, delete, or edit content as you would on any non-template-based page. You can turn locked regions into editable regions using the New Editable Region command. To change an editable region back into a locked region, select the region, click Modify on the Menu bar, point to Templates, and then click Remove Template Markup.

Finding Downloadable Templates

It is not necessary to create all of your templates from scratch or from existing pages. You can also use templates from outside sources, such as the Internet. A wide range of templates is available for web page components, such as buttons, Flash intros, and logos, as well as entire websites. These can include sites for businesses, charities, events, and many other venues. Some websites offer free templates for downloading and some offer them for sale. Go to your favorite search engine and type website templates in the Search text box. For example, templatemonster.com offers many types of templates, both free and for sale.

DREAMWEAVER 12-16   *Creating and Using Templates*

Updating All Pages Based on a Template

One of the greatest benefits of working with templates is that any change you make to a template can be made automatically to all nested templates and pages that are based on the template. A **nested template** is a template based on an existing template, called a **root template**. When you save a template that you have modified, the Update Template Files dialog box opens, asking if you want to update all the files in your site that are based on that template, as shown in Figure 15. When you click Update, the Update Pages dialog box opens and provides a summary of all the files that were updated.

Figure 15 *Update Template Files dialog box*

Files based on activities_pages template:
- golfing.html
- fishing.html
- cruises.html

POWER USER SHORTCUTS	
To do this:	**Use this shortcut:**
Open the New Editable Region dialog box	[Ctrl][Alt][V] (Win) or ⌘ [Alt][V] (Mac)
Make a link	[Ctrl][L] (Win) or ⌘ [L] (Mac)
Remove a link	[Ctrl][Shift][L] (Win) or ⌘ [Shift][L] (Mac)
Add a non-breaking space	[Shift][Ctrl][Spacebar](Win) or [Shift] ⌘ [Spacebar](Mac)

© Cengage Learning 2013

Make changes to a template

1. Open the activities_pages template from the Templates folder. (*Hint*: You may have to click the plus sign to expand the Templates folder first.)
2. Click to place the insertion point after the second link, add a space, insert an **em dash**, then add another space.
3. Create a third link using the word **Golfing**, link it to the golfing page, then compare your screen to Figure 16.
4. Select the **Spry Menu bar**, select the **Activities menu item** in the first column in the Property Inspector, click the **Add menu item button** above the second column, then type **Golfing** in the Text text box.
5. Use the **Browse for file button** next to the Link text box, then link the new Golfing menu item to the golfing page, as shown in Figure 17.
6. Open the fishing page.

   The new link at the bottom of the page does not appear because you have not yet saved the template and updated the site.
7. Close the fishing page.

You opened the activities_pages template, added a new link, then modified the Spry Menu bar to include the golfing page in the Activities submenu.

Update all template-based pages in a site

1. Click **File** on the Menu bar, then click **Save All**.

   The Update Template Files dialog box opens, as shown in Figure 18.

(continued)

Figure 16 *activities_pages template with new link added*

New link added to template

Figure 17 *Updating the Spry Menu bar*

New submenu item added to Spry Menu bar

Link to golfing page

Golfing label for the submenu item

DREAMWEAVER 12-18

Creating and Using Templates

Figure 18 *Update Template Files dialog box*

Figure 19 *Fishing page with template changes incorporated*

New link to golfing page displays on fishing page

2. Click **Update** to open the Update Pages dialog box, then click **Close** after it has finishing updating the pages. (*Note*: This may take several seconds. If you click the Show Log check box, you can watch the progress as it updates each file.)

3. Open the fishing, cruises, and golfing pages, then compare your screen to Figure 19.

   The fishing page, the cruises page, and the golfing page in the website now show the new link. The Activities link in the menu bar has three submenu items now that you can see in Live View or a browser.

4. Close all open pages.

5. Open the activities page, click to place the insertion point at the end of the paragraph with the links to the fishing and cruises pages, press **[spacebar]**, then type **We can also arrange tee times for you at area golf courses**.

   This new sentence provides text for a link to the golfing page.

6. Link the text **tee times** to golfing.html, then save the activities page.

7. Repeat Steps 4 and 5 on the previous page to add the golfing submenu item to each menu bar on the activities, about_us, cafe, index, and spa pages, then save and close each page. (*Hint*: You can also just modify one menu bar, then use it to replace each of the other menu bars.)

You saved the activities_pages template and used the Update Template Files dialog box and the Update Pages dialog box to specify that all pages in the site based on the template be updated to reflect the template modifications. You also added text to the activities page that was used to provide a link to the golfing page. You then opened each of the other pages in the site that are not based on a template and modified each of their menu bars.

Lesson 3   Use Templates to Update a Site

DREAMWEAVER 12-19

LESSON 4

Use Advanced
TEMPLATE OPTIONS

What You'll Do

In this lesson, you will learn about advanced template settings that can be used for more complex templates.

Setting Parameters for Optional Regions

If your template will be used by many people, it might be a good idea to include several optional regions in it so that template content contributors can pick and choose from a wide range of content elements. For example, on a retail site, you might have an optional region for each department to advertise a sale promotion. You would display the optional region for the department you want to feature during the time that department is having its sale. When the sale is over, you would hide that optional region. You might also want to set parameters for optional regions, specifying that they are displayed or hidden based on specific conditions. For instance, let's say you have two optional regions named shoe_sale_text and shoe_images. You could set the shoe_images optional region parameter to shoe_sale_text so that the shoe_images optional region would appear only when the shoe_sale_text optional region is showing, and would be hidden only when the shoe_sale_text optional region is hidden. Use the Advanced settings in the New Optional Region dialog box to set the parameters of an optional region. You can also write a conditional expression based on JavaScript. For instance, you could write an expression to specify that an optional region appear only when a related optional region is hidden.

Nesting Templates

If you are working on a complex website that has many different pages used by different people or departments, you might need to create **nested templates**, which are templates that are based on another template. Nested templates are helpful when you want to define a page or parts of a page in greater detail. An advantage of using nested templates is that any changes made to the original template can be automatically updated in the nested template.

To create a nested template, create a new page based on the original template, then use the Save as Template command to save the page as a nested template. You can then make changes to the nested template by adding or deleting content and defining new editable regions. Note that editable regions in the original template are passed on as editable regions to the nested template. However, if you add a new editable or optional region to an editable region that was passed on from the original template, the original editable region changes to a locked region in the nested template.

Creating Editable Attributes

There might be times when you want content contributors of your template to be able to change certain attributes of an element in a locked region. For instance, perhaps you want to give them the ability to change the cell background color of the top row in a repeating table, or change the source file for an image in a locked area of the template. You can use the Editable Tag Attributes dialog box, shown in Figure 20, to specify that certain attributes of locked regions be editable. To do this, choose an attribute of a selected element, make it editable, assign it a label, and specify its type and its default setting. For instance, in Figure 20, a link was first selected in a template. Then, the Editable Tag Attributes dialog box was opened by clicking Modify on the Menu bar, pointing to Templates, and then clicking Make Attribute Editable. From that dialog box, you can choose the attribute and settings that you want to make editable. When you define editable attributes of elements in locked regions, template users can make changes to the element's attributes using the Template Properties dialog box.

Figure 20 *Editable Tag Attributes dialog box*

SKILLS REVIEW

Create templates with editable regions.

1. Open the Blooms & Bulbs website, then open the plants page.
2. Save the plants page as a template called **plant_categories** and update the links.
3. Delete the heading, text, horizontal rule, video, and images in the content container. You should have only the banner, menu bar, sidebar with the contact information, the footer with the last updated statement, and copyright statement left on the page. (*Note*: Go to code view and delete any leftover code between the opening and closing section tags or any empty paragraph tags.)
4. Delete the copyright statement at the bottom of the page, then type **Annuals - Perennials - Water Plants**. (*Note*: Make sure there is a space before and after each hyphen.)
5. Link the Annuals text to the annuals.html page, the Perennials text to the perennials.html page, and the Water Plants text to the water_plants.html page.
6. Use the Tag Selector to select the article.content div, then create an editable region with it named **descriptions**. Switch to code view, locate the opening sidebar1 div tag, and delete the code style="height:850px". This deletes the internal style so that the external style will determine the height of the sidebar.
7. Return to Design view, then save and close the plant_categories template.

Use templates to create pages.

1. Create a new page from the plant_categories template, then save it as **annuals.html**, overwriting the existing file.
2. Drag the coleus.jpg file from the website assets folder into the content div and type **Coleus** as the alternate text.
3. Deselect the image, import the file annuals.doc from the drive and folder where you store your Chapter 12 data files and place the text under the image (Win), or use a word processing progam to copy and paste the text onto the page (Mac).
4. Clean up the Word HTML. If you see a message explaining that part of the code is locked, that means that it will not check the locked regions, which is fine.
5. Apply the img_left_float rule to the image.
6. Apply the Heading 3 format to the Annuals heading, then save and close the page.
7. Repeat Steps 1 through 6 to create a new page based on the plant_categories template, then save it as **perennials**, overwriting the existing page and using the fiber_optic_grass.jpg file and the perennials.doc text. Format the text and graphics consistently based on the annuals.html page.
8. Repeat Steps 1 through 6 to create a new **water_plants** page based on the plant_categories template, using the water_lily.jpg file and the water_plants.doc text, formatting the text and graphics consistently to match the other pages based on the template. (Remember to add alt text to each image.)
9. Save and close all open pages.
10. Close the Word files and the word processing program if necessary.

SKILLS REVIEW
(CONTINUED)

Use templates to update a site.

1. Open the plant_categories template, then delete the two hyphens and the spaces between the three links in the footer div, replacing them with three non-breaking spaces. (*Hint*: Use the Insert, HTML, Special Characters, Non-Breaking Space command or the keyboard shortcut [Shift][Ctrl][Spacebar](Win) or [Shift][command][Spacebar](Mac).)
2. Edit the height of the sidebar1 rule to 275px, save the template and the style sheet file, then update all files in the site that are based on the template.
3. Preview the annuals.html, perennials.html, and water_plants.html pages in your browser, compare your perennials page to Figure 21, close the browser, then close all open pages.

Figure 21 *Completed Skills Review*

PROJECT BUILDER 1

In this Project Builder, you use a template to enhance the TripSmart website. Use Figure 22 as a guide as you work with the template.

1. Open the TripSmart website.
2. Open the peru page, save it as a template named **destination_pages**, and update the links.
3. Select the content div and create an editable region named **trip_description**.
4. Save the template, leaving the existing content on the page.
5. Create a new page based on the template named **peru.html**, overwriting the existing peru page.
6. Close the peru page.
7. Open the galapagos page, then copy all the content in the article.content div.
8. Close the galapagos page.
9. Create a new page based on the destination_pages template.
10. Replace all content in the article.content div with the content you copied from the original galapagos page, then save it as galapagos.html, overwriting the exisiting galapagos file.
11. Close the galapagos page.
12. Create a new page based on the destination_pages template, then save it as **scotland.html**.
13. Edit the heading to read **Destination: Scotland**.
14. Delete the rest of the content in the article.content div.
15. Click under the heading, then import the Word file scotland.doc.
16. Use the Clean Up Word HTML command to remove any extra formatting.
17. Insert the images castle.jpg and sheep.jpg, including appropriate alternate text and and CSS formatting.
18. Save and close the scotland page.
19. On the destination_pages template, edit the content in the left sidebar to reflect the addition of the new tour. Compare your screen to Figure 22 for ideas.
20. Edit the Spry Menu bar to include the scotland page as an item under the Tours menu.
21. Save and close the template, updating all pages based on the template.
22. Open each page in the site that is not based on the destination_pages template and modify the menu bar to include the three child menus under the Tours menu. Note that the Scotland page link for pages based on the template should be ../scotland.html; for all other pages, it should be scotland.html. Verify that each of the destination pages was updated correctly.
23. Save all pages and preview them in the browser, testing each link.

PROJECT BUILDER 1
(CONTINUED)

Figure 22 *Sample Project Builder 1*

Creating and Using Templates

DREAMWEAVER 12-25

PROJECT BUILDER 2

In this Project Builder, you continue your work on the Carolyne's Creations website. Carolyne would like to make sure that the pages in the site have a consistent appearance. She has asked you to create a template based on the recipes page to use for adding new recipes to the website.

1. Open the Carolyne's Creations website, then create a new template from the recipes page named **recipes** and update the links.
2. Select the content in the article.content div and create an editable region from it named **name_description_recipe**.
3. Place the insertion point at the top of the right sidebar div and type **Featured Recipes:** enter a paragraph break, type **Caramel Coconut Pie** enter a paragraph break, type **Fried Green Tomatoes**, enter a paragraph break, then insert a horizontal rule below the text.
4. Apply a heading to format the text "Featured Recipes", then save and close the template.

(*Hint*: If the last ingredient does not appear in the bulleted list, it will on the pages based on the template when viewed in Live View or in a browser. The links to the two recipes will not show as linked text yet.)

5. Create a new file based on the recipes template and name it **recipes.html**, overwriting the original recipes.html file.
6. Close the new recipes page.
7. Create another new page based on the recipes template, and name it **fried_green_tomatoes.html**.
8. Replace the editable region text in the fried_green_tomatoes.html file with the fried_green_tomatoes text from the Word file, located in the drive and folder where you store your Data Files, then clean up the Word HTML.
9. Replace the coconut_pie.jpg image with the fried_green_tomatoes.jpg image from the Chapter 12 Data Files, apply the img_left_float rule, then change the alternate text to **Fried Green Tomatoes**.
10. Apply the same rules to each paragraph and heading that you used on the recipes page.
11. Save your work, preview the page in either Live View or your browser, make any alignment, style, and spacing adjustments of your choice, then save your work.
12. Open the recipes template and link the text under the menu bar as follows: Caramel Coconut Pie to recipes.html, and Fried Green Tomatoes to fried_green_tomatoes.html, as shown in Figure 23.
13. Save and close the template, updating the pages based on the template.
14. Save all files, preview the fried_green_tomatoes page in the browser, then compare your screen to Figure 24.
15. Test all links, close the browser, then close any open files.

PROJECT BUILDER 2
(CONTINUED)

Figure 23 *Completed Project Builder 2*

Figure 24 *Completed Project Builder 2*

DESIGN PROJECT

There are many web sources for Dreamweaver page templates. Many of them are free and many are available for nominal fees. One such site is moonfruit. The website pictured in Figure 25 was built from a template from the moonfruit website.

1. Connect to the Internet, then go to www.moonfruit.com.
2. Spend some time exploring the templates on this site by previewing several of them.
3. Think of an idea for a new site that you would like to create. The site can be for a club, organization, event, or any topic or person that interests you. Draw an outline and a sketch of the site, including the content that will be on each page.
4. After you have completed your sketch, look through the moonfruit templates available, then choose an appropriate template for your site.
5. Explain why you chose this particular template.
6. Search for other sites on the Internet that offer templates for downloading.
7. List three sites that you found and the prices listed for downloading each template.

Figure 25 *Design Project*
Table 22 website used with permission from Table 22 - table22branson.com

PORTFOLIO PROJECT

In this assignment, you continue to work on the website that you created in earlier chapters, enhancing it by using templates. You first create a template from one of your existing pages and define editable regions in it. You then apply the template to a page and add content to the editable regions.

1. Consult your wireframe and decide which page you would like to use as a template. You will use the template to create at least one other page in your site.
2. Create a sketch of the template page you will create. Mark the page elements that will be in locked regions. Identify and mark at least one area that will be an editable region.
3. Create a new template, then define the editable regions in the template.
4. Make any necessary formatting adjustments to make sure it looks attractive, and then save the template. Create a new page based on the template, using the same name as the page on which the template is based, so that the earlier version of the page is overwritten.
5. Apply the template to another existing page in the site, making sure to delete all repeating elements contained in the template.
6. Review the template(s) and the template-based pages, and decide if you need to make improvements. Use the checklist in Figure 26 to make sure you completed everything according to the assignment.
7. Make any necessary changes.
8. Save your work, then close all open pages.

Figure 26 *Portfolio Project checklist*

```
                    Website Checklist
1. Does your template include at least one editable region?
2. Are all links on templates-based pages document-relative?
3. Do all editable regions have appropriate names?
4. Do all links work correctly?
5. Do all pages look good using at least two different browsers?
6. Are you happy with the overall appearance of each page?
```

ADOBE DREAMWEAVER CS6

CHAPTER **13** **WORKING WITH LIBRARY ITEMS AND SNIPPETS**

1. Create and modify library items
2. Add library items to pages
3. Add and modify snippets

CHAPTER 13
WORKING WITH LIBRARY ITEMS AND SNIPPETS

Introduction

When creating a website, chances are good that you will want certain graphics or text blocks to appear in more than one place in the site. For instance, you might want the company contact information in several different places, or a footer containing links to the main pages of the site at the bottom of every page. Library items and snippets can help you work with these repeating elements more efficiently.

Understanding Library Items

If you want an element to appear repeatedly, then it's a good idea to save it as a library item. A **library item** is content that can contain text or graphics that you plan to use multiple times in your website and that is saved in a separate file in the Library folder of your website. When you need to use a library item on a web page, you can easily select it from the list of available library items in the Library category in the Assets panel. In addition to being readily available, another advantage of using library items is that when you make a change to the library item and then update the site, all instances of that item throughout the website will be updated to reflect the change.

Understanding Snippets

Another way to use the same content repeatedly throughout a site is to insert code snippets. **Code snippets** are ready-made, reusable pieces of code you can insert on a page. Dreamweaver provides a variety of code snippets you can use to create footers, drop-down menus, headers, and other page elements. Code snippets are stored in the Snippets panel and can be used on any open page in any website.

In this chapter, you will work with library items and code snippets to enhance The Striped Umbrella website.

TOOLS YOU'LL USE

Library button

Snippet

New Snippet button

Edits the original version of this library item button

LESSON 1

Create and Modify
LIBRARY ITEMS

What You'll Do

In this lesson, you will create a text-based library item. You will also create a library item that contains an image in the activities_pages template. You will then edit both library items and update the site to reflect those edits.

Understanding the Benefits of Library Items

Using library items for repetitive elements—especially those that need to be updated frequently—can save you considerable time. For instance, suppose you want to feature an employee of the month photograph on every page in your site. You could create a library item named employee_photo and add it to every page. Then, when you need to update the site to show a new employee photo, simply replace the photo contained in the library item, and the photo would be updated throughout the site. Library items can contain a wide range of content, including text, images, tables, Flash files, and audio files.

Viewing and Creating Library Items

To view library items, open the Assets panel, then click the Library button. The library items appear in a list, and a preview of the selected library item appears above the list, as shown in Figure 1. To save text or an image as a library item, select the item in the Document window, and then drag it to the Library on the Assets panel. You can also click Modify on the Menu bar, point to Library, and then click Add Object to Library. The item that you added will appear in the preview window on the Assets panel and in the library item list with the temporary name Untitled (Win) or a numeral starting with "1" (Mac) assigned to it. Type a new name, and then press [Enter] (Win) or [return] (Mac) to give the library item a meaningful name. Library items on a web page appear in shaded yellow in the Document window, but not in the browser. When you click a library item in the Document window, the entire item becomes selected and the Property inspector changes to display three buttons that you can use to work with the library item, as shown in Figure 2.

QUICK TIP
You can also view a list of available library items by expanding the Library folder in the Files panel.

DREAMWEAVER 13-4

Working with Library Items and Snippets

Modifying Library Items

You cannot edit library items on an open web page. To make changes to a library item, you have to open it. To open a library item, select the item in the Document window, and then click Open in the Property inspector. The library item will appear in the Document window, where you can make edits or add content to it. When you are satisfied with your edits, save the library item using the Save command on the File menu. When you do this, the Update Library Items dialog box will appear, asking if you want to update all instances of the library item throughout the site.

Figure 1 *Library items in Assets panel*

Figure 2 *Web page containing library item*

Lesson 1 Create and Modify Library Items

DREAMWEAVER 13-5

Create a text-based library item

1. Open The Striped Umbrella website, then open the index page.

2. Create a new class rule in the su_styles.css file called **contact_number** with the following settings: Font-family = **Arial**, **Helvetica**, **sans-serif**, Font-size = **small**, Font-weight = **bold**, color = **#006**, Text-align = **center**.

3. Move the copyright and last updated statements under the contact information, as shown in Figure 3.

4. Type **The Striped Umbrella 555-594-9458** in their previous position in the footer, then apply the **contact_number rule**.

5. Click to place the insertion point before the telephone number, change to the Text category on the Insert panel, click the **Characters list arrow**, click **Em Dash**, then add a space after the Em dash, as shown in Figure 3. (You want a space both before and after the Em dash.)

TIP You can also insert an Em dash by clicking Insert on the Menu bar, pointing to HTML, pointing to Special Characters, and clicking Em-Dash.

6. Display the Assets panel, then click the **Library button**.

7. Select the line of text with the telephone number, then drag it to the Assets panel.

(continued)

Figure 3 *Inserting an Em dash*

Move Copyright and Last updated text here

Em dash inserted on page

Click to insert the Em dash

Figure 4 *Assets panel showing contact_info library item*

Preview of selected library item

Selected library item

Library button

Figure 5 *Viewing the contact_info library item in Code view*

Code for library item

Library item file extension

8. Click **OK** to close the dialog box warning you that the library item will be saved without the style information.

    The text that you dragged is now an untitled library item on the Assets panel.

9. Type **contact_info** in the Name text box to replace "Untitled" (Win) or a temporary number (Mac), press **[Enter]** (Win) or **[return]** (Mac) to name the library item, then compare your Assets panel to Figure 4.

    The text formatting appears on the page but not in the Assets panel. If you look closely, you will see that the contact information now has a lightly shaded yellow background on the page behind the text, indicating it is a library item.

TIP If you don't see the shading, deselect the text and make sure that Invisible Elements is checked on your View, Visual Aids submenu.

10. Switch to Code view to view the library item, as shown in Figure 5, then return to Design view.

    The library item file has the file extension .lbi. The yellow shading is easier to see in Code view.

11. Save your work.

You created a text-based library item from text on the index page.

Lesson 1 Create and Modify Library Items

DREAMWEAVER 13-7

Create an image-based library item

1. Click the **Templates button** on the Assets panel, then double-click the **activities_pages template** to open it.
2. Click the **Library button** on the Assets panel to display the library item.
3. Place the insertion point in the uneditable region to the left of the Cruises link, go to Code view, then click before the opening cruises link tag.
4. Insert the **su_logo.gif** from the website assets folder using the menu or the Insert panel (do not drag it), add **The Striped Umbrella logo** as the alternate text, deselect the logo code, return to Design view, then compare your screen to Figure 6.
5. Create a new class rule in the su_styles.css file named **img_middle_align** with the following properties: Block: Vertical-align = **middle** and Box: Margin Right = **20px**.
6. Apply the img_middle_align rule to the su_logo image.
7. Select the logo and drag the selection to the Library on the Assets panel, then click **OK** to close the dialog box warning you that the style was not copied.

   The image is stored as a library item and appears in the preview window at the top of the Assets panel. A new untitled library item appears selected in the library item list. (Refresh the Assets panel if it does not appear.)

   (continued)

Figure 6 *Viewing the Striped Umbrella logo on the activities_pages template*

Logo added to footer

Working with Library Items and Snippets

Figure 7 *logo library item added to Assets panel*

logo library item

Preview for logo library item

logo library item

Figure 8 *Update Pages dialog box with Library items and Templates check boxes checked*

Show log check box

Update check boxes

Look in list arrow

8. Type **logo** to replace the placeholder name, press **[Enter]** (Win) or **[return]** (Mac) to name the library item on the Assets panel, then compare your screen to Figure 7.

TIP You may need to scroll left in the panel to see the filename.

9. Save your changes, then click **Update** in the Update Template Files dialog box to open the Update Pages dialog box.

10. Click the **Look in list arrow**, click **Files that Use**, check the **Library items** and **Templates** check boxes, as shown in Figure 8, then click **Start**.

    Dreamweaver updates your files based on the changes made to the library item. If you select the Show log check box, you will see a list of the items that were updated.

11. Click **Close**, then open the cruises page to view the library item on the page.

    Because the cruises page was based on the activities_pages template, the page was updated to include the new logo library item.

12. Save all files, preview the cruises page in the browser, click the fishing and golfing links to view the logo on each of the pages, close your browser, and close all open pages except the activities_pages template.

You created a library item named logo that contains the resort logo in the activities_pages template. You then saved the template and updated all pages in the site that are based on the template.

Lesson 1 Create and Modify Library Items

DREAMWEAVER 13-9

Edit an image-based library item

1. Click the **logo library item** at the bottom of the activities_pages template.
2. Click **Open** in the Property inspector, as shown in Figure 9, to open the logo library item.

   The image appears in the Document window. The page tab displays the filename logo.lbi. The file extension .lbi denotes a library file.

   TIP You can also open a library item by double-clicking it on the Assets panel.

3. Click the image in the Document window, then click the **Crop button** in the Property inspector.
4. Click **OK** to the message warning "The action you are about to perform will permanently alter the selected image."

   An outline surrounds the image. The resizing handles on the outline let you crop the image.

5. Drag the right edge toward the center of the image to crop off the starfish on the right edge of the graphic, then drag the other three edges outward so the rest of the image is not cropped, as shown in Figure 10.
6. When you are satisfied with the crop, double-click the logo to execute the crop, then compare your screen to Figure 11.

   TIP You can also press [Enter](Win) or [return](Mac) to execute a crop.

You opened the logo library item, then cropped the image.

Figure 9 *Opening a library item*

Click to open a library item

Figure 10 *Cropping the logo*

Drag these center handles outward to leave the top, left, and bottom edges uncropped

Drag the right handle to crop the image

Figure 11 *Viewing the cropped logo*

The starfish is cropped out of the logo

Figure 12 *Activities_pages template showing the updated logo library item*

Logo is cropped

Update library items

1. Click **File** on the Menu bar, then click **Save** to open the Update Library Items dialog box.

   The dialog box asks if you want to update the library item on the pages shown.

2. Click **Update** to open the Update Pages dialog box.

3. Click the **Look in list arrow**, click **Files that Use**, check the **Library items** and **Templates** check boxes, then click **Start**.

   Dreamweaver updates the cruises, fishing, golfing, and activities_pages files based on the changes you made to the library item.

4. Click **Close**, then close the logo.lbi file.

   The activities_pages template page reflects the change you made to the logo library item.

5. Compare your screen to Figure 12.

6. Save and close the activities_pages template, updating the pages in the site again if prompted.

You saved the logo library item and updated all pages in the site to incorporate the changes you made.

Lesson 1   Create and Modify Library Items

DREAMWEAVER 13-11

Edit a text-based library item

1. Open the index page, then select the **telephone text** to select the contact_info library item.
2. Click **Open** in the Property inspector to open the contact_info library item.
3. Edit the telephone number to read **555-594-9458 or 888-594-9458 toll free**, then compare your screen to Figure 13.

(continued)

Figure 13 *Contact_info library item after editing*

The Striped Umbrella — 555-594-9458 or 888-594-9458 toll free

Toll free number added

Figure 14 *activities_pages template showing the updated logo library item*

Updated library item

4. Save your changes, update the site, then close the contact_info library item.
5. Compare your index page to Figure 14.

   The text reflects the edits you made to the contact_info library item.
6. Save and close the index page.

You edited the text in the contact_info library item, then saved the changes and updated the site.

Lesson 1 Create and Modify Library Items

LESSON 2

Add Library
ITEMS TO PAGES

What You'll Do

In this lesson, you will add the text-based library item you created to the about_us, activities, cafe, feedback, and spa pages. You will detach the library item on the index page and edit it. You will then delete one of the library items and restore the deleted item using the Recreate command.

Adding Library Items to a Page

Once you create a library item, it's easy to add it to any page in a website. All you do is drag the library item from the Assets panel to the desired location on the page. When you insert a library item, the actual content and a reference to the library item are copied into the code. The inserted library item is shaded in yellow in the Document window and is automatically updated to reflect any changes you make to the library item.

QUICK TIP

You can also insert a library item on a page by selecting the item on the Assets panel, then clicking Insert.

There may be times when you don't want content to be updated when you update the library item. For instance, suppose you want one of your pages to include photos of all past employees of the month. You would insert content from the current library item, but you do not want the photo to change when the library item is updated to reflect next month's employee photo. To achieve this, you would insert the content of a library item on a page, then click the Detach from original button in the Property inspector. The content from the library item will be inserted on the page, but it will not be linked to the library item.

Making Library Items Editable on a Page

There may be times when you would like to make changes to a particular instance of a library item on one page, without making those changes to other instances of the library item in the site. You can make a library item editable on a page by breaking its link to the library item. To do this, select the library item, and then click Detach from original in the Property inspector. Once you have detached the library item, you can edit the content as you would any other element on the page. Keep in mind, though, that this edited content will not be updated when you make changes to the library item.

Deleting and Recreating Library Items

If you know that you will never need to use a library item again, you probably want to delete it. To delete a library item, select it on the Assets panel, and then click the Delete button. Deleting a library item only removes it from the Library folder; it does not change the contents of the pages that contain that library item. All instances of the deleted library item will still appear in shaded yellow in the site unless you detach them from the original. Be aware that you cannot use the Undo command to restore a library item. However, you can restore a library item by selecting any instance of the item in the site and clicking Recreate in the Property inspector. You can also recreate a library item after you have exited and started Dreamweaver again, provided a deleted library item still has an instance remaining on a page. After you recreate a library item, it reappears on the Assets panel and you can make changes to it and update all pages in the site again. Figure 15 shows the Property inspector with Library item settings.

Figure 15 *Property inspector with Library item settings*

Click to open library item

Click to detach selected element from library item

Click to restore deleted library item

Add a library item to a page

1. Open the about_us page.
2. Delete the copyright and last updated statements at the bottom of the page.
3. Open the Assets panel, drag the **contact_info library item** from the Assets panel to the location from where you deleted the copyright statement, then click to deselect the library item.

   The contact_info item now appears where you placed it. It is shaded in yellow, indicating it is a library item.
4. Click to the right of the library item, then apply the **contact_number rule**.
5. Compare your screen to Figure 16.
6. Save and close the about_us page.
7. Repeat Steps 2 through 4 to add the **contact_info** library item to the activities page, as shown in Figure 17, then continue with the cafe, feedback, and spa pages.

   If the page has a copyright statement and a last updated statement, delete them before you add the library item.

   TIP If you have trouble dragging the library item on a page, use the Insert button on the Assets panel instead.

   (continued)

Figure 16 *About us page with library item added*

Library item

Figure 17 *Activities page with library item added*

Library item

DREAMWEAVER 13-16

Working with Library Items and Snippets

Figure 18 *Insert Div Tag dialog box*

ID = contact *Class = contact_number*

Figure 19 *Viewing the library items on the cruises page*

logo library item on cruises page *contact_info library item on cruises page*

8. Open the activities_pages template and place the insertion point to the right of the set of three links at the bottom of the page.
9. Click **Insert** on the Menu bar, point to **Layout Objects**, then click **Div Tag**.
10. Verify that At insertion point is selected in the Insert drop-down menu, click the **Class list arrow**, select **contact_number**, enter **contact** as the ID, as shown in Figure 18, then click **OK**.
11. Replace the placeholder text with the contact_info library item, save the activities_pages template, then update all files.
12. Open the cruises page to view the two library items at the bottom of the page, as shown in Figure 19.
13. Save and preview all of the edited pages in the browser, then close the browser.
14. Close all open pages.

You added the contact_info library item to the about_us, activities, cafe, feedback, and spa pages. You inserted a new div tag for the contact_info library item on the activities_pages template, then updated all pages based on the template.

Creating Library Items

Although you can create library items with images, text, or a combination of the two, you can use only items that are within the body tags. For instance, when editing a library item, the CSS Styles panel will be unavailable because style sheet code is embedded in the head section, rather than just the body section. Likewise, the Page Properties dialog box will be unavailable because library items cannot include a body tag attribute such as text color. You can apply a rule after you have placed the library item on the page.

Make a library item editable on a page

1. Open the index page, then click the **contact_info library item** in the page footer.

   The Property inspector displays three buttons relating to library items.

2. Click **Detach from original** in the Property inspector.

   A dialog box opens, warning you that the item will no longer be automatically updated when the original library item changes.

3. Click **OK**.

   Notice that the contact information no longer appears in shaded yellow, indicating it is no longer a library item.

4. Type **in Florida** after the first telephone number, then compare your screen to Figure 20.

   The contact information is edited on the page, and the library item and all the uses of it on other pages are unaffected.

5. Save and close the index page.

You detached the contact information from the contact_info library item to make the text editable on the index page. You then added two words to the contact information.

Figure 20 *Editing a library item on a page*

with beautiful birds, yet a short drive down the road from world-class shopping, restaurants, and entertainment. Bring a good book and leave your laptop at the office. You won't want to go home!

The restaurants at The Striped Umbrella are amazing. The Sand Crab Cafe can be enjoyed al fresco at The Terrace, poolside at The Cabana, and inside in The Dining Room. The Dining Room features fresh seafood and an extensive wine list. The Terrace offers more casual dining with sweeping views of the gulf and fabulous sunsets. The Cabana serves sandwiches, salads, and

The Striped Umbrella
25 Beachside Drive
Ft. Eugene, Florida 33775
555-594-9458
Club Manager

Copyright 2002 - 2015
Last updated on May 22, 2012

The Striped Umbrella — 555-594-9458 in Florida or 888-594-9458 toll free

"in Florida" added to text

DREAMWEAVER 13-18

Working with Library Items and Snippets

Figure 21 *Assets panel after deleting the logo library item*

logo no longer appears

Delete button

Figure 22 *Assets panel after recreating the logo library item*

Recreated logo library item

Delete a library item

1. Select the logo library item on the Assets panel.
2. Click the **Delete button** 🗑 on the Assets panel.

   A dialog box opens, asking if you are sure you want to delete the library item.
3. Click **Yes**, then compare your screen to Figure 21.

   The logo library item no longer appears on the Assets panel. Macintosh users may need to select the contact_info library item to see the change.

You deleted the logo library item on the Assets panel.

Recreate a library item

1. Open the activities_pages template.

   The logo still appears in shaded yellow, indicating it is still a library item, even though you deleted the library item to which it is attached.
2. Click the **logo** to select it.
3. Click **Recreate** in the Property inspector, then compare your Assets panel to Figure 22.

   The logo library item is added to the Assets panel.

   If you do not see the logo library item, refresh the Assets panel.
4. Close the activities_pages template.

You recreated the logo library item that you deleted in the previous set of steps.

Lesson 2 Add Library Items to Pages

DREAMWEAVER 13-19

LESSON 3

Add and Modify
SNIPPETS

What You'll Do

▶ In this lesson, you will add a predefined snippet from the Snippets panel to create a new footer for the index page. You will then replace the placeholder text and links in the snippet with appropriate text and links. Finally, you will save the modified snippet as a new snippet and add it to other pages.

Using the Snippets Panel

Creating a website is a huge task, so it's nice to know that you can save time by using ready-made code snippets to create various elements in your site. The Snippets panel, located in the Files panel group, contains a large collection of reusable code snippets organized in folders and named by element type. The Snippets panel is divided into two panes, as shown in Figure 23. The lower pane contains folders that can be expanded to view the snippets. The upper pane displays a preview of the selected snippet. Use the buttons at the bottom of the Snippets panel to insert a snippet, create a new folder in the Snippets panel, create a new snippet, edit a snippet, or remove a snippet.

Inserting and Modifying Snippets

Adding a snippet to a page is an easy task; simply drag the snippet from the Snippets panel to the desired location on the page. Once you position a snippet, you will need to replace the placeholder text, links, and images with appropriate content.

QUICK TIP

You can also add a snippet to a page by selecting the snippet in the Snippets panel, then clicking the Insert button on the Snippets panel.

DREAMWEAVER 13-20

Working with Library Items and Snippets

Creating New Snippets

Once you've modified a snippet so that it contains text and graphics appropriate for your site, you might want to save it with a new name. Doing this will save time when using this snippet on other pages. To save a modified snippet as a new snippet, select the snippet content in the Document window, and then click the New Snippet button in the Snippets panel to open the Snippet dialog box. Use this dialog box to name the snippet and give it a description. Because the Snippet dialog box displays the snippet code, you can make edits to the code here if you wish. Any new snippets you create will appear in the Snippets panel.

Figure 23 *Snippets panel*

Preview of selected snippet

Contents of expanded Footers folder

Selected snippet

New Snippet button

Lesson 3 Add and Modify Snippets

DREAMWEAVER 13-21

Add a predefined snippet to a page

1. Open the index page.
2. Scroll to the bottom of the page, click to the right of the contact telephone numbers, then add a paragraph break.
3. Click **Window** on the Menu bar, then click **Snippets** to open the Snippets panel.
4. Click the **plus sign (+)** (Win) or the **triangle** (Mac) next to the Footers folder in the Snippets panel to display the contents of the Footers folder.
5. Drag **Basic: Text Block** in the Footer folder to the bottom of the index page, under the contact telephone numbers, as shown in Figure 24.

   This text will serve as placeholder text until you replace it with the appropriate links for The Striped Umbrella website.

   TIP Having a navigation bar with plain text links on each main page of a website ensures maximum accessibility for users.

6. Save your changes.

You added a predefined navigation bar and text block from the Snippets panel.

Figure 24 *Index page after inserting snippet*

Basic: Text Block snippet dragged from the Snippets panel

Footers folder

Basic: Text Block snippet

DREAMWEAVER 13-22

Working with Library Items and Snippets

Figure 25 *Index page after editing snippet placeholder text*

Move the copyright statement from this location

Placeholder text is replaced with current copyright statement

Modify snippet text

1. Select the placeholder paragraph under the placeholder links, including the paragraph break after "Consectetur," then press **[Delete]**.

    You will use the current copyright statement rather than the placeholder text.

2. Cut the current copyright statement (which is under the Club Manager email link), add a line break after the Snippet placeholder links, then paste the copyright statement under the Snippet placeholder links, as shown in Figure 25.

3. Save your work, then preview the page in the browser to make sure the contact_info library item is not behind the first AP div.

4. Close the browser, make any spacing corrections necessary, then save any changes made.

You edited the placeholder text contained in the navigation snippet on the index page.

Lesson 3 Add and Modify Snippets

DREAMWEAVER 13-23

Modify snippet links

1. Select the Lorum placeholder link, then type **Home**.
2. Replace the Ipsum placeholder link with **About Us**, replace the Dolor placeholder link with **Sand Crab Cafe**, replace the Sic Amet placeholder link with **The Sea Spa**, then replace the Consectetur placeholder link with **Activities**.
3. Move the contact_info embedded rule to the su_styles.css file, select all of the text in the snippet (including the copyright statement if necessary), and apply the **contact_info** rule.
4. Display the Files panel, select the **Home link text** in the footer at the bottom of the home page, then use the Point to File icon in the Property inspector to set the Link property to the index page, as shown in Figure 26.
5. Use the Point to File icon to set the Link property for the About Us, Sand Crab Cafe, The Spa, and Activities links.
6. Save your changes, preview the Index page in your browser, test all the new navigation links, then close your browser.

You changed the names of the placeholder links and used the Point to File icon to create links to the five main pages in The Striped Umbrella website.

Create a new snippet

1. Select the **navigation footer** on the index page in Code view, as shown in Figure 27, being sure to select the entire div tag code so both lines of text and their formatting are selected.

(continued)

Figure 26 *Using the Point to File icon to create document-relative links in the new navigation links*

Selected text for link to home page

Point to File icon

Drag Point to File icon to index.html file

Figure 27 *Selecting the code for the snippet*

Select beginning div tag code

Include ending div tag code

DREAMWEAVER 13-24

Working with Library Items and Snippets

Figure 28 *Snippet dialog box*

Name text box

Description text box

Code starts with <div

2. Select the Footers folder in the Snippets panel, then click the **New Snippet button** to open the Snippet dialog box.
3. Type **su_footer** in the Name text box.
4. Type **This is a text-based navigation bar and copyright statement**. in the Description text box, compare your screen to Figure 28, then click **OK**.

   The new snippet is added to the Snippets panel.
5. Open the about_us page, change to Design view, place the insertion point to the right of the telephone contact information, insert a line break, select the **su_footer** from the Snippets panel then click the **Insert button** on the Snippets panel to insert the snippet on the page.
6. Repeat Step 5 to insert the **su_footer snippet** on all pages in the website, including the activities_pages template, then use the Point to File button to relink the links in the footer on the activities_pages template.
7. Save and preview all site pages in the browser, close the browser, make any necessary spacing adjustments, then close all open pages.
8. Recreate the site cache, run reports for Untitled Documents, Missing Alt Text, Broken Links, and Orphaned Files, then correct any errors.

   Water.jpg and two_dolphins_small.jpg are listed as orphaned files. You may also see the crabdance.fla file if you completed the Flash editing steps. These files are no longer needed, so you can move them, delete them, or leave them in the site.
9. Publish your site, then exit Dreamweaver.

You copied the text-based navigation bar from the index page and saved it as a snippet called su_footer. You then copied it to the rest of the main pages.

Lesson 3 Add and Modify Snippets

DREAMWEAVER 13-25

SKILLS REVIEW

Create and modify library items.

1. Open the Blooms & Bulbs website, then open the index page.
2. Create a new class rule in the blooms_styles.css file called **telephone** with the following settings: Font-family: Verdana, Geneva, sans-serif; Font-size: 14 pixels; Font-weight: normal; Font-style: normal; Color: #000; Text-align: center.
3. Delete the last updated statement.
4. Insert a new paragraph above the copyright statement, type **Blooms & Bulbs (555) 248-0806**, then apply the telephone rule to the text.
5. Select the text you typed in Step 4 if necessary, drag it to the Assets panel with the Library category displayed to create a new library item, then name it **telephone**.
6. Select the copyright statement, then create a new library item named **copyright**.
7. Edit the telephone library item to remove the parentheses around the area code and add a hyphen, then save the library item, update the index page, save the index page, then close the library item.
8. Open the newsletter page, insert three line breaks after the last link in the sidebar, insert blooms_logo.jpg from the drive and folder the drive and folder where you store your Data Files, then type **Blooms & Bulbs logo** as the alternate text. (*Hint*: If your logo covers the right sidebar border, go to Code view and move the ending </p> tag before the two line breaks.)
9. Drag the logo to the Assets panel to create a new library item, then name it **logo**.
10. Save and close the newsletter page.

Add library items to pages.

1. Open the workshops page, then delete the copyright and last updated statements.
2. Insert the telephone library item where you just deleted the copyright statement, click to the right of the library item, then apply the telephone rule to it.
3. Enter a paragraph break, insert the copyright library item under the telephone library item, then apply the small_text rule.
4. Repeat Steps 1, 2, and 3 to add the telephone and copyright library items to the newsletter, plants and tips pages and to the plant_categories template under the set of three links, then apply the telephone style and the small_text rules to the library items on each page. Delete any existing copyright statements and update the template-based files after you add the library items to the template page.
5. Save all pages.
6. Delete the telephone library item from the Assets panel.
7. Switch to the index page, select the telephone library item on the page, then re-create it.
8. Save your work and preview all pages in the browser, then make any necessary adjustments to improve spacing.

Add and modify snippets.

1. At the bottom of the index page, insert a paragraph break before the telephone library item.
2. Insert the Basic: Text Block snippet in the new line using the Insert button on the Snippets panel.

SKILLS REVIEW
(CONTINUED)

3. Replace the placeholder links in the footer with text to link to the home, newsletter, plants, tips, and workshops pages.
4. Create a link for each page name in the navigation bar to the appropriate page.
5. Delete the paragraph under the links in the snippet along with the paragraph return above the paragraph.
6. Create a new snippet from the nav bar in the footer you just inserted. Place it in the footer folder. Name the snippet **blooms_nav_bar**, give it an appropriate description, then apply the telephone rule to the footer.
7. Insert the new blooms_nav_bar at the bottom of the newsletter, plants, tips, and workshops pages above the telephone library item, and apply the telephone rule to each of them if necessary.
8. Insert the blooms_nav_bar at the bottom of the plant_categories.dwt page (you may need to use the Insert button instead of dragging), replacing the set of three links to the individual plant pages, apply the telephone rule, reset the links in the footer, then update all pages based on the template.
9. Save all pages, then preview each page in the browser to test the links in the footer to make sure they work correctly. See Figure 29. (*Hint*: If your AP divs cover up any of the footer text, reposition them until they are clear of the text.)
10. Close the browser, then close all open pages.
11. Run reports for Missing Alt Text, Untitled Documents, Broken Links, Orphaned Files, then correct any errors that you find. The butterfly.jpg file is listed as an orphaned file. You can delete it, move it to another folder, or leave it in the website if you wish. It is not needed at this time, as it was replaced with two new images used in a rollover. You can also delete the SpryEffects.js file since the water_plants page does not have a behavior now.
12. Publish your completed site, then exit Dreamweaver.

Figure 29 *Completed Skills Review*

PROJECT BUILDER 1

In this Project Builder, you will continue your work on the TripSmart website. You have been given the TripSmart logo to use in the website and decide to create a library item from the logo combined with the copyright statement.

1. Open the TripSmart website, then open the index page.
2. Delete the last updated statement, place the insertion point after the copyright statement, then enter a paragraph break.
3. Insert the file tripsmart_logo.jpg from the drive and folder where you store your Data Files onto the page, adding **TripSmart logo** for the alternate text.
4. Drag the copyright statement to the right of the logo.
5. Create a new class rule named **contact** in the tripsmart_styles.css style sheet with the following settings: Font-family: Arial, Helvetica, sans-serif; Font-size: 12 pixels; Font-weight: bold; Color: #330.
6. Apply the contact rule to the copyright statement.
7. Select both the logo and copyright statement, then use them to create a new library item named **logo**.
8. Save all files, preview the index page in the browser, make any necessary spacing adjustments to improve the page appearance, compare your screen to Figure 30, then close the browser.
9. Open the services page, replace the existing copyright and last updated statements with the logo library item, then apply the contact rule.
10. Repeat Step 9 to add the logo library item to the rest of the pages in the website. (*Hint*: To add the logo library item to the galapagos, peru, and scotland pages, add it to the destination_pages.dwt file, replacing the existing copyright statement.)
11. Save all files, then preview the pages in the browser.
12. Close the browser, then make any necessary adjustments to improve the page appearance.
13. Close all files, run reports for Missing Alt Text, Untitled Documents, Broken Links, and Orphaned Files, then correct any errors that you find. The tripsmart_gradient and galapagos_trip.html are listed as orphaned files. You can delete them, move them to another folder, or leave them in the website if you wish. They are not needed at this time.
14. Publish your completed site, then exit Dreamweaver.

Figure 30 *Completed Project Builder 1*

PROJECT BUILDER 2

In this Project Builder, you will continue your work on the Carolyne's Creations website. Chef Carolyne has asked you to add some plain text links at the bottom of each page to provide users with more accessible links that do not depend on the image map at the top of each page.

1. Open the Carolyne's Creations website.
2. Open the index page, then delete the last updated statement.
3. Insert a paragraph break before the copyright statement in the footer.
4. Create a snippet of your choice to serve as a text-based menu bar at the bottom of the content div, then save the snippet as **cc_nav_bar**.
5. Compare your screen to Figure 31.
6. Save your work, then preview the page in the browser.
7. Close the browser, then insert the navigation bar snippet at the bottom of the adults, children, classes, catering, recipes template, and shop pages. (Remember to reset your links in the footer in the recipes template.)
8. Rename the recipes page **pie.html**, then update all the files in the site.
9. Make any adjustments to the pages to improve the appearance, save your work, then preview each page in the browser.
10. Close the browser, then close all open pages.
11. Run reports for Untitled Documents, Missing Alt Text, Broken Links, and Orphaned Files, then correct any errors.
12. Publish your completed site, then exit Dreamweaver.

Figure 31 *Completed Project Builder 2*

Working with Library Items and Snippets

DESIGN PROJECT

Library items and snippets are commonly used in websites to ensure that repetitive information is updated quickly and accurately.

1. Connect to the Internet, then go to www.usa.gov as shown in Figure 32.
2. Spend some time exploring the pages of this site to become familiar with its elements. Do you see many repeating elements?
3. If you were developing this site, which images or text would you convert into library items? Print two pages from this website and write a list of some of the text and visual elements from these pages that you would make into library items.

Figure 32 *Design Project*
USA.gov website – www.usa.gov

PORTFOLIO PROJECT

In this project, you will continue to work on the website that you created in Chapter 1.

You will continue to enhance your website by using library items and snippets.

1. Consult your wireframe and decide which text and graphic elements in the site should be converted into library items. Write a list of these items.
2. Discuss what content to include in a footer that you will add to each page of the site using a snippet.
3. Convert all the text elements you identified in your list into library items.
4. Insert the library items that you created in Step 3 in appropriate places in the website.
5. Convert all the graphic elements you identified in Step 1 into library items.
6. Insert the graphic library items that you created in Step 5 in appropriate places in the website.
7. Edit two of the library items that you created, then save and update all instances of the library item in the site.
8. Add a footer to the website using one of the snippets in the Footers folder of the Snippets panel. Replace all placeholder links with appropriate links to each major page in the site and replace placeholder text with text that is suitable for your site.
9. Create a new snippet from the footer that was created in Step 8. Insert this snippet on the other pages of the site.
10. Save your work, preview all pages in a browser, then test all the links. Use the checklist in Figure 33 to make sure your website is complete.
11. Make any necessary changes, then save and close all open pages.
12. Run reports for Untitled Documents, Missing Alt Text, Broken Links, and Orphaned Files, then correct any errors that you find.
13. Publish your completed site, then exit Dreamweaver.

Figure 33 *Portfolio Project checklist*

> **Website Checklist**
> 1. Have you converted all repeating text elements into library items?
> 2. Have you converted all repeating graphic elements, such as logos, into library items?
> 3. Did you save and update the library items after making edits to them?
> 4. Do all links work correctly?
> 5. Did you add a footer to all pages in the website?
> 6. Did you run the appropriate reports and correct any errors that you found?

ACA CERTIFICATION GRID

You can use the information in this table to study for the Adobe Web Communication Using Dreamweaver exam, used to obtain ACA (Adobe Certified Associate) Certification. Objectives covered in the exam are listed on the left; chapters and page numbers are listed on the right. Remember that many objectives are built on information found in other sections of the book, so the best way to use the book is to read it and follow the keystrokes from start to finish, and then use this table for review. For more information on Adobe certification, go to http://www.adobe.com/education/resources/certificate-programs.html.

(ACA) ADOBE WEB COMMUNICATION USING DREAMWEAVER CS6 OBJECTIVES		Chapter(s)	Page(s)
Domain 1.0 Setting Project Requirements			
1.1	**Identify the purpose, audience, and audience needs for a website.**		
	1.1a Identify information that determines purpose, audience, and audience needs for a website.	1, 2, Glossary	1-19, 2-5 to 2-6, Glossary-43
1.2	**Identify web page content that is relevant to the website purpose and appropriate for the target audience.**		
	1.2a Identify criteria for determining whether content is relevant to the website purpose.	1, 2	1-19, 2-6
	1.2b Identify criteria for determining whether content is appropriate for the target audience.	1, 2	1-19, 2-6
1.3	**Demonstrate knowledge of standard copyright rules (related terms, obtaining permission, and citing copyrighted material).**		
	1.3a Use copyright terms correctly, such as "copyrighted," "fair use doctrine," "intellectual property," and "derivative works."	7	7-36 to 7-39
	1.3b Identify when permission must be obtained to use copyrighted material.	7	7-36 to 7-39
	1.3c Identify methods used to indicate content as copyrighted.	7	7-36 to 7-39
	1.3d Recognize proper methods for citing websites, images, sounds, video, and text from the Internet.	7	7-39
1.4	**Demonstrate knowledge of website accessibility standards that address the needs of people with visual and motor impairments.**		
	1.4a Define website accessibility.	2	2-5
	1.4b Demonstrate knowledge of W3C Priority 1 Checkpoints and the W3C Priority 2 POUR principles for making a website accessible.	2, 4	2-5, 2-19, 4-13, 4-22

ACA CERTIFICATION GRID
(CONTINUED)

(ACA) ADOBE WEB COMMUNICATION USING DREAMWEAVER CS6 OBJECTIVES

		Chapter(s)	Page(s)
1.4c	Explain why including accessibility in website design matters to clients and the target audience.	2, 7	2-5, 2-6, 2-19, 7-6
1.4d	Identify elements of an HTML page that can be read by screen readers.	2, 4, 9, 11	2-4, 4-13, 9-13, 9-18, 11-5
1.4e	Demonstrate knowledge of Web Accessibility Initiative's Accessible Rich Internet Applications (WAI-ARIA) specification.	5	5-18
1.5	**Make website development decisions based on your analysis and interpretation of design specifications.**		
1.5a	Demonstrate knowledge of the relationship between end-user requirements and design and development decisions.	2, 7	2-6, 7-5, 7-40, 7-41
1.5b	Identify page elements that are affected by end-user technical factors such as download speed, screen resolution, operating system, browser type, and device.	2, 4, 7, 11	2-2, 2-5, 2-6, 2-10, 2-11, 2-30, 2-31, 2-33, 4-4, 7-5, 11-4
1.6	**Understand project management tasks and responsibilities.**		
1.6a	Identify items that might appear on a project plan.	1	1-18 to 1-21
1.6b	Identify phases that might appear on a project plan.	1	1-18 to 1-21
1.6c	Identify deliverables that might be produced during the project.	1	1-19, 1-21
1.6d	Identify common problems and issues in project management.	1, 7	1-21, 7-5, 7-11, 7-22, 7-23

ACA CERTIFICATION GRID
(CONTINUED)

(ACA) ADOBE WEB COMMUNICATION USING DREAMWEAVER CS6 OBJECTIVES

		Chapter(s)	Page(s)
Domain 2.0 Planning Site Design and Page Layout			
2.1	**Demonstrate general and Dreamweaver-specific knowledge of best practices for designing a website, such as maintaining consistency, separating content from design, using standard fonts, and utilizing visual hierarchy.**		
2.1a	Identify attributes of a website that demonstrate consistency.	1, 2, 3, 12	1-26, 2-2, 2-5, 2-6, 3-2, 3-10, 3-11, 12-2
2.1b	Identify techniques used to maintain consistency.	1, 2, 3, 6, 8, 12, 13	1-26, 2-2, 2-6, 2-10, 2-11, 2-32, 3-2, 3-19, 3-20, 6-4, 6-8, 8-2, 8-4, 8-5, 8-11, 8-18, 12-2, 12-4, 12-12, 13-2 to 13-19
2.1c	Identify the benefits of consistency.	2, 3, 8, 12	2-2, 3-2, 8-2, 8-4, 12-2
2.1d	Demonstrate knowledge of Cascading Style Sheets (CSS).	2, 3, 6, 8	2-11, Chapter 3, 6-1 to 6-21, Chapter 8
2.1e	Identify benefits of using CSS styles.	2, 3, 6, 8	2-11, 3-2, 3-6, 3-10, 3-11, 6-4, 8-2, 8-4
2.1f	Demonstrate knowledge of the different levels of CSS and the different features and capabilities of CSS2 and CSS3.	3	3-31
2.1g	Identify features used to maintain page structure and content hierarchy.	2, 3	2-11, 2-16, 3-2, 3-5, 3-8, 3-9
2.1h	Demonstrate knowledge of fixed and flexible page sizing.	6, 8	6-4, 6-6, 6-19, 6-25, 8-18, 8-19, 8-20
2.1i	Demonstrate knowledge of page layout and CSS design decisions that affect how a web page will print.	6, 8	6-25, 8-29
2.1j	Demonstrate knowledge of CSS best practices.	8, 10	8-2, 8-4, 8-18, 10-14, 10-19

ACA CERTIFICATION GRID (CONTINUED)

(ACA) ADOBE WEB COMMUNICATION USING DREAMWEAVER CS6 OBJECTIVES

		Chapter(s)	Page(s)
2.2	**Produce website designs that work equally well on various operating systems, browser versions/configurations, and devices.**		
2.2a	Demonstrate knowledge of different devices for viewing web content.	2, 4, 8	2-31, 2-32, 4-4, 8-19 to 8-22
2.2b	Demonstrate knowledge of web page elements that may not appear the same in different browsers, operating systems, or on different devices.	2, 7, 8	2-5, 2-10, 7-5, 8-21, 8-22
2.2c	Demonstrate knowledge of CSS3 media queries.	2, 8	2-32, 8-19, 8-20, 8-21
2.2d	Demonstrate knowledge of BrowserLab online service for cross-browser compatibility testing.	7, 8	7-5, 8-21
2.3	**Demonstrate knowledge of page layout design concepts and principles.**		
2.3a	Demonstrate knowledge of graphic design elements and principles.	2, 4, 9, 10, Glossary	2-2, 2-5, 2-32, 4-18, 4-19, 4-20, 9-4, 10-5, Glossary-37
2.3b	Identify examples of horizontal symmetry, vertical symmetry, diagonal symmetry, radial symmetry, and asymmetric layout.	2	2-32
2.3c	Recognize examples of page designs that violate design principles or best practices.	2, 4	2-2, 2-5, 2-6, 4-2
2.4	**Identify basic principles of website usability, readability, and accessibility.**		
2.4a	List elements used to improve website usability.	1, 2, 3, 4, 5, 8, 9	1-26, 2-2, 2-10, 2-14, 3-13, 4-22, 5-30, 8-2, 9-4
2.4b	Demonstrate knowledge of text formatting guidelines that improve readability.	2, 3, 4	2-5, 2-16, 3-2, 3-4 to 3-9, 3-13, 4-22

ACA CERTIFICATION GRID (CONTINUED)

(ACA) ADOBE WEB COMMUNICATION USING DREAMWEAVER CS6 OBJECTIVES

			Chapter(s)	Page(s)
	2.4c	Identify specific techniques used to make a website accessible to viewers with visual and motor impairments.	2, 4, 6, 9, 11, 13	2-14, 2-16, 4-22, 6-23, 9-13, 9-18, 11-4, 13-22
	2.4d	Identify elements of a website that by default are not read by screen readers.	4, 11	4-13, 11-5
2.5		**Demonstrate knowledge of flowcharts, storyboards, and wireframes to create web pages and a site map (site index) that maintain the planned website hierarchy.**		
	2.5a	Demonstrate knowledge of flowcharts.	1	1-19, 1-20
	2.5b	Demonstrate knowledge of storyboards.	1	1-19, 1-20
	2.5c	List items that appear on a website design storyboard.	1	1-19, 1-20
	2.5d	Demonstrate knowledge of wireframes.	1, 5, 6	1-19, 1-20, 5-32, 6-23
	2.5e	Recognize a website that follows the planned website hierarchy.	1, 5, 7	1-19, 1-20, 5-32, 7-40
2.6		**Communicate with others (such as peers and clients) about design plans.**		
	2.6a	Demonstrate knowledge of techniques for gathering feedback on design plans from others (such as peers and clients).	7	7-5, 7-22, 7-40, 7-41

ACA CERTIFICATION GRID
(CONTINUED)

(ACA) ADOBE WEB COMMUNICATION USING DREAMWEAVER CS6 OBJECTIVES

		Chapter(s)	Page(s)
Domain 3.0 Understanding the Adobe Dreamweaver CS6 Interface			
3.1	**Identify elements of the Dreamweaver interface.**		
3.1a	Identify and label elements of the Dreamweaver interface.	1, 8, 10	1-3, 1-4, 1-5, 1-6, 8-11, 8-12, 8-13, 8-21, 10-6, 10-7, 10-19
3.1b	Demonstrate knowledge of the differences between Design view, Code view, Split view, and Live view.	1, 8, 9, 10, 11	1-6, 1-9, 1-11, 1-15, 8-15, 8-23, 9-31, 10-16, 11-13
3.1c	Demonstrate knowledge of the Workspace Switcher.	1	1-10
3.1d	Demonstrate knowledge of working with related files and the Code Navigator.	1, 3	1-5, 3-16, 3-17, 3-21, 3-25
3.2	**Use the Insert bar.**		
3.2a	Identify types of content that can be created or inserted by using the Insert bar.	1, 2, 4, 9, 10, 11, 12, 13	1-4, 2-7, 2-8, 2-20, 2-22, 2-29, 4-6, 4-8, 9-8, 9-12, 9-14, 9-19 to 9-24, 9-26, 9-28, 9-29, 10-4, 10-6, 10-17, 11-4, 11-6, 11-10, 11-12, 11-20, 12-4, 12-9, 13-6
3.2b	Demonstrate knowledge of how to change between the categories on the Insert bar.	1, 2, 10, 11, 12	1-4, 2-7, 2-8, 2-16, 2-20, 2-22, 2-29, 10-6, 10-17, 10-19, 11-6, 11-10, 11-12, 11-20, 12-4, 12-7, 12-9

ACA CERTIFICATION GRID
(CONTINUED)

(ACA) ADOBE WEB COMMUNICATION USING DREAMWEAVER CS6 OBJECTIVES		Chapter(s)	Page(s)
3.3	**Use the Property inspector.**		
	3.3a Demonstrate knowledge of the various functions of the Property inspector.	1, 2, 4, 5, 8, 9, 10, 12, 13	1-6, 1-31, 2-6, 2-11, 2-13, 2-16, 2-21, 2-26, 4-6, 4-9, 4-16, 4-26, 5-6, 5-7, 5-8, 5-13, 5-14, 5-19, 5-20, 5-26 to 5-29, 8-6, 9-6, 9-9, 9-19, 9-21, 9-22, 9-26, 9-28, 9-29, 10-7 to 10-13, 10-16, 10-18, 12-9, 12-18, 13-15
3.4	**Use the Assets panel.**		
	3.4a Demonstrate knowledge of the Site and Favorites lists on the Assets panel.	4	4-4, 4-5, 4-7, 4-19
	3.4b Identify types of content that can be accessed by using the Assets panel.	2, 4, 5, 11, 12, 13	2-23, 4-4, 4-5, 4-7, 4-22, 5-9, 5-31, 11-6, 12-5, 12-6, 12-12, 13-14, 13-19
	3.4c Demonstrate knowledge of how to apply assets from the Assets panel to a web page.	4, 11, 12	4-5, 11-6, 12-12
3.5	**Use the Files panel.**		
	3.5a Identify uses of the Files panel.	1, 2, 4, 5, 7, 8, 12	1-2, 1-20, 1-22, 1-23, 1-27, 1-28, 1-32, 1-33, 2-14, 2-16, 4-4, 4-19, 4-22, 5-5, 5-6, 7-15, 7-16, 7-19 to 7-21, 8-8, 12-12
3.6	**Customize the workspace.**		
	3.6a Demonstrate how to open, minimize, collapse, close, resize, dock, and undock panels; how to access preset workspaces; how to change document views; how to save a custom workspace.	1, 2	1-9, 1-10, 1-14, 1-15, 2-28

ACA CERTIFICATION GRID
(CONTINUED)

(ACA) ADOBE WEB COMMUNICATION USING DREAMWEAVER CS6 OBJECTIVES		Chapter(s)	Page(s)
Domain 4.0 Adding Content by Using Dreamweaver CS6			
4.1	**Demonstrate knowledge of Hypertext Markup Language.**		
	4.1a Demonstrate knowledge of HTML1.x, HTML4, and HTML5 and their differences.	6	6-12, 6-23, 6-31, 6-34
	4.1b Demonstrate knowledge of HTML5 capabilities.	5, 6, Glossary	5-16, 6-4, 6-12, Glossary-37
4.2	**Define a Dreamweaver site.**		
	4.2a Demonstrate knowledge of the terms "local site," "remote site/folder," "web server," and "root folder."	1	1-20, 1-21, 1-24, 1-25
	4.2b Demonstrate knowledge of the steps for defining a new Dreamweaver site.	1	1-24, 1-25, 1-29
4.3	**Create, title, name, and save a web page.**		
	4.3a Demonstrate knowledge of the steps used to create, save, and name a new HTML page.	1, 2, 6	1-30, 1-32, 1-33, 2-14, 6-6, 6-7, 6-8
	4.3b Demonstrate knowledge of rules for naming HTML files.	2	2-15
	4.3c Demonstrate knowledge of best practices for naming HTML files.	2	2-15
	4.3d Identify the result of naming an HTML file "index.htm(l)" or "default.htm(l)."	1, 2	1-27, 2-15
	4.3e Differentiate between document filenames and document or page titles.	1, 2	1-32, 2-4
	4.3f Demonstrate knowledge of how to assign a document or page title.	2	2-6

ACA CERTIFICATION GRID
(CONTINUED)

(ACA) ADOBE WEB COMMUNICATION USING DREAMWEAVER CS6 OBJECTIVES

		Chapter(s)	Page(s)
4.4	**Add text to a web page.**		
	4.4a Demonstrate knowledge of how to add text to an HTML page.	2, 6	2-10, 2-12, 2-15, 2-16, 2-20, 6-10, 6-11
	4.4b Demonstrate knowledge of the effect of a Return keypress and a Shift-Return keypress when typing text on an HTML page.	2, 5	2-12, 5-18
4.5	**Insert images and apply alternative text on a web page.**		
	4.5a Demonstrate knowledge of the steps for inserting images.	1, 4, 10, 12	1-31, 4-5, 4-6, 4-9, 4-10, 10-16 to 10-18, 12-14, 12-15
	4.5b Demonstrate knowledge of how to add alternative text to images.	4, 10, 12	4-6, 4-8, 4-10, 4-13, 4-17, 10-16, 12-14, 12-15
	4.5c Identify image file types that can be viewed in all browsers.	4	4-2, 4-4
	4.5d Demonstrate knowledge of image file types and their uses.	4	4-4
	4.5e Demonstrate knowledge of using Photoshop Smart Objects.	4	4-15
	4.5f Identify purpose and benefits to using In Context Editing.	6, 12	6-6, 6-10, 12-9
4.6	**Link web content, using hyperlinks, e-mail links, and named anchors.**		
	4.6a Demonstrate knowledge of terms "hyperlink," "e-mail link," and "named anchor."	1, 2, 5	1-12, 2-18, 5-10
	4.6b Demonstrate knowledge of hyperlinks, including the differences between absolute, site-root-relative, and document-relative hyperlinks.	5	5-4, 5-5

ACA CERTIFICATION GRID
(CONTINUED)

(ACA) ADOBE WEB COMMUNICATION USING DREAMWEAVER CS6 OBJECTIVES

			Chapter(s)	Page(s)
	4.6c	Demonstrate knowledge of how to link text and images to another web page of the same site.	2, 4, 5, 9, 12	2-21, 2-22, 4-24, 4-26, 5-4, 5-5, 5-8, 5-16, 5-19, 5-20, 5-28, 5-29, 5-32, 9-32, 12-9, 12-11, 12-12, 12-14
	4.6d	Demonstrate knowledge of how to link text and images to another website.	5	5-6, 5-7
	4.6e	Demonstrate knowledge of how to link text or images to an e-mail address.	2	2-18, 2-22
	4.6f	Demonstrate knowledge of how to create and link to a named anchor.	5	5-10 to 5-15
	4.6g	Demonstrate knowledge of how to target links.	5	5-28
4.7	Include video and sound in a web page.			
	4.7a	Identify benefits of using HTML5 to include video in a web page.	11	11-4, 11-8
	4.7b	Identify best practices when including HTML5 video in a web page.	11	11-18
	4.7c	Identify best practices when including audio in a web page.	11	11-22, 11-23
	4.7d	Demonstrate knowledge of how to add HTML5 video to a web page.	11	11-18 to 11-21
	4.7e	Demonstrate knowledge of how to add audio to a web page.	11	11-22, 11-23

ACA CERTIFICATION GRID
(CONTINUED)

(ACA) ADOBE WEB COMMUNICATION USING DREAMWEAVER CS6 OBJECTIVES

			Chapter(s)	Page(s)
4.8		**Add animation and interactivity to content.**		
	4.8a	Demonstrate knowledge of tools for creating animation and interactive content.	11	Chapter 11
	4.8b	Identify best practices when including animation in a web page.	11	11-4 to 11-6
	4.8c	Demonstrate knowledge of how to add SWF files to a web page.	11	11-4 to 11-9
	4.8d	Demonstrate knowledge of how to view SWF files in Live Mode.	9, 11	9-31, 11-9
4.9		**Insert navigation bars, rollover images, and buttons created in a drawing program on a web page.**		
	4.9a	Demonstrate knowledge of how to insert navigation bars, rollover images, and buttons.	5	5-16 to 5-25
4.10		**Build image maps.**		
	4.10a	Demonstrate knowledge of the terms "hotspot" and "image map" as used in web page design.	5	5-26 to 5-29
	4.10b	Demonstrate knowledge of how to create an image map.	5	5-26 to 5-29
	4.10c	Identify best practices when creating image maps.	5	5-26
	4.10d	Demonstrate knowledge of how to set properties for a hotspot by using the Property inspector.	5	5-28, 5-29

ACA Certification Grid

ACA CERTIFICATION GRID
(CONTINUED)

(ACA) ADOBE WEB COMMUNICATION USING DREAMWEAVER CS6 OBJECTIVES

		Chapter(s)	Page(s)
4.11	**Import tabular data to a web page.**		
4.11a	Demonstrate knowledge of how to import tabular data.	2, 6	2-16, 6-34, 6-35
4.11b	Demonstrate knowledge of table, cell, row, and column properties.	6	6-22, 6-24, 6-25, 6-34, 6-36
4.11c	Demonstrate knowledge of how to set and change table, cell, row, and column properties.	6	6-22 to 6-29, 6-31, 6-36, 6-37
4.11d	Demonstrate knowledge of sizing methods used for tables.	6	6-24, 6-25
4.11e	Demonstrate knowledge of how to insert and delete columns and rows.	6	6-26, 6-39
4.11f	Demonstrate knowledge of how to merge and split cells.	6	6-26 to 6-29
4.12	**Import and display a Microsoft Word or Microsoft Excel document to a web page.**		
4.12a	Demonstrate knowledge of how to add Word or Excel content to a web page	2	2-15, 2-16
4.12b	Demonstrate knowledge of the correct settings to use when importing a Word document, based on the content in the document.	2	2-10, 2-16
4.12c	Demonstrate knowledge of how to link to a Word or Excel document from a web page.	2	2-16
4.13	**Create forms.**		
4.13a	Demonstrate knowledge of which form inputs are appropriate for collecting various types of information.	9	9-16 to 9-18
4.13b	Demonstrate knowledge of how to use Dreamweaver to insert various form elements on a page.	9	9-13 to 9-29
4.13c	Demonstrate knowledge of methods used to transmit form data.	9	9-4 to 9-7

ACA CERTIFICATION GRID (CONTINUED)

(ACA) ADOBE WEB COMMUNICATION USING DREAMWEAVER CS6 OBJECTIVES

		Chapter(s)	Page(s)
Domain 5.0 Organizing Content by Using Dreamweaver CS6			
5.1	**Set and modify document properties.**		
5.1a	Identify document properties that can be set or edited globally by using the Page Properties dialog box.	2, 4	2-4, 2-9, 4-18, 4-20, 4-21
5.1b	Demonstrate knowledge of how to set or modify global page properties, and global CSS styles, including those for text, links, and background.	2, 3, 4, 8, 10	2-4, 2-9, 3-10, 3-18, 4-5, 4-18, 4-19, 4-20, 4-21, 8-2, 8-4, 8-5, 10-19
5.1c	Differentiate the uses of global CSS rules and CSS rules for div tags.	8	8-2, 8-4, 8-5
5.2	**Organize web page layout with relative and absolutely positioned div tags and CSS.**		
5.2a	Demonstrate knowledge of how to insert a div tag in standard mode.	10	10-4 to 10-7
5.2b	Demonstrate knowledge of the advantages of using div tags instead of tables for page layout.	6	6-2
5.2c	Demonstrate knowledge of the distinctions among absolute, relative, fixed, and static positioning.	10, Glossary	10-2, 10-9, 10-20, 10-21, 10-24, Glossary-36, Glossary-42
5.2d	Demonstrate knowledge of div tag attributes such as height, width, margin, and padding.	10	10-5, 10-7, 10-8, 10-9, 10-14
5.2e	Demonstrate knowledge of how to modify div tag attributes.	10	10-5, 10-7 to 10-13, 10-22, 10-23, 10-25

ACA CERTIFICATION GRID
(CONTINUED)

(ACA) ADOBE WEB COMMUNICATION USING DREAMWEAVER CS6 OBJECTIVES

			Chapter(s)	Page(s)
	5.2f	Demonstrate knowledge of how to display overlapping content on a web page using div tags.	10	10-2, 10-4, 10-9, 10-12, 10-13
	5.2g	Demonstrate knowledge of how to use external style sheets	3, 8	3-10, 3-12 to 3-25, 8-2, 8-4, 8-5
	5.2h	Demonstrate knowledge of how to create CSS rules in the property inspector.	8	8-15
	5.2i	Demonstrate knowledge of how to define, modify, and check CSS rules.	3, 6, 8,	3-16, 3-21, 3-25, 6-4, 6-5, 6-15, 6-16, 8-12 to 8-17, 8-18 to 8-25, 8-27
	5.2j	Demonstrate knowledge using CSS3 to organize web page layout.	8	8-19
5.3	**Modify text and text properties.**			
	5.3a	Demonstrate knowledge of fonts, including what viewers see if they do not have the selected font installed or if "Default Font" is selected as the font type.	2	2-10, 2-11
	5.3b	Demonstrate knowledge of how to reference font libraries in a web page.	2, 3, 8	2-10, 3-19, 3-31, 8-18
	5.3c	Demonstrate knowledge of how to change font, font size, and color.	3	3-13, 3-15, 3-17, 3-18, 3-19, 3-22
	5.3d	Demonstrate knowledge of how to apply a paragraph style to a paragraph of text.	2, 3	2-16, 3-9
	5.3e	Demonstrate knowledge of how to indent text to set off a block quotation.	5	5-15
	5.3f	Demonstrate knowledge of how to align paragraphs.	2, 6	2-11, 6-15, 6-19

ACA CERTIFICATION GRID (CONTINUED)

(ACA) ADOBE WEB COMMUNICATION USING DREAMWEAVER CS6 OBJECTIVES

		Chapter(s)	Page(s)
5.3g	Demonstrate knowledge of ordered, unordered, and definition lists.	3	3-2, 3-4 to 3-9
5.3h	Demonstrate knowledge of how to create unordered and ordered lists and how to set properties for a list by using the List Item button in the Property inspector.	3	3-4 to 3-9
5.3i	Demonstrate knowledge of how to create definition lists.	3	3-2, 3-5
5.3j	Demonstrate knowledge of how to apply emphasis to text by using the Insert menu or the Property inspector.	2, 3	2-13, 3-9
5.3k	Demonstrate knowledge of how to create a custom font stack using the Edit Font list command in the Properties Inspector or for the font-family property in the CSS rule definition dialog box.	2, 3, Glossary	2-11, 3-13, Glossary-36
5.4	**Modify images and image properties.**		
5.4a	Demonstrate knowledge of the capabilities and limitations of editing or modifying images in Dreamweaver.	4	4-12, 4-15
5.4b	Demonstrate knowledge of how to scale an image.	4, 13	4-12, 13-10
5.4c	Demonstrate knowledge of editing static and interactive assets with Fireworks, Photoshop, and Flash from inside Dreamweaver.	4, 11	4-12, 4-15, 11-8, 11-9

ACA Certification Grid

ACA CERTIFICATION GRID
(CONTINUED)

(ACA) ADOBE WEB COMMUNICATION USING DREAMWEAVER CS6 OBJECTIVES	Chapter(s)	Page(s)
5.5 Create web page templates.		
5.5a Demonstrate knowledge of Dreamweaver templates.	2, 6, 12	2-6, 6-8, Chapter 12
5.5b Demonstrate knowledge of how to create a new Dreamweaver template.	12	12-4, 12-6, 12-10
5.5c Demonstrate knowledge of how to save an existing HTML file as a Dreamweaver template.	12	12-2, 12-4 to 12-6
5.5d Demonstrate knowledge of how to create and edit editable regions on a template.	12	12-7, 12-10
5.5e Demonstrate knowledge of how to apply or build pages from templates, and how to detach a template from a page.	12	12-11, 12-12, 12-13
5.6 Use basic HTML tags to set up an HTML document, format text, add links, create tables, and build ordered and unordered lists.		
5.6a Demonstrate knowledge of HTML tags, including HTML, HEAD, TITLE, BODY, H1-H6, P, EM, STRONG, A HREF, TABLE, TR, TD, OL, LI, UL.	2, 3, 4, 5, 6, 8	2-11, 2-12, 3-6, 3-7, 4-21, 4-27, 5-4, 5-5, 6-25, 6-29, 8-12

ACA CERTIFICATION GRID (CONTINUED)

(ACA) ADOBE WEB COMMUNICATION USING DREAMWEAVER CS6 OBJECTIVES

		Chapter(s)	Page(s)
5.7	**Add head content to make a web page visible to search engines.**		
5.7a	Demonstrate knowledge of head content, meta tags, and tag inspector	2	2-4, 2-6, 2-7, 2-8
5.7b	Demonstrate knowledge of how to add and edit head content using the Common category in the Insert bar.	2	2-7, 2-8
5.8	**Use CSS to implement a reusable design.**		
5.8a	Demonstrate knowledge of how to create inline styles and external style sheets.	3, 8	3-10, 3-11, 3-12 to 3-19, 3-25, 3-27, 8-2, 8-4, 8-5
5.8b	Demonstrate knowledge of how to use CSS to set properties for text and HTML tags.	8, 10	8-4, 8-5, 8-12, 8-13, 8-14 to 8-17, 10-14, 10-19
5.8c	Demonstrate knowledge of the advantages of using CSS for design.	6, 8	6-4, 8-2, 8-4, 8-5
5.8d	Demonstrate knowledge of how to use CSS Starter Layouts.	6	6-2, 6-4 to 6-7
5.8e	Demonstrate knowledge of how to use different selector types such as descendent selectors, classes, the tag selector, pseudo class selectors, and group selectors.	8, Glossary	8-7, 8-28, Glossary-35
5.8f	Demonstrate knowledge of how to troubleshoot CSS issues by using Visual Aids.	6	6-5, 6-16, 6-40

ACA CERTIFICATION GRID
(CONTINUED)

(ACA) ADOBE WEB COMMUNICATION USING DREAMWEAVER CS6 OBJECTIVES

		Chapter(s)	Page(s)
Domain 6.0 Evaluating and Maintaining a Site by Using Dreamweaver CS6			
6.1	**Conduct technical tests.**		
6.1a	Demonstrate knowledge of how to check spelling on a web page.	2, 9	2-17, 9-31
6.1b	Demonstrate knowledge of how to test links by using the Check Links Sitewide command.	5, 7	5-30, 5-31, 7-2, 7-4, 7-6
6.1c	Demonstrate knowledge of how to preview a web page in a browser.	2, 7, 8, 10	2-30, 2-31, 2-32, 2-33, 7-5, 8-21, 10-17, 10-25
6.1d	Demonstrate knowledge of how to preview a website for multiscreen designs.	2, 8, Glossary	2-31, 2-32, 8-19, 8-20, 8-21, Glossary-39
6.1e	Demonstrate knowledge of how to test a website against a storyboard.	5, 7	5-32, 7-40
6.1f	Demonstrate knowledge of how to test CSS layouts across web browsers.	6, 8, 10	6-4, 6-15, 6-16, 6-40, 8-21, 10-17
6.2	**Identify techniques for basic usability tests.**		
6.2a	Demonstrate knowledge of elements involved in conducting a website usability test.	7	7-18
6.3	**Identify methods for collecting site feedback.**		
6.3a	Demonstrate knowledge of methods for collecting viewer feedback and site evaluation information to determine if the site meets intended goals and user needs.	2, 7, 8, 9	2-7, 2-18, 7-5, 7-18, 8-20, 8-21, 8-25, 9-2, 9-4, 9-30, 9-32, 9-33

ACA CERTIFICATION GRID (CONTINUED)

(ACA) ADOBE WEB COMMUNICATION USING DREAMWEAVER CS6 OBJECTIVES		Chapter(s)	Page(s)
6.4	**Manage assets, links, and files for a site.**		
6.4a	Demonstrate knowledge of how to delete files by using the Files panel.	1, 4, 7	1-27, 4-19, 4-22, 7-4
6.4b	Demonstrate knowledge of how to rename files and update links by using the Files panel.	1	1-27
6.4c	Demonstrate knowledge of how to link files by dragging, using the Point-to-File icon in the Property inspector and the Files panel.	5, 12	5-14, 12-12
6.4d	Demonstrate knowledge of the terms "Get," "Put," "Check In," "Check Out," "Publish," and "Remote Server" as they apply to managing files and publishing a website	7	7-14 to 7-26
6.4e	Demonstrate knowledge of expanding and collapsing the Files panel to access features such as the site map, get and put, check in and out, and refreshing the Files panel.	7	7-19, 7-20, 7-22 to 7-26
6.4f	Demonstrate knowledge of using file management techniques such as Subversion control and check-in/check-out when working in teams.	7	7-21, 7-22 to 7-31
6.4g	Demonstrate knowledge of using the Related Files toolbar.	1, 3	1-5, 3-21, 3-25
6.4h	Demonstrate knowledge of FTP server and Web server relationships to a Dreamweaver site.	1, 7	1-21, 1-24, 1-25, 7-14 to 7-21
6.5	**Publish and update site files to a remote server.**		
6.5a	Demonstrate knowledge of how to set up a connection to a remote server.	1, 7	1-21, 1-24, 1-25, 7-17 to 7-21
6.5b	Demonstrate knowledge of how to publish files to a remote server.	1, 7	1-21, 1-24, 7-14 to 7-21
6.5c	Demonstrate knowledge of how to use the Files panel to connect to and disconnect from a remote site, how to upload files to a remote site, and how to download files from a remote site.	1, 7	1-21, 1-24, 7-15, 7-20

DATA FILES LIST

Read the following information carefully.

Find out from your instructor the location where you will store your files.

- To complete many of the chapters in this book, you need to use the Data Files provided on Cengage Brain. To access the Data Files on Cengage Brain:
  1. Open your browser and go to http://www.cengagebrain.com
  2. Type the author, title, or ISBN of this book in the Search window. (The ISBN is listed on the back cover.)
  3. Click the book title in the list of search results.
  4. When the book's main page opens, click the Access button under Free Study Tools
  5. To download Data Files, select a chapter number and then click on the Data Files tab on the left navigation bar to download the files.
  6. To access additional materials, including information about ACE certification, click the Additional Materials tab under Book Resources to download the files.

- Your instructor will tell you where to save the data files and where to store the files you create and modify.
- All the Data Files are organized in folders named after the chapter in which they are used. For instance, all Chapter 1 Data Files are stored in the chapter_1 folder. You should leave all the Data Files in these folders; do not move any Data File out of the folder in which it is originally stored.

Copy and organize your Data Files.

- Copy the folders that contain the Data Files to a USB storage drive, network folder, hard drive, or other storage device.
- As you build each website, the exercises in this book will guide you to copy the Data Files you need from the appropriate Data Files folder to the folder where you are storing the website. Your Data Files should always remain intact because you are copying (and not moving) them to the website.
- Because you will be building a website from one chapter to the next, sometimes you will need to use a Data File that is already contained in the website you are working on.

Find and keep track of your Data Files and completed files.

- Use the **Data File Supplied** column to make sure you have the files you need before starting the chapter or exercise indicated in the **Chapter** column.
- Use the **Student Creates File** column to find out the filename you use when saving your new file for the exercise.

DATA FILES LIST
(CONTINUED)

ADOBE DREAMWEAVER CS6				
Chapter	**Data File Supplied**	**Student Creates File**	**Used In**
Bridge	blooms_banner.jpg		
	blue_footed_booby.jpg		
	boardwalk.jpg		
	boats.jpg		
	brunch.jpg		
	butterfly.jpg		
	cafe_logo.gif		
	cafe_photo.gif		
	cc_banner.jpg		
	cc_banner_with_text.jpg		
	children_cooking.jpg		
	chives.jpg		
	chocolate_cake.jpg		
	club_house.jpg		
	coleus.jpg		
	cookies_oven.jpg		
	family_sunset.jpg		
	fiber_optic_grass.jpg		
	fish.jpg		
	fisherman.jpg		
	gardening_gloves.jpg		

DATA FILES LIST (CONTINUED)

ADOBE DREAMWEAVER CS6

Chapter	Data File Supplied	Student Creates File	Used In
Bridge, continued	iguana_and_lizard.jpg		
	lady_in_red.jpg		
	llama.jpg		
	machu_picchu_from_high.jpg		
	machu_picchu_ruins.jpg		
	map_large.jpg		
	map_small.jpg		
	marshmallows.jpg		
	peruvian_appetizers.jpg		
	peruvian_glass.jpg		
	pie.jpg		
	plants.jpg		
	pool.jpg		
	rose_bloom.jpg		
	rose_bud.jpg		
	ruby_grass.jpg		

DATA FILES LIST (CONTINUED)

ADOBE DREAMWEAVER CS6

Chapter	Data File Supplied	Student Creates File	Used In
Bridge, continued	sea_lions_in_surf.jpg		
	sea_spa_logo.png		
	spacer_30px.gif		
	su_banner.gif		
	su_logo.gif		
	trees.jpg		
	tripsmart_banner.gif		
	tripsmart_gradient.jpg		
	tulips.jpg		
	two_dolphins_small.jpg		
	two_roses.jpg		
	two_roses_large.jpg		
	walking_stick.jpg		
	water.jpg		
	water_lily.jpg		

DATA FILES LIST (CONTINUED)

ADOBE DREAMWEAVER CS6			
Chapter	**Data File Supplied**	**Student Creates File**	**Used In**
Chapter 1	dw1_1.html		Lesson 2
	assets/pool.jpg		
	assets/su_banner.gif		
	dw1_2.html	about_us.html	Lesson 4
	assets/su_banner.gif	activities.html	
		cafe.html	
		cruises.html	
		fishing.html	
		index.html	
		spa.html	
	dw1_3.html	annuals.html	Skills Review
	dw1_4.html	index.html	
	assets/blooms_banner.jpg	newsletter.html	
	assets/tulips.jpg	perennials.html	
		plants.html	
		tips.html	
		water_plants.html	
		workshops.html	

DATA FILES LIST (CONTINUED)

ADOBE DREAMWEAVER CS6

Chapter	Data File Supplied	Student Creates File	Used In
Chapter 1, continued	dw1_5.html	catalog.html	Project Builder 1
	assets/tripsmart_banner.jpg	galapagos.html	
		index.html	
		newsletter.html	
		peru.html	
		services.html	
		tours.html	
	dw1_6.html	adults.html	Project Builder 2
	assets/cc_banner.jpg	catering.html	
		children.html	
		classes.html	
		index.html	
		recipes.html	
		shop.html	
	none		Design Project
	none		Portfolio Project

Data Files List

DATA FILES LIST (CONTINUED)

ADOBE DREAMWEAVER CS6

Chapter	Data File Supplied	Student Creates File	Used In
Chapter 2	spa.doc		Lesson 2
	assets/sea_spa_logo.png		
	gardening_tips.doc		Skills Review
	assets/butterfly.jpg		
	none		Project Builder 1
	none		Project Builder 2
	none		Design Project
	none		Portfolio Project
Chapter 3	questions.doc		Lesson 1
		su_styles.css	Lesson 2
		blooms_styles.css	Skills Review
	dw3_1.html		Project Builder 1
		tripsmart_styles.css	
	assets/tripsmart_banner.jpg		
	dw3_2.html	cc_styles.css	Project Builder 2
	assets/cc_banner.jpg		
	assets/pie.jpg		
	none		Design Project
	none		Portfolio Project

DATA FILES LIST (CONTINUED)

ADOBE DREAMWEAVER CS6			
Chapter	**Data File Supplied**	**Student Creates File**	**Used In**
Chapter 4	dw4_1.html		Lesson 1
	assets/boardwalk.png		
	assets/club_house.jpg		
	assets/su_banner.gif		
	assets/su_logo.gif		
	assets/water.jpg		Lesson 3
	starfish.ico		Lesson 4
	assets/map_large.jpg		
	assets/map_small.jpg		
	assets/spacer.gif		
	dw4_2.html		Skills Review
	flower.ico		
	assets/blooms_banner.jpg		
	assets/lady_in_red.jpg		
	assets/rose_bloom.jpg		
	assets/rose_bud.jpg		
	assets/two_roses.jpg		
	assets/two_roses_large.jpg		

DATA FILES LIST
(CONTINUED)

ADOBE DREAMWEAVER CS6			
Chapter	**Data File Supplied**	**Student Creates File**	**Used In**
Chapter 4, continued	dw4_3.html		Project Builder 1
	airplane.ico		
	assets/blue_footed_booby.jpg		
	assets/iguana_and_lizard.jpg		
	assets/tripsmart_banner.jpg		
	dw4_4.html		Project Builder 2
	assets/cc_banner.jpg		
	assets/brunch.jpg		
	assets/peruvian_glass.jpg		
	none		Design Project
	none		Portfolio Project
Chapter 5	dw5_1.html		Lesson 1
	assets/family_sunset.jpg		
	assets/su_banner.gif		
	assets/two_dolphins_small.jpg		
	SpryAssets/SpryMenuBar.js	SpryAssets/SpryMenuBar.js	Lesson 3
	SpryAssets/SpryMenuBarDown.gif	SpryAssets/SpryMenuBarDown.gif	
	SpryAssets/SpryMenuBarDownHover.gif	SpryAssets/SpryMenuBarDownHover.gif	

DATA FILES LIST (CONTINUED)

ADOBE DREAMWEAVER CS6

Chapter	Data File Supplied	Student Creates File	Used In
Chapter 5, continued	SpryAssets/SpryMenuBarHorizontal.css	SpryAssets/SpryMenuBarHorizontal.css	
	SpryAssets/SpryMenuBarRight.gif	SpryAssets/SpryMenuBarRight.gif	
	SpryAssets/SpryMenuBarRightHover.gif	SpryAssets/SpryMenuBarRightHover.gif	
	dw5_2.html		Lesson 5
	dw5_3.html		
	assets/boats.jpg		
	assets/fisherman.jpg		
	dw5_4.html		Skills Review
	dw5_5.html		
	dw5_6.html		
	dw5_7.html		
	assets/blooms_banner.jpg		
	assets/coleus.jpg		
	assets/fiber_optic_grass.jpg		
	assets/plants.jpg		
	assets/ruby_grass.jpg		

Data Files List

DATA FILES LIST
(CONTINUED)

ADOBE DREAMWEAVER CS6

Chapter	Data File Supplied	Student Creates File	Used In
Chapter 5, continued	assets/trees.jpg		
	assets/water_lily.jpg		
	SpryAssets/SpryMenuBar.js	SpryAssets/SpryMenuBar.js	
	SpryAssets/SpryMenuBarDown.gif	SpryAssets/SpryMenuBarDown.gif	
	SpryAssets/SpryMenuBarDownHover.gif	SpryAssets/SpryMenuBarDownHover.gif	
	SpryAssets/SpryMenuBarHorizontal.css	SpryAssets/SpryMenuBarHorizontal.css	
	SpryAssets/SpryMenuBarRight.gif	SpryAssets/SpryMenuBarRight.gif	
	SpryAssets/SpryMenuBarRightHover.gif	SpryAssets/SpryMenuBarRightHover.gif	
	dw5_8.html		Project Builder 1
	dw5_9.html		
	dw5_10.html		
	assets/llama.jpg		
	assets/machu_picchu_from_high.jpg		
	assets/machu_picchu_ruins.jpg		
	assets/sea_lions_in_surf.jpg		
	assets/tripsmart_banner.jpg		

DATA FILES LIST
(CONTINUED)

ADOBE DREAMWEAVER CS6			
Chapter	**Data File Supplied**	**Student Creates File**	**Used In**
Chapter 5, continued	SpryAssets/SpryMenuBar.js	SpryAssets/SpryMenuBar.js	
	SpryAssets/SpryMenuBarDown.gif	SpryAssets/SpryMenuBarDown.gif	
	SpryAssets/SpryMenuBarDownHover.gif	SpryAssets/SpryMenuBarDownHover.gif	
	SpryAssets/SpryMenuBarHorizontal.css	SpryAssets/SpryMenuBarHorizontal.css	
	SpryAssets/SpryMenuBarRight.gif	SpryAssets/SpryMenuBarRight.gif	
	SpryAssets/SpryMenuBarRightHover.gif	SpryAssets/SpryMenuBarRightHover.gif	
	dw5_11.html		Project Builder 2
	dw5_12.html		
	dw5_13.html		
	assets/cc_banner_with_text.jpg		
	assets/children_cooking.jpg		
	assets/cookies_oven.jpg		
	assets/fish.jpg		
	assets/peruvian_appetizers.jpg		
	none		Design Project
	none		Portfolio Project

DATA FILES LIST (CONTINUED)

ADOBE DREAMWEAVER CS6			
Chapter	**Data File Supplied**	**Student Creates File**	**Used In**
Chapter 6	cafe.doc		Lesson 2
	assets/cafe_logo.gif		
	assets/cafe_photo.jpg		
	assets/chocolate_cake.jpg		Lesson 6
	composting.doc		Skills Review
	assets/chives.jpg		
	assets/gardening_gloves.gif		
	assets/tripsmart_gradient.jpg		Project Builder 1
	walking sticks.doc		
	assets/walking_stick.jpg		
	marshmallows.doc		Project Builder 2
	assets/marshmallows.jpg		
	none		Design Project
	none		Portfolio Project

DATA FILES LIST (CONTINUED)

ADOBE DREAMWEAVER CS6

Chapter	Data File Supplied	Student Creates File	Used In
Chapter 7	none	The Striped Umbrella.ste	Lesson 5
	none	Blooms & Bulbs.ste	Skills Review
	none	TripSmart.ste	Project Builder 1
	none	Carolyne's Creations.ste	Project Builder 2
	none		Design Project
	none		Portfolio Project
Chapter 8	striped_umbrella folder with new website files		Lesson 1
	blooms folder with new website files		Skills Review
	tripsmart folder with new website files		Project Builder 1
	cc folder with new website files		Project Builder 2
Chapter 9	dw9_1.html	feedback.html	Lesson 1
	assets/su_banner.gif		

DATA FILES LIST
(CONTINUED)

	ADOBE DREAMWEAVER CS6		
Chapter	**Data File Supplied**	**Student Creates File**	**Used In**
Chapter 10	assets/heron.jpg		Lesson 3
	assets/two_girls.jpg		
	assets/white_ibis.jpg		
	assets/spring_bloom.jpg		Skills Review
	assets/eilean_donan_castle.jpg		Project Builder 1
	assets/cs_logo.gif		Project Builder 2
Chapter 11	crabdance.fla		Lesson 1
	crabdance.swf		
	assets/one_dolphin.jpg		Lesson 2
	assets/two_dolphins.jpg		
	dw11_1.html	wildlife_message.html	Lesson 3
	umbrella_anchor_video.mp4		Lesson 4
	interviews.mp3		Lesson 5
	dw11_2.html		Skills Review
	garden_quote.swf		
	hanging_baskets.mp4		
	seeds_audio.mp3		
	assets/butterfly1.jpg		

DATA FILES LIST
(CONTINUED)

ADOBE DREAMWEAVER CS6

Chapter	Data File Supplied	Student Creates File	Used In
Chapter 11, continued	assets/butterfly2.jpg		
	sea_lions_video.mp4		Project Builder 1
	suspiro.mp4		Project Builder 2
Chapter 12		activities_pages.dwt	Lesson 1
	golf.doc		Lesson 2
	assets/golfer.jpg	golfing.html	
	assets/ladies_group.jpg		
	annuals.doc		Skills Review
	perennials.doc	plant_categories.dwt	
	water_plants.doc	water_plants.html	
	scotland.doc		Project Builder 1
	assets/castle.jpg		
	assets/sheep.jpg		
	fried_green_tomatoes.doc	fried_green_tomatoes.html	Project Builder 2
	assets/fried_green_tomatoes.jpg	recipes.dwt	
Chapter 13	assets/blooms_logo.jpg		Skills Review
	assets/tripsmart_logo.gif		Project Builder 1

Data Files List

DREAMWEAVER 35

GLOSSARY

A

Absolute path
A path containing an external link that references a link on a web page outside of the current website, and includes the protocol "http" and the URL, or address, of the web page.

Absolute positioning
Refers to the way that a page element, such as an AP element, is locked in a fixed position on a page.

Accordion
A CSS3 feature that uses buttons that, when clicked, open up like an accordion to display information that drops down below the button.

Action property
A form property that specifies the application or script that will process the data in a form.

ActionScript
A Flash scripting language developers use to add interactivity to movies, control objects, exchange data, and create complex animations.

Active Server Pages (ASP)
Server-side application used for processing data in a form.

Adaptive website
A website that adjusts or modifies the page content to fit the user's needs and device type used to view the site.

Add-on
Program extensions that add features to an existing application. Also called a plug-in.

Adobe AIR
An Adobe product used for developing content that can be delivered with a browser or as a desktop application.

Adobe Bridge
An application that serves as the hub for the Adobe Creative Suite 6. Can be used for file management tasks such as opening, viewing, sorting, and rating files.

Adobe BrowserLab
An Adobe online service for cross-browser and cross-platform compatibility testing.

Adobe Business Catalyst
A hosted application for setting up and maintaining an online business.

Adobe Edge
An Adobe program that combines the new capabilities of HTML5, CSS3, and JavaScript, but uses a program interface similar to Flash.

Adobe Flash video
See FLV.

Align
Position an image on a web page in relation to other elements on the page.

All rules pane
The top half of the CSS Styles panel that displays a list of the style sheets and rules for the open page when the Switch to All (document) Mode button is selected.

AP div tag
A div that is assigned a fixed (absolute) position on a web page.

AP element
The container that an AP div tag creates on a page. *See also* AP div tag.

AP Elements panel
Panel in the CSS panel group that is used to control the visibility, name, and Z-Index stacking order of AP elements on a web page.

Apache web server
A public domain, open source web server that is available using several different operating systems, including UNIX and Windows.

Application bar (Win)
In Dreamweaver, the toolbar located above the Document window that includes menu names, a Workspace switcher, and other application commands. In Bridge, the toolbar that contains the navigation buttons, the Workspace buttons, and the Search text box.

Assets
Files that are not web pages, such as images, Flash files, and video clips.

Assets folder
A subfolder in the local site root folder in which you store most of the files that are not web pages, such as images, Flash files, and video clips. This folder is often named images, but can be assigned any name.

Assets panel
A panel that contains nine categories of assets, such as images, used in a website. Clicking a category button displays a list of those assets.

Asynchronous JavaScript and XML (AJAX)
Method for developing interactive web pages that respond quickly to user input, such as clicking a map.

Audio Visual Interleave
See AVI.

AVI
Acronym for Audio Visual Interleave; the Microsoft standard for digital video format.

B

Background color
A color that fills an entire web page, frame, table, cell, or CSS layout block.

Background image
A graphic file used in place of a background color.

Banner
An image that generally appears across the top or down the side of a web page and can incorporate a company's logo, contact information, and links to the other pages in the site.

BaseCamp
A web-based project collaboration tool.

Behavior
Simple action scripts that let you incorporate interactivity by modifying content based on variables like user actions; tells a page object to respond in a specific way when an event occurs, such as when the mouse pointer is positioned over the object.

Blog
A website where the website owner regularly posts commentaries and opinions on various topics.

Blue drop zone
See Drop zone.

Body
The part of a web page that appears in a browser window. It contains all of the page content that is visible to users, such as text, images, and links.

Border
An outline that surrounds a cell, a table, or a CSS layout block.

Breadcrumb trail
A list of links that provides a path from the initial page opened in a website to the page being currently viewed.

Broken link
A link that cannot find the intended destination file for the link.

Browser Compatibility Check (BCC)
A Dreamweaver feature that checks for problems in the HTML code that might present a CSS rendering issue in some browsers by underlining questionable code in green.

Buffer
A temporary storage area on your hard drive that acts as a holding area for Flash content as it is being played.

Bullet
A small dot or similar icon preceding unordered list items. See also Bulleted list.

Bulleted list
An unordered list that uses bullets. See also Bullet.

C

Camera Raw file
A file format that contains unprocessed data and is not yet ready to be printed, similar to a negative from a film camera.

Cascading
The way styles are ranked in order of precedence as they are applied to page elements.

Cascading Style Sheet
A set of formatting attributes used to format web pages to provide a consistent presentation for content across a website.

Cell
A small box within a table that is used to hold text or graphics. Cells are arranged horizontally in rows and vertically in columns.

Cell padding
The distance between the cell content and the cell walls in a table.

Cell spacing
The distance between cells in a table.

Cell walls
The edges surrounding a cell in a table.

CGI
Acronym for Common Gateway Interface; a server-side application for processing information.

Check box
A form object used to create a list of options from which users can make multiple selections.

Check box group
A group of check boxes. See also Check box.

Child container
A container, created with HTML tags, whose code resides inside a parent container. Its properties are inherited from its parent container unless otherwise specified. See also Parent container.

Child keyword
In Bridge, a keyword that is a subcategory of a parent keyword. Also known as a subkeyword.

Child page
A page at a lower level in a web hierarchy that links to page at a higher level called a parent page.

Class type
A type of style that can contain a combination of formatting attributes that can be applied to a block of text or other page elements. Custom style names begin with a period (.). Also called a custom type.

Clean HTML code
Code that does what it is supposed to do without using unnecessary instructions, which take up memory.

Client-side scripting
A form processing method in which the user's computer processes a form, rather than a web server.

Clip property
A property that determines the portion of a AP div's content that will be visible when displayed in a web browser.

Cloak
To exclude from certain processes, such as being transferred to a remote site.

Code hint
An auto-complete feature that displays lists of tags that appear as you type in Code view.

Code Inspector
A separate floating window that displays the current page in Code view.

Code snippet
Ready-made, reusable pieces of code you can insert on a web page.

Code view
The Dreamweaver view that shows the underlying HTML code for the page; use this view to read or edit the code.

Coding toolbar
A toolbar that contains buttons you can use when working in Code view.

Cold Fusion
A server-side application used for processing data in a form.

Collections panel
In Bridge, a panel used to group assets located in different locations into a single collection.

Column
Table cells arranged vertically.

Common Gateway Interface
See CGI.

Compact mode
A Bridge mode with a smaller, simplified workspace.

Compound type
A type of style that is used to format a selection.

Content panel
In Bridge, the center pane, where thumbnails of files from the selected drive and folder in the Folders panel appear.

Controller
A graphic element that contains playback controls for video or audio files.

Copyright
A legal protection for the particular and tangible expression of an idea; the right of an author or creator of a work to copy, distribute, and modify a thing, idea, or image; a type of intellectual property.

CSS layout block
A section of a web page defined and formatted using a Cascading Style Sheet.

CSS Layout Box Model
CSS layout blocks defined as rectangular boxes of content with margins, padding, and borders.

CSS page layout
A method of positioning objects on web pages through the use of containers formatted with CSS. *See also* Cascading Style Sheets.

Custom button
In a form, a button that triggers an action, which you specify, on the page.

Custom type
See Class type.

D

Debug
To find and correct coding errors.

Declaration
The property and value of a style in a Cascading Style Sheet.

Default font
The font a browser uses to display text if no other font is assigned.

Default link color
The color a browser uses to display text if no other color is assigned.

Delimited file
A database, word processing, or spreadsheet file that has been saved as a text file with data separated with delimiters such as commas or tabs.

Delimiter
A comma, tab, colon, semicolon, or similar character that separates tabular data.

Deliverables
Products that will be provided to the client at the product completion such as pages or graphic elements created.

Dependent file
A file that another file needs to be complete, such as an image or style sheet.

Deprecated
Code that is no longer within the current standard and in danger of becoming obsolete.

Derivative work
An adaptation of another work, such as a movie version of a book; a new, original product that includes content from a previously existing work.

Descendant selector
A selector that includes two or more selectors that form a relationship and are separated by white space.

Description
A short summary that resides in the head section of a web page and describes the website content. *See also* Head content.

Design Note
A separate file in a website file structure that contains additional information about a page file or a graphic file.

Design view
The Dreamweaver view that shows the page as it would appear in a browser and is primarily used or creating and designing a web page.

Div tag
An HTML tag that is used to format and position web page elements.

Dock
A collection of panels or panel groups.

Document toolbar
A toolbar that contains buttons and drop-downmenus for changing the current work mode, checking browser compatibility, previewing web pages, debugging web pages, choosing visual aids, and viewing file management options.

Document window
The large area under the Document toolbar in the Dreamweaver workspace where you create and edit web pages.

Domain name
An IP address expressed in letters instead of numbers, usually reflecting the name of the business represented by the website; also referred to as a URL.

Download
The process of transferring files from a remote site to a local site.

Dreamweaver workspace
The entire window, from the Application bar (Win) or Menu bar (Mac) at the top of the window, to the status bar at the bottom border of the program window; the area in the Dreamweaver program window that includes all of the menus, panels, buttons, inspectors, and panes that you use to create and maintain websites.

Drop Zone
A blue outline area that indicate where a panel can be docked.

Dual Screen Layout
A layout you can utilize when using two monitors while working in Dreamweaver.

Dynamic content
Content that allows the user to interact with the page by clicking or typing, and then responds to this input in some way.

---------------- E ----------------

Editable optional region
An area on a template where users can add or change content, and that users can also choose to show or hide.

Editable region
An area in a template where users of the template can add or change content.

Embedded style sheet
A style that is part of an HTML page rather than in a separate file. Also called an internal style.

Essentials workspace
In Bridge, the default workspace that includes all of the menus, panels, buttons, and panes used to organize media files.

Export
To save data that was created in Dreamweaver in a special file format so that you can open it in another software program.

Extensible Metadata Platform (XMP) standard
The standard Adobe uses to save metadata.

External link
A link that connects to a web page in another website or to an e-mail address.

Export panel
In Bridge, a panel used to optimize images by saving them as JPEGs for use on the web.

External style sheet
Collection of styles stored in a separate file that controls the formatting of content on a web page. External style sheets have a .css file extension.

Glossary

F

Facebook
A social networking site that let users interact as an online community through the sharing of text, images, and videos.

Fair use
A part of copyright law that allows a user to make a copy of all or part of a work, even if permission has not been granted.

Favicon
Short for favorites icon, a small image that represents a website and appears in the address bar of many browsers.

Favorites
Assets that are used repeatedly in a website and are included in their own category in the assets panel.

Favorites panel
In Bridge, a panel used to quickly access folders that are designated as frequently used.

Fieldset
An HTML tag used to group related form elements together.

File field
Form object that allows users to upload files to a web server.

File Transfer Protocol (FTP)
The process of uploading and downloading files to and from a remote site.

Files panel
A window similar to Windows Explorer (Windows) or Finder (Macintosh), where Dreamweaver displays and manages files and folders. The Files panel contains a list of all the folders and files in a website.

Filter panel
In Bridge, a panel used to filter files to view in the Content panel.

Fixed layout
A fixed page layout that expresses all container widths in pixels and remains the same size regardless of the size of the browser window.

Fixed position
A CSS property that places an element relative to the browser window.

Flash button
A button made from a small, predefined Flash movie.

Fluid Grid Layout
A system for designing layouts that will adapt to multiple screen sizes.

FLV
Acronym for (Adobe) Flash Video; a video format you can link or embed on a web page.

Focus group
A marketing tool that asks a group of people for feedback about a product, such as the impact of a television ad or the effectiveness of a website design.

Fold line
A term from the newspaper business that indicates where the paper is folded in half. The most important information appears above the fold line.

Font libraries
Collections of fonts such as typekit.com or google.com/webfonts; accessed by browsers for specified WOFF fonts. *See also* WOFF font.

Font-combination
A set of font choices that specifies which fonts a browser should use to display text, such as Arial, Helvetica, sans serif. Also known as a font stack. Font combinations that a user creates are called custom font stacks.

Font stack
See Font-combination.

Form control
See Form object.

Form element
See Form object.

Form field
See Form object.

Form input
See Form object.

Form label
A label that identifies a form object by its function.

Form name property
A form property that specifies a unique name for the form.

Form object
An object on a web page, such as a text box, radio button, or check box, that collects information from users. Also called a form element, form control, form field, or form input.

FTP
See File Transfer Protocol.

G

GET method
A form property that specifies that ASCII data collected in the form will be sent to the server appended to the URL or to the file included in the Action property.

GIF
Acronym for Graphics Interchange Format file. A type of file format used for images placed on web pages that can support both transparency and animation.

Global CSS rule
A rule that affects all website content.

Global Positioning System
See GPS.

Google Video Chat
A video sharing community hosted by Google.

GPS
Acronym for Global Positioning System. A device used to track your position through a global satellite navigation system.

Graphic
A picture or design element that adds visual interest to a page.

Graphic design elements
Elements that combine to promote a pleasing page design, such as the way lines, shapes, forms, textures, and colors are used to create and place elements on a page.

Graphic design principles
The use of emphasis, movement, balance, unity, symmetry, color, white space, alignment, line, contrast, rule of thirds, proximity, and repetition to create an attractive and effective page design.

Grid
Horizontal and vertical lines that fill the page and are used to place page elements.

Group selector
A multiple selector that shares common properties and values.

Guide
A horizontal or vertical line that you drag from the rulers onto the page to help you align objects.

— H —

Head content
The part of a web page that includes the page title that appears in the title bar of the browser, as well as meta tags, which are HTML codes that include information about the page, such as keywords and descriptions, and are not visible in the browser.

Height (H) property
A property that specifies the height of a div either in pixels or as a percentage of the screen height.

Hex triplet
A color value expressed with three characters that represents the amount of red, green, and blue present in a color. Also known as an RGB triplet.

Hexadecimal RGB value
A six-character value that represents the amount of red, green, and blue in a color and is based on the Base 16 number system. If expressed in three characters instead of six, it's called an RGB triplet or a hex triplet.

Hidden field
Form object that makes it possible to provide information to the web server and form-processing script without the user knowing that the information is being sent.

History panel
A panel that contains a record of each action performed during an editing session, and allows you to undo actions; up to 1000 levels of Undo are available through the History panel (20 levels by default).

Home page
The first page that is displayed when users go to a website.

Hotspot
A clickable area on an image that, when clicked, links to a different location on the page or to another web page.

HTML
Stands for Hypertext Markup Language, the language web developers use to create web pages.

HTML5
The current version of HTML that added new ways to incorporate interactivity with tags that support semantic markup. Examples of added tags are <header>, <footer>, <article>, <section>, <video>, <hgroup>, <figure>, <embed>, <wbr>, and <canvas>.

HTTP
See HyperText Transfer Protocol.

Hyperlink
An image or text element on a web page that users click to display another location on the page, another web page on the same website, or a web page on a different website; also known as a link.

Hypertext Transfer Protocol (HTTP)
The transfer method specified by the Method property to send form data to a server.

Hypertext Transfer Protocol Secure (HTTPS)
The protocol for transferring secure information over the Internet.

Glossary

I

ID type
A type of CSS rule that is used to redefine an HTML tag.

Image
A graphic such as a photograph or a piece of artwork on a web page; images in a website are known as assets.

Image field
A form field that can contain a graphic.

Image map
An image that has one or more specially-designated areas, each of which serves as a link.

Image placeholder
A graphic the size of an image you plan to use that holds the position on the page until the final image is placed.

Import
To bring data created in one software application into another application.

InContext Editing (ICE)
An online service that users can log into and be allowed to make changes to designated editable regions on a page while viewing it in a browser.

Inherit
A property that specifies that the property and value are applied from a parent container.

Inheritance
The CSS governing principle that allows for the properties of a parent container to be used to format the content in a child container.

Inline style
A style whose code is placed within the body tags of a web page.

Insert panel
A panel with nine categories of buttons for creating and inserting objects displayed as a drop-down menu: Common, Layout, Forms, Data, Spry, jQuery Mobile, InContext Editing, Text, and Favorites.

Inspect mode
A Dreamweaver viewing mode that works together with Live View to help you identify HTML elements and their associated CSS styles.

Internal link
A link to a web page within the same website.

Internal style sheet
A style sheet whose code is saved within the code of a web page, rather than in an external file. Also called an embedded style.

Internet Service Provider (ISP)
Internet Service Provider. A service to which you subscribe to be able to connect to the Internet with your computer.

IP address
An assigned series of numbers, separated by periods, that designates an address on the Internet.

J

Java Server Page
See JSP.

JavaScript
A web-scripting code that interacts with HTML code to create dynamic content, such as rollovers or interactive forms on a web page; also called Jscript.

JavaScript Object Notation (JSON)
A subset of JavaScript, used by Adobe Edge.

JPEG or JPG
An acronym for Joint Photographic Experts Group; refers to a type of file format used for images that appear on web pages. Many photographs are saved with the JPEG file format.

Jscript
See JavaScript.

JSP
Acronym for Java Server Page; a server-side application for processing information.

Jump menu
A navigation menu that lets users go quickly to different pages in a site or to different sites on the Internet.

K

Keyword
In Dreamweaver, a word that relates to the content of a website and resides in the head section of a web page. In Bridge, a word that is added to a file to identify, group and sort files.

Keywords panel
In Bridge, a panel that lists the keywords assigned to a file.

L

Label tag
A form attribute that assigns a descriptive label to a form object.

LAN
Acronym for Local Area Network, a network that is not connected to the Internet.

Left property (L)
The property that specifies the distance between the left edge of an AP div and the left edge of the page or parent AP div that contains it.

Library item
Content that can contain text or graphics that you plan to use multiple times in your website and that is saved in a separate file in the Library folder of your site.

Licensing agreement
The permission given by a copyright holder that conveys the right to use the copyright holder's work.

Line break
Places a new text line without creating a new paragraph.

Link
See Hyperlink.

Liquid layout
A page layout that expresses all container widths in percents and changes size depending on the size of the browser window.

List
A form object for listing several options; the user can select one or more of the listed options.

Live view
A Dreamweaver view that displays an open document as if you were viewing it in a browser, with interactive elements active and functioning.

Local root folder
See Local site folder.

Local site folder
A folder on a hard drive, Flash drive, or floppy disk that holds all the files and folders for a website; also called the local root folder.

Locked region
An area on a template that cannot be changed by users of the template.

Low-bandwidth animation
Animations that don't require a fast connection to work properly.

---- M ----

Mailto: link
An e-mail address formatted as a link that opens the default mail program with a blank, addressed message.

Match.com
A social networking site that lets users share information in order to establish relationships.

Media object
A combination of visual and audio effects and text to create a fully engaging experience with a website.

Media queries
A Dreamweaver feature that uses files that specify set parameters for displaying pages on separate devices, such as tablets or smartphones.

Media-dependent style sheet
A style sheet tool for identifying the device being used and formatting the page appropriately.

Menu
A form object for listing several options; the user can only choose one.

Menu bar
In Dreamweaver, an area on a web page that contains links to the main pages of a website; also called a navigation bar. In Bridge, a bar at the top of the Bridge workspace with the program commands.

Merge cells
To combine multiple adjacent cells in a table into one cell.

Meta tag
An HTML code that resides in the head section of a web page and includes information about the page, such as keywords and descriptions. *See also* Head content.

Metadata panel
In Bridge, a panel that lists the metadata for a selected file. *See also* Metadata.

Metadata
Information about a file, such as keywords, descriptions, and copyright information, that is used to locate files.

Method property
A form property that specifies the HyperText Transfer Protocol (HTTP) used to send the form data to a web server.

MOV
The Apple Quick Time video format.

Multiscreen Preview
A Dreamweaver feature that allows you to see what a page would look like if it were viewed on a mobile hand-held device, such as a phone or tablet. Also known as a 3-up preview.

---- N ----

Named anchor
A specific location on a web page that is used to link to that portion of the web page.

Navigation bar
See Menu bar.

Navigation structure
A set of text or graphic links usually organized in rows or columns that users can use to navigate between pages of a website. *See also* Menu bar.

Glossary

Nested AP element
An AP div whose HTML code is included within another AP div's code.

Nested table
A table within a table.

Nested tag
A tag within a tag.

Nested template
A template based on another template.

No right-click script
JavaScript code that will block users from displaying the shortcut menu when they right-click an image on a web page.

Numbered list
See Ordered list.

―――――― O ――――――

Ogg
A free, open source container video format developed by the Xiph.Org Foundation.

Online community
Social website you can join, such as Facebook and Twitter, where you can communicate with others by posting messages or media content such as images or videos.

Opacity
Degree of transparency.

Optional region
Region in a template that template content contributors can choose to either show or hide.

Ordered list
A list of items that are placed in a specific order and preceded by numbers or letters; sometimes called a numbered list.

Orphaned file
Files that are not linked to any pages in the website.

Overflow property
A property that specifies how to handle excess content that does not fit inside an AP div.

―――――― P ――――――

Panel
A tabbed window in Dreamweaver that displays information on a particular topic or contains related commands.

Panel groups
Sets of related panels that are grouped together and displayed through the Window menu; also known as Tab groups.

Parent container
A container created with HTML tags, in which other containers fall between its opening and closing tags. *See also* Child container.

Parent keyword
In Bridge, the top level for a keyword with child keywords under it.

Parent page
A page at a higher level in a web hierarchy that links to other pages on a lower level, called child pages.

Path
The location of an open file in relation to its place in the folder structure of the website.

Path bar
In Bridge, the bar where the path of the selected folder in the Folders panel appears.

Permissions process
The process to obtain permission to use content legally.

Pinterest
A social networking site that lets users interact as an online community through the sharing of crafts, recipes, and other items of interest.

Plug-in
See Add-on.

PNG
The acronym for Portable Network Graphics File, a file format used for images placed on web pages; capable of showing millions of colors but is small in file size. PNG is the native file format in Fireworks.

Podcast
"Pod" is an acronym for Programming On Demand, in which users can download and play digitally broadcasted files using devices such as computers or MP3 players.

Point of contact
A place on a web page that provides users with a means of contacting the company.

POST method
A form property that specifies that the form data should be sent to the processing script as a binary or encrypted file, allowing you to send data securely.

POWDER
The acronym for Protocol for Web Description Resources; an evaluation system for web pages developed with the World Wide Web Consortium (W3C) that provides summary information about a website.

Preview panel
In Bridge, a panel where a preview of a select file appears.

Programming On Demand
See Podcast.

Progressive video download
A download type that will download a video to a user's computer, and then allow the video to play before it has completely downloaded.

Properties pane
The bottom half of the CSS Styles panel that lists a selected rule's properties.

Property inspector
In Dreamweaver, a panel that displays the properties of a selected web page object; its contents vary according to the object currently selected.

Protocol for Web Description Resources
See POWDER.

Pseudo class style
A style that determines the appearance of a page element when a certain condition from information external to the HTML source is met.

Public domain
Work that is no longer protected by copyright; anyone can use it for any purpose.

Publish
To make a website available for viewing on the Internet or on an intranet by transferring the files to a web server.

R

Radio button
A form object that provides an option for selecting one form item; displays as a small circle in a form.

Radio group
A group of radio buttons used to provide a list of options from which only one selection can be made.

RDS
Acronym for Remote Development Services; provides access control to web servers using Cold Fusion.

Related file
A file that is linked to a document and is necessary for the document to display and function correctly.

Related Files toolbar
A toolbar located below an open document's filename tab that displays the names of any related files.

Relative path
A path used with an internal link to reference a web page or graphic file within the website.

Remote server
A web server that hosts websites and is not directly connected to the computer housing the local site.

Remote site
A website that has been published to a remote server. *See also* Remote server.

Rendering
The way fonts are drawn on a screen.

Reset button
A button, that, when clicked, will clear data from a form and reset it to its default values.

RGB triplet
See Hex triplet.

Rich media content
Attractive and engaging images, interactive elements, video, or animations.

Rollover
A special effect that changes the appearance of an object when the mouse pointer moves over it.

Rollover image
An image that changes its appearance when a mouse pointer is placed over it in a browser.

Root folder
See Local site folder.

Row
Table cells arranged horizontally.

RSS
Acronym for Really Simple Syndication, a method websites use to distribute news stories, information about upcoming events, and announcements, known as an RSS Feed.

RSS feed
A way to distribute news stories through websites. *See also* RSS.

Rule
Sets of formatting attributes that define styles in a Cascading Style Sheet.

Rule of thirds
A design principle that entails dividing a page into nine squares and then placing the page elements of most interest on the intersections of the grid lines.

Rules pane
The middle pane of the CSS Styles panel that displays the location of the currently selected rule in the open document.

S

Sans-serif font
A font with block-style characters; commonly used for headings and subheadings.

Scope creep
A situation that occurs when impromptu changes or additions are made to a project without corresponding increases in the schedule or budget.

Secure FTP (SFTP)
A method for transferring files with encryption to protect the file content, user names, and passwords.

Secure Socket Layer
See SSL.

Selector
The name of the tag to which style declarations have been assigned.

Semantic markup
Coding to emphasize meaning.

Serif font
An ornate font that has a tail, or stroke, at the end of some characters. These strokes lead the eye from one character to the next, making it easier to recognize words; therefore, serif fonts are generally used in longer text passages.

Server-side scripting
A method used to process information a form collects using applications that reside on the web server.

Set up a site
Specify a website's name and the location of the local site root folder using the Dreamweaver Manage Sites dialog box.

SFTP
See Secure FTP.

Show Code and Design views
A combination of Code view and Design view. The best view for correcting errors.

Site definition
Contains important information about a website, including its URL, preferences that you've specified, and other secure information, such as login and password information.

Site map
A graphical representation or a directory listing of how web pages relate to each other within a website.

Skin
A controller graphic element placed over or below a video.

Skype
A video sharing application.

Slider
The small indicator on the left side of the History panel that you can drag to undo or redo one or more actions.

Smart object
An image layer that stores image data from raster or vector images.

Social networking
The grouping of individual web users who connect and interact with other users in online communities.

Split a cell
To divide table cells into multiple cells.

Spry
See Spry framework for AJAX.

Spry data set
A JavaScript object that stores data in rows and columns.

Spry effect
Screen effects such as fading and enlarging page elements.

Spry Framework
A JavaScript library that provides access to reusable widgets that you can add to web pages.

Spry framework for AJAX
Open source code developed by Adobe Systems to help designers quickly incorporate dynamic content on their web pages; also called Spry.

Spry menu bar
One of the preset widgets available in Dreamweaver that creates a dynamic, user-friendly menu bar that is easy to insert and customize.

Spry Validation Field widget
A form field that displays valid or invalid states when text is being entered in a form on a web page.

Spry widget
A page element that enables user interaction on a web page.

SSL
Acronym for Secure Socket Layer, the industry standard for viewing and sending confidential information over the Internet by encrypting the data.

Standard toolbar
A toolbar that contains buttons you use to execute frequently used commands that are also available on the File and Edit menus.

State
In a browser, the condition of an item in a Spry menu bar in relation to the mouse pointer.

Static content
Page content that does not change or allow user interaction.

Static position
A CSS property that places an element in order with the document flow.

Status bar
In Dreamweaver, the bar that appears at the bottom of the Dreamweaver document window; the left end of the status bar displays the tag selector, which shows the HTML tags being used at the insertion point location. The right end displays the window size and estimated download time for the page displayed.

Step
Each task performed in the History panel.

Streaming video download
Similar to a progressive video download, except streaming video downloads use buffers to gather the content as it is downloading to ensure a smoother playback.

Style Rendering toolbar
A toolbar that contains buttons that allow you to render (display) a web page as different media types (e.g., handheld).

Submit button
A button which, when clicked, sends user data from a form on a web page to a web server to be processed.

Summary for selection pane
The top half of the CSS Styles panel that displays a selected rule's properties when the Switch to Current Selection Mode button is selected.

Swap Image behavior
JavaScript code that directs the browser to display a different image when the mouse pointer is rolled over an image on a web page.

Swap Image Restore behavior
JavaScript code that directs the browser to restore a swapped image back to the original image. *See also* Swap Image behavior.

Synchronize
A Dreamweaver command that compares the names, dates, and times on all files on a local and remote site, then transfers only the files that have changed since the last upload.

––––––––––––– T –––––––––––––

Tab groups
See Panel groups.

Table
Grids of rows and columns that can be used either to hold tabular data on a web page or as a basic design tool for data placement.

Table caption
Text at the top of a table that describes the table contents; read by screen readers.

Table header
Text placed at the top or sides of a table on a web page; read by screen readers to help provide accessibility for table content.

Tabs
A CSS3 feature that is used to organize content into tabs similar to file folder tabs.

Tag (HTML)
The individual pieces of code that specify the appearance for page content when viewed in a browser.

Tag selector
The left side of the status bar that displays HTML tags used at the insertion point location.

Tag type
A style type used to redefine an HTML tag.

Target
The location on a web page that the browser displays when users click an internal link.

Target audience
The characteristics that make up the population that will be using a website, taking into consideration such factors as age, occupation, sex, education, residence, race, and computer literacy.

Target property
A property that specifies the window in which a form's data will be processed.

Template
A web page that contains the basic layout for each page in the site, including the location of a company logo, banner, or navigation links.

Terms of use
The rules that a copyright owner uses to establish how users may use his or her work.

Testing server
A server that is used to evaluate how a website is functioning before it is published.

Text area field
A form text field that can store several lines of text.

Text field
A form object used for collecting a string of characters such as a name.

Thumbnail image
A small version of a larger image.

Tiled image
A small graphic that repeats across and down a web page, appearing as individual squares or rectangles.

Top property (T)
The property that specifies the distance between the top edge of an AP div and the top edge of the page or a parent AP div.

Tracing image
An image that is placed in the background of a web page as a guide to create page elements on top of it, similar to the way tracing paper is used.

Trademark
An indicator that protects an image, word, slogan, symbol, or design used to identify goods or services.

Tumblr
A blog where users can post and share text, photos, music, and videos.

Tweet
A short message posted on the Twitter website that is no more than 140 characters.

Twitter
A website where viewers can post short messages up to 140 characters long, called "tweets."

Glossary

U

Uniform Resource Locator (URL)
An address that determines a route on the Internet or to a web page. See Domain name.

Unordered list
A lists of items that do not need to be placed in a specific order and are usually preceded by bullets.

Unvisited link
A link that the user has not yet clicked, or visited. The default color for unvisited links is blue.

Upload
The process of transferring files from a local drive to a web server.

URL
See Uniform Resource Locator.

V

Validate markup
To submit files to the W3C Validation Service so it can search through the code to look for errors that could occur with different language versions, such as HTML5.

Vector-based graphic
Scalable graphics that are built using mathematical formulas, rather than with pixels.

Vidcast
See Vodcast.

View
A choice for displaying page content in the Document window; Dreamweaver has three working views: Design view, Code view, and Show Code and Design views.

Vis property
A property that lets you control whether a selected AP div is visible or hidden.

Visited link
A link that has been previously clicked, or visited. The default color for visited links is purple.

Vodcast
Short for Video podcast. Also called a vidcast.

VSS
Acronym for Microsoft Visual SafeSource, a connection type used only with the Window operating system.

W

Web 2.0
The evolution of web applications that facilitate and promote information sharing among Internet users.

Web browser
A program, such as Microsoft Internet Explorer, Apple Safari, Google Chrome, or Mozilla Firefox, that displays web pages.

Web cam
A web camera used for video conferencing with a high-speed Internet connection.

Web server
A computer dedicated to hosting websites; it is connected to the Internet and configured with software to handle requests from browsers.

WebDav
Acronym for Web-based Distributed Authoring and Versioning, a type of connection used with the WebDav protocol, such as a website residing on an Apache web server.

WebM
An open, royalty-free media format sponsored by Google.

Website
A group of related web pages that are linked together and share a common interface and design.

White space
An area on a web page that is not filled with text or graphics.

Widget
A piece of code that allows users to interact with a program, such as clicking a menu item to open a page.

Width (W) property
The property that specifies the width of a div, either in pixels or as a percentage of the screen width.

Wiki
Named for the Hawaiian word for "quick," a site where a user can use simple editing tools to contribute and edit the page content in a site.

Wikipedia
An online encyclopedia that allows users to contribute to site content.

Wireframe
A prototype that represents every page and its contents in a website. Like a flowchart or storyboard, a wireframe shows the relationship of each page in the site to all the other pages.

WOFF
Acronym for Web Open Face Format; describes fonts available through font libraries for embedding in web pages through the CSS3 @font-face property.

WOFF font
Fonts available through font libraries for embedding in web pages through the CSS3 @font-face property.

World Wide Web Consortium (W3C)
An international community that develops open standards for web development.

Workspace switcher
A drop-down menu located in the top right corner on the Menu bar that allows you to change the workspace layout.

WYSIWYG
Acronym for What You See Is What You Get, where a web page looks the same in a browser as it does in a web editor.

—————————— X ——————————

XHTML
The acronym for eXtensible HyperText Markup Language, the current standard language used to create web pages.

XML
Acronym for Extensible Markup Language, a type of language that is used to develop customized tags to store information.

XSL
Acronym for Extensible Stylesheet Language, which is similar to CSS; the XSL style sheet information formats containers created with XML.

XSLT
Acronym for Extensible Stylesheet Language Transformations; interprets the code in an XSL file to transform an XML document, much like style sheet files transform HTML files.

—————————— Y ——————————

YouTube
A website where you can upload and share videos.

—————————— Z ——————————

Z-index property
A property that specifies the vertical stacking order of AP divs on a page.

INDEX

Note: Page numbers preceded by BR refer to the Bridge chapter; those preceded by DW refer to Dreamweaver chapters.

absolute paths, DW 5–5
absolute positioning, AP divs, DW 10–8
accessibility
    tables, DW 6–23
    validating standards, DW 7–6
    WCAG guidelines, DW 4–13
    web pages, DW 2–5
accordions, CSS3, DW 8–19
action(s), DW 11–14—15
    undoing. *See* undoing actions
Action property, forms, DW 9–5—6
ActionScript, DW 10–2
Active Server Pages (ASPs), DW 9–5
ActiveX controls, DW 11–2
adaptive websites, DW 8–20
add-ons, DW 11–2
    form objects, DW 9–18
    playing, keyboard shortcut, DW 11–21
Adobe Bridge. *See* Bridge
Adobe Bridge Preferences dialog box, BR 1–2
Adobe BrowserLab, DW 2–33, DW 7–5, DW 8–21

Adobe Business Catalyst, DW 6–10
Adobe Dreamweaver Exchange, DW 9–18, DW 9–26
Adobe Edge, DW 11–7
Adobe Exchange website, DW 11–6
Adobe Flash video (FLV) format, DW 11–18
Adobe Marketplace & Exchange, DW 9–18, DW 9–26
AIF or AIFF (Audio Interchange File Format), DW 11–22
AJAX (Asynchronous JavaScript and XML), DW 11–15
aligning
    content, editing block properties for, DW 6–15—16
    images in table cells, DW 6–30—31, DW 6–33
    images on web pages, DW 4–5, DW 4–11
    text, keyboard shortcut, DW 3–29
All Rules pane, CSS Styles panel, DW 8–12

alternate text, DW 4–13
    displaying in browser, DW 4–17
    editing, DW 4–16
    missing, checking for, DW 7–7
    setting accessibility option, DW 4–17
American Psychological Association (APA) guidelines, DW 7–39
animations, low-bandwidth, DW 11–4
AP div(s), DW 10–1—27
    adding behaviors, DW 10–2
    content. *See* AP div content
    creating using HTML tags, DW 10–5
    CSS layout blocks, DW 10–2
    defining, DW 10–7
    div tags, DW 10–2
    drawing, DW 10–6
    formatting, DW 10–5
    inserting, DW 10–4—5
    positioning. *See* positioning AP divs
    properties. *See* AP div properties
    uses, DW 10–2

AP div content, DW 10–5, DW 10–14—19
    images, DW 10–15, DW 10–16—17
    setting background images,
        DW 10–18
    text, DW 10–19
AP div properties, DW 10–20—25
    adding borders, DW 10–25
    renaming AP elements, DW 10–22
    setting relative to containers,
        DW 10–20—21, DW 10–24
    setting using AP Elements panel,
        DW 10–20
    visibility, DW 10–23
AP div tags, DW 6–4
AP elements, DW 6–4, DW 10–4.
    See also AP div(s)
    adding borders, DW 10–25
    content, DW 10–14—15
    nested, DW 10–20
    renaming, DW 10–22
AP Elements panel, DW 10–20,
    DW 10–23
APA (American Psychological
    Association) guidelines, DW 7–39
Apple Quick Time (MOV) format,
    DW 11–18
Application bar, BR 1–5. *See also*
    Menu bar

ASPs (Active Server Pages), DW 9–5
assets, DW 1–20
    organizing for quick access,
        DW 4–7
    removing from websites, DW 4–19
assets folders, saving image files,
    DW 2–14—16
Assets panel, DW 4–10, DW 5–6
    adding assets to web pages,
        DW 4–5
    category buttons, DW 4–4
    images, DW 4–4—5
    library items, DW 13–5, DW 13–7,
        DW 13–9, DW 13–19
    links, DW 5–31
    organizing assets for quick access,
        DW 4–7
    panes, DW 4–4—5
    templates, DW 12–5, DW 12–6
    URL category, DW 2–25
    viewing links, DW 5–9
    website maintenance, DW 7–4
Asynchronous JavaScript and XML
    (AJAX), DW 11–15
Attach External Style Sheet dialog box,
    DW 3–20
Attach Style Sheet button, DW 3–20,
    DW 3–24

attribution for material, DW 7–39
Audio Interchange File Format (AIF or
    AIFF), DW 11–22
Audio Visual Interleave (AVI) format,
    DW 11–18
AVI (Audio Visual Interleave) format,
    DW 11–18

background color, websites, DW 2–4,
    DW 2–9
background images
    AP div content, DW 10–18
    inserting, DW 4–18, DW 4–20—21
    removing, DW 4–21
banners, DW 1–12
BCC (Browser Compatibility Check)
    feature, DW 6–5, DW 6–15,
    DW 8–27, DW 8–29
behaviors, DW 10–2, DW 11–14—17
    actions and events, DW 11–14—15
    adding, DW 11–16
    adding interactive elements,
        DW 11–14
    adding to AP divs, DW 10–2
    Behaviors panel, DW 11–14,
        DW 11–15, DW 11–17
    editing, DW 11–17
    JavaScript, DW 6–2

rollover images, DW 11–11
Spry framework, DW 11–15
Behaviors panel, DW 11–14, DW 11–15
    Servers Behaviors panel compared, DW 11–17
blogs, DW 5–35
body, websites, DW 2–4
boldfacing text, keyboard shortcut, DW 3–29
borders
    AP elements, DW 10–25
    images, DW 4–12, DW 4–14
    tables, DW 6–22
braces, balancing, keyboard shortcut, DW 8–24
breadcrumbs trails, DW 5–30
Bridge, BR 1–1—15
    accessing, BR 1–2
    browsing in, keyboard shortcut, DW 4–17
    changing modes, BR 1–7
    Compact mode, BR 1–4
    inserting files, DW 4–5
    inserting images, DW 4–10
    metadata. *See* metadata
    starting, BR 1–6
Bridge Essentials workspace, BR 1–4—7
    Application bar, BR 1–5

Menu bar, BR 1–5
panes, BR 1–4—5
Path bar, BR 1–5
broken links, DW 2–20
browser(s)
    displaying alternate text, DW 4–17
    playing Flash movies, DW 11–7
    testing web pages in different browsers, DW 2–32—33
    viewing web pages, DW 2–32—33
    web page appearance in, DW 8–29
Browser Compatibility Check (BCC) feature, DW 6–5, DW 6–15, DW 8–27, DW 8–29
Browser Compatibility panel, DW 7–5
BrowserLab, DW 2–33, DW 7–5, DW 8–21
browsing in Bridge, keyboard shortcut, DW 4–17
buffers, DW 11–19
bullet(s), unordered lists, DW 3–4
bulleted lists, DW 3–4

Camera raw file formats, DW 4–5
captions, tables, DW 6–23
Cascading Style Sheets (CSSs), DW 2–4, DW 3–2, DW 3–10—19
    advantages, DW 3–11

choosing fonts, DW 3–13
converting styles, DW 3–27
CSS3. *See* CSS3
CSS Styles panel, DW 3–10
evolution, DW 3–31
formatting forms, DW 9–11
formatting menu bars, DW 5–20—25
formatting ordered lists, DW 3–5
formatting tables with CSS3, DW 6–23
formatting text, DW 2–10—11
rules. *See* CSS rule(s)
semantic tag appearance, DW 3–6
style sheets. *See* style sheets
types, DW 3–10
validating, DW 7–9
viewing code, DW 3–11, DW 3–16
cascading styles, DW 8–26
case-sensitive links, DW 5–8
cell content, DW 6–34—41
    formatting, DW 6–34, DW 6–36, DW 6–39
    inserting text, DW 6–34, DW 6–35
    modifying, DW 6–39
cell padding, DW 6–22
cell spacing, DW 6–22
cell walls, DW 6–22

CGI. *See* Common Gateway Interface (CGI) scripts
check boxes, forms, DW 9–16, DW 9–22—23
Check browser compatibility button, DW 7–5
Check Links Sitewide feature, DW 5–30
Check Out feature, enabling, DW 7–23, DW 7–24
Check Spelling dialog box, DW 2–19
Checkbox Group dialog box, DW 9–22
checkbox groups, forms, DW 9–22—23
checking files out and in, DW 7–22—26
    enabling Check Out feature, DW 7–23, DW 7–24
    keyboard shortcuts, DW 7–35
    Subversion control, DW 7–23
checking links, DW 5–30, DW 5–31, DW 7–4, DW 7–6
    for broken links, DW 7–6
    keyboard shortcuts, DW 5–33, DW 7–35
child containers, DW 6–17
child keywords, BR 1–8
child pages, DW 1–20
Circle Hotspot tool, DW 5–26
citing sources, DW 7–39

class rules, adding to style sheets, DW 3–22—23
class selectors, DW 8–7
class styles, DW 8–5
    creating, DW 8–10
Class type CSSs, DW 3–10
clean HTML code, DW 2–10
Clean Up Word HTML dialog box, DW 2–17
clients, presenting websites to, DW 7–40—41
client-side script(s), DW 10–2. *See also* JavaScript (Jscript)
client-side scripting, DW 9–5
Clip property, AP divs, DW 10–5
Cloaked assets folder, File panel, DW 7–29, DW 7–30, DW 7–31
cloaked files, DW 7–2
cloaking files, DW 7–28—31
    selected file types, DW 7–29, DW 7–31
    uncloaking, DW 7–29
cloaking folders, DW 7–28—29, DW 7–30
closing files, DW 1–35
    keyboard shortcut, DW 5–33
code
    collapsing selections, keyboard shortcut, DW 8–24

    CSS, DW 3–11, DW 3–16, DW 6–9
    expanding, DW 3–29
    expanding, keyboard shortcut, DW 8–24
    expanding selections, keyboard shortcut, DW 8–24
    indenting, keyboard shortcut, DW 8–24
    outdenting, keyboard shortcut, DW 8–24
    viewing, DW 3–11, DW 3–16
code hints, DW 3–27
    refreshing, keyboard shortcut, DW 8–24
    showing, keyboard shortcut, DW 8–24
Code Inspector
    showing and hiding, keyboard shortcut, DW 2–29
    using, DW 2–29
    viewing HTML code, DW 2–26—27
Code Navigator
    editing rules, DW 3–17
    viewing CSS code, DW 3–16
code snippets, DW 13–2, DW 13–20—25
    inserting, DW 13–20
    modifying links, DW 13–20, DW 13–24

modifying text, DW 13–20, DW 13–23
new, creating, DW 13–21, DW 13–24—25
predefined, adding to pages, DW 13–22
Snippets panel, DW 13–20, DW 13–21
Code view, DW 1–6
   CSS code, DW 6–9
   switching between Design view and, DW 1–35
Coding toolbar, DW 1–5—6, DW 1–7, DW 3–26
coding tools, DW 3–26—31
   code hints, DW 3–27
   collapsing code, DW 3–27, DW 3–28
   converting styles, DW 3–27
   expanding code, DW 3–29
   moving embedded styles to an external CSS, DW 3–30—31
   navigating code using, DW 3–27
Cold Fusion, DW 9–5
Collapse Full Tag, DW 3–27
Collapse Selection buttons, DW 3–27
collapsing
   code, DW 3–27, DW 3–28
   code, keyboard shortcut, DW 8–24
   tags, keyboard shortcut, DW 8–24

Collections panel, BR 1–4
color(s)
   to convey information on web pages, DW 2–5
   WCAG guidelines, DW 4–22
   web page background, DW 2–4, DW 2–9
   website color palettes, DW 4–19, DW 4–23
Color Cubes color palette, DW 2–5
"come back later" web pages, DW 2–32
comments, inserting, DW 2–31
Common Gateway Interface (CGI)
   scripts, DW 9–5, DW 9–7
   using, DW 9–9
Compact mode, Bridge, BR 1–4
compound selectors, DW 8–7
Compound type CSSs, DW 3–10
conflicting styles, DW 8–26—29
   checking for, DW 8–27, DW 8–29
   comparing, DW 8–28
   order of precedence, DW 8–26—27
   tools for managing styles, DW 8–27
Connect to Remote Server button, DW 7–15
containers, positioning AP divs relative to, DW 10–20—21, DW 10–24

content
   AP divs. See AP div content
   AP elements, DW 10–14—15
   div tags, DW 6–8
   dynamic, testing, DW 9–31
   Flash, inserting, DW 11–4—6
   static, DW 9–31
   web pages, collecting, DW 1–21
Content panel, BR 1–4—5
Continuous Tone color palette, DW 2–5
control(s), forms. See form objects
controllers
   sound, DW 11–23
   video, DW 11–18
copying
   keyboard shortcut, DW 2–29
   Spry menu bars, DW 5–17, DW 5–25
copyright, DW 7–2, DW 7–36—37
   posting notice, DW 7–38—39
CSS Advisor, DW 6–15
CSS code
   CSS layout blocks, DW 6–9
   viewing, DW 3–11, DW 3–16
CSS Form Builder, DW 9–26
CSS layout blocks
   adding images, DW 6–12—13
   adding text, DW 6–10—11
   AP divs, DW 10–2

CSS code, DW 6–9
div tag content, DW 6–8
editing content, DW 6–14—16
editing page properties,
   DW 6–20—21
editing properties, DW 6–18—19
editing type properties, DW 6–17
viewing, DW 6–5
viewing options, DW 6–16
CSS Layout Box Model, DW 6–16
CSS page layout(s), DW 6–2,
   DW 6–4—21
   creating pages with, DW 6–6—7
   CSS layout blocks. *See* CSS layout
     blocks
   div tags, DW 6–2, DW 6–4
   fixed, DW 6–4
   liquid, DW 6–4
   predesigned, DW 6–4
CSS page layout blocks, DW 2–4
CSS Property inspector, DW 3–12
CSS rule(s), DW 3–10
   applying, DW 3–14
   disabling properties, DW 8–27
   editing, DW 3–15, DW 3–17
   global, DW 8–2
CSS Rule Definition dialog box,
   DW 3–10, DW 4–11, DW 8–6

CSS Styles panel, DW 3–10, DW 3–12,
   DW 4–20, DW 6–14, DW 8–12—13
CSSs. *See* Cascading Style Sheets (CSSs)
CSS3, DW 8–18—19
   adding tags, DW 8–22—23
   modifying tags, DW 8–24
   uploading files for validation,
     DW 8–25
   validating for CSS3 standards,
     DW 8–20—21
CSS3 tags
   adding, DW 8–22—23
   modifying, DW 8–24
custom styles. *See* class styles
cutting. *See also* deleting; removing
   keyboard shortcut, DW 2–29

data loss, preventing, DW 2–22
date objects, inserting, DW 2–31
debugging, DW 1–6
declaration, CSS code, DW 3–11
default font, DW 2–5
default link colors, DW 2–5
defining AP divs, DW 10–7
definition lists, DW 3–5
deleting. *See also* cutting; removing
   embedded styles, DW 8–17
   library items, DW 13–15, DW 13–19

table columns, keyboard shortcut,
   DW 6–36
table rows, DW 6–26
table rows, keyboard shortcut,
   DW 6–36
delimited files, DW 6–35
delimiters, DW 6–35
dependent files, DW 7–16
description(s), web pages, DW 2–7,
   DW 2–8
Description dialog box, DW 2–8
Design Notes, DW 7–5
   associating with a file, DW 7–11
   editing, DW 7–12—13
   enabling, DW 7–10
Design view, DW 1–6
   switching between Code view and,
     DW 1–35
detaching templates from pages,
   DW 12–12
diagonal symmetry, web page design,
   DW 2–34
Director movies, DW 11–2
Disable/Enable CSS feature, DW 8–27
disabling CSS rule properties, DW 8–27
displaying. *See also* viewing
   Files tab, keyboard shortcut, DW 5–33
   guides, keyboard shortcut, DW 10–22

Index

DREAMWEAVER 55

panel groups, DW 1–10
panels, DW 1–35
rulers, keyboard shortcut, DW 10–22
toolbars, DW 1–7
div tags, DW 6–2, DW 10–2
    AP, DW 6–4
    content, DW 6–8
    tables vs., for page layout, DW 6–2
    uses, DW 6–33
docking panel groups, DW 1–11
document(s), Microsoft Office, importing and linking, DW 2–18
Document toolbar, DW 1–4, DW 1–7
Document window, DW 1–4
document-relative paths, DW 5–5
domain names, DW 1–22
downloadable templates, finding, DW 12–16
downloading
    files, DW 7–16
    legal use of media, DW 7–36
Draw AP Div button, DW 10–4
drawing, AP divs, DW 10–6
Dreamweaver, integrating with Photoshop, DW 4–15
Dual Screen layout, DW 1–9
dynamic content, testing, DW 9–31

editable optional regions, DW 12–5
editable regions, templates, DW 12–2, DW 12–4, DW 12–7
    creating, DW 12–7
    defining, DW 12–4
    editable optional regions, DW 12–5
    modifying, DW 12–10, DW 12–14
Editable Tag Attributes dialog box, DW 12–21
editing. *See also* modifying
    behaviors, DW 11–17
    content, CSS layout blocks, DW 6–14—16
    CSS rules, DW 3–15, DW 3–17
    Design Notes, DW 7–12—13
    embedded styles, DW 8–12, DW 8–14, DW 8–17
    ICE, DW 12–9
    image settings, DW 4–15
    image-based library items, DW 13–10
    making library items editable on a page, DW 13–14, DW 13–18
    page properties, CSS layout blocks, DW 6–20—21
    page titles, DW 2–6
    properties, CSS layout blocks, DW 6–18—19

site preferences, DW 7–27
    text-based library items, DW 13–12—13
    type properties, CSS layout blocks, DW 6–17
email link(s), DW 2–20, DW 2–24—25
    viewing in Assets panel, DW 2–25
Email Link dialog box, DW 2–24
embedded style(s), DW 8–2, DW 8–4—17
    applying, DW 8–11
    creating, DW 8–4—7, DW 8–10
    CSS Styles panel, DW 8–12—13
    deleting, DW 8–17
    editing, DW 8–12, DW 8–14, DW 8–17
    moving styles to an external CSS, DW 3–30—31
    redefining HTML tags, DW 8–12, DW 8–15—16
embedded style sheets. *See* internal style sheets
errors. *See also* checking links
    spelling, checking for, DW 2–19, DW 2–29
    undoing with History panel, DW 2–26

Essentials workspace. *See* Bridge Essentials workspace
events, DW 11-14—15
exiting Live view, keyboard shortcut, DW 11-21
Expanded Tables mode, DW 6-22, DW 6-23, DW 6-24
expanding tags, keyboard shortcut, DW 8-24
Export command, DW 7-32, DW 7-33
Export panel, BR 1-4
exporting
    data from tables, DW 6-35
    site definitions, DW 7-32, DW 7-33
Extensible Markup Language (XML), DW 2-8, DW 6-6
Extensible Metadata Platform (XMP) standard, BR 1-8
Extensible Stylesheet Language (XSL), DW 6-6
Extensible Stylesheet Language Transformations (XSLT), DW 6-6
external editors, resizing images, DW 4-12
external links, creating, DW 5-4, DW 5-6—7
external style(s), DW 8-5

external style sheets, DW 3-10, DW 3-20, DW 8-2
    moving embedded styles to, DW 3-30—31

Facebook, DW 5-34
fair use, DW 7-37
favicons, DW 4-24—25, DW 4-27
favorites, Assets panel, DW 4-4—5
Favorites option, Assets panel, DW 4-7
Favorites panel, BR 1-4
fieldsets, grouping form objects, DW 9-10
file(s)
    checking out and in. *See* checking files out and in
    cloaked, DW 7-2
    cloaking. *See* cloaking files
    closing, DW 1-35
    comparing for differences in content, DW 7-17
    creating, DW 1-35
    delimited, DW 6-35
    dependent, DW 7-16
    downloading, DW 7-16
    filtering. *See* filtering files
    groups, labels, BR 1-8
    labeling, BR 1-12

    opening, DW 1-35
    orphaned, DW 5-30, DW 7-6
    rating, BR 1-12
    related, DW 1-5, DW 3-21, DW 3-25
    saving. *See* saving files
    synchronizing, DW 7-16, DW 7-21
    transferring to and from a remote site, DW 7-15—16
    uncloaking, DW 7-29
    uploading. *See* uploading files
File Activity dialog box, DW 7-15
file fields, forms, DW 9-17
file formats
    images, DW 4-2, DW 4-4
    inserting audio, DW 11-22
    inserting video, DW 11-18
file management, using, DW 1-29
File panel, Cloaked assets folder, DW 7-29, DW 7-30, DW 7-31
File Transfer Protocol (FTP), DW 1-21, DW 7-15
filenames, web pages, DW 2-17
Files panel, DW 1-2, DW 1-20
    creating a local site folder, DW 1-23
    file management using, DW 1-29
    selecting a drive, DW 1-22
    viewing an open website, DW 1-24

Index

Files tab, displaying, keyboard shortcut, DW 5–33
Filter panel, BR 1–4
filtering files
    keywords, BR 1–11
    labels and ratings, BR 1–11
Fireworks
    inserting menu bars, DW 5–20
    media objects, DW 11–2
fixed layouts, DW 6–4
Flash, DW 11–4—9
    inserting Flash content, DW 11–4—6
    modifying files in Dreamweaver, DW 11–8—9
Flash buttons, DW 11–5
Flash movies, DW 11–5
    adding to web pages, DW 11–5, DW 11–6
    playing in browsers, DW 11–7
    playing in Dreamweaver, DW 11–7
    workspace, DW 11–5
Flash objects, collecting, DW 11–6
Flash Paper, DW 11–2
Flash Player, DW 11–2, DW 11–4
Fluid Grid Layout, DW 6–19
FLV (Adobe Flash video) format, DW 11–18

focus groups, DW 2–7
fold lines, DW 10–5
folders
    adding to websites, DW 1–28—29, DW 1–30
    cloaking, DW 7–28—29, DW 7–30
    images, setting default, DW 1–31
    local. *See* local site folders
    network, setting up web server connections, DW 7–18
    saving image files, DW 1–33
    uncloaking, DW 7–30
Folders panel, BR 1–4
font(s)
    changing, DW 2–11
    changing sizes, DW 2–11
    default, DW 2–5
    sans serif, DW 3–13
    serif, DW 3–13
    WOFF, DW 3–19, DW 8–18
Font combinations, DW 2–11
font libraries, DW 8–18
form(s), DW 9–1—35
    adding tables, DW 9–12
    CGI scripts, DW 9–7
    creating, DW 9–4—5
    formatting, DW 9–11
    inserting, DW 9–8

    labels, DW 9–2, DW 9–10—11, DW 9–13—14
    laying out using tables, DW 9–10
    linking files, DW 9–32—33
    planning, DW 9–4
    secure, DW 9–26
    setting properties, DW 9–5—7, DW 9–9
    spell checking, DW 9–31
    Spry data sets, DW 9–32
    Spry Validation Field widgets, DW 9–33
    testing dynamic content, DW 9–31
    user-friendly, DW 9–30
    using to collect information, DW 9–2
    visual clues, DW 9–30, DW 9–31
form controls. *See* form objects
form elements. *See* form objects
form fields. *See* form objects
form inputs. *See* form objects
form labels, DW 9–2, DW 9–10—11, DW 9–13—14
Form name property, DW 9–6—7
form objects, DW 9–2, DW 9–16—29. *See also* form(s)
    adding labels, DW 9–10—11
    add-ons, DW 9–18

checkbox groups, inserting, DW 9-22—23
grouping using fieldsets, DW 9-10
hidden fields, adding, DW 9-28
menus, adding, DW 9-26—27
multiple-line text fields, inserting, DW 9-21
radio groups, adding, DW 9-24—25
Reset buttons, adding, DW 9-29
setting attributes, DW 9-17—18
single-line text fields, inserting, DW 9-19—20
Submit buttons, adding, DW 9-29
form tables
  adding form labels, DW 9-13—14
  adding to forms, DW 9-12
  creating rules, DW 9-15
formatting
  AP divs, DW 10-5
  cell content, DW 6-34, DW 6-36, DW 6-39
  cells, DW 6-34, DW 6-37—38
  forms, DW 9-11
  menu bars using CSSs, DW 5-20—25
  ordered lists, DW 3-5, DW 3-9
  paragraphs, DW 2-11

Spry menu bars, using CSSs, DW 5-20—25
tables with HTML5 and CSS3, DW 6-23
text. *See* formatting text
formatting text
  AP divs, DW 10-19
  with HTML vs. CSS, DW 2-10—11, DW 2-12, DW 2-13
  as lists. *See* list(s)
  unordered lists, DW 3-4—5
FTP (File Transfer Protocol), DW 1-21, DW 7-15
FTP sites, setting up web server connections, DW 7-17

Get property, forms, DW 9-6
getting items, keyboard shortcut, DW 7-35
GIF (Graphics Interchange Format), DW 4-2, DW 4-4
global CSS rules, DW 8-2
Global Positioning System (GPS), DW 5-34
go to, keyboard shortcut, DW 8-24
Google Video Chat, DW 5-35
GPS (Global Positioning System), DW 5-34

graphics, vector-based, DW 11-4
graphics file formats, DW 4-2, DW 4-4
Graphics Interchange Format (GIF), DW 4-2, DW 4-4
grids, positioning page contents, DW 6-32
guides
  AP divs, DW 10-4—5
  locking, keyboard shortcut, DW 10-22
  positioning page contents, DW 6-32
  showing, keyboard shortcut, DW 10-22

Hand tool, DW 1-6
headers, table, DW 6-23
Height property (H), AP divs, DW 10-9, DW 10-11
Help system, DW 1-13, DW 1-16—17
  accessing, DW 1-35
hexadecimal RGB values, DW 2-9
hidden fields, forms, DW 9-17, DW 9-28
hiding
  panels, DW 1-35
  toolbars, DW 1-7
  visual aids, keyboard shortcut, DW 5-33, DW 10-22

History panel, DW 2–26, DW 2–27,
    DW 2–28
  clearing, DW 2–28
  features, DW 2–26
  slider, DW 2–26, DW 2–28
home pages, DW 1–12
  creating, DW 1–29, DW 1–32
horizontal rules, inserting, DW 2–22
horizontal symmetry, web page design,
    DW 2–34
hotspots, DW 5–26, DW 5–28
  creating, DW 5–26
  properties, DW 5–29
  targets, DW 5–28
HTML, DW 1–2
  body tags, DW 4–21
  clean HTML code, DW 2–10
  evolution, DW 6–12
  formatting text, DW 2–10—11,
    DW 2–12, DW 2–13
  table tags, DW 6–27
HTML Property inspector
  creating internal links, DW 5–5
  formatting paragraphs,
    DW 2–11
HTML Reports, DW 7–6
HTML tags
  creating AP divs using, DW 10–5
  formatting tags, DW 2–12

HTML5, DW 11–4
  redefining, DW 8–12, DW 8–15—16
HTML5, DW 6–12
  formatting tables, DW 6–23
  validating markup, DW 6–41,
    DW 7–8
HTML5 tags, DW 11–4
HTTP (Hypertext Transfer Protocol),
    specifying, DW 9–6
hyperlinks. See link(s)
Hypertext Transfer Protocol (HTTP),
    specifying, DW 9–6
Hypertext Transfer Protocol Secure,
    DW 9–26

ICE (InContext Editing), DW 6–10,
    DW 12–9
.ico file extension, DW 4–24
ID selectors, DW 8–7
image(s), DW 1–12, DW 1–20,
    DW 4–1—29
  adding to CSS layout blocks,
    DW 6–12—13
  aligning in table cells, DW 6–30—31,
    DW 6–33
  aligning on web pages, DW 4–5,
    DW 4–11
  AP div content, DW 10–15,
    DW 10–16—17

Assets panel, DW 4–4—5
background. See background images
  editing settings, DW 4–15
  enhancing, DW 4–12—13,
    DW 4–14—15
  enhancing web pages, DW 4–2
  file formats, DW 4–2, DW 4–4
  graphics vs., DW 4–2
  inserting, keyboard shortcut for,
    DW 4–17
  inserting in table cells, DW 6–30,
    DW 6–32
  inserting in web pages, DW 4–5,
    DW 4–6—7
  managing, DW 4–18—19
  placeholders. See image
    placeholder(s)
  removing from web pages,
    DW 4–19, DW 4–21
  resizing using an external editor,
    DW 4–12
  rollover, DW 11–10—13
  thumbnail. See thumbnail images
  tracing, DW 6–5
  website, protecting,
    DW 4–25
image fields, forms, DW 9–17
image files, saving in assets folders,
    DW 1–33, DW 2–14—16

image maps, DW 5–26—29
    creating, DW 5–28—29
        hotspot tools, DW 5–26—27
        hotspots, DW 5–26, DW 5–28
Image Orientation dialog box, DW 4–15
image placeholder(s), DW 4–5
    inserting, DW 4–8
    replacing with an image, DW 4–9
Image Placeholder dialog box, DW 4–8
image-based library items
    creating, DW 13–8—9
    editing, DW 13–10
images folder, default, setting, DW 1–31
Import Site dialog box, DW 7–32, DW 7–34
importing
    data from tables, DW 6–35
    Microsoft Office documents, DW 2–18
    site definitions, DW 7–32, DW 7–34—35
    text, DW 2–10, DW 2–17
Inconsistent Region Names dialog box, DW 12–12
InContext Editing (ICE), DW 6–10, DW 12–9
indenting text, keyboard shortcut, DW 3–29

inherited properties, formatting cell content, DW 6–39
inline styles, DW 3–10, DW 8–4, DW 8–5
Insert Date dialog box, DW 2–31
Insert panel, DW 1–4
Insert Spry Menu Bar command, DW 5–16
Inspect mode, DW 8–27
intellectual property, DW 7–36
internal links
    creating, DW 5–4—5, DW 5–8
    named anchors. *See* internal links to named anchors
internal links to named anchors, DW 5–10—15
    creating, DW 5–10—11, DW 5–14—15
    inserting names anchors, DW 5–12—13
internal style(s). *See* embedded styles
internal style sheets, DW 3–10, DW 3–20
    moving styles to an external CSS, DW 3–30—31
Internet Service Providers (ISPs), DW 1–21
IP addresses, DW 1–22

ISPs (Internet Service Providers), DW 1–21
italicizing type, keyboard shortcut, DW 3–29

Java applets, DW 11–2
Java Server Page (JSP), DW 9–5
JavaScript (Jscript), DW 9–5
    adding behaviors to AP divs, DW 10–2
    behaviors, DW 6–2
    no right-click script, DW 4–25
JavaScript functions, DW 2–27
JavaScript Object Notation (JSON), DW 11–7
JPEG or JPG (Joint Photographic Experts Group) file format, DW 4–2, DW 4–4, DW 4–25
Jscript. *See* JavaScript (Jscript)
JSON (JavaScript Object Notation), DW 11–7
JSP (Java Server Page), DW 9–5
jump menus, forms, DW 9–17

keyboard shortcuts, DW 1–35, DW 2–29, DW 3–29, DW 4–17, DW 5–33, DW 6–36, DW 7–35, DW 8–24, DW 10–22, DW 11–21, DW 12–17
    text, DW 2–12

Index

DREAMWEAVER 61

keywords, DW 2–4
   child, BR 1–8
   filtering files, BR 1–11
   parent, BR 1–8
   sub, BR 1–8
   web pages, DW 2–7
Keywords panel, BR 1–5

label(s)
   form objects, DW 9–10—11
   forms, DW 9–2, DW 9–10—11, DW 9–13—14
   groups of files, BR 1–8
Label button, DW 9–14
labeling files, BR 1–12
LANs (local area networks), DW 7–15
layout(s), web pages. *See* CSS page layout(s); page layouts
Layout Objects, AP Div command, DW 10–4
Left property (L), AP divs, DW 10–9, DW 10–10
library items, DW 13–2
   adding to pages, DW 13–14, DW 13–16—17
   benefits, DW 13–4
   creating, DW 13–4, DW 13–6—9
   deleted, restoring, DW 13–15
   deleting, DW 13–15, DW 13–19
   image-based, creating, DW 13–8—9
   image-based, editing, DW 13–10
   making editable on a page, DW 13–14, DW 13–18
   modifying, DW 13–5
   opening, DW 13–10
   recreating, DW 13–15, DW 13–19
   text-based, creating, DW 13–6—7
   text-based, editing, DW 13–12—13
   updating, DW 13–11
   viewing, DW 13–4
licensing agreements, DW 7–37—38
line breaks, keyboard shortcut, DW 2–29
link(s), DW 1–12, DW 2–5, DW 5–1—38
   breadcrumbs trails, DW 5–30
   broken, DW 2–20. *See also* checking links
   case-sensitive, DW 5–8
   checking. *See* checking links
   creating, keyboard shortcut, DW 5–33
   creating in template-based pages, DW 12–11, DW 12–14
   email (mailto:). *See* email link(s)
   external. *See* external links
   hotspots. *See* hotspots
   internal. *See* internal links; internal links to named anchors
   to larger image, adding, DW 4–24, DW 4–26
   making, keyboard shortcut, DW 12–17
   managing, DW 5–30—33
   menu bars, DW 2–20—21, DW 2–22
   point of contact, DW 2–20
   removing, keyboard shortcut, DW 5–33, DW 12–17
   site maps, DW 5–30
   viewing in Assets panel, DW 5–9
   WCAG accessibility, DW 2–21
   to web pages, DW 2–20, DW 2–23
Link Checker panel, DW 5–31, DW 7–2, DW 7–4
link colors, default, DW 2–5
linking
   files, forms, DW 9–32—33
   Microsoft Office documents, DW 2–18
liquid layouts, DW 6–4
list(s), DW 3–2, DW 3–4—9
   bulleted, DW 3–4
   definition, DW 3–5

forms, DW 9–16—17
ordered, DW 3–5, DW 3–8—9
unordered, DW 3–4—5,
  DW 3–6—7
List Values dialog box, DW 9–27
Live view, DW 1–5, DW 1–11, DW 9–31
  enabling, keyboard shortcut,
    DW 11–21
  exiting, keyboard shortcut,
    DW 11–21
local area networks (LANs), DW 7–15
local root folder, DW 1–25
local site folders, DW 1–20, DW 1–25
  creating, DW 1–23—24
  setting up web server connections,
    DW 7–18
locked regions, templates, DW 12–2
locking, guides, keyboard shortcut,
  DW 10–22
low-bandwidth animations,
  DW 11–4

mailto: links. *See* email link(s)
Match.com, DW 5–34
media objects, DW 11–2
  adding using HTML5 and Adobe
    Edge, DW 11–7
Media Queries, DW 8–19

menu(s)
  forms, DW 9–16—17,
    DW 9–26—27
  jump, forms, DW 9–17
Menu bar, BR 1–5, DW 1–4
menu bar(s), DW 1–12. *See also* Spry
  menu bar(s)
  Fireworks, inserting, DW 5–20
  links, DW 2–20—21, DW 2–22
merging table cells, DW 6–26, DW 6–29
  keyboard shortcut, DW 6–36
meta tags, DW 2–4
metadata, BR 1–2, DW 7–11
  adding, BR 1–9—10
  viewing, BR 1–9—10
Metadata panel, BR 1–5, BR 1–8
Method property, forms, DW 9–6
Mini Bridge, BR 1–2
MLA (Modern Language Association)
  guidelines, DW 7–39
mobile devices, testing web pages as
  rendered in, DW 2–33
Modern Language Association (MLA)
  guidelines, DW 7–39
modifying. *See also* editing
  cell content, DW 6–39
  code snippet text, DW 13–20,
    DW 13–23

editable regions, templates,
  DW 12–10, DW 12–14
Flash files from Dreamweaver,
  DW 11–7
library items, DW 13–5
links, code snippets, DW 13–20,
  DW 13–24
Spry menu bars, DW 5–17
templates, DW 12–8—9,
  DW 12–16, DW 12–18
web pages, DW 2–32, DW 2–34
Motion Picture Experts Group (MPEG)
  format, DW 11–22
MOV (Apple Quick Time) format,
  DW 11–18
movies. *See* Flash movies
MP3 file format, DW 11–22
MPEG (Motion Picture Experts Group)
  format, DW 11–22
Multiscreen Preview, DW 2–33
Multiscreen Preview command, DW 8–19

named anchor(s), DW 5–10
  inserting, DW 5–12—13
  inserting, keyboard shortcut,
    DW 5–33
  internal links. *See* internal links to
    named anchors

Named Anchor dialog box, DW 5–10, DW 5–12
navigation bars. *See* menu bar(s)
navigation structure, DW 1–12
    design, DW 5–30
    intuitive, DW 2–2
    links. *See* link(s)
nested AP elements, DW 10–20
nested tables, DW 6–22, DW 6–27
nesting templates, DW 12–20—21
network folders, setting up web server connections, DW 7–18
New CSS Rule dialog box, DW 3–12, DW 4–11, DW 8–4, DW 8–5, DW 8–10
New Document dialog box, DW 2–14, DW 12–10, DW 12–13
New Editable Region command, DW 12–16
New Editable Region dialog box, DW 12–4, DW 12–7
    opening, keyboard shortcut, DW 12–17
New Optional Region dialog box, DW 12–4, DW 12–5
New Workspace command, BR 1–4
no right-click script, DW 4–25

non-breaking spaces
    adding, keyboard shortcut, DW 12–17
    inserting, keyboard shortcut, DW 10–22
numbered lists. *See* ordered lists

object(s)
    date, inserting, DW 2–31
    Flash, collecting, DW 11–6
    form. *See* form objects
    media. *See* media objects
Ogg format, DW 11–18, DW 11–22
onClick event, DW 11–14—15
online communities, DW 5–2
onLoad event, DW 11–15
onMouseOver event, DW 11–15
opening
    files, DW 1–35
    library items, DW 13–10
    New Editable Region dialog box, keyboard shortcut, DW 12–17
    panels, DW 1–6
    web pages, DW 1–12, DW 1–14
optional regions, templates, DW 12–2, DW 12–4, DW 12–5
    editable, DW 12–5
    setting parameters, DW 12–20

ordered lists
    creating, DW 3–5, DW 3–8
    formatting, DW 3–5, DW 3–9
orphaned files, DW 5–30
    checking for, DW 7–6
outdenting text, keyboard shortcut, DW 3–29
Overflow property, AP divs, DW 10–5

page contents, positioning, DW 6–32
page layouts, DW 2–2
    checking, DW 6–40
    design principles, DW 2–34
    new page options, DW 6–8
    tracing images, DW 6–5
Page Properties dialog box, DW 13–17
page titles
    adding to websites, DW 1–34
    editing, DW 2–6
panel(s), DW 1–6. *See also specific panels*
    Bridge, resizing, BR 1–4
    opening, DW 1–6
    showing and hiding, DW 1–35
    viewing, DW 1–10—11
panel groups, DW 1–6
    displaying, DW 1–10
    docking, DW 1–11

paragraphs, formatting, DW 2–11
parent containers, DW 6–17
parent keywords, BR 1–8
parent pages, DW 1–20
pasting
    keyboard shortcut, DW 2–29
    Spry menu bars, DW 5–25
path(s), DW 5–5
Path bar, BR 1–5
permission process, DW 7–38
PFWG (Protocols and Formats Working Group), DW 5–18
Photoshop, integrating with Dreamweaver, DW 4–15
PICS (Platform for Internet Content Selection), DW 2–8
Pinterest, DW 5–34
placeholders, images. *See* image placeholder(s)
planning forms, DW 9–4
planning websites, DW 1–18—19
    basic structure, DW 1–19—20
    checklist, DW 1–19
    choosing window size, DW 2–35
Platform for Internet Content Selection (PICS), DW 2–8
playing
    Flash movies. *See* Flash movies

plug-ins, keyboard shortcut, DW 11–21
    stopping add-ins from, keyboard shortcut, DW 11–21
plug-ins. *See* add-ons
PNG (Portable Network Graphics) file format, DW 4–2, DW 4–4, DW 4–25
podcasts (Programming On Demand), DW 5–34
point of contact, DW 2–20
Pointer Hotspot tool, DW 5–27
Polygon Hotspot tool, DW 5–26, DW 5–27
Portable Network Graphics (PNG) file format, DW 4–2, DW 4–4, DW 4–25
positioning
    objects using AP divs. *See* AP div(s)
    page contents, DW 6–32
positioning AP divs, DW 10–4
    absolute positioning, DW 10–8
    relative to containers, DW 10–20—21, DW 10–24
    setting positioning attributes, DW 10–8—11
    setting Z-index value, DW 10–12—13
POST method, forms, DW 9–6
POUR (Putting People at the Center of the Process) Principles, DW 2–5

POWDER (Protocol for Web Description Resources) authentication, DW 2–8
predefined code snippets, adding to pages, DW 13–22
presenting websites to clients, DW 7–40—41
Preview panel, BR 1–5
printing
    code, keyboard shortcut, DW 5–33
    problems, DW 8–29
Programming On Demand (podcasts), DW 5–34
progressive video downloads, DW 11–18—19
project management with a team, DW 1–21
properties
    forms, setting, DW 9–5—7, DW 9–9
    text, setting, DW 2–18—19
    web pages, setting, DW 2–4—5
Properties pane, DW 1–6
    CSS Styles panel, DW 8–12, DW 8–17
Property inspector, DW 1–6
    AP divs, DW 10–7
    applying CSS or HTML formatting, DW 2–11

CSS, DW 3–12
HTML. *See* HTML Property inspector
Library item settings, DW 13–15
setting form properties,
   DW 9–5—7
Protocol for Web Description Resources (POWDER) authentication, DW 2–8
Protocols and Formats Working Group (PFWG), DW 5–18
pseudo class styles, DW 8–26—27
public domain, DW 7–37
publishing websites, DW 1–21, DW 1–25
   preparing for, DW 7–2
   synchronizing files, DW 7–16
   transferring files to and from remote sites, DW 7–15—16
   viewing remote sites, DW 7–15
   web servers. *See* web servers
putting items, keyboard shortcut, DW 7–35
Putting People at the Center of the Process (POUR) Principles, DW 2–5

radio buttons, forms, DW 9–16
radio group(s), forms, DW 9–16, DW 9–24—25
Radio Group dialog box, DW 9–24

rating files, BR 1–12
Real Simple Syndication (RSS), DW 5–34
real-world process, transitioning to, DW 3–18
recreating library items, DW 13–15, DW 13–19
Rectangle Hotspot tool, DW 5–26
redefining HTML tags, DW 8–12, DW 8–15—16
redoing actions, keyboard shortcut, DW 5–33
reference(s), DW 7–39
Reference panel, DW 2–27, DW 2–30
refreshing views, keyboard shortcut, DW 3–29, DW 4–17, DW 5–33
related files, DW 1–5, DW 3–21, DW 3–25
Related Files toolbar, DW 1–5
relative paths, DW 5–5
remote servers, DW 1–25
removing. *See also* cutting; deleting
   assets from websites, DW 4–19, DW 4–22
   images from web pages, DW 4–19, DW 4–21
   links, keyboard shortcut, DW 5–33, DW 12–17

renaming AP elements, DW 10–22
Reports dialog box, DW 7–7
Reset buttons, forms, DW 9–17, DW 9–29
resizing
   fonts, DW 2–11
   image using an external editor, DW 4–12
   panels in Bridge, BR 1–4
restoring deleted library items, DW 13–15
Results panel, DW 7–7
rich media content, DW 1–12—13
rollover images, DW 11–10—13
root folder, DW 1–20
root templates, DW 12–17
root-relative paths, DW 5–5
RSS (Real Simple Syndication), DW 5–34
RSS feeds, DW 5–34
rule(s), CSS. *See* CSS rule(s)
rule(s) (lines), horizontal, inserting, DW 2–22
rule of thirds, DW 2–34
rulers, showing, keyboard shortcut, DW 10–22
Rules pane, CSS Styles panel, DW 8–13

sans-serif fonts, DW 3–13
Save As Template command, DW 12–4, DW 12–6
Save As Template dialog box, DW 12–6
Save Style Sheet File As dialog box, DW 8–5
saving files
    image files in assets folder, DW 1–33
    image files in assets folders, DW 2–14—16
    preventing data loss, DW 2–22
Search text box, Help feature, DW 1–13
secure forms, DW 9–26
secure FTP (SFTP), DW 7–15
Secure Socket Layer (SSL), DW 9–26
Select External Editor dialog box, DW 4–15
Select tool, DW 1–6
selecting
    cells, keyboard shortcut, DW 6–36
    keyboard shortcut, DW 2–29
selectors
    CSS code, DW 3–11
    types, DW 8–7
"semantic web," DW 3–6
serif fonts, DW 3–13

servers
    remote, DW 1–25
    testing, DW 9–31
    web. See web servers
Servers Behaviors panel, Behaviors panel compared, DW 11–17
server-side controls, DW 11–2
server-side script(s), DW 10–2
server-side scripting, DW 9–5
Set Magnification menu, DW 1–6
setting up access, DW 1–26—27
setting up websites, DW 1–20, DW 1–25
SFTP (secure FTP), DW 7–15
Shockwave movies, DW 11–2
Show Code view, DW 1–6
simplicity, websites, DW 2–2
site definition(s), DW 7–32—35
    exporting, DW 7–32, DW 7–33
    importing, DW 7–32, DW 7–34—35
Site Definition dialog box, DW 9–31
site maps, DW 5–30
Site option, Assets panel, DW 4–7
site reports, DW 7–4—5
Site Setup dialog box, DW 7–14
skins, DW 11–18
Skype, DW 5–35
slider, History panel, DW 2–26, DW 2–28

snap to guides, keyboard shortcut, DW 10–22
snippet(s). See code snippets
Snippet dialog box, DW 13–21, DW 13–25
Snippets panel, DW 13–20, DW 13–21
social networking, DW 5–2, DW 5–34
sound, DW 11–22—25
    controllers, DW 11–23
spaces, non-breaking
    adding, keyboard shortcut, DW 12–17
    inserting, keyboard shortcut, DW 10–22
spell checking, DW 2–19, DW 2–29
    forms, DW 9–31
Split view, DW 1–10
splitting table cells, DW 6–28
    keyboard shortcut, DW 6–36
Spry data set(s), DW 9–32
Spry Data Set dialog box, DW 9–32
spry effects, DW 11–15
Spry framework, DW 5–16, DW 9–33
Spry framework for AJAX, DW 11–15
Spry menu bar(s), DW 5–16—25
    adding items, DW 5–20
    copying, DW 5–17, DW 5–25

creating, DW 5–16—17, DW 5–18—19
formatting using CSSs, DW 5–20—25
modifying, DW 5–17
pasting, DW 5–25
Spry Menu Bar dialog box, DW 5–16, DW 5–18
Spry Validation Field widgets, DW 9–33
Spry widgets, DW 9–33, DW 11–15. *See also* Spry menu bar(s)
SpryAssets folder, DW 5–16
SSL (Secure Socket Layer), DW 9–26
Standard mode, DW 6–23
    creating tables, DW 6–22—23
Standard toolbar, DW 1–5, DW 1–7
starting
    Bridge, BR 1–6
    Dreamweaver, DW 1–7—8
states, menu bar items, DW 5–16
static content, DW 9–31
status bar, DW 1–6
streaming video downloads, DW 11–19
style(s)
    cascading, DW 8–26
    class (custom). *See* class styles

conflicting. *See* conflicting styles
embedded (internal). *See* embedded style(s)
inline, DW 8–4, DW 8–5
Style Rendering toolbar, DW 1–5, DW 1–7, DW 3–17
style sheets. *See also* Cascading Style Sheets (CSSs)
    adding class rules, DW 3–22—23
    advantages, DW 3–11
    attaching, DW 3–20, DW 3–24
    existing, adding tag selectors, DW 3–18—19
    external. *See* internal style sheets
    internal (embedded). *See* internal style sheets
    viewing with Related Files toolbar, DW 3–25
sub keywords, BR 1–8
Submit buttons, forms, DW 9–17, DW 9–29
Summary for Selection pane, CSS Styles panel, DW 8–12—13
Swap Image behaviors, DW 11–11
Swap Image Restore behaviors, DW 11–11
SWF files, inserting, keyboard shortcut, DW 11–21

Switch Design View to Live button, DW 9–31
switching views, DW 1–9, DW 3–29
    keyboard shortcut, DW 3–29, DW 4–17
Synchronize command, DW 7–16
Synchronize Files dialog box, DW 7–16, DW 7–21
synchronizing files, DW 7–16, DW 7–21

tab(s), CSS3, DW 8–19
table(s), DW 6–2, DW 6–22—43
    adding and deleting rows, DW 6–26
    adding to forms, DW 9–12
    borders, DW 6–22
    cell content. *See* cell content
    cells. *See* table cells
    columns. *See* table columns
    creating, DW 6–22—23, DW 6–24—25
    div tags vs., for page layout, DW 6–2
    form. *See* form tables
    formatting with HTML5 and CSS3, DW 6–23
    importing and exporting data, DW 6–35
    inserting, keyboard shortcut, DW 6–36

inserting text, DW 6–34, DW 6–35
modes, DW 6–22. *See also* Expanded Tables mode
nested, DW 6–22, DW 6–27
rows. *See* table rows
setting accessibility preferences, DW 6–23
setting properties, DW 6–25
table tags, DW 6–27
widths, setting, DW 6–25
table captions, DW 6–23
table cells, DW 6–2
   adding form labels, DW 9–13
   aligning images, DW 6–30—31, DW 6–33
   cell padding, DW 6–22
   cell spacing, DW 6–22
   cell walls, DW 6–22
   content. *See* cell content
   formatting, DW 6–34, DW 6–37—38
   inserting images, DW 6–30, DW 6–32
   merging, DW 6–26, DW 6–29
   merging, keyboard shortcut, DW 6–36
   splitting, DW 6–28
   splitting, keyboard shortcut, DW 6–36

table columns, DW 6–2
   deleting, keyboard shortcut, DW 6–36
   increasing or decreasing span, keyboard shortcut, DW 6–36
   inserting, keyboard shortcut, DW 6–36
Table dialog box, DW 6–22, DW 6–23, DW 6–24
table headers, DW 6–23
table rows, DW 6–2
   adding and deleting, DW 6–26
   deleting, keyboard shortcut, DW 6–36
   inserting, keyboard shortcut, DW 6–36
tag(s)
   collapsing, keyboard shortcut, DW 8–24
   CSS3. *See* CSS3 tags
   HTML. *See* HTML tags
Tag Inspector panel group, DW 11–14
tag selectors, DW 1–6, DW 8–7
   adding to existing style sheets, DW 3–18—19
Tag type CSSs, DW 3–10
target(s), hotspots, DW 5–28

Target property, forms, DW 9–7
teams
   managing websites with, DW 7–22
   project management with, DW 1–21
template(s), DW 2–6, DW 12–1—21
   attaching to existing pages, DW 12–12
   converting existing pages to template-based pages, DW 12–15
   creating editable attributes, DW 12–21
   creating from existing pages, DW 12–4, DW 12–6
   creating links in pages based on, DW 12–11
   creating pages using, DW 12–10—15, DW 12–13
   definition, DW 12–2
   detaching from pages, DW 12–12
   downloadable, finding, DW 12–16
   editable regions. *See* editable regions, templates
   locked regions, DW 12–2
   modifying, DW 12–8—9, DW 12–16, DW 12–18
   nesting, DW 12–20—21

optional regions. *See* optional regions, templates
root, DW 12–17
updating sites using, DW 12–16—19
uses, DW 12–2
Template Properties dialog box, DW 12–21
Templates folder, DW 12–4, DW 12–6
testing
   dynamic content of forms, DW 9–31
   servers, DW 9–31
   web pages. *See* testing web pages
   websites for usability, DW 7–18
testing web pages, DW 1–21, DW 2–32, DW 7–5
   Adobe BrowserLab, DW 2–33
   different browsers and screen sizes, DW 2–32—33
   as rendered in mobile devices, DW 2–33
   by viewing in browser, DW 2–35
   against wireframe, DW 5–32
text, DW 3–1—33
   adding to CSS layout blocks, DW 6–10—11
   aligning, DW 3–29

alternate. *See* alternate text
AP div content, DW 10–19
boldfacing, DW 3–29
boldfacing, keyboard shortcut, DW 3–29
code snippets, modifying, DW 13–20, DW 13–23
creating, DW 2–10
CSSs. *See* Cascading Style Sheets (CSSs)
entering, DW 2–12
fonts. *See* font(s)
formatting. *See* formatting text
formatting paragraphs, DW 2–11
importing, DW 2–10, DW 2–17
indenting, DW 3–29
inserting in tables, DW 6–34, DW 6–35
italicizing, DW 3–29
keyboard shortcuts, DW 2–12
lists. *See* list(s)
outdenting, DW 3–29
saving files, DW 2–14—16
setting properties, DW 2–18—19
spell checking, DW 2–19, DW 2–29
text area fields, forms, DW 9–16

text fields
   forms, DW 9–16, DW 9–19—21
   multiple-line, inserting in forms, DW 9–21
   single-line, inserting in forms, DW 9–19—20
text-based library items
   creating, DW 13–6—7
   editing, DW 13–12—13
themes, consistent, DW 2–2
thumbnail images, adding links to larger images, DW 4–24, DW 4–26
toolbars, DW 1–4, DW 1–5
   displaying, DW 1–7
   hiding, DW 1–7
Top property (T), AP divs, DW 10–9, DW 10–10
tracing images, DW 6–5
trademarks, DW 7–36
Twitter, DW 5–35
type, CSS layout blocks, editing properties, DW 6–17
TypeKit, DW 2–10

uncloaking files, DW 7–29
"under construction" web pages, DW 2–32
Undo command, DW 13–15

undoing actions
    keyboard shortcut, DW 5–33
    Undo command, DW 13–15
Universal Resource Locators (URLs), DW 5–4
unordered lists
    bullets, DW 3–4
    creating, DW 3–4, DW 3–6—7
    formatting, DW 3–4—5
untitled documents, checking for, DW 7–7
Update Library Items dialog box, DW 13–5
Update Pages dialog box, DW 12–17, DW 13–9
Update Template Files dialog box, DW 12–17, DW 12–19
updating
    library items, DW 13–11
    sites using templates, DW 12–16—19
    web pages, DW 5–32—33
uploading entire sites, DW 7–16
uploading files, DW 7–15—16
    to remote server, DW 7–20
URL(s) (Universal Resource Locators), DW 5–4
    typing, DW 5–7

URL category, Assets panel, DW 2–25
usability testing, DW 7–18
user-friendly forms, DW 9–30

validating for CSS3 standards, DW 8–20—21
    uploading files for, DW 8–25
validating markup, DW 7–5
    accessibility standards, DW 7–6
    CSS, DW 7–9
    for HTML5 standards, DW 7–8
vector-based graphics, DW 11–4
Version Cue, DW 7–11
vertical symmetry, web page design, DW 2–34
video, DW 11–18—21
    controllers, DW 11–18
video downloads
    progressive, DW 11–18—19
    streaming, DW 11–19
view(s), DW 1–6. *See also* switching views; *specific views*
viewing. *See also* displaying
    alternate text in a browser, DW 4–17
    CSS code, DW 3–11, DW 3–16

CSS layout blocks, DW 6–5
email links in Assets panel, DW 2–25
HTML code in Code Inspector, DW 2–26—27
imported sites, DW 7–35
library items, DW 13–4
links in Assets panel, DW 5–9
metadata, BR 1–9—10
pages in Live view, DW 1–11
panels, DW 1–10—11
position of a guide, keyboard shortcut, DW 10–22
Reference panel, DW 2–30
remote websites, DW 7–15
styles with related Files toolbar, DW 3–25
web pages in a browser, DW 2–32—33
websites on remote servers, DW 7–19
Vis property, AP divs, DW 10–5
visibility, AP divs, DW 10–23
visual aids, hiding, keyboard shortcut, DW 5–33, DW 10–22
Visual Aids menu, DW 5–12
visual clues, forms, DW 9–30, DW 9–31
Visual Safe Source (VSS), DW 7–16

WAI-ARIAA (Web Accessibility Initiative Accessible Rich Internet Applications Suite), DW 5–18
WAV (Waveform Extension) format, DW 11–22
WAVE (Web Accessibility Evaluation Tool), DW 2–5
Waveform Extension (WAV) format, DW 11–22
WCAG. *See* Web Content Accessibility Guidelines (WCAG)
Web Accessibility Evaluation Tool (WAVE), DW 2–5
Web Accessibility Initiative Accessible Rich Internet Applications Suite (WAI-ARIAA), DW 5–18
web browsers, DW 1–2
web cams, DW 5–35
Web Content Accessibility Guidelines (WCAG), DW 2–5, DW 4–13
   color use, DW 4–22
   links, DW 2–21
   window size, DW 2–35
Web Open Font Format (WOFF), DW 3–19, DW 8–18
web page(s)
   accessibility, DW 2–5
   adding assets, DW 4–5
   adding to websites, DW 1–34—35
   adding white space, DW 4–12, DW 4–14
   aligning images, DW 4–5, DW 4–11
   appropriate content for target audience, DW 2–6
   child, DW 1–20
   choosing filenames, DW 2–17
   collecting content, DW 1–21
   colors to convey information, DW 2–5
   "come back later," DW 2–32
   content. *See* web page content
   creating, DW 1–20—21
   creating head content, DW 2–4
   descriptions, DW 2–7, DW 2–8
   elements, DW 1–12—13, DW 1–14—15
   enhancing with images, DW 4–2
   images. *See* image(s)
   inserting images, DW 4–5, DW 4–6—7
   keywords, DW 2–7
   links to, DW 2–20, DW 2–23
   modifying, DW 1–21, DW 2–32, DW 2–34
   opening, DW 1–12, DW 1–14
   page layout. *See* CSS page layout(s); page layouts
   parent, DW 1–20
   removing images, DW 4–19, DW 4–21
   "semantic web," DW 3–6
   setting properties, DW 2–4—5
   testing. *See* testing web pages
   text. *See* text
   titles. *See* page titles
   "under construction," DW 2–32
   updating, DW 5–32—33
web page content
   appropriate for target audience, DW 2–6
   creating head content, DW 2–4
   legal use, DW 7–36—39
web servers, DW 1–21, DW 7–14—15
   setting up access, DW 1–26—27
   setting up connections on FTP sites, DW 7–17
   setting up connections to local or network folders, DW 7–18
   synchronizing files, DW 7–16, DW 7–21
   uploading files, DW 7–20
   viewing websites, DW 7–19
Web 3.0, DW 5–35

Web 2.0, DW 5–34—35
WebAIM site, DW 2–5
WebAssist, DW 9–26
Web-based Distributed Authoring and Versioning (WebDave), DW 7–16
WebDave (Web-based Distributed Authoring and Versioning), DW 7–16
WebM format, DW 11–18
website(s), DW 1–2
    adaptive, DW 8–20
    adding folders, DW 1–28—29, DW 1–30
    adding pages, DW 1–29, DW 1–34—35
    background color, DW 2–4, DW 2–9
    body, DW 2–4
    effective navigation structures, DW 1–28
    imported, viewing, DW 7–35
    links. *See* link(s)
    local site folders, DW 1–23—24
    page titles. *See* page titles
    planning. *See* planning websites
    presenting to clients, DW 7–40—41
    publishing. *See* publishing websites
    selecting location, DW 1–22
    setting up, DW 1–20, DW 1–25
    themes, DW 2–2
    uploading entire sites, DW 7–16
website color palettes, DW 4–19, DW 4–23
website development process, DW 1–18
website maintenance, DW 7–4—13
    Design Notes. *See* Design Notes
white space
    adding to web pages, DW 4–12, DW 4–14
    effective use, DW 2–2
widgets, DW 5–16
    Spry, DW 9–33, DW 11–15. *See also* Spry menu bar(s)
Width property (W), AP divs, DW 10–9, DW 10–11
wiki(s), DW 5–34
Wikipedia, DW 5–34
window size, choosing, DW 2–35
wireframes, DW 1–19—20
    testing web pages against, DW 5–32
WOFF (Web Open Font Format), DW 3–19, DW 8–18
workspace, DW 1–4—11
    choosing layout, DW 1–10
    Coding toolbar, DW 1–5—6
    Document toolbar, DW 1–4, DW 1–5
    Document window, DW 1–4, DW 1–5
    Dual Screen layout, DW 1–9
    Live view, DW 1–4—5
    panels, DW 1–6
    Property inspector, DW 1–6
    Related Files toolbar, DW 1–5
    Standard toolbar, DW 1–5
    Style Rendering toolbar, DW 1–5
    views, DW 1–6
Workspace switcher, DW 1–10
World Wide Web Consortium (W3C), DW 2–5
    CSS3, DW 8–18
    PFWG, DW 5–18
    WCAG. *See* Web Content Accessibility Guidelines (WCAG)
WC. *See* World Wide Web Consortium (W3C)
WYSIWYG environment, Standard mode, DW 6–23

XHTML, DW 1–2
XML (Extensible Markup Language), DW 2–8, DW 6–6

XMP (Extensible Metadata Platform) standard, BR 1–8
XSL (Extensible Stylesheet Language), DW 6–6

XSLT (Extensible Stylesheet Language Transformations), DW 6–6

YouTube, DW 5–35

Z-index property, AP divs, DW 10–9, DW 10–12—13
Zoom tool, DW 1–6